LANCASTER
AGAINST
YORK

LANCASTER AGAINST YORK

THE WARS OF THE ROSES AND THE FOUNDATION OF MODERN BRITAIN

TREVOR ROYLE

palgrave
macmillan

LANCASTER AGAINST YORK
Copyright © Trevor Royle, 2008.

All rights reserved.

Where this book is distributed in the UK, Europe and the rest of the world, this is by Palgrave Macmillan, a division of Macmillan Publishers Limited, registered in England, company number 785998, of Houndmills, Basingstoke, Hampshire RG21 6XS.

Palgrave Macmillan is the global academic imprint of the above companies and has companies and representatives throughout the world.

Palgrave® and Macmillan® are registered trademarks in the United States, the United Kingdom, Europe and other countries.

ISBN-13: 978–1–4039–6672–8
ISBN-10: 1–4039–6672–9

Library of Congress Cataloging-in-Publication Data

Royle, Trevor.
    Lancaster against York: the Wars of the Roses and the foundation of modern Britain / by Trevor Royle.
        p. cm.
        ISBN 1–4039–6672–9
        1. Great Britain—History—Wars of the Roses, 1455–1485.
    2. Great Britain—History—Lancaster and York, 1399–1485. I. Title.

DA250.R79 2008
942.04—dc22   2008000333

A catalogue record of the book is available from the British Library.

Design by Newgen Imaging Systems (P) Ltd., Chennai, India.

First edition: August 2008

10 9 8 7 6 5 4 3 2 1

Printed in the United States of America.

CONTENTS

PREFACE AND
ACKNOWLEDGMENTS

Seen from the distance of the modern period, the Wars of the Roses seem inchoate and barely fathomable as even their antecedents were spread over several lifetimes. At the heart of the conflict was the dynastic dispute that divided the Royal House of Plantagenet, England's ruling family since 1154, the year of the accession of its founder King Henry II, the eldest son of Geoffrey Plantagenet, Count of Anjou. By the reign of Richard II, who succeeded to the throne in 1377 while still a boy, the Plantagenet succession was in trouble as the king struggled to keep his nobles in check and found himself under threat from his cousin Henry Bolingbroke, eldest son of John of Gaunt, King Edward III's third son. In 1399, having failed to exert himself and having thoroughly alarmed the nobles with his weakness and vacillation, Richard was forced to abdicate in favor of Bolingbroke, who promptly had him imprisoned at Pontefract—where he died—to cement the claims of the House of Lancaster. It was not the first time in history that the English throne had been disputed or that kings had been forced to fight for their crowns. Richard's great-grandfather, Edward II, was an inadequate ruler who antagonized the nobility and was deposed by his wife Isabella and murdered in 1327. Further back, Henry II's son John plunged the country into an unnecessary war with his barons in 1215. What made the struggle for the Plantagenet succession so awkward and so bruising was that it brought two rival and powerful families and their supporters—the House of Lancaster, represented by Henry Bolingbroke's line, and the claims of his kinsman Richard, Duke of York—into direct confrontation. Both lines were descended from King Edward III, and by the early part of the fifteenth century, when Bolingbroke's ineffective grandson Henry VI was on the throne, the scene was set for a tumultuous power struggle only one house could win.

From that clash came the name by which the conflict is best known, the Wars of the Roses. The origin of the term has been hotly debated, and some historians have argued that it is misleading or that the wars should be given some other description, but over the years the nomenclature has stuck. The philosopher David Hume referred to the "wars of the two roses" in his *History of England*, published in 1726, and another Scot, the novelist Sir Walter Scott, is also credited with introducing the concept in his novel *Anne of Geierstein* (1829), in which he speaks about "the civil discords so dreadfully prosecuted in the wars of the White and Red Roses." By the nineteenth century, the term was widely used to describe the dynastic struggle between the two rival lines, and it is now too late to change such a well-known title.

Even if the historical accuracy of the description is in doubt, its floral symbolism is compelling. Over the centuries, it has come to symbolize the struggle between the families: the white rose represents the Yorkists, and the red rose, the Lancastrians. Purists have protested that there is little evidence to suggest that either side fought under the symbol of a different colored rose. It is equally clear that the term Wars of the Roses does not come from the period when the civil war was actually being fought, but the symbolism of red and white roses is still central to the conflict. The House of York had a white rose as one of its many badges, and red was associated with Lancaster. When William Shakespeare wrote *Part One of Henry VI* at the end of the sixteenth century, he inserted a crucial scene in the Old Temple Gardens in London where the plucking of red and white roses by the rival supporters indicates the opposition of Lancaster and York. Although the action is completely fictitious, it established the relationship in a dramatic way and contemporary audiences would have understood it.

Shakespeare also returned to the symbolism in *Richard III* when the Tudor King Henry VII, the ultimate victor of the Wars of the Roses, expresses his desire to "unite the white rose and the red," and later Tudor imagery made much of the fact that under their family's rule, the red and white roses had been brought together in harmony. Other contemporary or near contemporary sources also refer to "the roses" as being central to the conflict. The anonymous chroniclers at Croyland (or Crowland) Abbey made several references to the rival roses in their account of the war; in the sixteenth century, the humanist historian Polydore Vergil claimed that both sides were represented by different-colored roses, and a century later at the time of the next civil war, the diarist Sir John Oglander, a Royalist, mentioned "the quarrel of the warring roses."

The use of the roses was also prompted by Tudor propaganda. Although the House of York had won back the throne from the Lancastrians with the accession of Edward IV, it was lost by his brother Richard III in 1485 after facing a challenge from Henry Tudor, the Earl of Richmond, who had a shaky claim to the throne by virtue of being the great-grandson of an illegitimate son of a younger son of Edward III. Richard's defeat and his death at the Battle of Bosworth effectively ended the Wars of the Roses, although Henry did not feel completely secure until he had quelled unrest in the north and west and defeated two pretenders to his throne. Following the years of discord, England was in need of harmony, and it was in the Tudors' interests to describe the wars as an unbroken conflict over two centuries (from the abdication of Richard II to the reign of Richard III) which was caused by the disastrous dynastic quarrel between the rival houses. It was only later that the conflict was seen on a larger scale and in a more tragic context; the man most responsible for instilling it in the national consciousness in those terms was Shakespeare.

His cycle of history plays chronicles the long collapse of Plantagenet power from *Richard II* through *The Two Parts of Henry IV*, *Henry V*, and *The Three Parts of Henry VI* to *Richard III*, and in so doing it cemented the concept of the Wars of the Roses as a long and bloody business that blighted English history as the rival houses of York and Lancaster vied for the crown. For many people, the plays form their only knowledge of the period, and half-remembered quotations and vividly drawn personalities provide clues to the main events. There is no reason why the plays should not be enjoyed in their own right as powerful pieces of drama, but such was Shakespeare's capacity to recreate the actual world inhabited by his characters that the plays have often been regarded as a realistic and honest account of what actually happened during that tumultuous period.

In writing this book I have made full use of the evidence supplied by contemporary or near-contemporary chroniclers. Many of the latter had access to eyewitnesses of the action, and while the subsequent accounts are not always accurate or show some bias, they still present vivid and diverse accounts of the events as recorded by the writer in question, be he a cloistered monastic chronicler such as Thomas Walsingham or a visiting Italian humanist like Dominic Mancini. Their works are listed in the bibliography together with the principal and most recent studies of the period that have provided the main sustenance during the writing of this book. All quotations from the plays of William Shakespeare have been taken from the Royal Shakespeare Company edition (see bibliography).

As ever I am grateful to the National Archives in Kew and the National Library of Scotland in Edinburgh. In both places, my research has been aided, abetted, and made more pleasurable by the kindness and helpful ministrations of their thoroughly professional staffs. At Palgrave Macmillan, Alessandra Bastagli acted as mentor and saw the book into being, but the original idea was encouraged by Michael Flamini, who wanted me to travel further back in time after writing revisionist histories of the Crimean War and the Wars of the Three Kingdoms.

During the writing of the book my youngest son Patrick collapsed and died in Oxford after taking part in a charity bicycle ride from London on an achingly hot July afternoon. As a military historian I must have written about and described the deaths of many young people—usually in a clinical and detached way—and this book is littered with examples. The loss of Patrick changed many of my perceptions by underlining just how arbitrary, unfair, and unnecessary so many such deaths are, be they intentional or accidental. As with so many things since his unseasonable death in the summer of 2006, this is for Patrick.

—TREVOR ROYLE
EDINBURGH/ANGUS
SUMMER 2007

War of the Roses (1455-1485) Family tree for the Houses of York and Lancaster

Edward III Plantagenet
1312-1327-1377

Philippa of Hainault

(2) Constance of Castile

(3) Katherine Swynford

Others

John of Gaunt
Duke of Lancaster

The Beauforts

Isabella
of Castile

Edmund of Langley
Duke of York

(1) Blanche of Derby

+ 10 others

Elizabeth

Philippa

Others, died
young

Henry IV Plantagenet
"Bolingbroke"
1366-1399-1413

Edward, Prince of Wales
the Black Prince

Anne of Bohemia

Mary de Bohun

Humphrey, Duke
of Gloucester

(1) Anne of Burgundy

(2) Owen Tudor

Joan, the Fair
Maid of Kent

Richard II Plantagenet
1367-1377-k.1400

Thomas, Duke
of Clarence

Edward

Philippa

Eric VII, King
of Denmark

John, Duke
of Bedford

Catherine of Valois
princess of France

Margaret d'Anjou

Edmund Tudor
Earl of Richmond

Blanche

(2) Jacquetta of
Luxemburg

(1) Henry V of Lancaster
1387-1413-1422

Henry VI of Lancaster
1421-1422-1461;
1470-1471-k.1471

Edward,
Prince of Wales

Margaret Beaufort

Henry VII Tudor
1457-1485-1509

Richard of York,
Earl of Cambridge

Anne Mortimer

Cecily Neville

Margaret

Isabella Neville

Edward,
Duke of York

Richard,
Duke of York

Edmund, Earl
of Rutland

+ 6, died
young

George, Duke
of Clarence

Elizabeth

Elizabeth Woodville

Elizabeth of York

Isabella

Richard III of York
1452-1483-kb.1485

Edward IV of York
1442-1461-1470;
1471-1483

George, Duke
of Bedford

Anne

Anne Neville

Edward, Prince of Wales

+ 4 girls

Edward V of York
1470-1483-k.1483

Catherine

Richard,
Duke of York

I

Woe to the Land in Which a Boy Is King

*I*n purely military terms, the conflict known as the Wars of the Roses properly began in the middle of the fifteenth century during the reign of Henry VI, with the First Battle of St. Albans, and lasted some 30 years. To understand why two English armies found themselves facing one another in the streets of a Northamptonshire town in May 1455 it is necessary to go back to 1399, when the country's anointed king, Richard II, the second son of Edward of Woodstock, also known as the Black Prince, and grandson of the great Plantagenet King Edward III, was forced to abdicate the throne. This untimely demission was to usher in a century of turbulence that threatened the collapse of the English body politic as a succession of rulers failed to deal with an "over-mighty" aristocracy. England was plunged into a series of violent encounters that were nasty and brutish but rarely decisive. Richard had the misfortune to be crowned king in 1377 while still a ten-year-old boy, and therefore still a minor; his reign did not recover from that unhappy start.

It was unfortunate that he ever became king in the first place. Not only was he a second son, but his father, the charismatic Black Prince, had predeceased him in 1376 and his older brother Edward of Angoulême should have preceded him as king, but his death five years earlier, at the age of six, prevented the natural succession. As a result of these early deaths, young Richard was propelled to an early throne. Clearly, the boy king needed guidance, but his grandfather's extensive progeny complicated the question of who would be the best mentor. Edward III had fathered thirteen children, and five of the sons had grown to maturity, becoming potent figures in their own right. With their wealth from carefully planned marriages and their noble blood—all had been made dukes—they enjoyed great temporal power and were almost independent of the crown. Edward, the Black Prince, had been the oldest and therefore heir to the throne, but his brothers were equally powerful, and as influential magnates, they entertained their own ambitions. It was only natural that they should have seen in their young nephew's plight an opportunity to enhance their own standing.

The second surviving son of Edward III was Lionel, Duke of Clarence, who had made a good match by marrying Elizabeth de Burgh, the heiress of William de Burgh, Earl of Ulster. Through her mother, she was descended from Henry III, another English king who had succeeded to the throne during his minority, in October 1216. (Elizabeth died in 1363, and Clarence married for a second time, Violante Visconti, daughter of the Duke of Milan.) Although Clarence had died in 1368, and was therefore not a contender at the time of Richard's accession, his daughter Philippa had married into the powerful Mortimer family, who were (English) Earls of March and would play a considerable role in the dynastic struggles ahead. Descended from Ralph Mortimer, who had crossed to England with William the Conqueror, the family owned large tracts of land on the Welsh borders and had also acquired property in Ireland.

Third in line was John of Gaunt, who had made an advantageous marriage with Blanche, daughter of Henry of Grosmont, the first Duke of Lancaster, a distinguished soldier and diplomat who had served Edward III. Edmund Crouchback, the second son of King Henry II, had founded his family in the previous century. One of the great men of his age, John of Gaunt was born in Ghent (hence his name) and, like his father-in-law, was deeply involved in European affairs. Powerful in his own right, Lancaster was a palatinate (a region whose ruler enjoys considerable authority outside Royal jurisdiction) and enjoyed great wealth and authority in England. His second marriage to Constance of Castile in 1371 brought him Royal titles as putative King of Castile and Leon, and Duke of Aquitaine. With his acres in England and France, his huge retinue, his castles, his love of soldiering, his skills in diplomacy, and his courtly conduct, he would have been the natural choice to have acted as regent for the young king, but as one of the most powerful men in England, John of Gaunt was suspected of wanting the crown for himself. None of the contemporary records suggest that there was any truth to the rumors, but they stuck, and it was Gaunt's misfortune to be identified with plots against the throne while loyally doing his utmost to protect his young nephew.

After John of Gaunt was Edmund of Langley, Earl of Cambridge and later Duke of York, the founder of the House of York, who was married to Isabella, daughter of Pedro the Cruel of Castile. Close to his older brother the Black

Prince, Edmund had fought in France, and at the time of Edward III's death he was acting as governor of Dover. Then there was Edward III's youngest son, Thomas of Woodstock, Earl of Buckingham and later (1385) Duke of Gloucester. He was perhaps the most feline of the brothers and later emerged as a keen threat to Richard's crown.

With the clash of family interests and rivalries potentially spilling over into bloodshed, it was clear that no one brother could claim the title of regent, even though John of Gaunt was the best qualified for the role. Instead there was a compromise. A "continual council" of 12 leading magnates was formed to decide policy and to advise the king's ministers, but it was a mixed blessing. While the arrangement avoided unnecessary splits during Richard's minority and prevented any of the Royal uncles from gaining the ascendancy, it also produced a political paralysis at a time when the country's fortunes were going badly, not just at home but in England's relations with France.

Since the previous century, both countries had been in a state of on–off conflict over the status of Aquitaine, an independent duchy within the kingdom of France that, together with other holdings, was under the suzerainty of England. In 1137 Eleanor, daughter of the French Duke of Aquitaine, had married King Henry II (having divorced Louis VII of France), and as a result of their marriage alliance, successive English kings, as Dukes of Aquitaine, owed homage to the French throne. However, as Henry II and his lineal descendants were sovereign rulers within their own right, French kings feared, not unreasonably, that their English counterparts would take steps to consolidate their power in France. At the same time, the English kings were unhappy with their subordinate position. England had been extending its commercial interests with the weavers and burghers of Flanders, who had become important trading partners. They also considered themselves to be natural allies of the English, and their support had encouraged Edward III to claim the French throne and to quarter the French coat-of-arms with his own. Another factor in this Anglo-French enmity was the "Auld Alliance": the mutually advantageous relationship whereby France gave support and assistance to Scotland as a counterweight to English ambitions in France.

The confrontation between England and France lasted over a hundred years, with eight periods of all-out warfare between 1337 and 1453. It is generally referred to as the Hundred Years War—a Victorian concept still in use although its timescale is not strictly accurate—and it influenced the contemporaneous dynastic struggles in England. Philip IV of France instigated the first period in 1337 after he announced that all English holdings south of the River Loire were forfeit. In response, Edward III established bases in Flanders to mount military expeditions into northern and northeastern France. Following a decisive naval victory at Sluys in 1340, a truce was declared only for war to break out again six years later after the French invaded Gascony, a French region between the Pyrenees and the River Garonne. Edward III's rejoinder was to invade France with an army of 10,000 archers, 3,000 cavalry, and 4,000 infantry. The first major engagement was the Battle of Crecy, fought on August 26, 1346, which left the French badly beaten, with 1,542 lords and knights dead and a casualty list of up to 20,000 foot soldiers and archers. The victory was followed by the English occupation of Calais and the agreement for a further truce that lasted until 1355.

During this interlude, between 1348 and 1349, Europe was ravaged by one of the periodic outbreaks of plague known as the Black Death that halved England's population and left hardly any country unscathed. Conflict was resumed in 1356 when Edward III and his sons again defeated the French at Poitiers. As the French realized that they could not beat the English in set-piece battles, the war descended into stalemate, and the resulting Treaty of Brétigny settled the territorial arguments: England gave up her claim to Normandy, while her holdings in Aquitaine and Calais were recognized by the French.

Desultory warfare continued in the period between 1368 and 1396 when the Constable of France Bertrand de Guesclin carried on a war of attrition against English holdings, gradually winning back possessions and extending French authority in Aquitaine. By the time that Richard II came to the throne, the war against the French was still a live issue, but it was expensive and becoming increasingly difficult to maintain. The Black Prince's victories in France had been extremely popular, as they enhanced national prestige. How to pay for them, however, was another matter, and it was one of the many problems Richard had to confront when he came of age.

Even so, despite the underlying tensions caused by the relationship with France, the boy king's reign got off to a good start with his coronation, which, by general agreement, was a sumptuous occasion masterminded by John of Gaunt. It lasted two days, the first taken up with a magnificent formal procession from the Tower of London to Westminster, the participants riding through "the crowded streets of the city of London, which were so bedecked with cloth of gold and silver, with silken hangings, and with other conceits to entertain the onlookers, that you might suppose you were seeing a triumph of the Caesars or ancient Rome in all its grandeur." The recorder of the event was Thomas Walsingham, Benedictine precentor of St. Albans and one of the main chroniclers of the period, who built on the *Chronica Majora* written by his predecessor, Matthew Paris, an earlier chronicler and monk of St. Albans. Walsingham also noted that the coronation was exceptionally well ordered; the procession provided a mirror of English society at the time, with the various earls, barons, knights, and squires riding or walking according to their station. The whole party dressed with white hoods to represent the king's innocence, and they were greeted by cheering crowds whose enthusiasm was no doubt helped by the wine that had replaced spring water in the conduits and flowed freely for at least three hours. At Cheapside they passed a specially constructed castle where four beautiful girls stood on the battlements, and "as the king approached they wafted down golden leaves before him, then, as he drew nearer they scattered imitation golden florins on him and his horse."

Inside Westminster Abbey, Richard was put through the ancient ceremony that anointed him king. Holy oil was poured, the crown was placed on his head, the scepter was put in his right hand, and the golden rod in his left. After the boy king was enthroned on the coronation chair, the *Te Deum* was sung and mass was celebrated. So exhausted was Richard by the rigors of the ceremonial that he had to be carried on the shoulders of his tutor and the chamberlain of his household, Sir Simon Burley, into neighboring Westminster Hall where a huge banquet awaited.

The proceedings must have left a lasting and profound impression on a boy who, from an early age, was acutely aware of his surroundings and of his own position within them. Already solitary and introverted, with no siblings to divert him, he was spoiled by his mother Joan of Woodstock, also known as the Fair Maid of Kent. Joan was one of the great beauties of her day, and she had had a colorful past: She had married her cousin the Black Prince in 1361 following the death of her second husband Sir Thomas Holland, and, being a granddaughter of Edward I, she was a powerful figure in her own right. From her, Richard understood the primacy of his position, and from an early age she encouraged her son to accept the idea that he was in a unique position as an absolute monarch with limitless powers. Through the efforts of Burley and Sir Guichard d'Angle, Earl of Huntingdon, another strong-minded tutor, he had been instructed in the absolute sanctity of his office, namely that he enjoyed a unique and mysterious status that from the very outset had been blessed by God. At his birth in Bordeaux in 1367 three kings had been present—those of Spain, Portugal, and Navarre—and the symbolism of their presence was so powerful that the young prince developed an intense and lifelong fixation with the feast of the Epiphany, the Adoration of the Magi commemorating the manifestation of Christ, celebrated on January 6. From the example of his coronation with its regalia, its blessings, anointment, and religious symbolism, Richard came to believe at an early age that his tutors' teachings must be true, that he was indeed God's anointed vessel.

All this mattered. At this time, the king was not just a figurehead, he was the embodiment of supreme authority on earth. For the people of England, he was the personification of all their hopes and fears; he could intervene decisively in their lives, and he was the ultimate authority in the land. As such, he had to maintain a physical presence that announced that he was king, as well as the mental agility to keep himself one step ahead of the requirements of kingship. In that sense, it was not surprising that Richard believed so strongly in the principle of divine right: everything he experienced as a boy encouraged him to accept that concept. But being king did not mean that he had to act alone.

Like his predecessors, Richard enjoyed the advice of a council whose members were drawn from the upper reaches of the nobility or were familiars—men of good quality—who helped him form policy and then execute it. There was also a representative parliament to raise taxes and pass laws. It had evolved from its medieval beginnings as a "model" assembly consisting of two knights from each shire and two burgesses from selected boroughs to become an effective council whose members gave consent on taxation and other matters on behalf of those who sent them. By the time of Richard's reign, the term "Commons" was being used—the body met in centers other than London—and the first Speaker was chosen in 1376. One of the two great officers of state was the chancellor, who was head of chancery and keeper of the Great Seal. As the senior legal officer of the realm, he presided in parliament, and the appointment was usually given to a trusted senior church figure. The second of the two great officers was the treasurer, responsible for the exchequer. The king also benefited from the services of his own household of trusted retainers and servants, the cost being met by the public purse and therefore a constant source of financial difficulties. Beyond them, to administer the country at national and local level there was an array of judges, sheriffs, justices of the peace, coroners, and customs officials. But at the apex of English society and responsible for its good governance stood the figure of the king. Not only was it vital that he play the role of supreme arbiter, he also had to look the part and behave as a true ruler of his kingdom.

On that point Richard scored well. Contemporary portraits show him to have been a pleasant-looking young man, tall, fair-skinned, and blond-haired, with an obvious love of fine clothes. Although his weak chin, thin beard, and sly smile betray a less than manly aspect, Richard stares out of his state portrait in Westminster Abbey spirited and alert, a man keenly aware of his position. Dress sense was important to him; he was a dandy who luxuriated in fine clothes and was uninterested in their cost, an affectation that led to growing discontent about the cost of maintaining his court. Little is known about the years of the king's minority, but the fragility of his position was underlined by the Bishop of

Rochester, Thomas Brinton, who preached a sermon on the day following the coronation exhorting the nobility to support the new king during the perilous years of his youth and to ensure the safety of the kingdom. Inevitably Richard's closest companions and those who exerted the most influence over him were his tutors, who largely owed their positions to the earlier patronage of the Black Prince. This led to a belief that a gulf had developed between the Royal household, which was perceived to be all-powerful, and the successions of continual councils that were responsible for ruling the country.

Matters came to a head at the second parliament of the young king's reign, held in Gloucester in October 1378, when Sir Peter de la Mare, the speaker of the Commons, questioned the validity of England's present governance and asked to be informed about the role played by "the king's councillors and governors of his person," the inference being that the system was not working. A compromise was reached when two new councillors, Sir Aubrey de Vere and Sir Richard Rous, were appointed to the third council in the following month, but this did not dim the growing dissatisfaction with the arrangement. There were concerns, too, about the costs of the Royal household and the means of maintaining it. At the time, money was raised by a poll tax that was paid at a standard rate of one groat (four cents), by all men and women aged over 14, with graduated rates for richer taxpayers. While the taxation system raised sufficient funds to meet expenditure, it was unpopular, and the third parliament of Richard's reign, held in April 1379, was quick to voice its dissent, not least because it seemed that the country was getting little in return for the burden of heavy taxation required for England's strategic commitments in France and along the border with Scotland. In an attempt to bring financial matters under control, parliament appointed an assessor, but little seems to have been done, and the matter was simply allowed to simmer, to no one's advantage.

Part of the problem was undoubtedly the extravagance of the Royal court. From an early age, Richard demonstrated that he was not averse to enjoying the fruits of his divine rule. His clothes were well-cut and fashionable in the style known as International Gothic—coats with padded shoulders and high collars, and tight two-colored hose and pointed shoes. Men at court dressed for effect and not for comfort or practicality. The king has also been credited with the invention of the handkerchief, although it is not clear if this emerged for health or sartorial reasons. With his interest in clothes, there was a strong narcissistic element to Richard's personality, and this manifested itself through both his appearance and his passion for artistic excellence. A contemporary critic complained that the clothes were "cut all to pieces," a reference to the leaf shapes that were cut into hems and sleeve edges "full of slashes and devils." Women, too, joined in the fashion revolution, wearing dresses with longer trains and sporting increasingly elaborate headdresses that caused a good deal of contemporary comment, much of it unkind. (As the headdresses became more elaborate and outrageous, the resultant confections were thought, wrongly, to be breeding grounds for mice.)

Partly, too, the extent and size of Richard's kingdom meant that the country was difficult to maintain. In effect, there were a number of different regions, and each contained substantial differences. For example, the English west country had very few similarities, cultural or linguistic, with the northern areas along the border with Scotland. To get from Exeter to Newcastle was a major expedition. Scotland and Ireland and, to a lesser extent, Wales, were separate entities. Throughout the reigns of the Plantagenet kings there had been periods of expansionism that had been engineered through dynastic marriages and by dint of an aggressive foreign policy. Henry II had conquered Ireland at the end of the twelfth century, although repeated attempts to bring it under complete control had mixed success, and, at the beginning of Richard's reign, it was largely in the hands of individual Irish chieftains.

As we have seen, there were still extensive holdings in France, although there had been a gradual decline in English prestige, and the possessions around Calais and Bordeaux and Bayonne in Aquitaine were held only with difficulty. As a result of the need to guard the kingdom from attack, defense costs ate up much of the national budget and led to unpopular increases in taxation. It was a recipe for disaster.

The spark was the decision to raise the poll tax to one shilling (eight cents or $42 today) per head of population in 1380, a move that proved to be unacceptable and led to widespread unrest throughout rural England. Collectors were attacked in the course of their duties, and in the most volatile areas, Essex and Kent, the anger gave way to a popular uprising that became known as the Peasants' Revolt as men banded together in common cause against payment of the poll tax. The unrest coincided with a growing feeling of dissatisfaction with both the working conditions on the land and the workers' relationship with landowners at a time when serfdom was slowly declining following the widespread mortality caused by the Black Death. The sudden shortage of manpower gave the workforce, composed largely of villeins or tenant-farmers, an unlooked-for advantage because landowners were unable to fill vacant tenancies and villeins were now in a position to bargain for better terms. They were also able to travel to seek work elsewhere, and this mobility introduced new job opportunities, especially for women in domestic service. After years of paying heed to a social structure in which everyone knew their place and their degree, the world was gradually being turned upside down as the old order gave way to something new and unsettling. Attempts to enforce a maximum wage at pre-plague levels also proved difficult, although a 1351 parliamentary statute had backed it. Coming on top of the unpopularity of the continuous years of fighting in France, which seemed to benefit only the nobility, and dissatisfaction with the expense of maintaining the Royal court, the introduction of this latest tax increase proved to be the last straw.

The revolt began in June when a group of disaffected men marched to Rochester Castle in Kent to demand the release of prisoners being held for their refusal to pay taxes. From there the protestors moved on to Maidstone and Canterbury, where they threatened to kill the archbishop, Simon Sudbury, who was also the king's chancellor and therefore one of the authors of the tax increases. All the while the mob attracted more people anxious to join their cause, and a leader and spokesman emerged in Wat Tyler, a man of radical convictions who for a very short time had England's destiny in his hands. At the same time, a similar revolt took place in Essex—at Brentwood an inquiry into nonpayment of taxes led to the death of three jurors—and the two groups of protestors converged on Blackheath and Mile End, where, with the help of disaffected citizens, they were able to enter London on June 13. Among those who had been set free at Rochester was a religious demagogue called John Ball, who had been a thorn in Sudbury's side following his complaints about greed and corruption among the country's clergy. Ball's message was simple and dangerous, and it entailed a complete reversal of the current social situation. "Good people," he would say, "nothing can go well in England, nor ever will do, until all goods are held in common, until there is neither villein nor nobleman, until we are all one."

Tyler and Ball—a third leader, Jack Straw, might have been a later invention—were certain about one thing: Although they demanded social change and wanted to abolish all lordships, they claimed that they were not being disloyal to the king and that their quarrel was not with him. On the contrary, they took a common oath of loyalty to Richard, who, they believed, was surrounded by wicked advisers and needed to be saved from them. To their way of thinking, that predicament lay at the heart of the matter, and they were determined to find a solution, if need be, by addressing the king directly and encouraging him to meet their grievances at the stroke of a pen.

For the time being, actions had to speak for words, and, upon entering London, the rebels burned down the buildings of supposed enemies and pillaged their property. Particular animus was reserved for John of Gaunt, whose sumptuous palace at the Savoy on the north side of the Thames (on the site of the present-day Embankment) was an early target. Being out of London, however, the king's uncle escaped any personal harm. For two days London was in a state of anarchy: In addition to burning down the Savoy palace, the rebels opened the prisons at Fleet and Marshalsea and released their inhabitants, sacked the New Temple, and destroyed the chancery records at Lambeth. Richard would not have been human had he not been thoroughly alarmed by the rebellion that seemed to be directed against his authority. It was a concerted attempt to bring about far-reaching changes, and as some ten thousand people backed it— London's population was only four times larger—the rebels clearly posed a threat and enjoyed widespread popular backing. Prudently, on the first outbreak of trouble, the king had moved from Windsor to the Tower of London which was easily defended, but throughout the experience he seems to have remained calm and clearheaded, so much so that he was able to play the leading role in bringing the emergency to conclusion. He was only 14 years old, but contemporary accounts make it clear that he showed considerable courage and conviction in agreeing to meet the rebel leaders, a risky strategy that could have put his life in danger.

There are several suppositions that can be made about Richard's response to the revolt. Perhaps he understood the importance of his own position in the demands being made by Tyler and Ball, and he put his faith in the belief that their loyalty would be stronger than their grievances. Perhaps, too, there was a wider plan to buy time by negotiating with the protestors and lulling them into a false sense of security, but for the inexperienced boyking the taming of this revolt was to be a seminal moment in his life. On June 14, having announced his intention to meet the rebels, he rode from the Tower to Mile End to meet the Essex rebels, accompanied only by William Walworth, the mayor of London. As Richard approached the rebel camp he showed no fear, and in return, the leaders treated him with the respect due to their lawful king. They assured him that they wished for no other king but him and set out their grievances that included the abolition of villeinage, the opening up of the labor market, and the creation of fixed rents for agricultural land. It was a tense moment, and Richard responded to it by agreeing to all their requests, promising to confirm his decision later with letters carrying the Great Seal and allowing them to return to their homes under a general pardon.

Whatever their reasons for taking part in the mass protest, this was what the crowd wanted to hear, and Richard's action effectively ended the revolt of the Essex rebels, who were prepared to take the king at this word before returning to their homes. It was a victory of sorts, and as Richard and his small entourage headed back to the Tower, the young man might well have been pleased with what he had achieved. Not only had he persuaded his subjects to halt their attempted uprising, but he had displayed the power and authority of the crown: The rebels had taken him at his word and had bent to his will because he was their liege sovereign. They would not have listened to Sudbury or any other of the king's advisers whose downfall they sought, but the boy-king Richard was another and altogether more serious matter. It was a good beginning, but on his return to the Tower, Richard was given the painful lesson that honeyed words and the majesty of the king's person were not always enough to still men's anger. While he was absent, there had been further violence in London, and Tyler's men had managed to get into the Tower, where they had summarily executed Sudbury and the king's treasurer Sir Robert Hales, whom they held accountable for the increase in the poll tax.

The violence provoked another trial of strength between Richard and the rebels, but once again the king was able to exert his influence over events. This time, though, there was to be no subservience on the part of the rebels, and Richard was hard-pressed to make his position felt. When the two sides met again on June 15 at the cattle market at Smithfield, Tyler was in no mood to kowtow to the king. Instead of bowing or kneeling he stayed on his horse and greeted the king as an equal, taking him by the hand and addressing him familiarly as "brother." In itself this was hardly heinous behavior—Tyler did not attempt any violence—but by acting in that way the rebel leader had made it clear that he took no account of the king's majesty and had committed the crime of treating Richard as an equal. By addressing Richard as an ordinary man, not only was Tyler exposing his radical pretensions, but he was also challenging the status quo. His demands were equally outrageous. In addition to the ultimatum made by the men of Essex and accepted by Richard, he seems to have insisted on the abolition of all secular and religious titles and the confiscation of Church land. This was going too far, but once again Richard appeared willing to make concessions and studiously ignored Tyler's increasingly arrogant and impertinent demeanor. As the discussion continued, tempers among Richard's retinue frayed, and stung by Tyler's behavior, Walworth decided to act. With his supporters behind him, the lord mayor of London rode into the fray, drew his dagger, and killed Tyler, although, according to some accounts, someone else may have dealt the actual blow.

It was a rash move, and things could have turned out very badly for the Royal party. The leader of the rebels had been killed in front of his followers, Richard and his retinue were outnumbered and lightly armed and could easily have fallen victim to the crowd's revenge, but nothing happened. Displaying great personal courage—being so young, all the more praiseworthy—Richard rode toward the crowd saying, "I am your leader: follow me." The arrival of militia troops loyal to the king settled the matter, and the crowd was gradually and peaceably dispersed. Even if the outcome was not as melodramatic as some contemporary chroniclers suggest in their accounts of the incident, Richard's demeanor demonstrated to his advisers that he was fast growing up and was emerging as a true ruler. In so far as he had shown his mettle and demonstrated behavior fitting a king—it helped that the rebels held him in such high regard that they did not react to the killing of their leader—the confrontation with Tyler was an early milestone in Richard's development.

The incident also underlined the importance of the ruler's divine right and gave Richard a valuable insight into the effect he had on his subjects. At Smithfield, the rebels had greeted him with loyal words—"we will not have any other king over you"—and they had made it clear that their quarrel was not with him but with his "evil" advisers. When their leader was cut down and Richard rode toward them, they heeded his words and returned to their homes. All this suggested that the king's majesty was inviolate and that he, Richard, was different from other men, even from his closest family and advisers, who were the real object of the rebels' ire.

From a more practical point of view, the incident would also have told him that he had to guard against any activity that might threaten his rule. And he was right to be concerned because the unrest had not been confined to the mutinous move on London. There were outbreaks of trouble in Hertfordshire and Suffolk; in Cambridge, the university archives were burned in the Market Square, and there was a minor insurrection in Norfolk, where the bishop of Norwich was assassinated. Bearing those events in mind, Richard set about remedying the situation by making sure that nothing he had promised at Mile End or Smithfield would be put into practice. As the rebels left London they believed that Richard would keep his promises and that they would be granted the charters of freedom that he had pledged at both meetings. Not for the last time they soon found that Richard had no intention of keeping his word and that they had in fact been duped. Within a fortnight, a deputation seeking confirmation of the king's promises was told in no uncertain terms, "villeins you are, and villeins you shall remain," and on July 2, Richard issued a formal revocation of his promises. Some of the ringleaders, including John Ball, were rounded up and executed, although by the standards of the day the retribution was not particularly brutal, largely because Richard was not interested in getting his revenge. It had been enough that his prerogative had been obeyed.

The events of the Peasants' Revolt had a further bearing on Richard's life: They suggested to his advisers that the time had come to find him a wife. There were a number of contenders, including the beautiful Caterina, one of the Duke of Milan's 38 children, who would have brought grace and a large dowry to the marriage, but the most convenient match was with Princess Anne of Bohemia, a daughter of the Holy Roman Emperor Charles IV and the sister of King Wenceslas IV of Bohemia. From the point of view of prestige and winning international influence, the marriage had several advantages: It made Richard the son-in-law of the Holy Roman Emperor, and it would provide a new scoring point in England's rivalry with France, which had become further complicated by the events known as the Great Schism. From 1309 to 1377 the center of papal influence had been at Avignon in France, but all that ended in 1378 when Urban VI had been elected pope in Rome. Not only was he an Italian outsider, but also his views were unpopular and his election was contested largely as a result of his rigid philosophy, his violent temper, and his desire to reform the Church. As a result, the college of cardinals withdrew to Anagni, where they deposed Urban and elected a rival, Clement VII, who reigned as pope in Avignon. At the same time, Urban remained in Rome where he was isolated "like a sparrow on a housetop," and both popes were forced to look for secular support in Europe to further their cause.

As for the happy couple, they seem to have been just that. Although Richard was only a youngster when they married, and while it was hardly a love match, he grew genuinely fond of his young wife. The death of his mother Joan in 1385 also helped to cement the relationship, as she had been a formative and perhaps overbearing influence in Richard's life. Whatever else, Anne's presence stimulated court life. Her Bohemian entourage introduced a feminine ingredient, and she encouraged her husband's cultural and sartorial interests, adding to the sophistication that Richard wanted to be the keynote of his reign. From the evidence of her effigy in Westminster Abbey, where, touchingly, she lies hand-in-hand with her husband, Anne was no beauty, but her grace, dignity, and good sense brought much-needed stability to Richard's life as he passed from the shallows of privileged youth into the deeper waters of manhood and kingship.

2

CHOSEN BY GOD

*I*n the earliest days of Richard's reign there was much residual goodwill for the part he had played in coping with the Peasants' Revolt, and in the wake of his marriage to Anne, once the anti-Bohemian sentiments had receded, there was widespread confidence that a period of calm would follow, that the Royal couple would prosper and produce a family to ensure a settled succession. As the 1380s hit their stride, there was every reason to believe that Richard would emerge a sensible and stable ruler in the tradition cemented by his grandfather, Edward III, and hopes were high that he would add to the achievements of his forebears and his father, not least in the martial field.

Much of the confidence came from the fact that Richard's reign marked a new beginning. It is fair to say that there was probably a good deal of self-interest involved, as new kings bring with them possibilities of patronage and advancement for those close to the throne. As for Richard's style of leadership, it was guided by the belief that he was not like other men, that the sanctity of his office and the religious symbolism of his coronation marked him as being different and gave him a special place in life. It was a heady theory, bordering on reckless, and it encouraged him to think that he alone was responsible for all his actions and that in times of need, men would look to him as to the dawning sun. As a personal theory, it was all highly subjective, and there were no guarantees that others would follow his reasoning or even pay lip service to it; worse, it was to lead him into deep trouble and mental instability later in his reign.

That Richard was determined to follow his own star became clear when he selected those advisers and courtiers who would be closest to him. Sensible Simon Burley remained his main confidante and mentor, providing a link with the Black Prince and the comforting past, but two appointments signified a change of direction and demonstrated the new king's determination to set a personal seal on his court. When parliament appointed Michael de la Pole, a wealthy and influential supporter of John of Gaunt, and the Earl of Arundel to "advise and govern the king," the intention was to provide tutelage and to place a curb on Richard's wilder tendencies, but the appointments were soon used to the throne's advantage. Shortly afterward, in March 1383, the chancellor Richard Scrope criticized the king for awarding lavish grants to his followers. This rap on the knuckles, however, achieved nothing other than to have the perpetrator of the criticism sacked. Then Richard intervened to show that he was his own man and would not be hobbled by advisors: De la Pole was appointed in Scrope's place, and two years later he was created Earl of Suffolk, a position that gave him enhanced authority at court and direct access to the king. This, too, was a sign of the changing times; the de la Poles were not aristocrats but had made their way up in the world through commerce to gain powerful positions at court. The family originated in Hull, where Michael's grandfather Richard had come to prominence as a merchant financier; by lending large amounts of money to Edward III, Richard de la Pole gained Royal patronage, and in 1333 he left Hull for London, where he was appointed chief butler at court, a post that gave him access to revenues from customs duty on the sale of wine and, more importantly, brought him to public prominence.

A more pernicious influence was Richard's close relationship with Robert de Vere, 9th Earl of Oxford, a feckless and widely disliked young man who was soon a recipient of Royal favors and grants of land and titles. In 1385 he was made Marquess of Dublin and then Duke of Ireland, an extravagant title that bore no relation to de Vere's talents or contribution to public life and one that was greatly resented by the king's uncles, who, being Royal dukes themselves, were greatly offended by de Vere's rapid advancement. Without producing any hard evidence, Walsingham hinted that there might have been darker reasons for the elevation.

This action demonstrated the depth of King Richard's affection for this man, whom he cultivated and loved, not without a degree of improper intimacy, or so it was rumored. It also provoked discontent among the other lords and barons, who were angry that a man of such mediocrity should receive such promotion, for he was not superior to the rest of them in either nobility of birth or gifts of character.

In fact there is nothing to suggest a homosexual relationship between the two men—de Vere had already caused scandal by seducing Agnes de Launcekrona, one of Queen Anne's Bohemian ladies-in-waiting and making her his mistress—but the closeness of their friendship coupled with de Vere's butterfly personality and his capacity for toadying told against him. It was also an awkward reminder of Edward II's earlier and disastrous infatuation with his favorite Piers Gaveston, although de Vere did not possess the same degree of personal authority over Richard, being more of a close friend and confidante than an actual creator of policy. Nevertheless, the establishment of a Royal inner circle was not popular. Not only was it a foolhardy move—in promoting de la Pole, Richard had used his own prerogative and had ignored the wishes of parliament—but in de Vere's case his frivolous presence at court was a constant reminder of the king's recklessness and extravagance. In that respect, his creation of favorites meant that Richard enjoyed only the briefest of honeymoon periods with those who should have been his closest and most loyal supporters. Among those offended by Richard's actions were the Royal uncles and advisers from the days of the Black Prince, who were now pressing for the emergence of more aggressive foreign policy, particularly toward the French.

Normally war canceled all moral or social debts even if military campaigns were liable to be an expensive drain on the exchequer. Powerful kings were supposed to be good soldiers, and from the outset Richard was under pressure from his uncles to reopen hostilities in France at the head of an English army just as his forebears had done to maintain national prestige. It must also be said that a renewal of the conflict would have suited the magnates as all stood to benefit from any English gains in France. An opportunity to do just that came sooner than Richard might have expected or wanted.

In 1383 a revolt in Ghent was followed by the intervention of a French army in the area, and the subsequent disruption halted the wool trade in which English merchants had substantial financial interests. As the export trade in wool to Flanders was one of the main sources of England's wealth, this was a blow that could not be ignored, and the response quickly took on the character of a crusade—literally and metaphorically. Here was an early opportunity to gain military glory and at the same time to strike a blow to protect English commercial interests. Leadership of the campaign fell to Henry Despenser, bishop of Norwich, a professional soldier with recent experience of fighting in Italy. Using his influence in Rome, the bishop gained Pope Urban VI's sanction to classify the campaign as a crusade that would be fought with the Church's blessing and would be funded by contributions in return for plenary indulgences (unqualified remission of punishment in purgatory, at the time one of the great abuses in the Church).

The intervention in the Low Countries was well-intentioned, but the result was disastrous. Although Despenser did not lack courage and conviction, he was at the head of an army that was little more than a rabble and that a lacked experienced commanders, a workable plan, and decent weapons and equipment.

Having crossed over to Flanders and successfully taken Gravelines and Bourbourg in May 1383, Despenser laid siege to Ypres only to be forced to make preparations to withdraw at the approach of superior French forces under the command of Philip, Duke of Burgundy, one of the protectors of the new French boy king, Charles VI. No sooner had the French arrived, than they started offering bribes to the English captains, and as these were promptly accepted, there was no actual fighting. After sacking Gravelines in a token show of force and defiance, the bishop was forced to withdraw his army. It was a shameful episode that brought no credit to England, and far from being an honorable undertaking, the entire expedition was considered to be a complete waste of money.

On the army's return to England, Despenser was stripped of his bishop's position, but his disgrace was not the end of the matter. Quite apart from humiliating the national interest and doing nothing to help the wool trade, the continued French presence in Flanders gave rise to fears that an invasion was being planned and that, as had happened so often in the past, the Scots would take advantage of the situation to attack England from the north. Reports began arriving in London that French forces had been dispatched to Scotland under the command of Admiral Jean de Vienne; with a sizable French army assembling on the other side of the Channel, it made tactical sense for the English to deal first with the threat from Scotland. This time the army of some 12,000 men was under Richard's personal command, although prudently John of Gaunt accompanied the force and provided the bulk of the archers, the main strike force.

By the autumn of 1385 the English army had achieved most of its tactical aims but had failed to deliver a decisive blow against the enemy. Melrose, Edinburgh, Perth, and Dundee had been attacked and burned, but the Scots refused to offer a pitched battle, preferring a scorched-earth policy, much to the scorn of de Vienne's knights, who had to watch helplessly as the Scots burned their crops in the Lothians rather than let them fall into English hands. (The ignominy was compounded when their Scottish hosts billed their French allies for the costs incurred by the lost harvest and kept de Vienne as a hostage until the money was paid.) Such as it was, the campaign blooded Richard as a military leader, but the operation accomplished little other than to force the Scots to adopt Fabian tactics and remain north of the border. The only outcome of any note was the elevation of two of the king's uncles—Edmund of Langley as Duke of York and Thomas of Woodstock as Duke of Gloucester.

The Scottish adventure also marked a parting of the ways for John of Gaunt, who must have noted in which way the wind was blowing. With his nephew emerging as a headstrong ruler unwilling to take advice, he decided that his future lay in pursuing his claims to the throne of Castile, where King Juan ruled in place of Gaunt's father-in-law, Pedro the Cruel. Gaunt's allies in the venture were the Portuguese, recently freed from Castilian domination, but he required funds from parliament that had earlier blocked his attempts to gain financial support for the adventure. However, at the beginning of 1386, the situation had changed, and with the French again threatening to invade England, parliament reckoned that a military expedition in the southwest of France would alter the strategic balance to England's advantage. Gaunt received his funds and the blessing of his nephew: On March 8, 1386, Richard hailed John of Gaunt as King of Castile, a move that he had ample reasons for supporting as it would keep his uncle out of the country at a time when he was about to face the first domestic crisis of his reign.

At the sitting of parliament in October 1386, the Commons were confronted with a demand from the chancellor for an immediate increase in taxation to pay for the neglected sea defenses, the strengthening of the border with Scotland, and Gaunt's campaign in Castile. Against a background of gathering panic at the possibility of a French invasion, this fourfold hike in taxation was too much for parliament to bear. It was inevitable that someone had to shoulder the blame, and a scapegoat was found in Michael de la Pole, newly created Earl of Suffolk and an object of considerable envy and scorn among this fellow magnates. Supported by Gloucester and Arundel, the Commons demanded his removal as chancellor, and the ultimatum plunged the court into crisis. When the news reached Richard at his manor at Eltham near Greenwich, he refused point-blank the request for the removal of one of his favorites and sent back a tart rejoinder saying that not even a kitchen scullion would be removed from his household at parliament's request. The retort was typical of a growing recklessness on the king's part, and it brought a stern response. Accompanied by Thomas Arundel, bishop of Ely, and brother to the earl (later Archbishop of Canterbury), Gloucester rode to Eltham and reminded the king that he had a responsibility to call a parliament once a year and to attend its deliberations. Unless he did so within 40 days, parliament would end its sitting and disperse, with the result that Richard would receive no subsidy. According to the author of the *Eulogium Historiarum*, Richard asked Gloucester whether his companions were willing to take up arms against him, to which the duke replied: "We do not rebel or arm ourselves against the king except in order to instruct him." Once again, it was not the person of the king that was threatened, but his policies and those who advised him.

Unwisely, Richard then raised the stakes by petulantly countering that he would seek help from the king of France. It was an idle threat that no one could take seriously, but it stung Gloucester into reminding his nephew that a king could be deposed if he neglected his duties and chose to listen to evil advisers, the implication being that it had happened once before in the country's history when Edward II had been forced to abdicate in 1327 following an indictment that accused him of being "incorrigible without hope of amendment." Richard took the hint and dismissed Suffolk as well as two other officials, the treasurer and the keeper of the privy seal. Suffolk was impeached and condemned to a period of imprisonment, only to be pardoned and allowed to continue to bask in the king's favor. This was another foolish and ill-tempered action that achieved nothing other than to enrage further Richard's enemies, but it counted for little as parliament had already decided on a new strategy to curb the king's spending. A commission was established to review Royal finances and to oversee policy, and although it would exist only for a year, Richard had to undertake to agree to its findings.

The king's reaction was to distance himself from events, and so began his so-called gyration of 1387 when he took himself and his retinue out of London and began a great peregrination of the country that lasted from February to November. Ostensibly the move kept him out of London at a time when the commission was doing its work, but Richard was also looking ahead and planning his next moves. He had been humiliated by his opponents, the inviolability of his Royal office had been called into question, and clearly he felt threatened by the turn of events. By traveling through his realm he would be able to gauge if he had any support in the shires and to see for himself if he could use the opportunity to rally followers to his cause.

While this was happening, de Vere used his influence in the northwest to raise an armed force of Welsh archers and Cheshire foot soldiers, ostensibly for service in Ireland but in reality to protect the king's household. At the same time, Richard took legal advice from his senior judges, including Sir Robert Tresilian, the chief justice who had been responsible for dealing with the aftermath of the Peasants' Revolt. The intention was to discover how far the king's prerogative had been infringed by parliament's actions and to get a legal opinion on whether or not the commission had been imposed against Richard's will and, if so, the extent to which those responsible were guilty of treason. The judges found in the king's favor in August and September, but Richard was in no position to use the judicial findings to his own benefit until he returned to London, where he hoped that he would find himself in a stronger position.

The first indications were good. When he rode into the city on November 10, he was greeted by enthusiastic crowds, but as Walsingham noted, "these Londoners were as swallows, found at one time with the lords, at another with the king, never settled and untrustworthy." In other words, Richard found that the Londoners' expressions of loyalty and support were more for the office of the king and less for the person of the king. Although the Lord Mayor Nicholas Brembre rallied support for Richard, there was to be no general or widespread backing from the people of London, who had clearly decided to await the outcome of events. By then the weight of the disagreement was swinging in the direction of Gloucester and Arundel, who had been joined by another powerful magnate, Thomas Beauchamp, Earl of Warwick, in gathering support against the king, as much to curb Richard as to protect their own interests. They were well aware that a judgment had been made against them and had taken their forces north of London, first to Haringey and then to Waltham Cross, where they consolidated their position and sent letters to London setting out their complaints about the king's advisers.

Their next step was to issue a written appeal on November 14 indicting Suffolk, de Vere, Tresilian, Brembre, and Alexander Neville, the archbishop of York on the change of treason. Three days later the Lords Appellant (as they came to be known on account of their appeal or accusation) presented themselves in London to make their case in person, and to their surprise Richard immediately accepted their appeal. It was agreed that parliament should reconvene the following year, the date being set for February 3, 1388, but, of course, on the king's part there was never any intention of keeping his side of the bargain. Richard hoped to play for time, and while four of the accused went into hiding or exile, de Vere hurried north to raise his army and to recruit for the king's cause. On hearing the news, the Lords Appellant started gathering their own forces, and they were joined in their enterprise by two younger men—John of Gaunt's son Henry Bolingbroke, Earl of Derby, and Arundel's son-in-law, Thomas Mowbray, Earl of Nottingham. After half a century of calm, England suddenly found itself on the brink of civil war.

De Vere made the first move at the beginning of December by moving his force of 4,250 men south toward London, hoping to impose Royal authority on the capital before the Lords Appellant could intervene by offering protection to the Royal household. He did this not without hope. His Welsh archers were well trained and battle-hardened, many of them having fought in France, and they were commanded by an experienced soldier Sir Thomas Molyneux; however, he had to move quickly before the opposition blocked his path to London. By then it was already too late. Gloucester had moved his forces north of London to take up a defensive position at Northampton, forcing de Vere to take a more southerly route. The original plan had been to head toward Stow-on-the-Wold, taking the ancient Fosse Way that ran from Axminster to Lincoln through Bath and Leicester, but when de Vere approached Burford on December 20, he found that Bolingbroke and Thomas Mowbray had cut off the route across the Thames by encamping on the island between the Pidnell and Radcot Bridges on the Berkshire–Oxfordshire border, near Faringdon. The trap was then sprung. When de Vere's forces arrived at the two bridges they found that one had been sabotaged and the other was heavily guarded by Bolingbroke's men. Unable to cross the Thames, they were further thwarted by the arrival of Gloucester's men from the north. As the battle began, Gloucester's pikemen advanced and the outnumbered and surprised Royalists began surrendering in droves or desperately trying to cross the river to safety. The way was now open for the army of the Lords Appellant to move triumphantly toward London, where Richard had wisely taken refuge in the Tower.

As for de Vere, he thought only of his own safety, and he was one of the first to flee by mounting a fresh horse and getting across the wreckage of Pidnell Bridge. But it was a desperate move. The horse refused to jump, and de Vere took it into the river and rode upstream, lightening his load by removing his armor and sword. That these items were found the following day encouraged the rumor that de Vere had been drowned. In fact, by holding his nerve even when he came under heavy fire from a company of archers at Radcot Bridge, de Vere managed to escape in the gathering gloom. After taking shelter in the nearby woods he made his way westward and later managed to leave England for exile in France. Five years later he died in penury, having been savaged by a wild boar while hunting. Radcot Bridge does not figure greatly in the list of battles fought on British soil, but it was a turning point. It was more of a skirmish than a pitched battle, and without their leader, the Royalist army did not offer much opposition. Englishmen had taken up arms against Englishmen for the first time in over half a century since Queen Isabel and Roger de Mortimer had unseated Edward II after invading England in 1326, and for a time it looked as if history would repeat itself with the dethroning of another English king.

Richard was now at the mercy of the Lords Appellant, and there is evidence to suggest that they planned to depose him there and then and might even have done so had they been able to agree on a successor. Shortly after Christmas the two sides met to agree to terms, but, having defeated the Royalist army, all the cards were held by the Lords Appellant. Backed into a corner and surrounded by an army that had inflicted a decisive defeat on his own forces, Richard had no option but to concede all demands made to him. Parliament would be summoned, warrants would be issued for the arrest of the five accused, and others were added to the list including Simon Burley and the king's steward Sir John Beauchamp. To add salt to the wound, warrants were also issued for the arrest of the judges who had found in the king's favor over parliament's infringement of his prerogative.

Parliament duly opened in the palace of Westminster on the agreed date, and from the outset it was obvious that the Lords Appellant were in complete control. Richard was forced to listen to their lengthy appeal, which was two hours in the reading, and it was upheld, despite a legal challenge from the king's party arguing that it was without legal precedent. For the accused there could only be one sentence: The fugitives (Suffolk and de Vere) were sentenced to death in absentia, but the Archbishop of York escaped death by being outlawed— he was stripped of his honours and possessions—and his case was referred to Rome. Brembre made a spirited defence, but he followed Tresilian to the scaffold, the former chief justice having been forcibly removed from Westminster Abbey on Gloucester's orders. It was not the end of the bloodletting. Charges of "accroaching" the Royal power by taking advantage of his youth were raised against Burley and four other courtiers including Beauchamp, and all were sentenced to death. Anne pleaded desperately to save Burley's life, but in vain; the only concession was the decision to acknowledge his status by beheading him instead of hanging him from the public scaffold. As for the judges, they too were sentenced to death, but they were eventually spared and instead were sent to exile in Ireland. It had been a shocking episode, and one that brought no credit to any of the participants. The Lords Appellant had no legal backing for their actions, the so-called trials were a sham, and the death sentences made a mockery of justice, but by acting in that way and by coercing parliament Gloucester and his fellow rebels had shown that they wielded the real power in the land. It was not surprising that this meeting of parliament later became known as the Merciless Parliament.

And yet, amid the mayhem and the carnage, there was one saving grace. Although Richard had been humbled, no attempt had been made to interfere with his personal rule and no one had demanded that he be unseated. It was enough that the court had been cleansed of the king's advisers (like de Vere, de la Pole died in exile), that his regal powers had been curbed, and that his person had been humiliated. The moves by the Lords Appellant had also cleared the air and had given the king a chance to reassert his authority. A year later, on May 3, 1389, at the age of twenty-two and having passed his majority, Richard assumed responsibility for ruling the country as king, after asking the assembled nobles, "Why should I be denied a right which is granted to anyone of lower rank?" His first step was to appoint as chancellor William of Wykeham, an elder statesman who had also served Edward III and who had risen from a humble background to become one of the great patrons of education, having already founded New College at Oxford and a school for boys at Winchester. Other appointments to Richard's council also showed the king's independence of mind without offending the Lords Appellant, who had largely withdrawn from public life after getting their way at court. Yet despite his claims of maturity, Richard still needed a mentor, and he found one in the familiar figure of John of Gaunt, who returned from Spain in 1389 without his Castilian throne but boosted by substantial financial rewards. The king's uncle was getting older—he was approaching fifty—and in late life, he had cast off many of his early ambitions and was thinking of his legacy. Until the end of his life ten years later, John of Gaunt's loyalty to Richard was unquestioned, and he became a constant presence and close adviser.

The next five years of Richard's reign were marked by relative harmony interspersed with episodes that showed that the king had lost none of his impetuosity or his ability to choose the wrong option. The anticipated outbreak of hostilities with France had failed to materialize, and thanks to Gaunt's earlier diplomatic interventions, a truce held between the two countries. It helped that in 1392, Charles VI suffered the first of the periodic bouts of insanity that would disfigure his reign—he had declared himself king of France on coming of age in 1388—and France's allies the Scots were also quiet. At the time of the Merciless Parliament the Scots had taken advantage of England's internal problems by sending into Northumberland a strong raiding party which defeated the English defending forces led by Harry Hotspur, the Earl of Northumberland's eldest son and the warden of the East March. While a diversionary force attacked English positions in Ireland, the main thrust was led by the Earl of Fife and the Lord of Galloway, Archibald the Grim, who attacked Carlisle and ravaged the valley of the River Eden. At the same time, another force under the earls of March, Moray, and Douglas assembled at Jedburgh and swept through Northumberland with fire and sword to lay waste Durham. Newcastle was also threatened before the Scots retired northward, with forces led by Hotspur and his brother Ralph in pursuit. On August 5 (or according to English sources, August 19), the English had reached Otterburn in Redesdale to find the Scots camped to the north of the present A696 highway. Although it was late in the day and his men were exhausted, Hotspur decided on a preemptive strike, and the resultant battle was what the chronicler Froissart described as "one of the sorest and best foughten without cowardice or faint hearts." The battle was won for the Scots in the gloaming when Douglas led a ferocious charge into the English flanks, only to be axed to the ground during the attack. Despite his death, the defeat at Otterburn was a severe embarrassment to Richard, not least because Hotspur was captured and subsequently ransomed for a huge sum.

The relative domestic tranquillity of this period of Richard's life provides an attractive picture of the creative and artistic aspects of his personality. Court poets were encouraged and patronized, and in return they would read their work at Richard's table. While there was nothing new in this practice, the main development was that they wrote in English rather than in French, with the result that the native tongue gradually became acceptable at court. Richard, too, spoke English as well as French, and his positive attitude to the language helped its acceptance. The most eminent of those writing in English was Geoffrey Chaucer, whose career had begun in the reign of Edward III and who had enjoyed John of Gaunt's patronage earlier in his career. His elegy *The Book of the Duchess* was written in memory of Gaunt's first wife Blanche, and his own wife Philippa was the sister of Katherine Swynford, who became Gaunt's third wife in January 1396, after years as his mistress. One of Richard's first acts on his accession was to confirm Chaucer in his position of controller of Customs and Subsidy of Wools, Skins, and Hides, a lucrative appointment that brought him considerable wealth and political power in London. Chaucer had also been involved in a number of embassies in Europe, most notably in Italy in the winter of 1372–1373 when he came under the influence of contemporary Italian writing and may even have met Boccaccio and Petrarch.

In 1388, Chaucer seems to have suffered at the hands of the Lords Appellant when Royal appointments came under scrutiny, but he was back in the king's favor a year later. Appointed clerk of the King's Works, he was responsible for looking after the Tower, Westminster Palace, and other Royal residences, parks, and lodges, and he was in the post for just under two years. His last official position was as deputy forester of the Royal forest of North Petherton in Somerset, and the records show that he was in receipt of several gifts and stipends from Richard, including the annual presentation of a hogshead of wine. During Richard's reign Chaucer wrote *The Canterbury Tales*, the work for which he is best known. Written predominantly in rhyming couplets, it extends to 17,000 lines, and the general prologue describes the meeting of assorted pilgrims in the Tabard Inn at Southwark as they prepare to journey to Canterbury. Detailed portraits are provided of all the pilgrims who come from all walks of society, and the narrative is driven by the conceit that each should tell a story on the way (the original scheme was for four stories, two on the outward journey and two on the return), with the teller of the best tale receiving a free supper. Although the work is incomplete and there are doubts over the correct order of the stories, *The Canterbury Tales* provides an intimate picture of the various strands of English social life in Chaucer's day, from the courtly Knight with his experience of fighting in Europe to the virtuous Friar and the down-to-earth but lecherous Wife of Bath. Here is a summary of English society in the fourteenth century that covers the main representatives of the different social levels—the soldier, the learned professional, the landed gentry, agricultural laborers, the rising middle classes, the tradesmen, the monastic orders, and people from the provinces outside London. Nothing like this series of portraits had ever appeared before in European literature, and as a result *The Canterbury Tales* is one of the great ornaments of Richard's reign.

In addition to patronizing the arts and making his court a place of refinement and grace, Richard also developed a finely honed sense of himself and the strength of his Royal lineage. Of particular interest to him was the figure of Edward the Confessor, with whom he felt he enjoyed a mystical relationship and who had been canonized in 1161. As an outward manifestation of his respect, Richard had the Royal arms impaled with those of the saint and was responsible for the various manifestations of Edward the Confessor which were used in the rebuilding of Westminster Hall, the magnificent edifice, once the largest in Europe, which had been built in the eleventh century by William Rufus. Its centerpiece was the huge, braced, hammerbeam roof, designed by Henry Yevele, which dispensed with the need for the supporting arcades of columns, but Richard's stall was also worthy of note. Richly decorated, it was a monument to the king's personal vanity and to the importance he placed on his monarchy, dominated as it was by a huge full-length portrait. There he sits in all his glory, red-robed with the scepter and orbs of kingship in his hands, his face slightly puffy and a wispy boyish beard covering his weak chin. It is the earliest state portrait in English history—today it can be found inside the west door of Westminster Abbey—and with its rich use of hammered gold, the wonder is that it survived at all.

Two unfortunate incidents made an impact on this relatively benign phase of Richard's reign. In 1392 he quarreled with the city of London over the grant of a loan. The city was a wealthy cosmopolitan place that had benefited from its support of the king during the Peasants' Revolt, but it also proved to be a fickle partner, and the refusal to offer the king any financial support led to the imposition of a huge fine. It was not the end of the matter. Richard decided to punish the city further, unwisely dismissing the mayor and the leading magistrates and removing the law courts and the chancery to York. As Walsingham noted, "the innovation did not last long, for these institutions were brought back to London just as easily as they had been taken to York," but the king's rash behavior cooled his relationship with the city. The matter was papered over with the restoration of the loan, and the reconciliation was celebrated with a grand pageant in which the king played a leading role, but lasting damage had been done and Richard could never again count on London's fullest support.

Two years later he suffered a heavier blow when Anne died in June 1394 at the early age of twenty-seven. The loss unnerved Richard and left him prostrated by grief. Despite the unpromising start to their marriage, he had come to love her, and he seems to have been totally unprepared for her death. A huge state funeral was held for her in Westminster Abbey, where he created a joint tomb, the hands of their effigies clasped in eternal love. During the service Richard's grief and his capacity for impetuosity resurfaced when he struck the Earl of Arundel with a rod, in retaliation for the magnate's rudeness in arriving late and then asking permission to leave early. Arundel was clearly courting trouble by behaving in such a rude way, but the king's response outweighed the slight he had received and is an indication both of the pain he felt at his wife's passing and the inner rage that was never far from the surface. Further evidence of his unhinged mind came when he ordered the destruction of part of the Royal manor house at Sheen on the banks of the Thames in Surrey, a favorite residence where he had built a set of private apartments and chapel. So bitter was his sorrow at Anne's untimely death that he could not even bear to look again at the site of a place where he and his wife had enjoyed such intense happiness. Both episodes suggest an intemperate personality at work, and there is little doubt that Richard's immoderate approach to problems was a worrying behavioral flaw at a time when he needed to have all his wits about him.

3

ALL POMP AND MAJESTY
I DO FORSWEAR

ollowing Anne's untimely death, Richard went into a period of prolonged
mourning, but he could not ignore two pressing problems that impinged
on his rule and that required his urgent attention: France and Ireland.
From the evidence of the *Westminster Chronicle*, a contemporary record attrib-
uted to the monk Robert of Reading, it seems that Richard was fully aware of the
need to find some sort of accord with France that would end the quarrel or produce an honorable truce without either side losing too much face. Continuing
the struggle or mounting fresh military expeditions against the French invariably
meant raising taxes, an unpopular move that would inevitably harm his own
position. He had already witnessed the enforced removal from office of one
chancellor (de la Pole in 1386), and it is clear that he understood that "damaging
results" would follow the high costs of any new military campaign. The French,
too, were keen to find a compromise, as the constraints on the Flemish wool
trade were equally damaging to them at a time when Philip, the Duke of
Burgundy and uncle to Charles VI, was strengthening his interests in the area. In
1383 he had married Margaret of Flanders, thereby acquiring further land there
as well as in the French Comte, Artois, Hainault, and Brabant. In 1393, the two
sides began negotiations to find a solution to the question of English holdings in
Aquitaine, the real bone of contention between the two countries. Richard was
eager to settle the issue once and for all, and at one point agreed to the suggestion that he should pay liege-homage to the king of France (the practice whereby
one sovereign renders feudal allegiance to another), but when that proposal was
opposed by the English parliament, the negotiations came to a standstill.

Nonetheless, there was still a desire on both sides to reach a settlement, and Richard's freedom to enter into a new marriage produced the solution. In March 1396 the two kings concluded an agreement to work together to end the Great Schism that had divided the Catholic Church and to embark on a crusade at a later date to recover the Holy Land. There would be a truce lasting 28 years, and in return Richard consented to marry Isabella of Valois, the six-year-old daughter of Charles VI and his wife Isabeau of Bavaria.

The marriage took place in October 1396 but was not a popular union. Not only was the bride French, but being little more than a child it would take time before she was able to produce children to ensure the succession. But for Richard it was a tempting proposition. As part of the settlement Isabella brought a handsome dowry, and in the longer term, with the birth of children, the marriage promised to end once and for all the long and expensive confrontation with France. As Walsingham put it, the new relationship meant that "both monarchs could live in peace and tranquillity, and could secure a proper state of harmony between their two kingdoms for ever, and no more Christian blood would be shed." That was exactly what Richard desired: Unlike his forebears, he had no taste for warfare in general and was in no mood to go to war with France at a time when the confrontation was, in effect, in stalemate.

Having settled the relationship with France by means of the new period of truce and the marriage agreement, Richard was able to turn his attention to Ireland, another seemingly intractable problem in urgent need of attention. No English king since John in 1210 had taken the trouble to visit the Irish lordship, and in that time the country had almost become ungovernable. During Richard's minority Edmund Mortimer, 3rd (English) Earl of March, had been appointed to govern Ireland in 1379, but his period in office lasted barely two years. He was drowned while crossing a ford in County Cork, and his title and holdings had passed to his seven-year-old son Roger. As a result, Ireland was left rudderless, with English authority confined to parts of Ulster and Leinster. Even around Dublin in the area known as the Pale—at that time the medieval counties of Dublin, Meath, Louth, and Kildare—English rule was vulnerable to attack and disruption by the native Irish.

One of the chieftains in the Wicklow Mountains, Art McMurrough, styled himself as king of Leinster and "captain of his nation," and in that role he felt strong enough to attack English-held towns in Leinster and even to threaten Dublin. It was to curb that kind of lawless power that Richard set sail for Ireland in the autumn of 1394 at the head of a large army of 8,000 men. His tactics were straightforward and turned out to be reasonably successful: to confine McMurrough in the mountains of Wicklow and to restrict his movement as a prelude to pacifying Leinster and colonizing it with English settlers. The size of the English army made a huge impression on the Irish, who confined their attacks on it to ambushes that were quickly routed by the English archers. By the time Richard reached Dublin, the Irish were ready to submit to him. Contrary to the expectations of the Irish, Richard did not use his overwhelming superiority to punish the chieftains, but decided on a policy of appeasement. In return for the chieftains' oaths of allegiance, he promised to arbitrate on their problems with the English and to provide the necessary finance to revitalize English rule. McMurrough even consented to return land he had confiscated, and although this came to nothing, Richard's expedition must be counted a great success in that he had achieved most of his objectives. When he eventually left the country the following May, he did so in the belief that English rule had been reimposed and that the Gaelic revival had been checked.

As happened so frequently throughout the course of Richard's reign, it was all a mirage. Richard might have scored diplomatic and domestic successes, but the rapprochement with France was not universally popular because it seemed to place England in a subservient position to the French king. There was also disquiet about the religious and political ramifications associated with the king's marriage and the implied closer union with France. When parliament assembled in January it quickly quashed a proposal to send an English army to fight in support of Charles VI's territorial ambitions in northern Italy, where the French had a claim on the territory of the Duke of Milan. Once again Richard was seen to be responsible for introducing a reckless policy of appeasement as the offer had been made as the result of a rash promise that he had made to his future French father-in-law. Once again his reign was in danger of unraveling, largely as a result of his increasingly unbridled profligacy. Richard had always been extravagant, but his expenditure had generally been kept within bounds; now it was spinning out of control, forcing him to borrow, and, worse, a vainglorious side to his character was being revealed. About this time the author of the *Eulogium Historiarum* recorded a worrying new trend at court where the king "ordered a throne to be set up in his chamber on which he could sit after dinner until evening, showing himself. He would talk to no one but would look at people, and whoever he looked at, whatever his rank, he had to genuflect." Grandiose behavior of that kind was unlikely to add to his popularity or increase his support among the nobility, but in and of itself such behavior was not the ultimate cause of his eventual downfall. The king himself was solely responsible for what happened next.

For reasons that are not exactly clear, Richard decided to take revenge on his enemies, the Lords Appellant who had humbled him almost ten years earlier. His main targets were the leaders, Gloucester, Arundel, and Warwick. At the end of July 1397, all three were summoned to attend a banquet in London, but only Warwick accepted the invitation, and for his pains he was arrested and imprisoned in the Tower. Arundel followed next and was incarcerated in Carisbroke Castle. With Gloucester, Richard took no chances: At the head of a powerful force of armed men, he rode down to his uncle's residence at Pleshey in Essex and, having arrested him, arranged for him to be sent across the Channel to Calais for safekeeping. Richard had moved quickly and decisively against the three powerful magnates whom he perceived to be the deadliest of his enemies. Walsingham referred to the "king's scheming behavior" and suggested that he acted "without warning," but this seems unlikely. At that stage in his reign, Richard would hardly have taken such a crucial and far-reaching step without weighing the options. While it is fair to say that he intended to recover the position he felt he had lost at the time of the Merciless Parliament and overcome the humiliation he had suffered at the hands of the Lords Appellant—Arundel's insistence on Burley's execution still rankled—he could act against such powerful men, including his uncle, only from a position of strength.

More than any other factor, it is likely that Richard was determined to retain and strengthen the Royal prerogative that he felt had been violated in 1388. Ten years later he was in a position to do just that. The truce with France and the settlement of Ireland (chimerical though it was) had strengthened his hand, and he had used the intervening years to rebuild his retinue. Among those closest to him were his two half-brothers Thomas and John Holland, respectively the earls of Kent and Huntingdon (their father Thomas, Earl of Kent, had been married to Joan of Woodstock before she married the Black Prince). Gaunt also continued to support the king, as did John Beaufort, his eldest son from his relationship with Katherine Swynford. That same year all the Royal bastards had been legitimated when parliament allowed Gaunt to marry his long-term mistress, their children taking the name Beaufort from the castle in Champagne where they were born. Also included in the latest Royal entourage were Richard's cousins Edward of Norwich, the Earl of Rutland and eldest son of the Duke of York, and Thomas Mowbray, the Earl of Nottingham. Such was the closeness of relationships at Richard's court that when Richard decided to strengthen his position, the new affiliations pitched brother against brother (Gaunt and Gloucester), nephew against uncle (Rutland and Gloucester), and son-in-law against father-in-law (Nottingham and Arundel).

When parliament opened on September 17, there was a further show of Royal strength with the appearance of Richard's new bodyguards, who were described by Walsingham as "a savage crowd of Cheshire men, armed with axes, bows and arrows." In a grim reminder of past events, the procedure mirrored the actions taken by the Merciless Parliament, only this time the appellants were on the receiving end of an appeal against them. The first to be tried for treason was Arundel, who answered the indictment read by John of Gaunt with the retort that he had received a charter of pardon at the time of the Merciless Parliament and was also in receipt of the king's personal promise of safety. His protestations were to no avail, and Arundel was sentenced to death by the horrible method of being hanged, drawn, and quartered. (Reserved for traitors, this involved the victim being hung until barely conscious, and then cut down to have his genitals cut off and stuffed in his mouth, followed by evisceration.) Richard intervened to change the sentence to execution by beheading, and without further ado Arundel was led off to the Tower, where, according to witnesses, he met his end with grace and courage. Arundel's brother, now archbishop of Canterbury, was also arraigned, but his life was spared and he was sent into exile. Gloucester would have been next in line, but when his trial began, word arrived from Calais that he was dead. This was a fortunate outcome as his execution would have angered Gaunt. Either Gloucester had died from natural causes or, more probably, he was murdered by Mowbray on Richard's orders to save him the indignity of facing a trial for treason followed by inevitable execution. The last to be tried was Warwick, who immediately pleaded guilty and threw himself on the king's mercy. According to the chronicler Adam of Usk who was present at the trial, he behaved in an unmanly way, "wailing and weeping and whining, traitor that he was." He, too, was condemned to death, but Richard again interceded and Warwick was banished to the Isle of Man, where he faced harsh imprisonment at the hands of the Governor William le Scrope.

Having dispatched his enemies, Richard was able to consolidate his own position and to reward those who had supported him. There were dukedoms for those closest to him in his retinue: His half-brothers John and Thomas Holland were elevated as Dukes of Exeter and Surrey, Rutland became Duke of Albemarle, Mowbray became Duke of Norfolk, and Bolingbroke received the title Duke of Hereford. Richard also made sure that parliament was packed with his own supporters, but despite successfully eliminating his enemies, he was still intent on reinforcing his position. His mind went back to the defeat at Radcot Bridge, and those who had supported the Lords Appellant were forced to pay large fines in return for pardons, and there were collective fines for London and for those in Herefordshire and Essex who had ridden in Gloucester's armed forces. As if to bring home the fact that he was the master now, he ordered parliament to reassemble early in 1398, not in London but in Shrewsbury, close to the center of his military power in Cheshire and the Welsh borders. During the sitting, de la Pole was restored as Earl of Suffolk and all acts passed by the Merciless Parliament were repealed. Parliament also agreed to reiterate an oath, first sworn the previous September, that these changes would be upheld on penalty of accusation of treason. These were oppressive measures, but at the time Richard was able to do as he pleased as there was no opposition and his powers were more or less absolute. As Walsingham put it graphically, Richard "began to act the tyrant and oppress the people."

All seemed to be going Richard's way until the third day of the parliament when Bolingbroke reported a conversation he had had with Mowbray the previous December while both men were riding from Windsor to London. It seems that Mowbray had warned him that they were "on the point of being undone" for their participation at Radcot Bridge and that there was a plot to kill them as well as John of Gaunt and the king's two half-brothers with a view to confiscating the Lancastrian lands. As the accusation was only reported by Bolingbroke and does not exist in any extant form, the exact details are unclear, but he was sufficiently alarmed to take advice from his father, who in turn raised the matter with the king. Because Mowbray was not present to defend his name and was greatly angered that his confidential conversation had been reported to Richard, the matter was allowed to fester and descended into a quarrel between the two men, which quickly spiraled out of control. Mowbray was deprived of some of his offices, including the captaincy of Calais, and for a time was put in prison for his own safety. To safeguard their positions both men accused the other of treason, and, as the quarrel could not be decided by law, Richard ordered the matter to be settled by trial of battle at Gosford Green, Coventry, on September 16, 1398—this was a chivalric means of settling a dispute between social equals in which the winner either killed his opponent or disabled him and forced him to surrender by crying "Craven!"

If it had taken place, the tournament would have been one of the most colorful events of Richard's reign. Both participants were dukes, one of them (Bolingbroke) was the king's cousin, and quite possibly it could have been a battle to the death. Bolingbroke was already well versed in the practice of jousting and was an experienced soldier: In 1390 he had joined the Teutonic knights in their crusade against pagan Lithuania, where he took part in the siege of Vilnius. For his combat with Mowbray he went into training and ordered special armor to be made for him in Milan. Given his strength and expertise, it is probable that he would have gained the upper hand, but dramatically on the day of the confrontation Richard, who was arbitrating, threw down his staff and signaled that the contest was over and that there would be no trial by battle. Instead, Mowbray was sent into exile for life, while Bolingbroke received the more moderate sentence of ten years' exile. Again there was probably no single reason why Richard acted in this way, and it has to be said that his decision dismayed the onlookers, who had flocked to Coventry in expectation of a notable spectacle. It could hardly have been a desire to stop bloodshed. Despite his lack of military experience, Richard was no coward and knew how to act decisively and, when necessary, brutally. Neither of the men involved in the confrontation was particularly close to him, and Bolingbroke's lesser sentence was as much due to family ties as to the respect Richard felt for his uncle. (Gaunt was not present at the tournament.) More likely, he realized that neither man's triumph would suit him because at the time people believed that the outcome of a trial by battle revealed the truth of the allegations that had been made. If Mowbray won, then it would be acknowledged that his claims were just, namely that Richard had intended to punish both men for their roles at Radcot Bridge. If Bolingbroke won, equally awkward problems would have arisen. While it would have cleared Richard's name, a triumph in the jousting lists would have made Bolingbrook a popular figure, and the king could not afford that at a time when the Royal succession had not been settled, Isabella being still a child. In the event the only winner was Richard, who with one stroke managed to rid himself of the two remaining Lords Appellant who had defied him all those years ago.

Nevertheless the sentences also carried risks: Although Gaunt was ill, he was still alive, and the exile of his son was a double punishment for an old and increasingly frail man. Perhaps to soften the blow, Richard gave Bolingbroke a cash grant to cover his losses while he was in exile in France—he decided to take up residence in Paris—and more importantly, issued him with letters that would allow him to pursue for livery of his inheritance should Gaunt die within the next ten years. (The term "pursue for livery" applied to the process by which in the old feudal tenures, wards, whether of the king or another guardian, on arriving at legal age, could compel a delivery of their estates to them from their guardians.) In fact John of Gaunt died within six months of his son's exile, meeting his end at Leicester Castle "by a sudden languor, both for old age and heaviness." Gaunt's death presented Richard with both a problem and an opportunity. He could have pardoned Bolingbroke or even allowed him to attend his father's funeral, but he chose to do neither. Instead he decided to act against him. Knowing that he could not afford to have a wealthy rival and possible claimant to his throne living in France, Richard revoked the letters that would have allowed Bolingbroke to claim his inheritance. As an added punishment, he extended his exile to life. Apart from gaining further revenge, his reasoning was that while Bolingbroke was in France, his moves would be checked by the French, who were keen to keep the truce and would hardly rock the boat by condoning any plotting by an exiled

English magnate. In this as in so many other matters during his reign, Richard was mistaken.

Secure in the belief that he had settled the issue and had succeeded in protecting his own position, Richard made plans to return to Ireland. He had good reasons to go. The Irish had not lived up to their promises, Art McMurrough had recommenced military activities, and the (English) Earl of March had been killed trying to restore order in fighting near Kells. There was a clear need to stop the rot, and at the end of May, Richard assembled a new army numbering some 5,000 men and sailed over to Ireland determined to halt the violence and also to avenge the death of the Earl of March, his heir pre-sumptive. (Roger Mortimer's mother Philippa of Clarence was Edward III's granddaughter, and this relationship gave him a reasonable legal claim on the throne.) Once again, fate intervened and events elsewhere conspired against Richard. In Paris, the Duke of Orléans, the French king's brother, was in ascen-dancy over the Duke of Burgundy during the period of the regency caused by one of Charles VI's periodic bouts of insanity. This was to be a source of constant concern throughout the reign: Not only did it incapacitate the French king, but it led to an increasingly volatile quarrel between his brother Louis, Duke of Orleans, and Philip, Duke of Burgundy.

The reasons of Charles VI's incapacity are difficult to understand—schizo-phrenia, porphyria, and bipolar disorder have all been advanced as causes—but the first outbreak of insanity in 1392 was recorded. The attempted assassination of his friend and adviser Oliver de Clisson encouraged the king to mount an expedition into Brittany to apprehend the culprits, and during the progression Charles was unusually on edge. At one point during the journey the Royal party was stopped and warned by a stranger that the king was about to be betrayed by unknown assailants. This warning was dismissed, but there were terrible conse-quences. In the midday heat a page dropped the king's lance, and as it fell to the ground it made a mighty noise that unhinged Charles. Drawing his sword and shouting "Treason!" he rode through his escorts and started swinging wildly at them. A number were killed before he was overpowered. In the aftermath Burgundy assumed the regency, but it was the beginning of a litany of episodes in which the king would lose his mind and be incapable of ruling France. On another occasion, he was unable to remember his identity, and this was followed by periods when he refused to wash or change his clothes. Later he came to believe that he was made of glass and would break if people approached him.

The king's madness also affected events on the other side of the Channel. Being pro-war and against rapprochement with England, Orleans used his brother's incapacity to enter into an alliance with Bolingbroke, who had taken up residence at the Hotel de Clisson and was generally well received by the French court. Under the terms of the agreement with Orleans, which had been facilitated by Burgundy's absence from the French capital, each man pledged to be "the friend of the other's friends and well-wishers, and the enemy of the other's enemies." While Richard was dealing with his kingdom in Ireland, Bolingbroke decided to return to England to take advantage of what seemed to be a God-given opportunity to reclaim his rights. In weighing the odds he might also have been prompted into action by the young Earl of Arundel, who needed little encouragement to avenge the execution of his father, but the most probable reason for his decision to return to England was that he had been given a glorious chance to retrieve his inheritance and in so doing to take his revenge on Richard. The death of his father to whom he had always been close could also have been a factor: While John of Gaunt was in England, Bolingbroke took little part in public life and had only joined the Lords Appellant in 1388 while his father was out of the country.

Four weeks after Richard had arrived in Ireland, Bolingbroke left Paris and sailed from Boulogne accompanied by a small party of friends and retainers. After making landfall in Sussex, the party sailed north up the east coast of England and landed at Ravenspur just north of the Humber estuary, deep in Lancastrian territory. Bolingbroke was soon joined there by a number of powerful northern lords including Henry Percy, Earl of Northumberland, his son Henry Hotspur, and their cousin Ralph Neville, Earl of Westmorland. It is impossible to know if Bolingbroke left France intent on deposing Richard or if he only wanted to reclaim his inheritance—Henry is said to have made a promise at Doncaster in the presence of an assembly of lords including Northumberland, Hotspur, Westmorland, and the archbishop of Canterbury that his only motive was to retrieve his position in England. However, the support of the northern magnates and the speed with which other members of the nobility joined his cause, bringing with them men-at-arms, must have persuaded him that he had the numbers and the capacity to challenge the king. As his slowly burgeoning army made its way south toward Gloucester, Bolingbroke's cause was helped by the hopeless indecision shown by Edmund, Duke of York, who had been appointed keeper of the realm in Richard's absence. It took a week for the news of Bolingbroke's return to reach him, and his response was to send a warning to Richard while withdrawing his small forces west toward Bristol, where he hoped to meet up with the Royalist army returning from Ireland. But it was already too late. Delayed by a lack of ships, Richard was unable to get back to England until July 25, when he landed at Milford Haven only to find that his cause was collapsing. By then Bolingbroke had taken Berkeley Castle and had executed three of the king's leading councillors. Believing his way to be blocked, Richard then headed north to Conwy Castle in north Wales, where he hoped to gather support in Cheshire, whose people had always been loyal to his cause.

Once more he had been forestalled. Having marched his rebel army quickly north, Bolingbroke was already in Chester, and after his emissaries were arrested, Richard was left with no option but to attempt to broker an agreement. At first it seemed as if an understanding could be reached that would keep Richard on the throne and restore Bolingbroke, to his rightful position by ending his exile and letting him come into his inheritance. Northumberland conducted the negotiations for Bolingbroke, and during the discussions he seems to have done enough to persuade Richard that he would not be harmed and that his position would remain intact and unsullied. During the negotiations Northumberland himself seems to have sworn that Richard could retain his royal dignity and power if only the family estates and the hereditary stewardship were restored to Henry Bolingbroke. That might have been the intention, but the execution was rather different. Richard was escorted to Flint Castle where Bolingbroke was waiting, wearing full armor in the office of high steward of England as if to show the king that he was now the master and their positions had been reversed. From there they continued south to London, where Richard was locked in the Tower, a prisoner in his own country. By then it was all over for him. His supporters had melted away, and Bolingbroke and his backers clearly had the upper hand. All that remained for the usurpers was to produce a rationalization for what would happen next—the removal of a crowned king from his legal throne. One option would have been to keep Richard as the nominal king and to appoint a regent, but Bolingbroke had seen with his own eyes the support he had gathered, and by then he had been able to gauge the depths of Richard's unpopularity within the country.

What followed next was a mixture of persuasion and political fixing. While pressure was put on Richard to stand down, Bolingbroke's party stressed the continuity that he would bring to the throne and the prime importance of rescuing England from the autocratic rule of the king and his self-serving advisers. In particular, according to Adam of Usk, when Richard's record was investigated by Bolingbroke's followers they found that it provided sufficient grounds to depose him on the evidence of his "perjuries, sodomitical acts, dispossession of his subjects, reduction of his people to servitude, lack of reason and incapacity to rule." A total of 39 accusations were made against him based on the understanding that he had broken the terms of his coronation oath and that he preferred to rule "according to his own arbitrary will" instead of by upholding the laws of the country. There was also the precedent of Edward II to take into account, and when parliament was summoned on September 30, there was only one item for it to consider. On the day before it convened Richard had succumbed to pressure from a visiting deputation that included Bolingbroke and had agreed to resign as king. According to one contemporary record he did this "with a cheerful expression" and gave Bolingbroke his signet ring as a symbol of his wishes, but it is difficult to believe that version. Shakespeare probably came closer to the truth when he described an angry and frustrated Richard symbolically washing away his Coronation oil with his own tears. For Richard, giving up his crown would have been a painful business, and he was not the kind of man who would have made it any easier for himself or his usurpers.

After attending mass, Bolingbroke rode over to Westminster Hall and told the assembled members that he was making a challenge for the crown based on his blood rights through descent from Henry III, and that with the help of his kinsmen and followers he meant to recover his rightful inheritance, adding that the "realm was in point of being undone for default of governance and the undoing of good laws." As there was no one to speak for Richard, the assembly joined in acclaiming Bolingbroke the new king and declaring that Richard was deposed. They had no standing to do this as parliament had no authority without the king's presence, but the time for political niceties had passed, and a fortnight later Bolingbroke was crowned as King Henry IV. From the outset, he had proclaimed his willingness to forget the past and forge a new beginning, and Richard's closest supporters were merely stripped of their titles. It was as if the new king was intent on making good the promise given on his accession, that he was not intended to "disinherit any man of his heritage, franchise or any other rights that he ought to have, nor put him out of that that he has had by the good laws and custom of the Realm, except those persons that have been against the good purpose and the common profit of the Realm."

In fact Henry was as good as his word, and he proved to be surprisingly lenient, perhaps remembering the sentence of exile that he had received and Richard's refusal to allow him to claim his inheritance. There was, though, the question of what should be done with the anointed king, who was imprisoned first at Leeds Castle in Kent and then at Pontefract Castle in Yorkshire, following a short spell at Knaresborough. In the middle of February 1400 it was announced that Richard was dead, either deliberately or by his own hand. The official version was that he starved to death, although it is impossible to know if this was done with intent or if Richard decided to end it all by refusing to eat—Walsingham claimed that he killed himself by voluntary starvation, while Adam of Usk argued that the king's death was caused by a deliberate policy of starvation "as he lay in chains in the castle of Pontefract." His body was taken to

London, where he had expressed a wish to be buried alongside Anne in Westminster Abbey. However, Henry paid no attention to the king's last will and testament and had Richard buried in the priory at Kings Langley, and his body remained there until December 1413 when in an act of piety and reconciliation Henry's son Henry V had him reburied in Westminster Abbey.

Richard's fate cast a long shadow over the fifteenth century. Whatever else he had been, he was a usurped king, and it proved difficult for Henry IV and his successors to gloss over the fact that they had come to the throne not through inheritance but by deposing and perhaps killing one of their close relatives. In time, the feebleness and many blunders of Richard's reign were forgotten or ignored, as were his vanities and his extravagance, and he was remembered as the king who had lost his crown unnaturally and perhaps even illegally. Instead of living out his life and reign in tranquillity, with the comforting knowledge that he might have fathered an heir to confirm the succession, he had died under suspicious circumstances, shorn of his crown and his honor. It was a harsh fate for a man who believed that his existence was a divine mission and that he enjoyed powers denied to lesser men. To the very end Richard II seems to have clung on to his belief in the absolute monarchy, and although he eventually gave ground to Bolingbroke, his decision to abdicate was forced on him at a time when he was enfeebled and had no room to maneuver. Inevitably, the pathos of his position has colored history's verdict of a king who was brought down by his bad judgment and by his refusal to trim his beliefs or to cultivate working relationships with the powerful magnates who wielded such power in his kingdom.

Over the centuries his personality and psychological makeup have also been subject to investigation and conjecture. The findings have ranged from a belief that he might have been clinically insane to a more sober contention that he was rash and weak-willed and was liable to base his decisions on what he wanted to believe rather than on any rational conviction that he was doing the right thing. Certainly, during the last two years of his life when he alienated so many people who could have been useful to him, Richard frequently behaved in an irrational and intemperate fashion. Instead of showing the coolness and firm judgment that he brought to his affairs in Ireland or as a young man when he boldly confronted the rebellious peasants in London, he allowed himself to be seduced by the delusion of his own omnipotence. In particular, the decision to proceed aggressively against Gloucester, Arundel, and Warwick in 1397 left him vulnerable to attack and showed a lack of political judgment. As happened so often in his life, he had nothing much to gain by taking his revenge and a great deal more to lose by acting against them when he did.

Against that, like any other human being, Richard possessed attractive qualities, and in no other incident did he show his emotional side more clearly than in his grief at the death of his wife, Anne. With her moderating influence and good sense it is tempting to wonder if his life would have turned out differently had she survived. As a young man, not more than a boy, Richard's comportment during the Peasants' Revolt demonstrated that when the occasion demanded he was capable of showing good sense and moral courage. As a soldier and the grandson of the Black Prince, his conduct was blameless, and in Scotland and Ireland he demonstrated that he could be a leader of men, although his uncles would have preferred him to have done that by leading his armies against the French. On that score his great achievement in terms of foreign policy was his steadfast refusal to reignite the war in France, although latterly this was helped by the rapprochement brought about by his marriage to Isabella.

Richard's patronage of the arts also puts him in a good light, especially his support for the use of English, even though he often used the resultant expenditure to glorify his court at the expense of the public exchequer. His long fatherless childhood in preparation for assuming the crown must have affected him, and the charges brought against him by parliament at the time of his abdication suggest that he had never grown up mentally or accepted his responsibilities as king. But compared to many other rulers before or after him, Richard was not a particularly evil man. Unscrupulous and duplicitous, wrongheaded and convinced of his own infallibility: Those charges can be laid against him as evidence of his vanity and his irrationality, but he was very much a product of his background and upbringing. He made the mistake of alienating the very people who should have supported him; worse and all too often, he befriended those who only led him into deeper trouble. In the final analysis, Richard was doomed not by any particular aberration in his mental makeup but by his steadfast belief in his own supremacy as king and by his incapacity, or refusal, to produce good governance when it was most needed. More than any other factor, that failing helped to seal his fate.

4

THE USURPER KING

From the very moment he became king, Bolingbroke's reign was clouded with dark suspicions about his right to the throne. As a result there were always lingering misgivings that in the long term his authority might become untenable. In front of parliament he had claimed the crown as his by right of hereditary title, because he was descended "by right line of the blood coming from the good lord Henry the Third," but it was a statement dripping with insincerity and laden with half-truths. Not only had he seized the crown after declaring that he was justly pursuing his rights as Duke of Lancaster, but his statement to parliament was based on the spurious assumption that Edward of Lancaster and not Edward I was the eldest son of Henry III and that therefore he was the rightful heir through his mother Blanche of Lancaster. As this was little more than an idle legend, his claim did nothing to mask the fact that he was a usurper king.

Not even his coronation eased those doubts. Henry's coronation took place on St. Edward's Day (October 13), but although it was replete with religious trappings, the ceremony failed to reinforce his right to the crown. Even before he entered Westminster Abbey to sit on the throne there were problems about the key points of the ceremony.

So that the mystique of the divinely appointed king could be maintained, anointment was central to the proceedings. Richard had made much of that conceit when he was crowned, and matters were helped for Henry by the miraculous discovery of the fabulous golden eagle ampulla of sacred ointment that had been missing for many years—the symbolism of its unexpected reappearance in time for Henry's coronation is obvious. This sacred oil was supposed to have been presented by the Virgin Mary, who appeared in a vision to the martyred

Archbishop of Canterbury, Thomas Becket, in the twelfth century. For reasons that are unknown, it had been lost for many years and its sudden recovery should have been a good portent, but, on the contrary, the reappearance of the long-lost ampulla only made matters worse. When the Archbishop of Canterbury began the anointment it was discovered that the king's head was crawling with lice. And another bad sign followed when the newly crowned king's traditional gold coin fell from his hand at the offertory and despite strenuous efforts could not be recovered. All this was recorded by Adam of Usk, and to the superstitious the incidents were signs of ill omen that did not bode well for Bolingbroke's reign. Later, at the traditional banquet in Westminster Hall there was another awkward moment when Sir Thomas Dymoke the official champion challenged anyone to gainsay Henry's title: The new king simply said that he was prepared to defend it himself.

Nevertheless, even though Henry had seized the crown and even though his coronation seemed to suggest that his kingship might be built on unsound foundations, his reign got off to a reasonably good start. His accession and the deposition of Richard had been relatively popular—it helped that the former king was decidedly out of favor—and Henry showed that he was anxious to restore prestige to the throne and to reward those who had been loyal to him. The chronicler John Capgrave went so far as to compare the new king to Solomon, choosing "not wealth or honours but the succouring wisdom of God," and there were high hopes that his reign would usher in an age of achievement and blessings. On a more temporal level, one of Henry's first acts was to create a new order of chivalry, the Order of the Bath (this soon died out and was not restored until 1725), and two days after the coronation he proclaimed his eldest son Henry heir to the throne and made him Prince of Wales, a title first conferred on the Black Prince in 1343. In order to create an atmosphere of confidence, Henry repeated over and over again that he had no intention of being any different from his predecessors and that there would be no slackening of the traditional discretionary rights and privileges of the Crown, the so-called Royal prerogatives. He also took steps to ensure the future of his position in 1406 when his title to the Crown was cemented by an act of parliament, and a year later he introduced legislation to exclude his father's Beaufort children and their descendants from the succession. Cleverly, he avoided offense and potential family strife by confirming their legitimacy by letters patent, but by adding the words "excepting the royal dignity" he made sure that they would never succeed to the throne. This did not stop Henry from relying on his half-brothers John and Henry Beaufort, who both served on his council of advisers, but the step did provide a legal check on any ambitions they might have entertained as the offspring of John of Gaunt. Henry had good reason to be touchy about his position: King Charles VI of France refused to recognize him—after all he had usurped his son-in-law—and took to treating English envoys with more than usual contempt.

At the same time, during that honeymoon period in office, Henry chose to reward the loyalty of his supporters and to keep the allegiance of those who had been in Richard's employment. This meant giving grants of land and expensive annuities, the costs of which inevitably fell on the Royal exchequer. This profligacy was bound to lead to problems with parliament. In his own right, Henry was a wealthy man who enjoyed the income from his Lancastrian lands and properties as well as those of his wife Mary Bohun, younger daughter of the Earl of Hereford, whom he had married in 1380, and whose older sister Eleanor was married to Henry's uncle Thomas of Woodstock, Duke of Gloucester. From an early stage in his life Bolingbroke had come to rely on the large subventions made to him by John of Gaunt and was used to the trappings of wealth and power. On becoming king, he continued to regard his family wealth as his private income to be used at his pleasure and discretion; while this gave him the kind of affluence that had been denied to Richard, it did not solve the perennial problems of paying for the upkeep of the court. At the time, a king was supposed "to live of his own," that is, he was supposed to use his own revenues for his personal expenditure while using taxes to pay for the defense of the realm. In Henry's case though, there was a misunderstanding from the very beginning. His Lancastrian wealth could not be ignored, and it proved difficult to separate his private needs from his public position as head of state. In an attempt to fix the matter Henry argued that the cost of his household was a public expense that should be met from crown revenues but that he would "put the household in good and moderate governance." Despite those well-intentioned efforts, the finance of the Royal household remained a sensitive subject for much of Henry's reign.

In the first years of Henry's reign parliament showed a reluctance to grant taxes, offering the new king nothing more than the income from customs duties, which were themselves reduced as a result of the slump in the wool trade, and a year into his reign appeals to the church and the aristocracy for funds fell on deaf ears. Although the nobility and the princes of the church were agreed that Henry should be offered financial support, finding the money was another matter, and an indication of the problems facing the new king can be seen in the fact that he employed six treasurers during the first five years of his reign. It did not help matters that there was confusion over Henry's own position with regard to what should be done about taxation. While making his move to claim the throne, he had promised to reduce taxation, but his comments were taken to mean that he would not be raising taxes at all, and among many of his subjects that assumption came to be believed.

The fact that he had huge personal wealth must also have helped reinforce the idea that as far as finance was concerned, Henry's reign would be a golden age and there would be no repetition of Richard's profligacy and the abuse of the king's personal powers to raise funds. John Gower thought as much when he wrote his welcoming poem to the new king, and he went further, emphasizing his belief that Henry's claim to the throne came not only from Royal descent but also from the Almighty. However, from an early stage in the reign it became clear that Henry had an embarrassing lack of experience in administration and good governance. He was not short of courage or self-confidence and possessed a willingness to learn, but he had no training for the actual business of kingship. As a young man he had traveled extensively in Europe and had won renown as a soldier, but now he had to learn new administrative skills. Not surprisingly he relied heavily on the support of trusted Lancastrian retainers. Although experienced administrators like Sir Hugh Waterton and Sir Thomas Erpingham served him well, any king who leans on his own people to the exclusion of others creates suspicions among those who are outside what appears to be a charmed circle. That being said, in Henry's case his family patronage was an astute move, as throughout his reign the support of his Lancastrian retinue did much to shore up his position, especially when he faced the inevitable challenges against his authority. As Henry was soon to discover, it had been one thing to claim and win the throne, but it was quite another to hold on to it. Not only would he face a seemingly never-ending battle with parliament over money, but there would also be far too many occasions when he had to struggle with others to retain his own authority. Throughout his reign the threat of a descent into civil war was never far away.

The first challenge came on Twelfth Night in 1400—the so-called Epiphany Uprising—when a group of Richard's supporters led by the earls of Salisbury, Gloucester, Exeter, and Surrey attempted to assassinate Henry and his sons but were betrayed by Henry's cousin, the Earl of Rutland. Previously in Richard's camp, Rutland and his father York had transferred their loyalties to Henry on the new king's accession. The switch had brought them the contempt of the plotters, who paid with their lives for their disloyalty, while the House of York prospered as a result of supporting the king. On hearing of the plot Henry rode from Windsor to the safety of London, but he had no need to fear for his safety. There was no public support for the would-be rebels, who were quickly hunted down and subjected to mob justice. On being taken prisoner, the leaders were lynched by angry crowds who showed no sign of the devotion to Richard that a successful rebellion demanded, and the attempt on the king's life was crushed even before it began. Six days later, the other leading figures faced trial at Oxford, where 22 of their number were executed.

The plotters had clearly misjudged the mood of the country, and by acting within the bounds of the law—the lesser nobles were tried before a court of law—Henry had acted sensibly. Equally prudently he also spoke out against the peremptory executions of the ringleaders and stated that it was wrong to kill accused men without trial. Despite his sensible response, it was not the last effort to usurp his authority. As had happened before and as would happen again for many more centuries, the king had to face a fresh challenge from England's northern neighbors. In theory, Henry stated that his intention was to live in harmony with the Scots, but he had to face the fact that the Scottish king and his council refused to acknowledge his position as king of England. At the time Scotland was ruled by the elderly King Robert III, who was unable to prevent his relatives from plotting against him and had such low self-esteem that he condemned himself in his own words as "the worst of kings and most wretched of men in the kingdom." His eldest son had died in suspicious circumstances while under the protection of his uncle the Duke of Albany, and to prevent a similar fate befalling his second son, James, he was sent to the safety of the French court. Unfortunately James's ship was intercepted by English pirates in the North Sea, and the young Scottish prince fell into Henry's hands and became a hostage in England for the next 18 years.

To press his claims and to take advantage of perceived Scottish weaknesses, Henry raised an army and invaded Scotland in August 1400, and by the middle of the month the English forces had reached Edinburgh. Faced with this display of strength—there were over 2,000 feared archers in Henry's army—Albany took the path of least resistance. The Scots produced a vague suggestion that the issue should be settled by a fight between a limited number of knights, but this was rejected out of hand and eventually the Scots issued an equally ambiguous promise to recognize Henry as king of England. At the end of August, the English army started pulling out of the Scottish lowlands with nothing achieved other than the avoidance of unnecessary bloodshed. It was Henry's last visit to Scotland, and it was also the last time that an English king invaded Scotland at the head of an army, but it was not the end of his troubles with the Celtic nations.

While returning from Scotland, Henry received the disquieting news that an obscure Welsh landowner called Owen Glendower (properly Owain Glyn Dŵr) was causing trouble on the Welsh marshes following a quarrel with his English neighbor, the Lord Grey of Ruthin, and on September 16, 1400, had been proclaimed prince of Wales by his supporters. The local squabble quickly became a more general revolt to "free the Welsh people from the slavery of their English enemies," and it was clear that Henry had a major problem on his hands. The English response was to quell the trouble before it could spread and gain strength. Glendower was condemned as an outlaw and traitor, and instead of returning to London, Henry led an expedition into Wales in a major show of strength to overawe the inhabitants of the north, including those living in the fortified towns of Harlech and Caernarfon. It succeeded in its purpose in that Glendower's supporters melted away and refused battle, but as had happened in Scotland the lack of an outcome was not the end of the problem. Within a year, in the spring of 1401, the rebellion had broken out again throughout the country, and Glendower had emerged as a serious contender to make good his promise that he was the new ruler of Wales. On Good Friday 1401, Conwy Castle was seized and Henry was forced to reconsider the extent of the problem facing him. Not only was fighting a low-intensity war a difficult and time-consuming business, it was also expensive and a drain on an already over-stretched exchequer. Besides, Henry was a major landowner in Wales, and the suppression of the uprising would create unpopularity and lose him revenues in the disaffected areas. The following year he mounted two further punitive expeditions into Wales, but neither succeeded in bringing Glendower to heel.

Worse, they encouraged the Welsh to support Glendower's rebellion in greater numbers, and the rebel leader began finding friends outside the country. In Scotland, Glendower won the moral support of Robert III and his council, and by 1406 had entered into an alliance with Charles VI of France through a treaty known as the Pennal Policy that also contained proposals to recognize the Avignon papacy in return for the establishment of a Welsh Church free from Canterbury's control. These moves were backed by the creation of a Welsh parliament that met at Machynlleth and Dolgellau and, more importantly, by a major military victory over English forces led by Sir Edmund Mortimer at Pilleth in Radnorshire in June 1402.

The victory at Pilleth also gave Glendower a pawn in the shape of Edmund Mortimer, the uncle of the (English) Earl of March who was to play a leading role as the drama in Wales unfolded. Henry's response to the defeat was a late-summer military operation in Wales mounted by a huge army—some said 100,000 strong—which assembled in Chester, Shrewsbury, and Hereford. Unseasonable weather hindered its progress, and as it turned out no military gains were made because the Welsh showed an unwillingness to take part in pitched battles. Although the revolt posed a huge problem for Henry, it could have been kept in check but for the fact that Glendower was holding Edmund Mortimer for ransom. As a member of a leading family and one that had supported the succession, an important fact was that the (English) Earl of March had previously been named as Richard's heir presumptive; Mortimer was not without influence. Even so, Henry remained unwilling to enter into negotiations, and this refusal led to difficulties with the formidable Earl of Northumberland and his son Henry Hotspur, who was married to Mortimer's sister, Elizabeth.

Once again the Scots provided a flashpoint. Shortly before Glendower's victory at Pilleth, a Scots army under Archibald, Earl of Douglas, and the Earls of Angus and Moray mounted a large-scale raid into the north of England and pillaged the country as far south as Durham. While returning to Scotland with their plunder the Scots were intercepted by an army under Northumberland to the northwest of the town of Wooler. Acting in support of the English force was the (Scottish) Earl of March, and his expertise was to be a crucial feature in the resultant battle. He also had a score to settle with Douglas, who had been granted most of his lands following his desertion to Henry IV. Douglas faced a predicament. The opposition blocked his route back into Scotland, and, knowing that he had no option but to give battle, he deployed his slightly larger army on the steep slopes of the nearby Homildon Hill. With their bristling spears densely packed into the ground in front of them to form a defensive shield, the Scots seemed to have advantage, and, indeed, had Northumberland heeded the urgings of his son, who recommended an immediate frontal attack, they might have won the day. Instead, taking March's advice, Northumberland placed the bulk of his archers on Harehope Hill to the northwest while the rest of his army faced the Scots from the north. Because Harehope was at the same elevation as Homildon, it allowed the English archers to shoot their much-feared weapons with some hope of hitting their targets while preventing any counterattack by the Scottish cavalry. In the end it was the weight and accuracy of fire from the English archers that won the battle for the English. Firing 15 arrows a minute, the English archers poured their fire into the dense ranks of the enemy and caused havoc. Not only did the barrage kill hundreds of Scots, it encouraged the survivors to try to end their misery by rushing down the hill to attack their tormentors. For a short time it seemed that the English bowmen were unnerved by the assault, but they stood firm and their rapid fire ended all Scottish resistance.

Homildon Hill was hailed as a Percy victory and a fitting revenge for the earlier defeat at Otterburn in 1388. It also compared badly with the lack of success in Wales, but instead of using the victory to gain some kudos, Henry made matters worse by demanding that the prisoners should be sent to London, where they would be ransomed. This proved to be a terrible mistake. In the first place, it was an insult to Hotspur, who had been captured and ransomed at Otterburn, and he would not have been human had he not wanted to exact revenge from the

Scots for that earlier insult. There was also a question of unpaid salaries and expenses to the Percys, which would have been ameliorated by the Scottish ransoms. In the second place, the demand to ransom the Scots, plus the sums that would be raised, compared badly with Henry's refusal to negotiate with Glendower over the release of Mortimer, who was, after all, a kinsman of the Percys. If Henry had been looking for a quarrel with this proud and powerful northern family, he could not have a found a better way of provoking one.

The Percys had been snubbed by the king, and, added to their reservations about the legality of Henry's right to the kingship, they clearly believed that their honor had been impugned over a matter—control of the Scottish marshes—that they considered to be in their own bailiwick. Now, from Wales, there was an unexpected chance to do something positive to remedy the situation. In December, Mortimer threw in his lot with Glendower by marrying his daughter Katherine and announced his intention to support the struggle for the freedom of Wales. Furthermore, he decided to support his nephew, the (English) Earl of March, in his own claims for the English throne and asked the Percys to provide the necessary military backing. This was granted, not least because a fresh grievance had emerged over the payment of money for the protection of the Scottish border.

In an attempt to placate the Percys, Henry had granted them a tract of land on the other side of the Scottish border, but this needed financial and military support if it was to be taken over. That summer Hotspur was back in Scotland at Cocklaws, a fortified tower near Hawick, and he and his father made an immediate appeal to Henry for the necessary funds and support to complete the operation to grab the local land. The letter was written by Northumberland in respectful tones, and on receiving it Henry was minded to offer help by marching north with an army of 5,000 soldiers, but before the king could make good his promise Hotspur had decided to offer his support to Glendower. As he marched north Henry was greatly dismayed to hear news of the betrayal. He also discovered that Hotspur had not tarried but had acted immediately by quitting Scotland for the area around the old Royalist stronghold of Chester, where he had joined forces with his uncle Thomas Percy, Earl of Worcester and was busy proclaiming that Richard was alive and with him in his army. The rebels' intentions were to combine Glendower's and Hotspur's armies and then to defeat Henry before putting Mortimer's nephew on the throne.

To forestall them, Henry moved his army south and picked up more support in his Lancastrian heartlands. By the third week of July he was in Shrewsbury, and the two armies met three miles to the north of the city at Albright Hussey on the road to Whitchurch. The rebels lined up to the north—fighting with them was the Earl of Douglas, having switched his allegiance to his erstwhile Percy captors—while the Royalists were divided with the king's men on the right and those of the Prince of Wales (Henry) on the left. This was the first battle to be fought on English soil in which both sides were evenly matched as far as the numbers and efficiency of their archers were concerned, and in the opening rounds dreadful damage was done to both sides by those deadly weapons. If anything, the Cheshire bowmen under Hotspur were more lethal, and before too long men in the king's forces were falling "as fast as leaves fall in autumn under the hoar-frost." Men waiting under the arrow shower—knights, squires, and men-at-arms—could only stand and take what cover they could until the order was given to begin the charge. Then they moved forward with swords and axes to start the next and equally bloody phase of the battle as men fought hand-to-hand in the killing zone.

During this phase Hotspur charged with a small force of 30 handpicked men to attack the Royal standard, but although they killed the standard-bearer Sir Thomas Blount, the king was unscathed. Soon the shout was heard that Henry Hotspur was dead—later it emerged that he had indeed been killed—and despite the vociferous denials, his supporters started fleeing from the field. The day belonged to the king, who took immediate revenge by having Worcester executed. As for Hotspur, his body was found on the battlefield and was buried, but to prevent rumors of his survival, it was dug up again and covered in salt and put on display in nearby Shrewsbury. Then it was beheaded and quartered with the relevant body parts being sent to be displayed in London, York, Bristol, Chester, and Newcastle. Because Northumberland arrived late and took no part in the fighting he was pardoned, after being tried for the lesser crime of trespass, but the victory at Shrewsbury was not the end of Henry's troubles.

France once again became an irritant. Charles VI seems to have developed a real hatred of Henry, not just for seizing the English throne, but for taking the life of his son-in-law. On that score there was also a degree of French animus about the treatment of Queen Isabella, who remained in England after her husband's downfall and who was a drain on Henry's exchequer at a time when he was under pressure to reduce his household expenditure. An ill-advised attempt to have her married to the prince of Wales was brushed aside in Paris, and thereafter English diplomacy centered on having her returned to France as quickly as possible. In normal circumstances this would have been the ideal solution. At 11 she was still a girl, and if she was not to be married to Prince Henry, she was of little use to the English court. But she was a queen of England and a princess of France, and she could hardly be sent back to the land of her birth as if she were a nobody. There was also the question of her dowry, which the French wanted to be returned, but as those funds had been spent long ago, there was no expectation that Henry would make good the loss.

An agreement was eventually reached to allow her to return to France in the summer of 1401, but the absence of the dowry and the feeling that they had been belittled continued to rankle the French. Orleans was the prime mover in stirring up rancor, not least because he saw opportunities to retrieve land in Aquitaine, and the first steps in the confrontation were taken shortly after Isabella's return with an outbreak of French naval attacks on English vessels in the Channel. To put further pressure on Henry, France entered into a new alliance with the Scots, and to continue the Celtic connection, it was decided to send 2,500 French soldiers to help Glendower in Wales. At the same time English possessions in Aquitaine were attacked and Calais had to be reinforced, all of which added to Henry's financial problems with parliament and led to complaints of a repetition of Richard's extravagance. One positive upshot of the confrontation with France was Henry's marriage to Joan, the daughter of Charles II of Navarre and the widow of John de Montfort, Duke of Brittany. Henry had been a widower since 1394 when Mary Bohun had died, and the new alliance brought with it the promise of Breton support against France and the possibility of using their ports to put a stop to the piracy in the Channel. However, nothing came of those hoped-for benefits: The English were unpopular in Brittany due to the maritime problems, and Joan was forced to surrender her rights as regent of Brittany. One consequence was that she was forced to surrender her son to the safekeeping of Philip, Duke of Burgundy. Despite the absence of any benefits from the alliance, the marriage seems to have been a happy one, even though the actual process proved to be a prolonged business—the couple was married by proxy in April 1402, but the final ceremony did not take place until the following year in Winchester Cathedral.

None of this activity did anything to halt Henry's continuing problems with parliament over taxation. On the contrary, the confrontation with France and the threat of more to come hinted at the necessity for even greater expenditure, and when parliament met in January 1404, there were complaints both about the cost of maintaining Henry's court and the mismanagement of French depredations in the Channel. A second parliament held that same year, in Coventry in October, failed to resolve the financial difficulties, and Henry was left in the awkward position of having to meet his obligations as king—putting down rebellions, dealing with the French, the Scots, and the Welsh—while coping with a body which was seemingly indifferent to his financial inconveniences. Fortunately, at a personal level Henry enjoyed a reasonable relationship with parliament, most of whose members were loyal to him or were recipients of his annuities, and there was little of the squabbling that had clouded the previous reign. At the very least the Coventry parliament provided a grant for the continuation of the war against Glendower, and a new offensive was planned for the following year. The speaker Sir Arnold Savage was close to the Royal household, and Henry was careful to make requests for money only when his own resources had dried up, but for all the absence of direct confrontation between king and parliament over funding, worries over finance remained the biggest bugbear of Henry's reign.

The next year proved to be no better for Henry, with a fresh outbreak of rebellion, once again involving the Percy family, whose grievances against the king continued to fester. Even though Hotspur had been killed and his father humbled at Shrewsbury, Henry had been unable to curb Northumberland power in the north of England, where the castles of Alnwick and Warkworth were occupied by Percy forces and kept effectively outside the Royal writ. At the same time, Glendower had control of the Welsh fortresses at Harlech and Llanbadran and showed every sign of continuing his rebellion against Royal authority with the intention of gaining independence for his country. From a military point of view, if Henry wanted to regain his authority he would have to fight a war on two fronts. That fear became a reality in February 1405, when Glendower, Northumberland, and March entered into a new compact, the Tripartite Indenture, which proposed dividing England and Wales into three new areas of control. Glendower would be given Wales and most of the west of England, Northumberland would receive Norfolk, Leicestershire, Northamptonshire, Warwickshire, and all areas to the north, while the (English) Earl of March would be given control of the rest of southern England.

Now that parliament had provided the necessary funds, Henry's first inclination was to crush the rebellion in Wales once and for all. Before Easter he summoned a general muster of his forces, and following the Garter ceremony at Windsor on April 23, set out for Hereford on the Welsh marshes. While he was there he received information from his council that Thomas, Lord Bardolph, an important military supporter, had headed north to join Northumberland and that as a result a new northern revolt was a distinct possibility. Henry took his forces to Worcester before moving his army north and sent a party ahead to discover what was happening. By the time he reached Derby his worst suspicions were confirmed. Bardolph had indeed thrown in his lot with the Percys, and they had been joined by Thomas Mowbray, the Earl Marshal (son of Thomas Mowbray, the banished Duke of Norfolk), and by Richard Scrope, Archbishop of York, who had been a member of the delegation that accepted Richard's renunciation of his throne in the Tower of London. At the time, the archbishop had supported Henry, but for reasons that are unclear, Scrope had come to believe that Henry was in breach of the promise made at Doncaster that he would not make a claim for the throne of England and was therefore guilty of a major perjury. His support for the rebellion carried weight: He was a senior churchman who had read aloud to parliament Richard's statement of abdication and had assisted the Archbishop of Canterbury during the coronation. Not only was Scrope's defection an embarrassment to the king, but he and Mowbray had raised a force of several thousand local men, including a number of knights.

For the second time in his reign Henry was facing the possibility of a civil war, and this time he would be fighting on two fronts—against Glendower in Wales and against the Northumberland faction in the north of England. On his side he had the support of Westmorland, and it was this other important northern magnate who saved the day. With Henry's son Prince John he rode ahead with a small force and caught up with Scrope at Shipton Moor outside York. Following a short parley Westmorland agreed that Scrope's grievances would be considered and redressed—these included an end to undue taxation and restoration of peace in Wales, though it is unclear if the agreement included the allegation that Henry had broken his oath and should therefore stand aside in favor of Richard's heir, the (English) Earl of March. In return Scrope agreed to disband his army, but in so doing he fell into a trap; he and Mowbray were immediately arrested as traitors and taken back to York to await Henry's arrival. If the action smacked of sharp practice, it has to be remembered that Henry was fighting for his survival and could not afford to let Northumberland's revolt get out of hand: Arresting the archbishop was a pragmatic means of neutralizing a sizable force and its influential leader.

What followed next was equally brusque and to the point. On June 8, the feast of St. William the Confessor, Scrope, Mowbray, and one of the knights in their force, Sir William Plumpton, were tried for treason at the archbishop's palace of Bishopthorpe and all three were condemned to death. In Scrope's case the sentence was read by Sir William Fulthorp, a knight, as the chief justice William Gascoigne declined to act after telling the king: "According to the laws of the kingdom, neither you, my Lord King, nor any of your subjects acting in your name, can legally condemn any bishop to death." Scrope met his death by beheading with great dignity, excusing the executioner Thomas Alman and asking him to strike five blows, "for I long to bear them for the love of my Lord Jesus Christ, who, obedient to his Father even unto death, bore the first five wounds for our sake." The treatment meted out to Scrope was unusual by Henry's standards; the king was not a particularly vengeful man, and the execution of a prelate was held to be a sin for which the king could have faced excommunication. It is clear that Henry must have felt deeply betrayed as he chose to ignore the attempts at intercession made by Archbishop Thomas Arundel, who had rushed north in an unsuccessful attempt to change the king's mind.

On hearing of Scrope's fate, Northumberland and Bardolph fled north into Scotland and abandoned their attempted rebellion. Henry's pursuit was hampered by a sudden illness that struck him near Ripon, and he had to halt for a week in the village of Hamerton, where he was reported to be afflicted with "horrible torments." This could have been occasioned by stress or by feelings of guilt about the execution, but some contemporary documents allege that he had been struck down with "large leprous pustules" as a divine punishment for his actions. More unhappiness followed as the summer drew to a close. Although Northumberland's revolt had been nipped in the bud and the castles at Alnwick and Warkworth were back in Royal hands, the campaign in Wales faltered for the fourth year running. Carmarthen was retaken, as was the fortress at Coety in Glamorgan, but the campaign ended with Glendower still free and able to continue his rebellion. To cap it all, Henry's baggage train was lost in sudden floods and most of it fell into Welsh hands. It was a dispiriting end to a disappointing year.

5

UNEASY LIES THE HEAD

Henry cut a sorry figure when he returned to London at the end of 1405. The defeat of the northern rebels and the reimposition of his authority should have given him fresh confidence for the new year, but he was in poor physical shape following his collapse at Hamerton. While the allegations of leprosy were probably untrue, mischievous rumors, most likely in retaliation for Scrope's execution, Henry was suffering from some kind of skin ailment as well as a leg injury—Capgrave noted that "the King lost the beauty of his face" at this time of his life, and there also seem to have been problems with his heart and circulation. All these physical setbacks added to the strains of the later stages of his reign and caused procedural difficulties when the sixth parliament of his reign opened at Westminster on March 1.

Known as the "Long Parliament" due to the intermittent nature of its business, it sat until December 22, with breaks for Easter and the late summer harvest, and like its predecessors, its agenda was dominated by finance. There was also an urgent need to address the question of procedures. As the conduct of its business was hampered by interruptions caused by breakdowns in the king's health, parliament decided to create a small governing council to advise the king and to oversee Royal expenditure. Its members included Prince Henry; Archbishop Arundel; the Bishops of Winchester and London; Edward, Duke of York; and John Beaufort, Earl of Somerset, and its main aim was to reduce the costs of maintaining the Royal household. One measure was the expulsion of members of Queen Joan's Breton household, who were considered an unnecessary expense who had brought nothing in return for their keep. New regulations were also introduced to control defense expenditure by careful auditing, and taxation was extended "to be levied on chantry priests and mendicant friars and other religious men who celebrated anniversary masses."

The creation of the council did much to improve the governance of the country, not least in terms of the timeless question of Royal finances. The following year parliament met at Gloucester, and its members were able to ease some of the restrictions on Royal expenditure as well as take measures to keep taxation within agreed levels. One reason for this new and unexpected development was the efficiency of the smaller council; another was the reduction in the costs of defense. Northumberland's rebellion had been effectively crushed, thereby lessening the need to garrison the northern counties, and although Wales continued to present problems, it was by no means the drain on the exchequer that it had been at the height of Glendower's revolt. Following Northumberland's and Bardolph's flight into Scotland, and the confiscation of the former's estates, the grandiose plans for the dismemberment of the kingdom had lapsed and Glendower was left out on a limb. With the (English) Earl of March, he retired into the fastness of Harlech Castle, and although the French offered further intervention with attacks from the sea on Kidwelly and Caernarfon, the high-water mark of his revolt had already passed. Armed resistance continued to be a problem in the principality until 1409 when Harlech fell to Royalist forces commanded by Prince Henry. March was killed during the action, and the loss of Glendower's most important ally was a crushing blow from which the Welsh leader never recovered. Although he was able to continue a guerrilla war until 1410, his claim to be the rightful Prince of Wales died with the failure of his rebellion to make any headway against the English.

Much of the credit for the success of the Royalist cause was due to the legitimate Prince of Wales. By then, with his father ill and incapacitated, Henry had assumed overall command of the Royalist forces in Wales, and the experience left its mark on him. He learned about soldiering and about the need to create an effective system of command and control, he gained an understanding of the problems of organizing and administering a campaign, and during his time in the field he forged friendships that would last a lifetime. And just as important, he came to understand the relevance of making decisions and operating in isolation far removed from his home base without the ability to take advice from his superiors. All those lessons would stand him in good stead in the years ahead. As for Glendower, the collapse of his rebellion marked the end of his dreams, and he simply disappeared from sight, to live on in people's minds as a folk hero, an Arthurian figure who might one day reappear to help his country in its next hour of need. By 1413 the Welsh rebellion had petered out and Glendower went underground, never to be seen again. He may have died three years later, probably in one of his daughter's manor houses in Herefordshire.

By then Northumberland's fortunes were also on the wane. In 1408 he mounted one last desperate attempt to overthrow Henry by fomenting revolt in the Percy heartlands in the north, but nothing came of his efforts. On February 19, in driving snow, his small and unprepared army was defeated by Royalist forces under the command of the Sheriff of Yorkshire, Sir Thomas Rokeby, at the Battle of Bramham Moor to the southwest of Tadcaster near Haslewood Castle in West Yorkshire. Northumberland was killed during the battle, and his death and March's earlier disappearance from the scene meant that for the first time in Henry's reign the king could live without fear of civil war. It was also the last time that Henry involved himself in any military action. While he did not ride with Rokeby or take part in the fighting on Bramham Moor, he followed on behind with the Royalist army, and in the palace at Selby he meted out justice to those who had taken part in the revolt. Among those executed was the Abbot of Halesowen, who was discovered on the battlefield wearing armor, thereby demonstrating his culpability and his support for Northumberland, while the Bishop of Bangor was pardoned, having been captured after the battle wearing his clerical dress. It was the king's last hurrah as a soldier. According to a contemporary record, Henry purged the north of any further hopes of rebellion during his sitting at Selby, where "many were condemned, and diverse put to great fines, and the country brought to quietness."

Scotland, too, was proving to be less of a problem than it had been in the past, thanks to the renewal of a number of truces and more importantly to the continuing presence at Henry's court of James, the heir to the throne of Scotland. Even though the regent Albany showed little desire to bring about the prince's release—his own son Murdoch Stewart, Duke of Fife, had been captured after Homildon, but the ransom was paid in 1415 after Henry V became king— James proved to be an important bargaining counter. As long as he was in English hands the Scots held their peace, and, in their relations with France, James was a useful ally for the English in their attempts to stop Scottish mercenaries fighting in French service. There were benefits for the young Scottish prince as he used his 18 years in English confinement to improve himself and to complete his education at Henry's court. An intelligent youth, he showed an interest in English political institutions, especially parliament, and Henry also offered to help in his instruction, telling his council: "If the Scots were truly grateful they would have sent this young man to me to be educated, for I too know French."

There was also better news from France, where the hapless Charles VI continued to inhabit a twilit world of mental chaos leavened by increasingly few periods of lucidity. The power struggle between Burgundy and Orleans had dominated his reign and continued without remittance into the new century. In 1404, Duke Philip of Burgundy died and was succeeded by his son, John Sanspeur ("the Fearless"), and this first cousin of the king showed no sign of relaxing his family's ambitions to dominate the French court. Then, three years later, Louis of Orleans was killed in Paris and the assassination was blamed on the Burgundians. According to Walsingham, Orleans had been "taking his pleasure with whores, harlots, incest," and had committed adultery with the wife of a knight, who had killed him and who was then supported by Burgundy in getting his revenge. Following Orleans's murder the duke was succeeded by his son Charles, who had recently married Richard II's widow Isabella. Her untimely death during childbirth in 1409 led Charles into a second marriage to Bonne, a daughter of Bertrand, Count of Armagnac, one of France's great noble houses and a major power-broker in its own right. The marriage created an alliance that was notably anti-English in character, although that did not stop Charles from seeking an alliance with Henry IV, and in time the Armagnac, or Orleans, faction came to represent most of the nobility in the south and the west of the country.

The continuing friction in France was greatly beneficial to Henry, who had hoped that the return of Isabella would reduce tensions between the two countries and put a stop to the debilitating piracy in the Channel. To his pleasure he now found both French parties courting him assiduously. From his holdings in Flanders, Burgundy offered Henry possession of the towns of Gravelines, Dunkirk, Dixmude, and Sluys, which would be important acquisitions for providing additional links for the lucrative wool trade. In return, Burgundy requested military help to clear the Armagnac faction from Paris. This was given, and in the summer of 1411 a small English force crossed over to France under the command of the Earl of Arundel to join the Burgundians in the expulsion of the Armagnacs from the French capital. Walsingham's chronicle suggests that the operation was a resounding success and that those who took part in it were well rewarded by the Burgundians for their services.

The English soldiers sent out to forage decided to enter Saint-Cloud (a suburb of Paris and residence of the Duke of Orleans) but found that the bridge across the River Seine had been partially destroyed by their opponents. The enemy had spread over it some planks, which were narrow, but long enough to enable the townspeople to come out of the gates. They could then fend off the English or, according to what sort of encounter it was, retreat from the enemy if necessary.

A battle took place in which the French were forced to flee. In their terror they slipped on the narrow planks and drowned in the river. One thousand and three hundred were reported dead; the others fled into the town and told the weeping duke of the disaster. He saved his own life only by fleeing to a different part of the town. The English then looted Saint-Cloud, took many prisoners, and returned with them to Paris.

England, especially the Prince of Wales, who favored the Burgundian faction, welcomed the victory. Ideally, King Henry would have liked to secure a French match for his son, but nothing came of the proposals to marry the Prince of Wales to one of the Burgundian princesses. However, any arrangement would have probably foundered because in the following year the Duke of Orleans played his hand by sending an embassy to England offering a much bigger opportunity for Henry. Under the terms of a secret treaty agreed at Bourges, he offered to make territory in Aquitaine—Guyenne, Poitou, and Angoulême— available to Henry in return for military assistance against the Burgundians. The duke had seen the English soldiers in action at Saint-Cloud and clearly felt that they would be a notable asset. Henry was captivated by the idea, flimsy though it was; not only would it restore his reputation in France, but it might also produce a much-needed military triumph to bolster his reign at a time when he had been sidelined from national and international affairs. An agreement was signed, and an English army was dispatched to Normandy under the command of Henry's younger son Prince Thomas, the Duke of Clarence. At one point Henry announced his intention of leading the army himself, but with his broken health and lack of energy the idea was stillborn. By then the king was in a pitiful condition, unable to ride and a poor shadow of the gallant young man who had gone crusading in eastern Europe and who had been known throughout Europe for his skill on the jousting field.

It was perhaps as well that he did not undertake the operation, for unlike the previous year's canter, Clarence's campaign achieved very little. Having landed at Vaast-la-Hogue intending to raid suspected centers of piracy on the Normandy coast, the English forces remained somewhat aimlessly in the Cotentin peninsula until they were unexpectedly recalled to England. The decision was taken by Orleans, who had suddenly found himself in a state of new military confrontation with the Burgundians. On hearing about the secret Treaty of Bourges, John the Fearless denounced the Armagnacs as traitors and prepared an army to drive them out of the south. Faced by the possibility of civil war, Charles VI, happily in a lucid state, ordered Orleans to renounce the agreement and peace of a kind was restored. Under an agreement signed at Auxerre that summer, the two sides were reconciled and agreed to pay off Clarence's army, which was preparing to march into Anjou. The whole incident was immensely embarrassing to the English, not least because the Prince of Wales had opposed the adventure from the outset as it compromised his preferred policy of dealing with the Burgundians.

This was a sensitive point. By the end of the decade, relations between Henry and his oldest son were tense and provided the potential for even greater disagreements. By that time the prince was well into his 20s, and having gained considerable experience of soldiering in Wales, he was keen to add to his knowledge and political skills. Since becoming a member of his father's council he had emerged as a thoughtful and energetic young man who clearly wanted to have a greater involvement in the governance of the realm. With him on the council he had the support of his father's half-brothers Henry and Thomas Beaufort and close allies such as Thomas Langley, Bishop of Durham, Richard Beauchamp, who had served with him in Wales, and Henry Chichele, a future Archbishop of Canterbury. Their task was to govern England efficiently and responsibly at a time when Henry's physical condition prevented him from accepting the full responsibilities of his Crown.

From a health point of view the king's last years were certainly unpleasant, and while it is difficult to understand the exact nature of his illness—leprosy, plague (which erupted again in 1408), and venereal diseases have all been suggested—it was clearly painful and debilitating: Adam of Usk described the ailment as "a rotting of the flesh, a drying up of the eyes and a rupture of the intestines." Rumors abounded about his condition: The French believed that his toes had dropped off, while the Scots were adamant that he had shrunk in size and was no bigger than a child. One thing is certain: The visible tumors, rashes, and suppurating flesh were dreadful to behold and tested even the strongest stomach. It did not help matters that Henry's illnesses were strangely spasmodic. One day he would be so weak that he appeared to be on the verge of death and would lie comatose on his bed; on the next, he would have recovered his powers and would be able to resume his duties as king. Unfortunately for everyone concerned, when Henry was in control of his mind and body he became increasingly fretful and dictatorial, especially in his dealings with his son.

Matters came to a head in the autumn of 1411 when Henry Beaufort suggested that the time might have come for the king to stand down from his throne in favor of his son the Prince of Wales. It was a serious point that was made to address a well-known problem—the king's physical condition could not be ignored—but coming on top of the recent disagreement over which faction should be supported in France, it was also was a direct challenge to Henry's throne, and like an old warhorse, he rose to meet it. In common with any other ruler who had supplanted his predecessor, Henry was intensely aware of the fragility of his position, and he understood only too well the uncomfortable truth that usurpers could themselves be usurped. Unwilling to stand aside and fearful perhaps that if he did not his son might act against him by using force to claim the Crown, Henry decided on preemptive action. When parliament opened on November 3, Henry was unable to attend, but two days later he rallied to tell the new speaker, Sir Thomas Chaucer, son of the poet, that he wanted "no novelties" but preferred to preserve his own prerogatives. The Beauforts were thanked for their services—a sure sign that they had been dismissed—and Henry packed the council with men who would be loyal to him, such as Archbishop Arundel as chancellor and Prince Thomas in place of the Prince of Wales. The decision caused an open breach between Henry and his eldest son, who responded by parading his men-at-arms in London in a show of force the following year. Nothing came of the confrontation, but there is little doubt that in 1411 and 1412 the relationship between the king and the Prince of Wales was at rock bottom.

During this period the king's closest associate and adviser was Thomas Arundel, brother of the Earl of Arundel and one of Henry's firmest supporters when he made his bid for the throne in 1399. Thanks to his influence as Archbishop of Canterbury, any opposition to the king from the church hierarchy was quickly stilled. The only main objector was Thomas Merks, the Bishop of Carlisle, who made a spirited protest about the usurpation and into whose mouth Shakespeare put the famous words about the act spawning the future civil wars in which "the blood of English shall manure the ground." It helped that Arundel had no love for the previous regime—his brother Richard had been executed on the orders of Richard II, and he himself had been sent into exile—but there seems to have been a genuine and lasting friendship between him and Bolingbroke. In his correspondence Henry referred to Arundel as his "true friend" and restored him to the see of Canterbury after he came to the throne, as well as appointing him chancellor. He also supported him in his lengthy and vigorous campaign to extirpate the heresy of Lollardy, the name given to those who espoused the teachings of John Wyclif, who had died in 1384 but still attracted a powerful following. The son of a Yorkshire landowner, Wyclif had attended Balliol College, Oxford, where he had propagated revolutionary doctrinal ideas that denied the theory of transubstantiation (the belief that during communion the bread and wine are transformed into Jesus Christ's body and blood) and argued that right of property depended on attaining a state of grace. As he argued that the church was not in that happy position, it thus should be disendowed and transformed into a state of purity and poverty. Wyclif's ideas were published in the two books *De Dominio Divino*, and *De Civile Dominio*, and their appearance led to him being expelled from Oxford, and he withdrew to live in Lutterworth in Leicestershire where his last years were spent translating the bible, which he believed to be "the one perfect word preceding from the mouth of God."

By the time Henry came to the throne, Lollardy enjoyed some support within the political establishment—John of Gaunt had been one of Wyclif's patrons, and the "Knights of the Lollards" represented a substantial following among the upper classes—although the term had also become a catchall phrase to describe any kind of behavior that seemed to go against the grain. As the historian Miri Rubin so splendidly puts it in her social history of the period, Lollardy was "a label attached to people who failed a number of tests of social acceptability through sexual incontinence, clerical wanderings, an outspoken manner in criticism of the clergy, suspicious puritanical yearnings, attachment to vernacular books, or distaste for ostentatious religious expression." In other words, anyone who was "different" or "strange" was looking for trouble and would promptly be written off as a "Lollard." Lollardy was a heresy that attracted a wide variety of vaguely antiestablishment manifestations, and in all those different guises it was a potential source of political and social unrest. As such it seemed to be a problem that needed to be addressed, especially in those difficult years after Richard had been usurped when there was a good deal of incontinent talk about him still being alive, and perhaps even returning to claim his rightful throne. Coupled with the physical assaults on Henry's own right to rule—from the Epiphany Uprising in the first days of his reign to the more serious confrontation mounted by the Percys and Glendower—Henry had a vested interest in making sure that any heresy, real or imagined, was contained. Under those circumstances it was all too easy to make the connection that anyone suspected of any kind of deviation was a potential traitor who had to be punished.

The result was the production of the statute *De Haeretico Comburendo* (On Burning Heretics) that was passed by parliament in 1401 to punish "divers false and perverse persons of a certain sect" who were suspected of preaching and teaching heretical doctrines: "They hold and exercise schools, they make and write books, they do wickedly instruct and inform people and . . . stir them to sedition and insurrections and make great strife and division among the people." The statute was aimed at Wyclif's followers, as one of the main tenets of the Lollards' belief was the importance of the bible and religious tracts to propagate the Christian religion. Instead of using the established Church and its priests as a conduit, the Lollards believed that the word of God could be distributed directly to the people or through unlicensed preachers. For the king and his bishops, though, this was not freedom but license, and because the propagation of unorthodox knowledge could lead to dissent and perhaps even rebellion, it had to be brought under control. Until the passing of the statute, ecclesiastical courts dealt with the phenomenon of blasphemy (it had never been a widespread problem in England), but they could not inflict punishments that took life or shed blood. Henry's laws changed all that by producing a procedure by which convicted heretics would be turned over to the local sheriff or mayor, who "caused them to be burnt before the people in a conspicuous place, that such punishment may strike fear into the minds of others." It was hoped that this legislation would concentrate the minds of those who caused trouble by demanding change or simply kicking against the established order.

For the first time church and state were brought together to punish those who might be guilty of spreading unorthodox opinions. In fact, not only were the dangers posed by Lollardy exaggerated at the time, but the passing of the statute led to a good deal of witch-hunting as the authorities went about the business of making people see the error of their ways or took their revenge on suspected troublemakers. All too often this enthusiasm developed into the persecution of people for no other reason than to destroy their reputations and to denounce those whose only fault was to be on the wrong side of those who accused them of heresy. Fortunately, the extreme penalty was rarely used, and the main import of the statute was to deter potential malcontents and to strike fear into anyone who might be troublesome in the early years of the new king's reign. For example, in Leicester, Philip Repton, an Augustinian canon, was accused of heresy but recanted and went on to become Abbot of St. Mary's in the same town and was later named Bishop of Lincoln. Others were less fortunate, but even so in the ten years after the statute was passed only two heretics were actually burned, and between 1423 and 1522 only 34 Lollards suffered the extreme penalty, while over 400 abjured their beliefs rather than face the flames. The two Lollards who were executed during Henry's reign were William Sawtry (or Sawtre), a priest from St. Margaret's Lynn in Norfolk, and John Badby, a tailor from Evesham, both of whom were burned at the stake for refusing to abandon their beliefs.

The first to die was Sawtry, who was cross-questioned by Arundel in St. Paul's Cathedral on February 23, 1401, before being taken to Smithfield by the civic authorities, who had paid for the costs of his execution and had provided the necessary combustible materials. Sawtry's "crime" was disputing transubstantiation and arguing that money spent on pilgrimages would be better spent on helping the poor at home. Arundel spent three hours attempting to persuade him to change his mind but to no avail, and Sawtry was duly burned to death. Nine years later Badby met a similar fate after facing the same process, but the manner of his death was vile even by the standards of the day. Once again Arundel gave him every opportunity to recant, as did the Prince of Wales, who was present at the trial and who interested himself in such matters, but Badby refused to go back on his belief that transubstantiation was a wicked heresy. Like Sawtry he was taken to the open tournament ground at Smithfield, but as the fire

was lit he started screaming. Thinking that the awful noise was the sound of
Badby repenting, the Prince of Wales ordered the execution to stop and Badby
was dragged from the flames. In return he was offered three pence a day as a pension for the rest of his life, provided that he recanted, but that proved to be no
incentive and, as Walsingham reported the incident, the execution was restarted:

> The wretched man, rekindling his breath, spat on this generous offer, doubtless
> because he was possessed of an evil spirit. So Prince Henry ordered him to be
> put back on the flames and to receive no more mercy. This trouble-maker died
> for his own sins, pitifully burned in the fire.

The presence of the Prince of Wales and his involvement in Badby's trial and
execution were powerful reminders that the state would not tolerate Lollardy or
any other kind of dissent. Heretics continued to be punished in this way
throughout the century, and the last to be burned was Joan Boughton in 1494, an
"old cankered heretic," who was punished for claiming that Wyclif was a saint.

It helped that Henry was a devout man who was anxious to maintain good
relations with the church, hence the importance of his close friendship with
Arundel. In return he received subventions that helped to ease the constant
financial burden, and in time he managed to survive the scandal caused by the
execution of Archbishop Scrope. Although those involved in the execution were
excommunicated by Pope Innocent VII, the continuation of the Great Schism
meant that the edict could be safely ignored, and in effect it lasted only until
1409 when the Council of Pisa deposed the Avignon and Rome popes and
elected a new pope to succeed both, thereby bringing to a temporary closure the
long-lasting split in the church by creating a third papal line at Pisa. An English
embassy sent by Henry attended the council, and this was to be one of his more
successful foreign policy initiatives. The alliance of Crown and Church, as
exemplified by the friendship between Henry and his archbishop, had other consequences. It meant that nothing came of several Lollard proposals in parliament
to sequester the church's riches, especially the immense wealth of the ecclesiastical sees, and it would be another century before religious endowments were
diminished through the dissolution of the monasteries. Arundel also received the
king's support when he insisted on making a "visitation" to Oxford as part of his
campaign to extirpate Lollardy. Although the archbishop's attempted interference was resisted by the university, which produced an earlier papal bull of
exemption in a last-ditch attempt to protect their interests, Henry backed the
procedure, and anyone who had supported Wyclif in any way at Oxford was
forced to recant. In the last years of the reign Arundel was forced to concede his

position as chancellor of the exchequer to the Beaufort faction, but it was a measure of his importance that he returned to influence during the brief emergence of Prince Thomas at court in 1412.

With a sad inevitability the last years of Henry's life were clouded both by the dreadful physical problems that afflicted him and by his tense relationship with Prince Henry. Equally inevitably, perhaps, the king's afflictions gave contemporaries and some later commentators the opportunity to see them as divine punishments for his act of usurpation and then for his illegal murder of an archbishop. What more could he have expected following his act of unseating a lawfully anointed king and then misusing his power and authority to execute a senior churchman? Such meanderings about cause and effect are not uncommon throughout history, and although they usually have no basis in fact, in this case they are irresistible. As a young man King Henry represented the flower of chivalry. Being powerfully built and possessing a commanding presence, he had all the kingly attributes that Richard lacked. He was courageous and dignified and much admired for his military skills. He was cultured and took an interest in literature and music. He was feted in European courts and was a wealthy and powerful man in his own right even before he became king. The son of a distinguished family, descendents of Edward III, who enjoyed great temporal and political power in England and throughout Europe, Henry had influential friends and supporters, and in his youth he even enjoyed the encouragement and backing of his kinsman, the king. But for Richard's foolhardy decision to exact revenge by sending him into exile and then to double-cross him by denying him his inheritance, Henry, as Bolingbroke, could have led a very different kind of life as a loyal supporter of the status quo and a true friend of the Royal house.

His troubles began when he seized the throne and continued after he put himself on it. From the very outset of his reign he was handicapped by the need to produce adequate funds and then to balance them; he was also hamstrung by the need to use armed force to protect what he held. At a time when the country's finances were in a perilous state, he found himself fighting a potentially disastrous and immensely expensive civil war on two fronts, confronting the Percys who had once supported him, and being forced into fighting a bitterly contested counterinsurgency war in Wales. For any king this unwanted exercise in crisis management would have been a trying beginning to his reign; for Henry it proved to be a fight for outright survival, for if he had failed, all would have been lost. And yet, at the very moment that he had overcome his worst difficulties, tragedy struck him down. Having crushed the last vestiges of the revolts against him in the north and in Wales, he was cut down by a wasting illness, and this meant that his last years were spent in a kind of limbo in which he struggled to keep his dignity and to maintain his prerogatives, while others were forced into action to make sure that the country was governed. It must have seemed dreadfully unfair. By then the Scots were no longer the problem they had been at the beginning of his reign, the Welsh had been brought under control, England was once again reasonably quiet, and there was no immediate danger of a fresh conflict with France.

Henry collapsed at the age of 47, on March 20, 1413, while he was praying at the shrine of Edward the Confessor in Westminster Abbey, and he was carried into the chambers of the nearby abbot's house to die. For a man who had longed to go on crusade to the Holy Land and still planned to put those dreams into effect, it was fitting, as Robert Fabyan opines, that the room in which he drew his last breaths should have had a suitably resonant name:

> At length when he [Henry] had come to himself, not knowing where he was, he asked of such as were about him, what place that was. They said to him that it belonged to the abbot of Westminster. As he felt himself so sick, he asked if that chamber had any special name: they answered that it was called Jerusalem. Then said the king, "Praise be to the father of Heaven, for now I know that I shall die in this chamber, according to the prophecy made about me before that I should die in Jerusalem."

At the time of his death Henry had finally come to terms with the Prince of Wales, and they seem to have reached a quietus that suited them both and that seems to have been constructed on something approaching affection. The dead king was carried by water to his palace at Faversham, and from there he was taken for burial within Canterbury cathedral, where he lies near the tomb of the Black Prince. After his death his executors discovered that the king who had begun his reign as one of the wealthiest men in England was virtually bankrupt. In his will he asked that his affairs be put in order, but the harsh reality was that King Henry was so much in debt that it was impossible to pay back everything that he owed.

It would be easy to regard Henry as the author of many of his own misfortunes. He seized the throne in a manner that suggested sleight of hand—as he showed after his arrival at Ravenspur in 1399, he was no stranger to devious behavior—and while he proved to be a master of his own destiny in actually carrying out the act of usurpation, he was less successful in the business of ruling the country as king. As has often been said of his reign, it had been easy enough for him to win the crown, but he found that it was much more difficult to wear it and then accept its many responsibilities. Lack of money proved to be a perennial problem and strained his relations with parliament, forcing him to accept compromises and to make requests only when no other means of support were available. This did not make him a constitutional monarch in the modern sense, but it is true that he tried to rule with the assent of parliament and did not seek any confrontation with it, preferring wherever possible to find consensus. It helped that the body was packed with Lancastrian appointees or supporters and that many of the speakers owed their positions to Royal patronage. In the latter days of his reign the ruling council proved to be an effective instrument, even if it never overcame the anomaly of its position, the king still being alive and mentally alert while it carried out the great business of the governance of England.

One fact was indisputable: At the time of Henry IV's death, his kingdom was at peace and his son faced no challengers to his throne. It was a solid foundation for the reign that followed.

6

No Tongue Can Tell
of His Renown

*P*rince Henry came to the throne of England blessed with a wide-ranging political intelligence and a sound knowledge of how the country should be governed. He had waited long for the moment and had spent the intervening period fruitfully and sensibly, quietly learning the realities of kingship. For two years he had served on the country's governing council and had reached a fine understanding of the mechanics of good government; he had also come to appreciate the need to surround himself with loyal advisers. As a soldier he had proved himself fighting against the Welsh, and, in his youth, he had been taken to Ireland as part of Richard II's military entourage. As an astute young man he had witnessed firsthand the effects of his father's frailties: his exile and dispossession followed by the seizure of the throne and the long fight to retain it. As he himself had lusted after his father's crown, he knew only too well what could happen to the unwary—his brother Clarence had marginalized him in the last years of their father's reign. One of his first steps as king was to ensure the solidity of his father's main Lancastrian supporters, namely his Beaufort relations and the Earls of Warwick, Arundel, and Westmorland.

Henry was crowned king on April 9, 1413, in Westminster Abbey, and the ceremony seems to have had a profound effect on him. Like Richard II he believed implicitly in the sanctity of his position and had already concluded that he had been divinely ordained to carry out God's great work. Later, as his reign progressed, this conviction was extended to embrace a more profound belief that England had been chosen by God to be a favored nation to humble the pride of France. On the day of the coronation it snowed, and this was taken as a sign that change was in the air and that better days lay ahead, although others regarded the snow not as a sign of purification but as an omen that boded ill for the country. Whatever the portents, the symbolism of the snow must have had some meaning for the new king and those who witnessed his coronation. Not only was it an unexpected change in the weather, its appearance coincided with a transformation in the young king's attitudes. During his youth Henry had enjoyed life to the full, and even if his experiences had not been as riotous as Shakespeare suggests in his portrayal of Prince Hal's antics with Falstaff and his crew, there is Thomas Elmham's evidence that Henry "found leisure for the excesses common to ungoverned age." His first biographer Tito Livio dei Fruolvisi, an Italian humanist who completed his work in 1437, confirmed that Henry became a reformed character on acceding to the throne and that after the death of his father "his life was free from every taint of lustfulness." The Italian also left an attractive portrait of the new king and his attributes:

> Let me describe the prince; he was taller than most men, his face fair and set on a longish neck, his body graceful, his limbs slender but marvelously strong. Indeed, he was miraculously fleet of foot, faster than any dog or arrow. Often he would run with two of his companions in pursuit of the swiftest does—he himself would always be the one to catch the creature. He had a great liking for music and found enjoyment in hunting, military pursuits and other pleasures that are customarily allowed to young knights.

Most contemporary descriptions of his life and reign deal only in superlatives, but, of course, there was another less pleasing side to the man. He could appear cold and aloof, and his well-advertised piety was often mistaken for excessive sanctimony. On occasion he could appear high-handed, with a cruel streak that manifested itself in the brutal treatment of anyone who opposed him or stood in his way. To Henry's credit, that harsher aspect of his character also gave him a single-mindedness of purpose and a common sense that stood him in good stead in the great business of ruling his country.

Shortly after becoming king, Henry was advised by Henry Beaufort to provide "bon governance," and that need to provide a sound administration became the watchword for the early years of his reign. In place of the endless profligacy of his father's period, Royal finances were brought under strict control, household expenses were reduced while revenues from land were increased. The stability of the realm was also addressed through a mixture of firmness and hard-nosed pragmatism. The young (English) Earl of March was released from house arrest and created a Knight of Bath even though his claim to the throne was well known. At the same time Harry Hotspur's son was restored to the earldom of Northumberland. Henry V clearly believed that it was better to keep potential enemies in sight and in his debt. In this case, however, there was also an ulterior motive at work in that he needed the Percy family to guard England's border with Scotland, their traditional duty and one that gave them great temporal power in the north. The young earl had been held hostage by the Scots, and Henry secured his release by exchanging him with Murdoch Stewart, Earl of Fife and son of the Duke of Albany, who had been in English hands since the Battle of Homildon Hill in 1402. No comparable steps were taken to release James Stewart, the rightful heir to the Scottish throne, and for the time being Scotland remained obdurately in the hands of the Albany faction. As for Wales, Henry introduced a policy of reconciliation: Corruption by officials in the north of the country was investigated and punished, and Welsh men were encouraged to serve in England as soldiers, notably and successfully as archers.

The long-term aim was to unite the country and to provide the people with a sense of purpose that had been lacking in his father's reign. And it succeeded. Henry restored gravitas as well as popularity to the kingship, his well-attested piety was much admired (the French thought he looked more like a priest than a soldier), he was conservative in religious matters, and he proved to be a great supporter and patron of the Catholic Church. Two religious houses were built close to the River Thames, one for the Carthusian order at Sheen and the second for the nuns of St. Brigit at Twickenham, given the name Syon. The idea was that he was to be prayed for perpetually, and bells would be rung at the end of prayers to start a new round of devotion. Henry was certainly religious-minded and set in his beliefs, but that adherence to a strict religious orthodoxy produced another aspect of his personality in his dislike of Lollardy and the vehemence he brought to extirpating it.

Twice in his reign Henry was forced into a position where he had to act appropriately to preserve his position, and on neither occasion did he flinch from doing what was expected of him. He had already demonstrated his dislike of the Lollards, first by attending the trial and execution of John Badby during his father's reign and then by putting down the attempted rebellion in early 1414 when a group of Lollards hatched a plot to take him and his brothers prisoner while they were in residence at Eltham. Although there is now some doubt about the extent of the Lollards' influence and the real danger posed by that attempt on the king's life, it did allow Henry to portray the incident as proof positive that the anointed king enjoyed God's favor and his divine protection. It also forced him to deal with the Lollards' main leader in parliament, Sir John Oldcastle, who supported Wyclif's proposals for the confiscation of the principal monastic houses. Henry admired Oldcastle as a soldier—he had served in the Welsh wars and had distinguished himself fighting in France under Arundel—but he could not stand by while he denounced the authority of the pope, which he did when he was arrested on charges of heresy in September 1413. The hearing took place in the chapter house of St. Paul's and was heard before a number of clerics including Archbishop Arundel and the Bishops of London and Winchester. Despite facing the full panoply of the church's learning, Oldcastle was obdurate. While he conceded his belief in the Eucharist, he denied the theory of transubstantiation: In his opinion, the bread remained bread, and the Church was wrong to claim its transformation in Christ's body. Then he refused to concede that confession was a necessary prelude to salvation, and to the horror of those present he called the pope the Anti-Christ and asserted that his cardinals and followers were his tail. This was heresy, and Oldcastle cannot have been surprised when Arundel handed him over to the legal authorities to be punished. He was sent to the Tower of London and given 40 days to change his mind.

The incident was thoroughly embarrassing for the king. He liked Oldcastle and admired his military virtues, but at the same time he could not agree with any of his religious views. He had vowed to crush the Lollards, yet here was a prominent leader making a public stand on a contentious religious matter and in so doing defying Royal authority. It seems that Henry genuinely wanted Oldcastle to recant and hoped that the period of grace would enable him to change his mind, but on the night of October 19, Oldcastle mysteriously disappeared from the Tower and vanished into thin air. Rumors persisted that the king had arranged the escape or that a member of the court had engineered it, perhaps Beaufort, but this is unlikely. Subterfuge of that kind was not in Henry's character, and it is difficult to believe that he would permit such a potentially dangerous personality to escape and propagate his heresies. That might explain why Henry acted so ferociously against the Lollards the following January. In the official indictment Oldcastle was named as the ringleader of the plot to kill the king and become regent in his stead. If that was the intention, the uprising or protest failed miserably, and although Oldcastle was not among those hunted down, tried, and executed, he remained at large until the end of 1417 when he was captured near the Welsh border and brought to London for trial. This time the authorities were taking no chances with a man who had become such a bugbear and a focus for further discontent. On December 14, Oldcastle was tried as a traitor and heretic, found guilty, and executed by being "hung and burnt hanging," a savage sentence.

By then Henry had faced a much more dangerous plot against his authority that may or may not have included Oldcastle among the conspirators. It had happened in the summer of 1415 when Henry was on the cusp of invading France and pressing his claims to the French throne. As his armed forces began assembling at Southampton he received the astonishing news from the (English) Earl of March that a well-organized plot to kill him was about to be put into effect by men who were thought to be loyal to the king. March was party to the plans but at the last minute thought twice about his involvement and confessed everything to Henry while he was staying at Porchester Castle on the night of July 31. What made the revelation so shocking was that the main instigators were all Lancastrians close to the king, and their loyalty should have been taken for granted. At the heart of the conspiracy was Henry, Lord Scrope of Masham, the nephew of the archbishop who had risen against Henry IV and a man described by Tito Livio as a "an ornament of chivalry." He had served as Henry's treasurer, and his motives are unfathomable, but he did enjoy close family connections with the other main conspirators—the Earl of Cambridge and Sir Thomas Grey of Heton, both of whom were influential noblemen with positions at court. All were connected one way or another, and through their relationship with March may have believed that they had a legitimate claim on the crown.

Richard, Earl of Cambridge, came from an impeccable background. He was the king's cousin, being the second son of Edmund, Duke of York, and he was a godson of Richard II. He was also the brother-in-law of the (English) Earl of March, having married the earl's sister Anne Mortimer in 1408. After her death in childbirth three years later, he married Matilda Clifford, the sister of Hotspur's brother-in-law John Clifford. To complete the circle, his son by Anne Mortimer, Richard, had been named as March's heir, the earl being childless. However, for all that Cambridge enjoyed strong family connections, he was a man with a grudge against the king. On being created Earl of Cambridge he found that he was in financial difficulties and could not meet all of his obligations. An endowment from the king would have eased his problems, but this was not forthcoming, and personal unhappiness with his lot seems to have turned into enmity toward the king. His first ally was Sir Thomas Grey of Heton, a powerful northern magnate who enjoyed family links with the Percys, and he needed little encouragement to throw in his lot with the conspirators. The idea was to bring March into the plot and to make him king in place of Henry, thereby confirming his position as Richard II's heir presumptive and putting an end to Henry IV's usurpation. If March failed to produce an heir there would be the happy result that Cambridge's son Richard Plantagenet would succeed to the throne—later, during the Wars of the Roses, he would be one of the main contenders for the Crown worn by Henry V's son.

It was all fantasy and it all ended messily. Having secured Grey's support, Cambridge rode south from his seat Conisburgh Castle in Northumberland and made contact with Scrope at Southampton. March was then admitted to the plot, but from the outset he seemed an unwilling participant even though his residence at Cranbury near Winchester was used for much of the planning. Like the earlier plots to get rid of Henry IV, it was planned as a nationwide uprising. Northumberland would seize the north of England, and March would be entrusted with raising the revolt in the west, where he would make contact with Oldcastle and even Glendower to secure Wales. The first day of August was fixed for the king's assassination, and March would be speedily enthroned as King Edmund I. However, March's nerve failed him. Given the king's memories of the earlier attempts to oust his father, Henry took this plot seriously, and after listening to March's revelations he acted swiftly and savagely. The three traitors were arrested and imprisoned. Grey was tried in Southampton the following day and, having made a full confession, was executed by beheading. Scrope and Cambridge exercised their right to be tried by their peers in front of 20 noblemen, but they too were found guilty and sentenced to death. Henry commuted Cambridge's sentence to beheading, but no such good fortune awaited Scrope, who was judged to be the most guilty and who was forced to face the traitor's fate, being hung, drawn, and quartered and his head put on public display in his home city of York as a warning to others.

For the others implicated in the plot Henry showed mercy. March was forgiven and remained loyal; having also been pardoned, Northumberland returned to the Royal fold, and in time Henry made his peace with the Oldcastle family. It had been an unsettling experience. Not only were the main plotters powerful magnates in their own right whose loyalties clearly lay not with the king but with their own interests, but the conspiracy had been hatched at the very moment that Henry was about to launch a military expedition against France. That was one reason why he acted so quickly and so decisively in trying and executing the leaders: Time was not on his side, as he had on his mind the great business of leading a major cross-Channel offensive against England's old enemies. On August 11, a week after the sentences had been carried out, Henry set sail with his army for France to carry out the most audacious foreign policy initiative of his reign—to break the truce brokered by Richard II in 1396 and to stake his entitlement to be the rightful king of France as originally claimed by Edward III.

His thinking was guided by several factors: As a result of his father's seizure of the throne in 1399, Henry had received the title Duke of Aquitaine, and he maintained a seigniorial interest in those lands. He also believed strongly that the French had reneged on the conditions of the Treaty of Brétigny that had been brokered in 1360 and that the failure to execute its main points had created a casus belli. This agreement had come about as a result of the capture of

King John II of France at the Battle of Poitiers four years earlier, an incident that produced an exceptionally strong bargaining position for the English negotiators when they met at Brétigny near Chartres. During the talks the principals were the Black Prince and the French Dauphin, and the main points agreed by them were supposed to bring the conflict to a mutually satisfactory conclusion. In return for renouncing the French crown and suzerainty over Brittany and Flanders, Edward III would be given full suzerainty over Aquitaine, Montreuil, Ponthieu, and the Calais Pale (Guines, Marck, and Calais). To cement the decision John II would be ransomed for three million gold crowns, to be paid in installments, and the French crown would drop its claim to the new English possessions. In the end, the renunciations were never carried out and the whole of the ransom was not paid, a state of affairs that led Henry to believe that he had a valid reason to go to war with France. A victorious campaign would have two advantages: it would bring about the restitution of the English claims, as well as the unpaid ransom.

Henry's French policy was also driven by a desire to enter into an alliance with the Burgundians at a time when the country's central government had been enfeebled by civil strife. From the outset of his reign Henry reckoned that the Burgundians were the better bet, not least because as the dominant force in the region they held the key to the security of Calais and its Pale. Also to be taken into account was the aggravation caused by French piracy and naval activities in the Channel that were injurious to English trade. The port of Harfleur at the mouth of the River Seine was a particular problem as it was the main French naval base in the area. Personality also influenced the king's thinking. Unlike Richard II, Henry was a soldierly individual, more like Edward III or the Black Prince, who believed that it was a king's duty to lead his armies to victory in battle. A campaign in France would test that concept to the full.

It was a bold plan and the time seemed right to execute it. Although Henry V's claims as the son of a usurper were weak, he understood that the muddled political conditions inside France had presented him with his best chance of success. While the French court was fractured and in disarray, he ruled a settled country. With Charles VI still enfeebled, the split between the Orleanists and the Burgundians was as pronounced as ever, and Henry could sense opportunities by exploiting the two factions. Initially, in the first year of his reign, he tried diplomacy and opened his account by making territorial demands in Aquitaine and asking for the hand of Princess Katherine of Valois, the French king's daughter. The demands were not disagreeable to the Orleanists, who would have welcomed a truce or a treaty based on marriage, but they were unwilling to discuss any move involving the sovereignty of France. Their intransigence on this point was revealed and made manifest during the final discussions held at Winchester at the end of June 1415, when one of the French envoys, the Archbishop of Bourges, responded to Henry's claims for the French throne with the retort that he was not even the rightful king of England. While these discussions continued Henry was also in contact with John the Fearless, Duke of Burgundy, who was keen to wrest control from Charles VI and regain Paris but was wary about entering into any alliance with the English. When the demand for support was pressed, Burgundy backed away and decided to throw in his lot with the Orleanists rather than support an English monarch in his attempt to seize the French throne.

All the time Henry had been preparing for war, almost as if he knew it was his manifest destiny to fight for what he believed were his legal rights. Weapons, especially bows and arrows, were stockpiled in the Tower of London, and siege machines were prepared for the capture of French towns. Ships were constructed or bought or hired in the Low Countries to take the armada across the Channel. When the force was finally brought together in the summer of 1415 it consisted of 105,000 fighting soldiers who were transported together with their horses and equipment on a total of 1,500 ships. The makeup of the force revealed its purpose and Henry's determination to make a lasting impression on his enemies. Under the terms of his compact (or indenture) with the nobility, barons and knights who served as his captains brought their own retinues of men, and these could range from 50 to 500, depending on the wealth and standing of those raising the force. Lesser captains had to recruit their men, while big landowners would find the men, from their own estates. Local sheriffs also acted as commissioners for the king to raise men for service in France. The entire force crossed to France on August 11, and as the fleet passed down Southampton swans accompanied it. This was taken to be a good omen.

Instead of pursuing the traditional English war-fighting policy of *chevauchées* (rapid, long-distance raids deep into French territory), Henry had decided to embark on a war of conquest and was determined to prepare the ground by securing base before engaging in more mobile operations. He could not afford to have extended lines of communication, and his invasion force would have to engage numerically superior French forces once they had landed at Harfleur, his chosen port of entry at the mouth of the Seine. Three days after setting sail, on August 14, his armada made landfall at Chef de Caux, and although the landing was unopposed, he had to lay siege to the huge and imposing fortress of Harfleur that was generally unassailable by besieging forces. It was a prize worth winning. If the port and its fortress could be captured, the way to Paris, 100 miles away, would be open and Henry would have secured a firm foothold on French soil.

However, the siege of Harfleur was not to be undertaken lightly. The fortifications were solid, and on the seaward side they stretched for over two miles. The Seine offered protection on the south, the River Lezarde was to the north, and a belt of marshes covered the eastern approaches. It took three days for the siege to begin and for three heavy guns to be dragged into position to begin their bombardment of the defenses. An attempt was made to mine the moat, but the French defenders fought this off with the creation of countermines and the English settled down to what would clearly be a lengthy affair. It also proved to be an unhealthy business: The marshes were home to millions of flies and mosquitoes, and in the summer heat, men quickly succumbed to illness. Dysentery was rife, and inadequate food supplies added to the army's woes. By the time the siege came to an end on September 22, over 2,000 of Henry's men had become casualties and many more had to be repatriated as a result of sickness.

The next stage of the operation should have been an immediate assault on Paris followed by a further attack south, deep into French territory toward Bordeaux, but the protracted battle for Harfleur made an ambitious move of that kind impossible. Henry had lost a third of his fighting men either to sickness or in battle, and he was reduced to leading a force that consisted of less than 1,000 men-at-arms and around 5,000 archers, many of them Welsh. Given the lateness of the year and the approach of the autumn rainy season, his best option might have been to return to England and leave Harfleur strongly garrisoned by English forces, but that would have represented a pyrrhic victory. More than anything else he wanted to engage the French in the set-piece battle that had been avoided during the recent siege. It was a high-risk strategy as the French forces would be superior in number, but at a council of war held on October 5, Henry came up with a compromise that would satisfy English honor and, so he hoped, keep his army safe. Instead of seeking an immediate engagement with the French in the vicinity of Harfleur, his army would march northeast through French soil toward Calais, a move that would bring them back to England and safety and one that would not give any hint of retreat. Four days later, the English forces began pulling out of Harfleur to begin a march of 120 miles that would take them across the great river barriers of Picardy, including the Somme, toward the Channel.

It was an epic undertaking. They were crossing hostile territory and the exact location of the French army was initially unknown, but Henry's men made good progress in the first week. They crossed the obstacles of the rivers Bresle and Bethune near Eu and covered 80 miles in five days. On approaching the estuary of the Somme on October 13, the first intelligence was received about the position of the enemy, and it also became clear that the chosen crossing at

Blanche-Taque was impassable, being heavily defended by 6,000 men. Undaunted, Henry led his army southeast along the southern bank of the Somme, passing Amiens and Abbeville until they came across two undefended causeways at Bethencourt and Voyennes. By then, October 19, the English had been on the march for ten days and were not only exhausted but also uneasily aware that a huge French force shadowed them on their right flank. The arrival of French heralds on October 21 with a challenge to fight provided confirmation that battle could not be avoided, but it was not until three days later, following further forced marches along a route to the south of Arras between Bapaume and Albert, that the two armies came into contact near the villages of Tramecourt and Agincourt on the road to Calais. On one side were the English, exhausted, hungry, and outnumbered at least six to one; the French were confident, well fed, superior in numbers, and defending their homeland. All that united the soldiers on both sides was the need for shelter from the incessant rain. As night fell on October 24, it was obvious that the French held the upper hand and that it would take a miracle, luck, or superior military judgment for the small and worn-out English forces to survive whatever the next 20 hours would bring them.

At dawn, the French were positioned to the north. Due to the lack of space in the open ground between the woods that surrounded Tramecourt and Agincourt, the French were drawn up in three battles, or columns, the first two composed of dismounted men-at-arms flanked by crossbow men and the third composed of cavalry. Count de Vendôme commanded the right flank, and Clignet de Brebant and Guillaume de Saveuse led the smaller left flank. Mounted troops also flanked the front battle. Against them, the English had also lined up in three battles, but their smaller numbers allowed them to deploy line abreast with the archers defending the flanks. Henry commanded the center, the Duke of York the right, and Lord Camoys the left (he had fought against the Scots and under John of Gaunt in Castile). The ground was little more than 1,000 yards wide, and as it had been freshly ploughed for winter wheat, it provided heavy going, especially as the recent torrential rains had turned parts of it into a quagmire. For three hours after sunrise, both sides held their ground in the cold damp air. It would have been a nerve-wracking experience especially for the English, who were tired and hungry. The French contemporary chronicler Jean de Waurin described the front ranks sitting down to eat and drink or to jostle for the best position, but that was on the French side. On short rations—the archers had managed to find some nuts and berries—the English could only watch and wait, alone with their fears of what lay ahead. At around 11 AM the first move was made when Henry ordered his army to move slowly forward across the sodden ground to take up a new position within 300 yards of the French lines.

When they came to a halt, the English line stretched over 900 yards, and the archers, the main strike force, took up position in echelons in front of the men-at-arms. Pointed stakes were hammered into the ground to form palisades that would protect their positions against cavalry attack. Their task was to fire into the French lines both to kill and to provoke the enemy into retaliation, and they did this by concentrating their fusillades on particular targets. Arrows were placed on the ground in front of each archer, bows were strung and had already been checked by Sir Thomas Erpingham, steward of the royal household; now they had to wait for the order to begin firing their missiles. When they did go into action, de Waurin claimed the "air was darkened by an intolerable number of piercing arrows flying across the sky to pour upon the enemy like a cloud laden with rain." It looked impressive, but at that stage in the battle the arrow shower did little damage as the mounted men-at-arms wore steel armor and were reasonably protected; only their horses would have fallen victim. But it was enough to provoke the French commander Charles d'Albret, the constable of France, to give the order for an advance across the front. As the dismounted men-at-arms began their ponderous move forward, the cavalry charged the English lines with the intention of sweeping the archers from the field. Another round of arrows was fired at them, but then, just before the point of impact, the English archers moved away to reveal their stakes. For the advancing cavalry moving at around 15 miles an hour on their big caparisoned hunter horses the momentum could not be stopped. Some crashed onto the defenses and were impaled, others fell to the ground to be bludgeoned to death by archers who had exchanged their bows for mallets and axes, while the lucky ones managed to rein in their horses and turn around toward their own lines. Some French cavalry got in among the English archers, but in this second phase of the battle they had been badly mauled and most retreated in disarray.

Worse, as the frenzied horses made their way back across the field they collided with the dismounted men-at-arms as they went into the attack. The interruption allowed the English archers to reopen fire on the advancing French lines, this time lowering the trajectory and using heavier arrow points; the French began to fall in numbers. Although most wore steel armor, there were weak points, and as the range decreased, many arrows were able to penetrate lighter steel. The heavy fire also channeled the French attack into a narrower front that gave them an initial advantage as the English moved back a spear's length to receive the charge, but it was also the cause of their undoing. As the two fronts clashed and the attacking French started falling to the ground, the weight of the attack pushed the French men-at-arms into close and deadly contact with their opponents. This must have been a horrible phase. Despite wearing steel armor, when men fell to the ground they were easy prey for the close-quarter weapons—the maces, bills, and battle-axes—to finish them off. As men stumbled around in their death throes, the rump of the attack following behind them fell over them and added to the slaughter. At this point the English archers rejoined the battle, once more exchanging their bows for handheld weapons to stand by their comrades in the killing zone. A second attack by the French second line under the command of the Duke of Alençon fared little better. Seeing what had happened to their comrades, the third line of cavalry held their ground and did not make the charge that could have done serious damage to the undefended and temporarily confused English lines. Men exhausted by the butchery would have been hard-pressed to withstand a determined cavalry attack, and by that stage in the battle the English archers would have been desperately short of arrows. Within an hour, around midday, the English had gained the upper hand and control of the battle.

By 3 PM, with dusk fast approaching, the battle petered out and peace of a kind returned to the battlefield. As was the custom of the period, the French heralds approached Henry to inform him that he had won the day and that the battle should be known as Agincourt. The grim task of counting the dead and tending to the wounded then began. English casualties were relatively light—they range from 400 to 1,600 (killed and wounded)—but among them were the Duke of York and the Earl of Suffolk. For the French, it had been a disaster. Of the Constable's army of 20,000 that had lined up earlier in the day, around a third were dead, most from dreadful blows to the body or from arrow wounds, and many more would die later of peritonitis or from their fractures. Many notable names were among the dead—the Constable, the Duke of Brabant, and the Count of Nevers, both brothers to Burgundy, and the Duke of Alençon. Among the French nobles who survived the battle but found themselves in English captivity were the Duke of Orleans, the Duke of Bourbon, and the counts of Vendôme, Richemont, Eu, and Boucicaut. By any standards, the battle, fought on the feast day of the saints Crispin and Crispinian, was a glorious victory for the English and a personal triumph for Henry, who had directed the forces. (The saints in question lived in Soissons in the third century and had been martyred for their Christian beliefs.) A superior French army had been defeated, and once again the skill and killing capacity of the English archers had sent a powerful message across Europe. Four days later Henry's little army had reached Calais, where they had to wait for shipment across the Channel, and it was not until November 23 that they were able return to London to a heroes' welcome. It was typical of Henry that he refused to accept any personal credit and preferred to offer thanks to God for his support in making the victory possible: The Archbishop of

Canterbury ruled that henceforth the feast day of Crispin and Crispinian was to be celebrated with due reverence, a move that underlined both the scale of the victory over the French and God's role in making it happen.

From that moment onward, the names of the king and the battle were to be linked for good or for ill. Agincourt defined Henry's career in that it seemed to reinforce the legitimacy of his reign and put a seal on the right of the Lancastrians to occupy the throne of England. Not only had he displayed great leadership on the field and immense personal bravery by leading from the front where he was often in the thick of the action, but by ascribing the victory to God it seemed that England had been granted divine protection and assistance. On a temporal level, Henry had shown that he was a leader of men and a worthy successor to Edward III; on a spiritual level, he had been revealed as a man doubly blessed. How else could so few have defeated so many unless they had divine protection? All this mattered: In the heady days following the return of the hero king and his victorious army, perception became more important that reality. No one could doubt Henry's right to wear the crown of England, and just as importantly there were no longer any qualms about his entitlement to claim the throne of France. The courage and steadfastness of around 6,000 Englishmen on a muddy autumn field in Picardy had seen to that.

7

THE MIGHTY AND
PUISSANT CONQUEROR

*a*t Agincourt, Henry had won a great victory, and his name and reputation as a great leader resounded through Europe; but the reality of his situation was rather different. He had launched the campaign to further his territorial ambitions in France, but apart from winning a single battle and crushing the opposition's army he had done nothing to encourage the French to make any concessions, and neither had he made any tangible gains in pursuit of his policy of conquest. All that he had in his possession was a town in France at the mouth of the Seine, and it was obvious that his opponents would soon take advantage of the garrison's precarious position and attempt to win it back.

The Orleanist faction, now led by Bertrand, Count of Armagnac, had refused to enter into new negotiations with Henry, and the Burgundians stayed aloof, preferring to push their own claims when and if the opportunity arose. They did not have long to wait. Shortly after Charles VI returned to Paris at the end of November 1415, the Duke of Burgundy tried to capitalize on the situation by forcing Armagnac out of the capital, but his bid failed and petered out altogether when the Dauphin suddenly died in mid-December. The French king's son and heir was succeeded by his younger brother John, and this subtle change in relationships encouraged the duke to remove his forces from the Paris area and take them back into Flanders. Not only did this strengthen his position—the new Dauphin John was married to Burgundy's niece—but it made him less likely to seek any compact with the English at a time when his main aim was to oust Armagnac from Paris. From the point of view of diplomacy none of this helped Henry, and he had further cause to be troubled when the French took steps to besiege Harfleur early in the following year.

Before the French intervened in earnest to win back their possession, the English garrison had been reinforced and placed under the command of the Earl of Dorset, but their safety was by no means guaranteed. That much became clear in March when an English foraging party narrowly avoided defeat at the hands of the French investigating army that was led by the Count of Armagnac, recently appointed the new Constable of France. In an attempt to bring the issue to a speedier conclusion Armagnac started hiring warships from Genoa and Castile and employed them to blockade the approaches to the Seine to prevent the English from getting supplies through to Harfleur. The new tactics worked—Harfleur was now under siege by land and sea—and it provoked the English to respond. Preparations were made for a new expedition, and on August 15, a naval force led by the king's brother, the Duke of Bedford, arrived off Harfleur to engage the French fleet. The subsequent action lasted six hours, and it ended in Bedford's favor: According to the Italian chronicler Antonio Morosini, it was one of the most vicious and hard-fought naval battles ever fought.

Although it was a welcome victory, the lifting of the siege of Harfleur does raise questions regarding Henry's foreign policy in 1416. Having defeated the French, he seemed to lose his nerve about what to do next. Finance was one reason: The previous year's expedition had been costly, and although parliament was of a mind to provide further subsidies, it would take at least another year before Henry could raise another army to launch a fresh attack on French soil. It is also possible that he had been unnerved by the circumstances of his victory at Agincourt. While he took it as a sign of God's grace and a reminder that his claim over France was a just one, he would not have been human had he not realized that his victory had been a close-run thing and that the battle could have been lost but for French pride, intransigence, and bad leadership. International diplomacy had also been brought into play. In that same year, 1416, Henry's attention had been diverted by the arrival of Sigismund, King of Hungary, and since 1411, Holy Roman Emperor, the titular ruler of large swathes of eastern and central Europe. A complicated man whose authority had been eroded by internecine fighting in Bohemia, Sigismund regarded himself as a European peacemaker, and his greatest diplomatic ambition was to bring to an end the Great Schism, which had plunged the Catholic Church into chaos. To that end he had summoned a General Council of the Church at Constance in November 1414, and in the intervening period he endeavored to convince the princes of the church to return to a single universally recognized papacy.

Part of that effort took him to Paris in March 1416—the aim being to persuade the French to withdraw support from Benedict XIII, the Avignon pope—and from there he continued across the Channel and reached Dover on

May 1. He arrived with the intention of acting as a peace-broker between the two countries, not just because they were in a state of conflict but also because French and English clerics continued the national rivalry at Constance. Voting at the General Council was in the hands of "nations" (English, French, German, and Italian), and because England and France were on separate sides of the schism, there was great scope for carrying on the war by other means, using the papal discussions as a proxy for the wider political disagreements. By visiting France and England, Sigismund saw an opportunity to bring the Council's work to fruition—he was keen to find a compliant pope who would validate his claims in Germany and Bohemia, where he was intent on suppressing the Hussites, followers of John Hus who had much in common with Wyclif—and at the same time he wanted to put a stop to the cross-Channel confrontation. With him he brought a French embassy headed by the Archbishop of Reims and a large retinue including the Duke of Berry.

Henry had high hopes that Sigismund would back his territorial claims in France, while the emperor hoped to add to his reputation as a diplomat, but neither side gained much from the discussions that lasted until late summer. On August 15, a treaty of mutual support was signed at Canterbury, on the same day that the Duke of Bedford had destroyed the French fleet at the Battle of the Seine. The treaty was couched in such general terms that there was a large question mark over whether or not Sigismund would have provided any military assistance to Henry as the alliance demanded, but the new relationship and the great naval victory gave considerable encouragement to the English king. Three weeks later he followed Sigismund over to Calais for fresh talks with the French ambassadors and a series of secret meetings with the Duke of Burgundy, whom he hoped to cajole into an alliance. Each side wanted something from the covert talks. Henry was keen to get the duke's support for his claim on the French crown; Sigismund desired the same outcome but for the different reason of making the Council of Constance work, while Burgundy simply wanted to understand how the Canterbury alliance would affect his own position in France. Of the three he had the most to put on the table, but apart from offering vague assurances about his own neutrality—the records of the meeting are unclear about the outcome—he made sure that no one knew what his position really was.

Nonetheless, the meetings in Calais did help to point Henry in the right direction. He had tried diplomacy, and it had achieved nothing other than to buy time, and it persuaded him that he had to regain the initiative by renewing hostilities with France. On his return to England he informed parliament that he intended to restart military operations in France the following summer and that he would require a double subsidy to fund the operations. This time Henry decided to invade Normandy to protect what he conquered by first pacifying the area and then bringing it under English control. Because he was planning for events in the longer term, he needed to create secure lines of communication for supply and resupply, and for that to happen the English had to retain control of the Channel. At the end of June 1417, an English naval force under the Earl of Huntingdon and Lord Castelhon destroyed four Genoese carracks in the mouth of the Seine, effectively giving the English naval supremacy along the French coast. When Henry landed at Toques, west of Honfleur, on August 1, he knew that he would now be able to maintain the logistic tail to keep his army of some 10,000 men (one in three of them archers) in the field for the rest of the year and perhaps even longer. His cause was helped by a fresh outbreak of hostilities between the Burgundians and the Armagnacs that resulted in Duke John's army surrounding Paris, a move that made it difficult for the Duke of Armagnac to respond to the English invasion.

A month after landing and following a grueling siege undertaken by forces under Clarence's command, Caen fell into English hands, and it was followed by the seizure of a number of smaller towns along the eastern Normandy border including Argentan and Falaise. Their capture provided Henry's forces with winter quarters and a springboard for the invasion of the Cotentin peninsula. As a warning to the other main towns in Normandy, Henry ordered the expulsion of those in Caen's population who refused to accept his rule. Cherbourg was besieged the following spring—it fell in September—and at the beginning of July 1418, the strategically important town of Pont-de-l'Arche fell into English hands. This had the significant outcome of cutting off Rouen, the capital of Normandy, from any support that may have been coming from Paris. In fact, the chance of Rouen receiving any military assistance had already crumbled. In May, Burgundy's armies had taken control of Paris, and during the fighting, the Count of Armagnac and many of his supporters were slaughtered. At the same time King Charles VI became a prisoner of the Duke of Burgundy, who emerged from the bloody incident as the virtual ruler of France.

The political pendulum had swung once more and had created a new set of alliances. The Dauphin John had died and was succeeded by his younger brother Charles, the third son of Charles VI, who was of the Armagnac faction, but due to his mother Isabeau's sexual improprieties his legitimacy was widely doubted. Not surprisingly the new Dauphin fled Paris when Burgundy arrived in the city on July 14, bringing with him Queen Isabeau, who had been proclaimed regent to rule in place of her incapacitated husband, while the duke rejoiced in his new title, Governor of France. The changes left the Burgundians in control of Paris, while the Dauphin joined the Armagnacs at Melun, where he assumed leadership of their party. Following Count Bernard's death, the Orleanist or Armagnac factions were also known as Dauphinists. While all this was happening Henry was encamped in Lower Normandy, where he was able to tighten his grip on his new holdings.

As for the people of Rouen, they were left with no hope of help from the outside and settled down for a long siege in their seemingly impregnable forti-fied city. Matters were complicated by the fact that Rouen was a Burgundian city. Enmeshed as he was in civil strife with the Dauphinists, the Duke of Burgundy found himself in a quandary. He was obliged to defend Paris against English attack, yet it was an affront to his dignity that Henry had put one of his key cities under siege at a time when he lacked the military capacity to come to its rescue. The only way out of the impasse was a realignment of his priorities, and he took that route by entering into peace talks with the Dauphin with the aim of forging an alliance to attack the English. Given the internal situation in France, the move reeked of pragmatism, but when the two sides met at Saint-Maur-des-Fossés that autumn, nothing came of the talks other than an outbreak of fresh diplomatic initiatives. Having failed to reach any agreement with his fellow countrymen, the Dauphin then made contact with Henry and held out the prospect of a fresh alliance against the Burgundians in return for meeting some of Henry's demands. For the Dauphin, anxious to reinforce his position and maintain his claim to his father's throne, this made sense, but once again the talks failed to achieve anything as the French were unwilling to entertain Henry's territorial demands in France.

Everything now turned on the siege of Rouen, which turned into a trial of strength between the defenders, who soon realized that no help would be com-ing their way, and the English, who were determined to bring the siege to a suc-cessful conclusion. Rouen was one of the most bitterly contested confrontations of Henry's second expedition in France, and it became a test of endurance for both sides. The siege had opened on July 31, 1418, and in the early stages the defenders were confident that they would be able to hold out and break the will of the English army. Not only had the huge fortress been strengthened to with-stand attack by siege engines and cannon, but shortly before the arrival of the English army the surrounding countryside had been razed by the French to deny the attackers access to foodstuffs. This meant that everything needed by Henry's army—food, fuel, and reinforcements—could not be foraged locally but had to be brought in from England, the main reason why naval control of the Channel was so important. Henry, though, decided to be patient. Rouen was surrounded, and the River Seine was closed to traffic by blocking it with chain booms and block ships to prevent it being used as a passage. Having encircled the city and cut it off from the outside world, Henry simply waited, secure in the knowledge that neither the Burgundians nor the Dauphinists would make any move to come to the rescue of their beleaguered countrymen.

It took five months before there was any move. That winter turned out to be one of the worst in living memory, and conditions inside Rouen became unbearable. Food, water, and fuel ran low, and with the population reduced to starvation, the commander of the garrison Guy de Bouteiller decided to release all the nonmilitary personnel, including many refugees from the surrounding countryside, who were unable to play any part in manning the defenses. Around 12,000 people were simply thrown out of the city and left to their own devices in a wintry wasteland. All that stood between them and a slow death was the mercy of the English army, but Henry decided to prevent them from escaping, and the hapless refugees were left to starve or freeze to death along the marshlands of the Seine within sight of the city's defenders.

As things finally fell apart and it became evident that further resistance was futile, de Bouteiller surrendered the keys of the city on January 19, 1419, and Rouen was in Henry's hands. He entered the city the following day and after a mass of thanksgiving set about establishing a new administration for his new duchy of Normandy. The idea was to run it as an efficient English bailiwick— taxes would be raised, there would be a sound system of government based on the former estates, and land would be granted to English colonists and to Normans thought to be loyal to the new setup. In short, Henry intended to win Norman hearts and minds as a prelude to renewing his claims on the French throne. The next step was to decide whether or not to attack Paris. In the longer term that must have been his ambition, but at the beginning of the new year following a long and grueling campaign to subdue Normandy, he lacked the military means to make a successful attack on the French capital. Instead, he turned once more to diplomacy. Henry's advisers attempted to convene a meeting with the Dauphin at Evreux in March, but this failed to materialize when the French side did not turn up on the appointed day. That failure drove Henry once more toward the Burgundian camp, and after the establishment of a two-month truce, the three sides met near Meulan at the end of May, the main protagonists being Henry, Burgundy, Queen Isabeau, her daughter Katherine of Valois, and her son the Dauphin. In all, eight meetings were held over a five-week period and the negotiations came tantalizingly close to reaching an agreement.

Henry's demands came straight to the point. For the first time he agreed to put aside his claims to the French throne, at least for the time being, but in return he wanted some major territorial concessions to match his military successes. Everything that he had captured since landing in France would remain in English hands, and, in addition, he laid claim to the territories that had been ceded to King Edward III as a result of the Treaty of Brétigny in 1360. Finally, he gave notice that he was serious in his intention to marry Princess Katherine of Valois, daughter of King Charles VI. The marriage had been considered an ideal possibility since 1408 when Henry was twenty-one and she was just eight, and it had also been central to the negotiations in 1414. Having met her for the first time at Meulan, Henry seems to have been sufficiently attracted to her to press the suit with considerably more firmness. All the sides had much to gain from reaching a workable agreement. The Burgundians would enter into a powerful new alliance with England, and Henry would achieve most of his territorial goals. The French wanted a solution, but there was the great stumbling block that it would be dishonorable and potentially fatal to cede so much land to an English king at a time when Henry had only postponed, not dropped, his claim to the French throne.

As the French were being asked to make most of the concessions, it is hardly surprising that the talks foundered and eventually broke down. A meeting fixed for July 3 failed to take place, and just as inevitably Duke John responded to the setback by making contact with the Dauphin and asking for a fresh reconciliation. Faced by the English demands, it was always possible that the Burgundians and the Dauphinists would unite in a common cause, and although their subsequent agreement was limited to a promise that neither side would enter into a treaty with Henry, it did put a stop to the cycle of negotiations. The English response was rapid and effective. On July 29, the day after a local truce ended with the Burgundians, an English force seized Pontoise, a strategically important town lying between Rouen and Paris, and by the middle of August, Henry's army was threatening the French capital, forcing the court to move to Troyes. There was panic everywhere. Adding to the confusion, Duke John was shockingly murdered by a follower of the Dauphin when the two men met at Montereau to the south of Paris during the second week of September. To the horror of those present, Duke John was killed as he knelt in front of the Dauphin when they met on the bridge over the River Yonne. Later, apologists for the Dauphin claimed that Duke John had been struck down because he was reaching for his sword, but it seems a far-fetched excuse for the attack that plunged the country into confusion. Whatever else, one thing was clear: The most powerful man in France had been killed and his death was blamed on his greatest rival.

The murder at Montereau changed everything. Burgundy was succeeded by his son Philip "the Good," an inexperienced young man upon whom the weight of ensuring his own family's position as well as protecting the French throne had been thrust. The Dauphin had weakened his faction's position by being associated with the murder at Montereau, and Queen Isabeau had to decide if it was in her interests to continue the Burgundian alliance. Only Henry emerged from the shameful events with his position enhanced. Suddenly he seemed to be the one person who could bring some order to the chaos and by doing so, strengthen his own position within France. Henry began negotiations with the new Duke Philip at the end of September, and he did so from a position of considerable strength. His opening gambit made it clear that he intended to press his own claim to the French throne by emerging as Charles VI's heir, with the Dauphin being disinherited, and that his position would be strengthened immeasurably by his marriage to Katherine. The two countries would be ruled by him and his successors, although each would be administratively independent of the other and French laws and institutions would be respected.

These were radical and far-reaching proposals, and it was to the credit of Duke Philip that he did not cave in immediately. However, he could only play for time because not only were conditions in Paris worsening due to the blockade by English forces, but there was also the very strong possibility that if nothing were decided, Henry might reopen negotiations with the Dauphin. The talks dragged on until Christmas Eve, when agreement was reached on Henry's terms and a general truce was signed between the two parties in Rouen. Under its provisions, Henry entered into an alliance with the Burgundians, each party agreed to lend assistance to the other, the blockade of Paris was lifted, and arrangements were set in motion for Henry's marriage with Katherine. A few months later, on May 20, 1420, the agreement was ratified by the Treaty of Troyes, which made the French Royal family party to the agreement. Although Charles was not well enough to sign the deed of ratification, this was done on his behalf by Queen Isabeau and Duke Philip. The diplomatic niceties having been completed, Henry married Katherine in the Church of St. John in Troyes in a simple ceremony on June 2.

For Henry, the Treaty of Troyes was a personal triumph and the diplomatic high-water mark of his reign. Through a mixture of warfare and diplomacy, with some good fortune added in, he had achieved a dynastic settlement that gave him most of what he wanted. He and his heirs would rule France, peace had been restored, both England and France would retain their integrity, and all had been achieved reasonably amicably. He had also succeeded in his aims while spending almost four years out of England, where his absence had been regretted but had not led to any local difficulties or scheming among the nobility. Given England's turbulent recent history, it was quite an achievement to leave the country and not face a challenge from a potential rival. As for the people of France, they appeared to accept the new dispensation largely because it brought peace after years of internecine warfare and also because those who supported the Burgundians, especially the Parisians, had come to believe that it was the only possible way forward. In return for that support, important and lucrative benefices were returned to them. The only opponents were those whose opinion had not been asked—those who supported the Dauphin, who had been disinherited by the treaty. However, he and his party still controlled much of the south and the area to the east of Paris where three fortified towns—Melun, Montereau, and Sens—still loyal to the Dauphinists were located. Under the terms of the treaty Henry was obliged to bring them under control to protect Paris and each was subjected to siege. Sens fell first, on June 10, followed by Montereau, the scene of Duke John's murder, but Melun held out until November. Having battered them into submission, Henry formally entered Paris on December 1, 1420, in the company of Charles VI and Duke Philip of Burgundy and a large English retinue.

The successful conclusion to the campaign allowed Henry to think about returning home to England. After spending the new year at Rouen the Royal couple made their way back to England, reaching Dover on February 1, 1421, to be greeted by a joyous and enthusiastic reception. Three weeks later Katherine was crowned queen in Westminster Abbey in a service conducted by the Archbishop of Canterbury. That done, Henry set off on a peregrination of England to revisit places he had not seen for many years and, just as importantly, to allow himself to be seen by his subjects following his long absence in France. He visited important shrines, and he and his retinue celebrated Easter with his wife, now pregnant, in Leicester, the burial place of his mother. Next on his itinerary was Beverley in Yorkshire, but the pilgrimage ended in calamity. Shortly afterwards Henry received the disastrous news of a heavy defeat of English forces in France. Just before Easter, the Duke of Clarence, his lieutenant-general in France, received intelligence that a large Dauphinist force was assembling at Baugé near Angers. Clarence was courageous and an experienced soldier, but he was also hot-headed. As he was not far away from Baugé, he decided on a preemptive strike and without further ado set out with a small force of mounted men-at-arms while the rest of his men followed. There was no reconnaissance of enemy dispositions or the lay of the land, and, fatally, Clarence pushed ahead without his archers. Although the smaller English force fought well when they engaged the opposition and believed that they were only encountering light resistance in the initial stages of the battle, they were soon overcome by a force which was three times stronger. In the melee Clarence was killed and a number of notable English nobles were taken prisoner.

The defeat was a serious setback—until there were any children born to the Royal marriage, Clarence was Henry's heir—and although the Dauphinists did not capitalize on their unexpected victory by marching on Paris, as might have seemed sensible, it did encourage them to think that the English were not invincible. Henry, too, seemed to realize that his authority had been checked, or at least brought into question, and set about creating a new army to bring his French kingdom under control. Money suddenly became a problem, as it had been in his father's reign, but parliament voted him funds and he raised the rest as loans or gifts from friends and supporters. By the beginning of June, the necessary forces were in place and he crossed to France with a retinue including the Duke of Gloucester and King James of Scotland, still in English captivity, who, Henry hoped, might be useful in persuading his fellow Scots to withdraw their support for the Dauphin.

On arriving back in France, Henry headed for Paris to make plain to the inhabitants that he was intent on avenging the setback at Baugé and meant to punish the Dauphinists for their presumption. He also had discussions with Duke Philip, who agreed to put down an unexpected upsurge of support for the Dauphin in Picardy while the English forces dealt with the Dauphinists south of the River Loire. It was to no avail. The Dauphin refused to engage in a set-piece battle, and although Henry got as far as Orleans, he was forced to return to Paris in September with his army weakened by illness. Frustrated by the lack of action he turned his attention to besieging the fortified town of Meaux, which lay to the east of Paris and guarded the lower reaches of the River Marne. Once it fell into his hands it would complete Henry's attempts to control the River Seine, but it proved to be a difficult operation. Once again Henry decided to use the tactics that had served him so well in the past. Instead of attempting to bludgeon Meaux into submission, his forces surrounded the town and set about starving the garrison by cutting off all access to the outside world. This time, though, it proved to be a more difficult task. Henry's besieging army came under attack from marauding Dauphinist cavalry forces, and the winter was unusually wet, with the result that foraging became a problem and supplies were soon running low. The garrison also proved to be more obdurate than expected, not least because it included a number of Scots who knew that they could expect no mercy if Meaux fell into English hands. It was turning into a long and hard affair, and the only good news came from London on December 6, when it was announced that Katherine had given birth to a baby boy, to be christened Henry.

Eventually Meaux fell in May 1422. English cannon were used to blast the weary garrison into submission, but it had been a hard-won victory that had taken up a good deal of energy and resources. Around a hundred Dauphinist prisoners were dispatched to England for imprisonment, and many more were expelled from the city and sent south to rejoin their leader. In the longer term, the fall of Meaux raised as many questions as it answered. While a sizable asset had been prised out of the Dauphin's hands, the siege had created huge problems for Henry's army in France. It was also an unpleasant reminder of the fact that while Henry and his heirs were titular kings of France, their writ did not extend over the whole country, large swathes of which were loyal to the Dauphin. Was that what lay ahead in the future: a succession of long and expensive campaigns to wear down the Dauphinists before Henry could call himself the rightful ruler of the whole of France? And before that came about, could he rely implicitly on the loyalty of the French people? The answers were probably yes and no. The Treaty of Troyes must have seemed like a distant triumph as Henry took stock of his position after Meaux had capitulated. Additionally, he took something else from the siege: an illness, probably dysentery, from the unsanitary conditions inside camp in the middle of winter.

Shortly after the end of the siege Katherine arrived from England and met up with her husband in Paris at Whitsun. From there they moved to Senlis, a small town to the northeast, where it became clear that Henry was ailing. Even so, he seemed to be fit enough to answer a request for military assistance from Duke Philip, who was engaged with Dauphinist forces near Bourges. Ever the soldier, Henry set off with Bedford and Warwick in attendance, but during the journey his condition worsened to such an extent that he had to change his horse for a litter. His condition was now critical, and he was moved to Vincennes where no one, least of all the king, could doubt the seriousness of his position. As his physical condition declined, he remained sufficiently lucid to put his affairs in order, but he was failing fast. He revised his will and placed his son in the protection of his brother Gloucester, who would be appointed warden or keeper of England, while the regency of France would be given to Duke Philip or, failing him, to Bedford. His old friend Thomas Beaufort was entrusted with Prince Henry's education. The end came on August 31, his last spoken thought being a regret that he had never fulfilled his wish to visit the Holy Land to rebuild the walls of Jerusalem. After his death, his sadly wasted body was embalmed and he was taken by river to Rouen, where the funeral obsequies lasted several days before he was finally moved to London for burial in Westminster Abbey on November 7. Walsingham's tribute was couched in conventional terms of piety, but across the centuries it still manages to reflect the great sense of loss and grief in England at the king's untimely passing:

> King Henry V left no one like him among Christian kings or princes: his death,
> not only by his subjects in England and France, but in the whole of

Christendom, was deservedly mourned. He was pious in soul, taciturn and discreet in his speech, far-seeing in counsel, prudent in judgement, modest in appearance, magnanimous in his actions, firm in business, persistent in pilgrimages and generous in alms; devoted to God and supportive and respectful of the prelates and ministers of the church; warlike, distinguished and fortunate, he had won victories in all his military engagements.

All that was true, and in a personal sense the encomiums were not misplaced. Of Henry's abilities as a soldier there can be no doubt. He learned the art of war the hard way by fighting as a young man in the counterinsurgency campaign against Owen Glendower, and in the fighting in France he emerged as a natural leader, a soldier who could enthuse others to rise above themselves and do more than they thought themselves capable of achieving. Never a faintheart, he knew when to be ruthless, and, although some of his actions bordered on the callous, he understood the necessity of firm and decisive action in warfare; having made up his mind about what needed to be done to win the day, he moved his army forward and pushed home any advantage as soon as it appeared. That ability to stand apart and to view events disinterestedly helped him as a commander, and at Agincourt it gave him the edge over his opponents.

On a more cerebral level, Henry's piety and devotion to his duty as a king cannot be doubted. Much of his personal life was guided by prayer, and even the way he ordered his personal matters in advance of his death indicates a mind that believed that there was more to a man's life than its earthly manifestation. When Henry put his trust in God in prayer he was not mouthing platitudes but enunciating a deeply held belief in the spiritual nature of the relationship between man and his maker. And as a king that orderliness of thought was matched by the stability and good sense he brought to his kingdom throughout his reign. Unlike his father, who was hamstrung by the belief that he had usurped a rightful king and was somehow dishonored by the action, Henry V was secure in his position and by personal example reinforced the family and tribal loyalties that supported him. In contrast to what happened in his father's day, Henry V's domestic reign was not unsettled or threatened by civil strife—other than the quickly quelled plot on the eve of the Harfleur expedition—and he provided an effective form of governance that unified his kingdom. In short, Henry deserves his reputation as one of England's greatest kings, above all perhaps for the victory he won against all odds at Agincourt.

And yet, Henry was not just a heroic figure. For all that he waged a successful war against France and for all that he exacted from his defeated enemy a peace treaty that gave him most of what he wanted, Henry's campaigns in France created as many problems as they solved. Imposing the conditions at Troyes was a diplomatic triumph, but it is impossible to know if the dual monarchy arrangement would have ever worked, even if Henry had not died so young. (The exact date of his birth and therefore his age at the time of his death are uncertain, 1386 and 1387 both being mooted. It was probably not recorded because he was never expected to become King of England.) Large parts of France remained under the Dauphin's control, and having been dispossessed, King Charles VI's son probably would not have accepted his inferior and debased position. There was also the question of national pride. Henry was admired by many French people and his death was mourned—the commemorations in Rouen were particularly sincere and sonorous—but there was also resentment. This was, after all, a relationship that had been imposed on the French people by force of arms. It would only have been natural had they kicked against it at some future juncture.

As for the war itself and the reasons for waging it, whatever problems it created for future generations, the conflict can be justified in the realpolitik of Henry's day. Although Henry based his French policy on the premise that possession of the country would secure England's future happiness and prosperity, he also believed that it was a legal war in that he had a rightful claim to the French throne following their refusal to honor obligations made to his great-grandfather in 1360. When events played into his hands at Agincourt and, later, through the death of Duke John of Burgundy, he had no option but to follow his destiny. In so doing, he came tantalizingly close to achieving his objectives before his unseasonable and, for England at least, tragic death.

8

A Scepter in a
Child's Hand

On Henry's death, his son Prince Henry was proclaimed king of England and France at the early age of nine months. For everyone connected to the English court, it was a trying moment as once again the country had a childking. Without a monarch, the country needed to be governed and steps had to be taken to forestall any outbreak of internecine fighting among those who might have believed that they had a better claim on the throne—notably the prince's uncles Bedford and Gloucester—or who thought to take their chances during this period of transition. Before his death, Henry V had made his wishes known for the protection and guidance of his realm during his son's minority, but whether or not his plan worked depended on the goodwill of those chosen by the king to carry out his plans. Fortunately there were enough building blocks in place to ensure the safety of the edifice that Henry had created. Although there was by no means a sense of complete common cause among all of the magnates, and there were times when hidden enmities almost rose to the surface to threaten the country's stability, the governance of England did not collapse and, by and large, the arrangements made by Henry survived the prince's minority. It was a tribute to the loyalty expressed by those who followed Henry V and to the maturity that had been the benchmark of the warrior king's reign that the country and most of France remained calm. In the days and months that followed his death there was none of the turmoil that might have arisen had the arrangements been weak or ineffective. Of course there were tensions. Not all of the personalities were on mutually friendly terms, and there was a sense that the younger magnates were marking time until Henry VI came into his own, but the years of the Royal infancy proved to be surprisingly tranquil and well ordered.

One of the beneficiaries of the new order was James I of Scotland, who had been in English captivity since 1406. Thinking that his release would guarantee Scottish neutrality at a time when Scots had been fighting in France, the council decided that he should be set free and returned to Scotland. During his years in English hands James Stewart had become thoroughly anglicized and had developed into an intelligent young man with strong literary and cultural tastes. He had also fallen in love with Lady Joan Beaufort, whom he married on February 2, 1424, shortly before he returned to Scotland. She was a daughter of John Beaufort, Duke of Somerset and a cousin of Henry V, and the English council had high hopes that the marriage to a leading member of the Beaufort family would produce a lasting period of peace with Scotland—in addition to agreeing to pay a ransom to cover the costs of his upkeep and education, James signed a seven-year truce—and for a while the policy worked. On regaining the Scottish throne, James imposed a centralist form of government and reestablished his authority by executing his rival to the throne Murdoch Stewart, Duke of Albany, and his two sons and confiscating their lands.

Under the terms of Henry V's final will, the king had made specific arrangements for his son's inheritance. As we have seen, the three most important personages trusted with looking after his infant son and the realm were his two surviving brothers Humphrey, Duke of Gloucester, and John, Duke of Bedford, and his Beaufort uncle, Thomas, Duke of Exeter, the youngest of John of Gaunt's three sons by his mistress Katherine Swynford. Surprisingly perhaps, the younger of the two brothers, Gloucester, was appointed guardian of the future king and warden of England, but that was probably due to the fact that he had been acting in that role at the time of Henry's death. Bedford, a more stable and upright character, was to take charge of France as regent until Prince Henry came of age. It was a task that Bedford accepted gladly as a sacred duty, and he proved to be both a wise administrator and a valiant protector of his country's interests—no easy matter considering that France had been ravaged by the long years of confrontation and warfare. Exeter was also a good choice, as Henry had trusted his Beaufort cousins, but he was an older man and was overshadowed by his younger brother Henry Beaufort, Bishop of Winchester, who had also been given a councillor role in the prince's upbringing. The bishop was one of the most influential men in England: Having made a huge fortune from the wool trade, he had helped Henry V with extensive loans, and according to the chronicler Edward Hall he was "rich above measure of all men."

There was one other important and constant factor in the infant king's life—his mother, Queen Katherine. Through her husband's will she had been denied any role in the regency, but she was entrusted with his upbringing while an infant. As Prince Henry's mother, she was responsible for looking after him while they were in residence at Windsor, and she proved to be an admirable Queen Dowager. She was still young, had retained her looks, and it was always possible that she might wish to remarry. If that happened, it would complicate matters as an ambitious new husband might want to exert his authority by making a claim on the throne. However, when Katherine did fall in love she proved to be remarkably discreet. While her son was still in his infancy, she entered into a relationship with a member of the Welsh gentry called Owen Tudor (properly Owen ap Maredudd ap Tewdwr), whose family had been involved in the Glendower rebellion against Henry IV. Next to nothing is known about their relationship: They may have married in secret, and they certainly had children, the eldest being Edmund Tudor who later became the Earl of Richmond. As Tudor occupied a modest position at court—he was Keeper of the Wardrobe— he was a social inferior and any relationship with the Queen Dowager was ill-advised. Surprisingly, there was no scandal attached to the affair, although the council seems to have accepted the fact that it existed. Against all the odds their secret relationship survived until her death in 1437. As for her lover, he was briefly imprisoned in Newgate and their sons Edmund and Jasper were placed in the care of Katherine de la Pole, the Abbess of Barking, and sister to the Earl of Suffolk.

Given the fact that Prince Henry's three principal advisers were all powerful and wealthy men within their own right, there was bound to be rivalry, and the wonder is that jealousy did not break out into something more serious. Each man was different from the others. Bedford was a soldier's soldier, an upright and loyal leader of men who had the complete trust of the soldiers under his command. He was also the right man to represent England's interests in France, and it helped that he was married to Anne, the sister of Philip of Burgundy. In return, Bedford carried out his duties with a light hand, keeping French administrators in their positions and maintaining an enlightened view of French institutions by ruling through a Grand Council in Paris. When his authority was challenged, he also knew when to use military force and revealed his strengths as a battlefield commander by inflicting a serious defeat on Scottish–Orleanist forces at Verneuil in August 1424.

Bedford's brother Gloucester was altogether different, although he was no less bellicose. Known to history as "the good Duke Humphrey," his personality belied that enviable description. His sudden and unexpected marriage to Jacqueline of Hainault and Holland had given him territorial claims in the Netherlands that he intended to pursue to prevent his wife's former husband the Duke of Brabant naming Philip of Burgundy as his heir. At one point, in 1424, the year of Verneuil, Gloucester rashly led an armed force into Hainault, a move that threatened the Burgundian alliance and enraged his brother Bedford at a time when he was attempting to consolidate English authority in France. Although Gloucester had his good points in that he was highly educated, widely read, intelligent, and a serious patron of the arts who encouraged several writers and helped to endow the Bodleian Library in Oxford, he was also irresponsible, self-serving, and extremely ambitious. While Henry V lived, his younger brother could be kept under control, but when Duke Humphrey was unsupervised, he was a menace. It did not help matters that he was jealous of Bedford's soldierly qualities and position in France or that he developed a dislike of his Beaufort relatives, particularly Henry, who became a cardinal in 1426. Their rivalry was intense and bitter and was to last a lifetime.

The three men nominated by Henry as advisers were also involved in the governance of the realm that was in the hands of the 17 members of a regency council during the king's minority. Their task was to continue the policies laid down by Henry V and, by directing the national finances and controlling foreign policy, to make sure that England remained unified and peaceful during the king's minority. Parliament remained responsible for taxation. One possible font of dissent was removed in January 1425, when the (English) Earl of March died of plague at Trim Castle in Ireland where he was fulfilling his duties as lord lieutenant. He was the last of the male line of the Mortimers, and with his passing his claim to the throne as heir-general to Richard II died with him, but, as we shall see, it did not disappear completely. As March died without an heir, his lands devolved to his sister's son, the 14-year-old Richard of Cambridge, Duke of York, whose father had been executed after plotting against Henry V on the eve of the Agincourt campaign. He was not allowed, however, to inherit immediately, and the Mortimer lands were held for the crown by Gloucester until York came of age. Nothing was said about any possible claim to the throne that he might have entertained after his Mortimer uncle's death. Not only was he related to March, but he was also descended from Edward III through both parents, his father being the son of that king's fourth son, Edmund of Langley, first Duke of York, and his mother the great-granddaughter of Edward's second son, Lionel of Antwerp, the Duke of Clarence.

As there was no single all-powerful regent, all of the council's decisions had to be taken in front of the baby king to maintain the belief that the person and office of majesty were inseparable. The great seal was placed in his possession, and to all intents and purposes the illusion was kept up that the infant king was the supreme authority while decisions were being made. Anything less would have damaged the legitimacy of the Lancastrian succession, and had either of

Henry V's brothers made any attempt to usurp the crown, it would have had disastrous consequences not just in England but also in France. This pretense had a unifying effect on the council that was responsible for all executive action, but Gloucester found it difficult to operate without hankering for the title and authority of regent, ruling in the place of the king. Not only was he sufficiently ambitious to want the position for his own purposes, but he believed that Henry V's wishes, as expressed in his will, gave him the authority to fulfill that role. From the outset of the new arrangements, Gloucester promoted his interests with a persistence that angered the other councillors, so much so that they were forced to declare that they were collectively responsible for the good governance of England until the king came of age. While this avoided an immediate confrontation with one of the most powerful councillors, it did not dampen Gloucester's aspirations, and gradually a split appeared in the council between him and Henry Beaufort. More than any other matter, one subject divided the two men: the question of what to do in France. Gloucester wanted to continue military operations and to defeat the Orleanists in order to cement the Treaty of Troyes, while Beaufort worried about the costs of waging war and preferred brokering an honorable peace. Inevitably, perhaps, France was to be the first great crisis of the infant king's reign.

Within six weeks of Henry V's death, Charles VI was also dead, a state of affairs that meant that all at once the agreement reached at Troyes would have to be put to the test. Throughout his life, the French king had been tormented by mental illness, and this had been exacerbated by his wife Isabeau's sexual improprieties. That he survived so long and was not deposed owed everything to the power of the Burgundians and to his wife's machinations, including the final détente with Henry V at Troyes. Under the treaty's terms, Charles's heir was now an eight-month-old English boy, the son of the man who had all but deposed him. However, that agreement held good only in Burgundian France. South of the Loire, the old Orleanist or Armagnac faction acknowledged the claims of the Dauphin Charles, the son of Charles VI who had finally convinced his supporters that he had a legitimate claim on the French throne in spite of the lingering doubts about his paternity. (His mother Isabeau had repudiated him as being illegitimate, the result of one of her numerous affairs.) It was one of the ironies of Henry V's life that had he lived but a few weeks longer he would have been able to claim the throne of the country he had tried so hard to bring under English control. Those two deaths, one early and unforeseen, the other predictable and largely unlamented, were to have a huge influence on the sons who followed them. One was King of France by right of treaty; the other believed himself to be King of France by rightful succession.

Following Henry V's death his infant son had been proclaimed king of England and France in succession to his father, but he was not crowned as such until November 6, 1429, shortly before his eighth birthday. As a young child, Henry's early years had been entrusted to his mother, who had a largely female retinue, and it was not until shortly before his second birthday that he made his first public appearance at the opening of parliament. Arrangements were also made for young Henry to have the company of boys his own age, and shortly after his fifth birthday he was taken out of the care of women so that his education could begin in earnest. By then his tutor and "master" was Richard Beauchamp, Earl of Warwick, one of the country's leading soldiers and a prominent diplomat who had served Henry IV at the Council of Constance. His role was to school his charge in the basics of kingship, to provide him with a rounded education, and to instruct him in the art of war. All these were attributes that every contemporary king needed if he were to survive and prosper, and in those respects, even down to his provision of a miniature suit of armor and appropriate weapons, Warwick was the ideal mentor. Earlier, Henry's governess, Dame Alice Butler, had begun his education along similar lines, and by the time the young prince was crowned he would have had a good enough concept of the responsibilities that lay ahead of him.

If he did not, then the solemnity of the coronation rituals would have reminded him that he was of Royal blood and an anointed theocratic king under God's protection and guidance. Like his grandfather, he was anointed with Thomas Becket's miraculous oil from the golden eagle ampulla that was borne into Westminster Abbey with great reverence. The whole service underscored the sanctity and regality of his office; it was a lengthy and, for a child, a time-consuming ceremony, but young Henry appears to have behaved with solemnity and good grace. No wine flowed as had always been the custom, but the crowds were large and appreciative, and later people remembered two things about him—the young king's pious aspect as he gazed on those attending his coronation and the fact that he was too small to wear the heavy crown with any comfort. One other fact intruded: The words of the ceremonial insisted that he was "born by descent and title of right justly to reign in England and in France," and to underline that fact the next stage was to have him crowned in his other kingdom.

Henry arrived in France, fittingly on St. George's Day, the following year (April 23, 1430), and his possessions in France consisted of Normandy, Gascony, and the Île de France including Paris, while his Burgundian allies brought the security of Picardy and Flanders. Bedford promised his young nephew that English policy "prospered" in France, but the realty was slightly different. For all that the regent had worked wonders in maintaining English authority and prestige, things were already in danger of falling apart largely as a result of the need to deal with the ever-present threat of the Dauphin's supporters. Bedford had already inflicted heavy defeats on the Scots–Orleanist forces, but he had been out of the country from most of 1426, and during that time the faction loyal to the Dauphin had regrouped. In the summer of 1428, Bedford summoned his main commanders, the Earls of Salisbury, Suffolk, and Warwick, and Sir John Talbot (later the Earl of Shrewsbury), to a war council in Paris where it was decided to take immediate steps to crush the Orleanists in their seat of power south of the Loire. Following a rapid campaign, Salisbury laid siege to Orleans with a joint English and Burgundian field army while the Dauphin was nearby at Chinon. The operations got off to a poor start when Salisbury was mortally wounded by a cannon-ball four days into the siege and command passed to Suffolk, a shrewd and competent soldier but lacking his predecessor's flair. His plan was to surround the city and starve it into submission, the tactics that had worked so well in the past, but the army available to Suffolk needed reinforcements from England that were not forthcoming due to the costs and the increasing unpopularity of waging war in France.

As the winter dragged on, the garrison inside Orleans showed no sign of surrendering. Also, to even the odds for those under siege, an English relief convoy was ambushed in February 1429 near Rouvray, five miles north of Janville, by a joint French and Scottish force. This was followed by a proposal from inside the city that they should surrender to the Duke of Burgundy, a request that was angrily dismissed by Bedford with the thought that "it was not honourable nor yet consonant to reason, that the king of England should beat the bush and the Duke of Burgoyne [sic] should have the birds." In disgust Burgundy withdrew his troops from the investing force. A few weeks later, in May, Suffolk had been forced to raise the siege and disperse his forces. It was not a good move: On June 12, he was defeated at Jargeau, a village close to the city, and fell into the hands of the Dauphin's forces.

By then, there was a new factor for Bedford to consider—the sudden appearance in the Dauphin's camp of a young peasant girl known as Joan of Arc (Jeanne d'Arc) who suddenly appeared to rally the French cause. One French courtier described her as "a girl who came from no one knows where and has been God knows what," but in fact quite a lot is known about this enigmatic figure who helped to change the course of French history. She was born in January 1412, in Domrémy near Vaucouleurs in Champagne, the daughter of a peasant farmer. In her early teens she came to believe that she had been born to do God's great work. This was not simply an inner belief but one that was inspired by the voices of St. Catherine, St. Margaret, and St. Michael, who had appeared to her in visions exhorting her to go to the aid of the Dauphin in Chinon and help him in his struggle against the suzerainty of the English. So persistent were these manifestations that Joan, a short, stocky girl, was convinced she had to act. An initial overture to the garrison commander at Vaucouleurs was rebuffed, but when she foretold the Battle of Rouvray, he was sufficiently convinced of her sincerity to send her with an escort to Chinon. It was at this point, early in 1429, that she started wearing men's clothes, as much to disguise her identity as to convince others of her martial abilities. Inevitably, as the chronicler Jean de Waurin makes clear, her arrival at Chinon did not immediately inspire the Dauphin or his closest advisers, who thought she was "a deluded lunatic."

However, the Dauphin eventually was sufficiently convinced by the girl's argument to have her interrogated at Poitiers by a committee of clerics and theologians, who pronounced that her mission was genuine and that she was spiritually sound. This was a time when the Dauphin's fortunes were at their lowest ebb. It was by no means certain that Orleans would survive the siege, and if it fell, the entire valley of the Loire would fall into English hands. The Dauphin's court was short of money and morale was low; it is not difficult to see why the Dauphinists came to put their trust in this strange peasant girl with her determination and her inner belief that she enjoyed divine favor. There was also the added bonus that Joan's intervention was taken to settle all doubts about the Dauphin's legitimacy: If she enjoyed God's favor, this could only be possible if Charles was the rightful heir to the throne of France. Having persuaded the Dauphin and his court that she was engaged on a divine mission, she was put in command of an army to relieve Orleans. Dressed in a suit of armor she managed to persuade the French soldiers under her command to take solemn vows to eschew robbery and fornication and to follow behind her as she marched along the Loire to meet their destiny.

Although she became known as *La Pucelle* (virgin or maiden) and was fully supported throughout the operations by the experienced Duke of Alençon, Joan proved to be a remarkably forceful and prescient military commander. Under her direction, the French attacked and captured the English blockading fort at St. Loup on May 4, and within a week the siege of Orleans was lifted, forcing the English army to disperse. A month later Suffolk had been defeated at Jargeau, and this was followed by a further victory over Talbot's army at Patay. Suddenly, within the space of eight weeks, everything foreseen by Joan had come true, and the Dauphin readily fell in with her proposal that without further ado he should be crowned King of France. From Tours the triumphant pair marched their forces to Rheims, the traditional coronation place of French kings, and it was there on July 17, 1429, that the Dauphin was crowned King Charles VII. At one stroke the conditions of the Treaty of Troyes had been shattered and the English position in France was facing a substantial threat. More than any other factor, the French coronation and Charles VII's subsequent proclamation promising to restore all French property persuaded the English to crown Henry VI before the year had come to an end. Now that events had moved so rapidly in France they had to act equally fast to reassert their authority before the new king and *La Pucelle* used their newfound strength and belief to retake Paris.

This was a golden opportunity for the house of Valois to reassert its claim on the French throne by retaking the French capital, but jealousies within Charles VII's camp prevented Joan of Arc from retaining the initiative. Bedford responded resolutely to the challenge that faced the English in France. While arrangements were being made for young Prince Henry to be crowned and to cross over to France the following year, Bedford moved forces to Compiègne in preparation for an attack on Rheims. At the same time Henry Beaufort (now Cardinal Beaufort) was charged with the responsibility of raising fresh forces for service in France. By acting firmly and by bringing the newly crowned Henry VI over to France for his French coronation, Bedford hoped to convince the Burgundians that their best option still lay in the Troyes agreement. For that reason it was vital to demonize Joan of Arc, who was dismissed by the English as "a creature in the form of a woman" or, as Bedford described her, "a disciple and limb of the fiend called *La Pucelle* that used false enchantments and sorcery." Unable to bear the thought that a French army led by a woman had chased them out of the Loire, the English encouraged rumors that Joan of Arc was at best a man and at worst, as Bedford hinted, an agent of the devil.

Despite those measures Henry and his retinue arrived in Calais in April 1430 to find that the situation was still too dangerous to allow them to travel to Paris, and he had to stay put in the Channel port until the beginning of the summer when he was moved to Rouen. While this was happening, Joan of Arc fell into the hands of John of Luxembourg, an ally of the Duke of Burgundy, on May 24 after she had rashly attacked Burgundian forces outside Compiègne on the River Oise.

Joan's fate was quickly sealed. Her captors haggled over her, and she was eventually sold to the English and sent in chains to Rouen. She was put on trial for heresy and witchcraft in February 1431, and appeared before a panel of inquisitors, but the proceedings were a travesty. Although Joan remained constant in her defense, the fact that she claimed to have engaged in direct communication with God through the saints told against her. She also stood condemned for wearing men's clothes as the practice hinted at loose morals. At one point toward the end of the trial Joan recanted and promised to dress as a woman in return for receiving

communion and accepting a life sentence, but that decision was quickly and pre-
dictably repudiated when the "voices" suddenly returned to chide her. This time
there could be no mercy. She was condemned as "a heretic, idolatrer, apostate and
relapsed; a liar, a pernicious miscreant; a blasphemer, cruel and dissolute." On
May 30, 1431, she was burned at the stake in the marketplace of Rouen, an act that
smacked of political expediency on both sides. The man she had put on the French
throne did nothing to try to help her, and it was not until 1456, at Charles VII's
instigation, that a papal court reversed the decision of the court at Rouen on the
grounds that it had come under undue English pressure and had ignored key
pieces of evidence. By then Joan of Arc was long dead, and her memory as France's
savior was more useful to the French king than had she lived.

Hers is the story of a meteoric intervention that had the desired effect of
restoring the fortunes of the Orleanists, for all that it was prompted by a mixture
of intense yet simplistic patriotism and a single-minded almost fanatical belief in
the workings of the supernatural. (Joan was canonized in 1920.) Through her
intervention, France had its own king again in Charles VII, national pride had
been restored during the miraculous summer campaign of 1429, and the dual
monarchy had been put under immediate and unwanted pressure from which it
would never recover. The unrest generated by her crusade meant that it had also
become impossible for the English to carry through their plan to crown Henry
at Rheims, a move that would have been a direct challenge to the Dauphinists,
and instead Bedford had to make do with Notre Dame in Paris. Even then he
had to secure the route to the French capital, and it was not until after Louviers
had been recaptured that Henry's party was able to make their way into Paris.
The ten-year-old boy was crowned king on December 16, 1431, in a ceremony
that started badly and ended up making a poor impression on the French, who
had already objected to the mass being taken by the Bishop of Winchester. To
them, the whole thing was considered alien and too English, and great offense
was taken when a large silver wine goblet was removed by the king's officers
instead of being returned to the canons, as was customary. Worse followed at the
coronation feast, which quickly degenerated into farce. While the Palais had
been sumptuously decorated, the food was badly cooked—a result of using
English cooks, according to a contemporary account published by the anonymous "Bourgeois of Paris"—and away from the high table there were no place
settings for the lesser guests. In return for the French hospitality and to celebrate
his coronation, Henry had been expected to grant favors such as lifting taxes and
releasing prisoners, but that aspect of the ceremonial was also botched, leaving
the people of Paris to feel that they had spent a great deal of money on an
increasingly unpopular king and had received nothing in return.

That belief was exacerbated when Henry and his court hurriedly left the city the day after Christmas, on St. Stephen's Day, and returned to England. It was destined to be Henry VI's only visit to his French kingdom. In planning the expedition and the coronation, Bedford had hoped to cement the Burgundian alliance and to emphasize the importance of the Treaty of Troyes, but the whole thing had been a fiasco. Shortly after Henry's departure, Burgundy signed a local truce with Charles VII. Slowly, but perceptibly, he was easing himself out of the English alliance, and his instincts were matched by a new mood that supported the House of Valois. Fifteen years had passed since the defeat at Agincourt, and people were tiring of English rule and wanted a new arrangement that would protect and enhance French interests. Henry's coronation was supposed to cement his French kingdom; instead it marked the beginning of the end of his father's peace settlement.

The need to continue the war in France, plus the costs of the king's coronation, proved to be a heavy financial commitment that had to be borne by funds raised in England and Normandy. An additional burden was the need to garrison the country to protect English interests, and it soon became clear that Bedford's forces were overstretched, with never more than 4,000 troops available to him. Disaffection with English rule prompted outbreaks of violence, and while much of Normandy remained quiescent in the aftermath of Henry's departure, there was unrest in Avranches and Caen, which broke out into violence and attacks on English possessions. Once again Bedford mounted operations against Valois holdings, mainly in Picardy and Maine, but it was becoming clear to him that Philip of Burgundy was increasingly less interested in making the alliance work. Having signed a new truce with Charles VII, Duke Philip pulled out of the next year's offensive on the Somme, which was purely an English concern. As a result they paid heavily for it. In the fighting at Gerneroi, the Earl of Arundel was killed and the towns of Ètaples and Le Crotoy fell into Valois hands. Slowly but with grim inevitability, Henry V's power-sharing agreement was collapsing under the weight of renewed Valois authority and the inability of the English to counter it in the field. A further blow had been struck in 1432 when Bedford's wife Anne died, thereby severing his family alliance with the Duke of Burgundy. The matter was exacerbated when Bedford remarried Jacquetta of Luxembourg: Although her family was Burgundian allies, it seems that the Duke Philip had not been consulted and took offense at the new liaison.

There is also evidence to suggest that Burgundy feared that one day Henry VI would make peace with Charles VII and leave him isolated. A Burgundian embassy sent to London was able to report that Henry would enter into negotiations with Charles only if he renounced the French crown, but the fear clearly preyed on Burgundy's mind. He was also under pressure from the pope to patch up his quarrel with the House of Valois and to repudiate the terms of the Treaty of Troyes, and this led to a new peace conference held in Arras in August 1435, which was held under papal auspices. With each delegation being represented by up to 800 representatives, it was one of the biggest diplomatic summits ever held in Europe, and its findings destroyed the dual kingship. Despite furious English protests and the withdrawal of their delegation led by Archbishop Kemp of Canterbury, the papal mediators found that the treaty was flawed and that the Duke of Burgundy could be released from its terms. In return, Charles VII promised to make atonement for the murder of Duke John of Burgundy at Meulan and to punish those responsible for committing the outrage. Burgundy's decision was confirmed in letters that were delivered in London in late September. It was a bad moment for the young king: When he read their contents, he found that he had not been addressed as Burgundy's sovereign but merely as King of England. Faced by the inescapable conclusion that his cause in France was as good as lost, tears welled in the young king's eyes as he contemplated the treachery of a man he considered to be a loyal kinsman bound by treaty to carry out an agreed policy. Henry VI was only 13 years old, but he never forgot or forgave what he considered to be a great betrayal.

Besides, he was already beginning to discover the full implications of kingship. Following his coronation, relations between Gloucester and Beaufort had reached a new nadir when the former failed to come to terms with the fact that he was no longer in the powerful councillor position he had occupied during the king's infancy. In an attempt to regain his position and weaken Beaufort, he produced evidence in November 1431 claiming that on becoming a cardinal Beaufort should have surrendered the see of Winchester along with its substantial revenues. Far from embarrassing Beaufort into quitting his office as Gloucester intended, the charges stung him into action and he fought back and made a successful appeal to parliament to maintain his rights. The decision was made conditional on the payment of loans to the king's exchequer, but at least Beaufort had not seen his position fatally weakened and he retained his precedence in council. Gloucester also quarreled with his brother Bedford, who returned from France at the end of 1433, for only the second time in ten years, to defend his record and to try to raise more money for military operations in France. He also found that he had to protect his position in council from his brother's troublemaking, and on one occasion the young king had to intercede to stop his uncles' incessant quarreling.

Now an adolescent, Henry was described as a robust, large-boned, and fine-looking young man with interests in hunting, "a very gracious and clever child," according to the Duke of Burgundy's ambassador. He had clearly received a good education under Warwick's direction and showed an enthusiasm for reading and learning that lasted a lifetime. History remembers him for the austerity and piety of his later years—he was given to wearing a hair shirt next to his skin—but as a youth he demonstrated a surprising interest in elegant clothes and fine hats. He was also capable of showing precocity. In a note to the council, Warwick said that Henry had "grown in years, in stature of his person, and also in conceit [learning] and knowledge of his Royal estate, the which cause him to grudge with chastising." As the young king's mentor Warwick had already been given the right to punish Henry and had exercised it on more than one occasion by administering a sound thrashing. In his teenage years that need to keep him in check had become more apparent. There were rumors that Henry was being badly influenced by his uncle Gloucester, and in the winter of 1433–1434 he was secluded at the Abbey of Bury St. Edmund where he was admitted into the fraternity of the foundation, an experience that left a lasting impression on him. It also helped him to understand more fully his position as king—how could it have been otherwise given the symbolism and ceremony of his coronations with their insistence on his divine right?—and by the early 1430s he was anxious to embrace his majority. At this stage in his life he was developing into an intelligent and potentially forceful young man, but as Warwick hinted to the council, he lacked subtlety and seemed to be easily influenced. Shortly after the congress at Arras the young king had more to weep over when he received news that Bedford, his uncle and most powerful supporter, had died suddenly at Rouen. A few weeks later, on October 1, Henry attended his first meeting of council in a role that was not simply ceremonial: The day was fast approaching when he would come into his own.

9

A MAN OF MILD AND PLAIN-DEALING DISPOSITION

On November 12, 1437, Henry brought his minority to an end when he received the full power of kingship. He was not long past his 16th birthday, still an adolescent, but he had been well schooled for the task that lay ahead—during the past two years he had been initiated in the workings of the council and had a reasonable understanding of his duties and responsibilities. The new order meant that the role of the council had to change to reflect the king's majority. Henceforth its task would be advisory, and it is to the great credit of those who had served on the body during the king's minority that the transition was a smooth one. Although they had enjoyed fifteen years of virtually autonomous rule and were not always in full agreement, they had kept to the letter and spirit of Henry V's wishes as expressed in his will. To reflect the new beginning four new councillors were appointed: Sir John Stourton; Thomas Rodbury, Bishop of St. David's; Richard Earl of Salisbury; and Robert Rolleston, Keeper of the Great Wardrobe.

However, differences remained, especially over the great matter of France, where Bedford's death in 1435 had changed the complexion of the English presence in the country. While Bedford lived, he stood at the apex of English power in France, controlling a system of patronage that gave military authority to a tightly knit Lancastrian circle of lords and captains in return for grants of land. Although this system remained in place, the defenses of Normandy were gradually coming under pressure from forces loyal to Charles VII, who reoccupied Paris in 1437, and there were worrying signs of local disaffection among some sectors of the population. Garrisoning Normandy was also hugely expensive, requiring subsidies from England, and inevitably the questions regarding its continuing viability refused to go away. To address the difficulty, the Duke of York had been appointed Lieutenant in France the year before Henry's accession—his wealth and temporal power made him an obvious candidate—and during his short time in charge of England's affairs in France he had managed to stabilize the position with the assistance of Suffolk and Talbot. He was succeeded for a short time by Warwick, who received the post not because he was suited for it but because he was being rewarded for his period of service as the king's tutor.

Scotland, too, was causing problems once more, and given the nature of its alliances with the French king, this impacted English rule in France. With Bedford no longer a factor, James was persuaded to pursue a more aggressively Francophile policy. In 1428, a marriage had been arranged between James's eldest daughter Margaret and the Dauphin (later Louis XI); at the same time, the military alliance with France was renewed and Scotland was promised the possession of French territory, the county of Saintonage and the Seigneurie of Rochfort. (The promises were never made good, although Scotland continued to press her claims until 1517.) However, the Scottish king's position was not unassailable: At the end of the year he celebrated Christmas in the Dominican friary at Perth, and it was there, outside the city walls, that he was murdered on the night of February 20, 1437. His assailants were rapidly hunted down and savagely executed. James's son, the future James II, was only six years old at the time, and Archibald, fifth Earl of Douglas, was appointed guardian with the title Lieutenant of the Realm. During the boy king's minority, the alliance with France was strengthened by his betrothal to Mary of Gueldres, a niece of Philip of Burgundy through his sister Isabella's marriage to Duke Francis of Brittany.

However, despite the slaying of James I and the potentially destabilizing effects of ruling through a regency, the truce with England held—apart from an outbreak of cross-border raids in 1448—and the main problem facing Henry continued to be France. In an attempt to find a way out of the impasse produced by the Arras agreement, a peace conference was held in Calais on July 10, 1439. Cardinal Beaufort led the English delegation, and he had been empowered to offer compromises on Henry VI's claim to the French throne in return for guarantees about the sovereignty of England's French possessions, but it soon became clear that the French were not interested in brokering a deal along those lines. Beaufort thought that he possessed powerful cards in the persons of the Dukes of Orleans and Angoulême, who had been captured at Agincourt and who were still being held as hostages in England, but he was mistaken. During the talks, Charles VII's advisers insisted that the English could hold land in France only as vassals of the French crown and that they would agree to the extension of the truce only if the English agreed to restore land in Normandy and surrendered the Duke of Orleans without a ransom. An attempt at finding a compromise by instituting another round of truces also failed, and Beaufort was left with little option but to return to England to allow the council to discuss the proposals.

Needless to say, the French terms were rejected out of hand and a fresh military campaign opened in 1440 with several Norman towns being restored to English control, including Harfleur and Pontoise. However, this succession of sieges and counter-sieges did not improve matters for the English: Nothing short of a complete victory over Charles VII would restore them to the position they had achieved under Henry V. The English position had also been weakened by the sudden death of Warwick in April 1439, less than two years into his assumption of the post of the king's representative in France, and by the delay in reappointing York as his successor. York was already beginning to demonstrate the headstrong stubbornness and single-mindedness that would mark his later career. Before accepting the post, he insisted on being given the same powers as Bedford, and he also demanded adequate funding for the task at hand. Still a relatively young man, he was only 29, his position in public life had been strengthened by his marriage to Cecily Neville, the daughter of the Earl of Westmorland and Joan Beaufort, daughter of John of Gaunt and Katherine Swynford. It was a fruitful union: Thirteen children were born to them of whom seven survived into adulthood, in stark contrast to the Lancastrian succession where the only surviving offspring of Henry IV consisted of Gloucester and Henry VI.

In the midst of these confusions the new king showed a precocious willing-ness to become involved in French policy, but it soon became apparent that his interference was not always helpful as it led to unforced changes of plan, the creation of policies on a whim, and undue meddling by members of his council.

At this unsettled time Gloucester should have come into his own. He was the surviving brother of Henry V and his counsel should have been valued, not least because he was vastly experienced in French affairs. But already his star was on the wane. Although he was opposed to the release of the Duke of Orleans as a means of showing good faith to Charles VII during the peace negotiations in Calais, this was approved by Henry VI, acting on the advice of Suffolk. Even so, the gesture did not help matters. On his return to France in 1440, Orleans was received with acclaim everywhere but in the court of Charles VII, who refused to receive him. This was a double disaster as Orleans had been an important diplo-matic pawn who had been granted his freedom in a bid to further the peace talks with the French king. Now he had been released to no avail, and, worse, he quickly became involved in a new series of internal plottings involving the

Burgundian camp—to Gloucester's ire, Orleans unexpectedly married Mary of Cleves, Burgundy's fourteen-year-old niece, and promptly withdrew to his estates, where he was of no use to either side. Gloucester had also reignited his feud with Cardinal Beaufort by accusing him of treachery for allowing the release of Orleans, but the heaviest damage to his reputation was done by his second wife, Eleanor of Cobham. To general astonishment, in the summer of 1441 she stood accused of practicing sorcery against the king's person by indulging in necromancy and the black arts, a serious business at a time when witchcraft was associated with the powers of the Devil.

The charges were thoroughly scandalous. In conjunction with other accomplices including Roger Bolingbroke, a well-known astrologer, and Margery Jourdemain, a self-confessed witch, Eleanor had attempted to use a horoscope to predict if she would ever become queen in the event of the young king's death. Given her husband's position as heir-presumptive, this was a possibility if Henry died unmarried and childless, but the conspirators went a step further by making a wax image of the king and burning it. The allusion was obvious and the discovery of the necromancy aimed against the king could have led to charges of treason, for which she would receive no mercy. For Gloucester her reckless behavior was a tremendous blow to his position and prestige at court— Bolingbroke had been a member of his household, and another conspirator, John Home, had acted as his secretary. In July, Eleanor and her accomplices were tried before an ecclesiastic court containing Gloucester's great enemy Cardinal Beaufort. For Bolingbroke and Jourdemain, also known as the Witch of Eyre, there could be no mercy—he was sentenced to the traitor's death of being hanged, drawn, and quartered, while the witch was burned at the stake. For Eleanor there was a different fate. In November she was forced to carry out three days of public penance walking through the streets of London with a lighted taper as if she were a common prostitute and not the wife of one of England's most powerful magnates. Thereafter she was sentenced to a lifetime's imprisonment in various isolated castles in England including Kenilworth, Peel Castle on the Isle of Man, and Beaumaris on the island of Anglesey. She was never released and died in 1452. Throughout her, ordeal, which Henry insisted upon, Gloucester did nothing to help her, and that public display of political and personal impotence was telling confirmation of his fall from grace.

It was not the end of the matter. After Eleanor's incarceration, Gloucester was denied access to the court as Henry himself became increasingly apprehensive that his uncle was trying to engineer his downfall, not an unnatural suspicion given what had happened. He became so convinced that Gloucester was plotting to have Eleanor released as a first step to taking over the throne from him that in

February 1447, he had his uncle and his retinue arrested during a session of the parliament held at Bury St. Edmunds. It was a thoroughly disagreeable and disreputable business. After arriving in the town on February 18, Gloucester was denied access to the king and was promptly detained along with the leading members of his entourage, who were then rapidly dispatched to places of imprisonment throughout England. For reasons that are impossible to verify but that are perhaps all too understandable, this sudden and unexpected turn of events so shocked Gloucester that he dropped dead five days later. There were no signs of violence on his body, which was placed on pubic view to allay suspicions—a contemporary French account alleged that he had been murdered by the singularly unpleasant method of driving a hot poker into his anus, and it was accompanied by the implication that the murder had been carried out on Henry's orders. Following on from the shock of his wife's incarceration and his realization that he could not influence policy, it is probable that Gloucester died of a stroke brought on by despair, knowing that he had little left to live for. Gloucester was the last Lancastrian prince of Royal blood, and with his death a link with John of Gaunt had been lost. Although Gloucester had been a pest as a politician with his scheming and his vacillation, he was remembered as a patron of the arts, and *Gregory's Chronicle*, a contemporary commonplace book detailing life in London, lamented the loss of "a man of letters, and a true enthusiast for learning, the faith, the church, the clergy and the realm."

By then, as part of the wider diplomatic game with France, the young king had taken a wife. He was of age and the Eleanor of Cobham affair had reinforced the need to produce an heir sooner than later, but the match was also dictated by realpolitik. Ideally, a marriage to one of Charles VII's many daughters would have created a strong alliance, but they were either betrothed or died young (a common Valois failing). There was also the case of sanguinity: A daughter of the French king would be Henry VI's cousin and the Valois family had an unfortunate history of mental disorders, most notably, as we have seen, in Charles VI. Instead, in 1444, the choice fell on Margaret of Anjou, the second daughter of René of Anjou, the brother of Charles VII's queen, Marie of Anjou. Described by a contemporary chronicler as a great beauty renowned for her "wit and her lofty spirit of courage," Margaret was a strong-willed young woman well versed in the ways of court life, and, importantly for the succession, she came from a fecund family. The embassy sent to France to arrange the match was directed by the Earl of Suffolk, who had been rising in the king's favor since returning from France. While serving there he had become friendly with the Earl of Salisbury, one of the better English commanders in France, and the relationship had brought him into the Beaufort faction. This alliance had then been strengthened in 1430 by his marriage to Salisbury's widow Alice Chaucer, the granddaughter of the poet. (Salisbury had been killed at the siege of Orleans two years earlier.) Suffolk's star had risen as a result of the king's friendship—Henry warmed to the man, making him the head of his household and paying attention to his advice—but his rise to power brought him into conflict with Gloucester. With good reason Suffolk was lukewarm about accepting the commission to arrange the king's marriage, as he did not want to be associated with any peace agreement that might affect Henry's claims to the French throne. However, the young king insisted that Suffolk lead the delegation and in return provided him with a written indemnity for his actions.

With a small group of advisers Suffolk crossed to France in March 1444, and received a surprisingly warm welcome from both Charles and Duke René. The marriage negotiation was concluded by the Treaty of Tours on May 22, but its terms were remarkably one-sided. Margaret agreed to surrender all claims to her father's possessions and there would be no dowry as Duke René was virtually penniless. A two-year truce was also concluded at this time, as well as a secret agreement by which Henry was prepared to cede to René the lands of Anjou and Maine. This latter concession had to be kept confidential as its exposure would have confirmed Gloucester's fears about the dangers of making peace with France—unlike Suffolk and Beaufort he believed that negotiations were a sign of weakness. Two days later in the church of St. Martin, Margaret was betrothed to Henry in a magnificent ceremony attended by the king and queen of France, with Suffolk standing proxy for the English king. It was not until the following year that arrangements were made for Margaret to move to England, and once again Suffolk was given the task of heading the embassy and standing in for his sovereign at the marriage ceremony that was held at Nancy and was followed by a week of festivities. From there she traveled to Paris, where York greeted her and escorted her to the English capital at Rouen where she prepared for the final stage of her journey to England. Her voyage proved to be a terrible experience. The Channel was hit by storms, and her ship was beached at Porchester, where there was no one to greet the party and the queen was forced to take refuge in a nearby cottage, Suffolk having been obliged to carry her ashore. Margaret had been prostrated by seasickness, and it took a further two days before she was strong enough to make her way to Southampton. According to Henry his new bride was "yet sick of the labour and indisposition of the sea," and it was not until April 23 that she finally met her husband at the Abbey of Titchfield in the New Forest, where they were formally married by the Bishop of Salisbury. At the end of May the Royal couple returned to London, where Margaret was finally crowned queen. It was a happy enough occasion, but the marriage of Margaret marked the beginning of a season of severe turbulence. In the space of nine years, England would see the loss of France, the eruption of a serious revolt, the emergence of contenders to the crown, and the king's descent into the madness inherited from his Valois genes.

What kind of a man had the 16-year-old French princess married? Due to the king's subsequent mental instability and the tragedy of his last years, including the loss of his crown, later chroniclers either pitied him or represented him as a saint or martyr, with the result that he appears to posterity in the words of John Rous's history of the kings of England as "a most holy man, shamefully expelled from his kingdom but little given to the world and worldly affairs." There is considerable contemporary evidence to suggest that Henry was indeed a simple man who practiced Christian virtues and took seriously his coronation oath to protect the faith and church. He also seems to have had a compassionate nature and displayed a sensitivity that made many of his acts of kindness appear simple-minded or merely excessive. He was certainly shy of women in his youth and was probably a virgin when he married. According to the evidence of John Blacman, who served him as a chaplain and who later wrote an account of the king's life, Henry was shocked to see women and men bathing naked when he visited Bath in 1449 and on another occasion angrily dismissed a Christmas pageant in which young women bared their breasts. In Blacman's considered opinion, Henry possessed great piety that made him more of a man of God than a king capable of dealing with worldly affairs:

> He was like a second Job, a man simple and upright, altogether fearing the Lord God, and departing from evil. He was a simple man, without any crook of craft or untruth, as is plain to all. With none did he deal craftily, nor would he say an untrue word to any, but framed his speech always to speak truth.

In no better action can Henry's basic goodness of heart be seen than in his creation of Eton College at Windsor and King's College at Cambridge, both monuments to his piety and interest in the advancement of learning. Eton came into being on October 11, 1440, with the foundation of the college that consisted of a provost, ten priests, four clerks, six choristers, and 25 poor scholars. In addition to being taught grammar, the scholars were to pray for the souls of Henry's forebears and in due course for the soul of the king himself. At the same time the king acquired land at Cambridge for the building of a university college, and the foundation stone was laid six years later. Henry's decision to found these educational centers was driven by a desire to commemorate his accession to power in a fitting way, and they remain as monuments to the only successful

personal initiatives of his reign. During his lifetime Henry relished every opportunity to visit Eton College to talk to the boys and to enjoin them not to neglect
their studies and to be "gentle and teachable."

Unfortunately, Henry seems to have been overly simplistic in his approach
to other matters and often appeared simple-minded in his dealings with the
council. All too often he agreed with the last piece of advice given to him and
then just as suddenly changed his mind. This was no way for a king of his period
to behave, and given his inability to impose himself in any meaningful way it was
perhaps inevitable that he was easily swayed by those closest to him, including,
in time, the woman he had just married. Suffolk was especially influential,
emerging as the leader of the court party, and, in alliance with the Beaufort faction, he had been vitally opposed to Gloucester, whose authority had waned as a
result of his wife's foolish machinations. Suffolk enjoyed considerable temporal
power and had the king's ear. The Burgundian chronicler Georges Chastellain
described him as being England's "second king," and he had cleverly reinforced
his position at court, through skilful patronage of allies in key positions who
endorsed his policies and prospered as a result. Here he was helped by Henry's
tendency to be far too free with his largesse: The king maintained a large and
lavish court, and the courtiers closest to him benefited accordingly. For his work
in brokering the Royal marriage Suffolk had been created a duke, a singular
honor usually given to a prince of the Royal blood, and in addition to his post as
chamberlain he was appointed Warden of the Cinque Ports and Constable of
Dover. A close friend of the recently released Duke of Orleans, Suffolk
supported the Beaufort policy of entering into a peace agreement with France,
and Gloucester's death in 1447 strengthened his position. He was also suspicious
of York, who was replaced as the King's Lieutenant in France by Edmund
Beaufort, the Earl of Somerset, who had succeeded his brother in 1444 and
formed part of the tightly knit Suffolk–Beaufort nexus that bolstered Henry's
power and authority.

The period immediately following Henry's marriage was the apogee of
Suffolk's power, but already the situation at court was degenerating into a factionalism that had been kept at bay by the unanimity of the magnates during the
king's minority. France proved to be the main stumbling block. Not only was the
secret agreement over Maine and Anjou a time bomb whose exposure would
outrage the country, but the English presence in France was becoming expensive
to maintain at a time when the exchequer was under strain as a result of the
increased size of the court following the Royal marriage. The factionalism had
been exacerbated by the decision to remove York from his position in France and
to send him to Ireland as the King's Lieutenant. The move embittered York, who

made an immediate claim for payment of salary and expenses. By then Charles VII had begun insisting that Henry should keep his promise to cede Maine and Anjou, and when that became known—the date for the transfer was set for November 1, 1447—English landowners in those provinces demanded compensation for their lost properties. To encourage the English to meet their commitments Charles VII had assembled an army of 6,000 soldiers and laid siege to Le Mans. Open warfare was avoided only when Henry dispatched envoys instructing the city to hand itself over to the French as part of the peace settlement. Fatefully for her future reputation, Margaret of Anjou also became involved by pressing her husband to make good his promises to the French king. As she told Charles VII, her uncle by marriage, "in this matter we will do your pleasure as much as lies in our power, as we have always done already."

It had not taken Margaret long to assert herself at court. On her marriage, Sir John Talbot, now promoted as the Earl of Shrewsbury, had presented her with a volume of illuminated French romances so that "after she had learnt English she might not forget her mother tongue." It turned out to be a prescient gift. Margaret did indeed learn English quickly, but it seemed to many of her enemies that she had not forgotten her native country. When the secession of Maine and Anjou became public knowledge, she was blamed for the decision that was widely regarded as a disastrous and shameful betrayal of English interests. Increasingly, she was also regarded as a liability. Besides being expensive to maintain, Margaret was also too keen to involve herself in court politics. Suffolk seems to have recognized the queen's quickening interest from the outset and took full advantage of it, treating her in a courtly manner and writing romantic verses in her honor. He was probably attracted to her too, despite the difference in their ages—one contemporary description by the chronicler Chastellain claimed that "she was indeed a very fair lady, altogether well worth the looking at." Suffolk was 48, she was 15 when they first met, and during his embassies in France to conclude the marriage agreement they had spent much time in each other's company. Before his death Gloucester claimed that the mutual attraction had led them to become lovers, but this seems unlikely. There was certainly a close connection between them that offended contemporary sensibilities, but it is more likely to have been fueled by the aphrodisiac of power. From the outset Margaret made it clear that she would not be a passive onlooker but fully intended to be a player in court politics, and things were made easier for her by her husband's quiet acquiescence and feeble grasp of affairs. In France the presence of a court party was a fact of life, and having become queen of England, Margaret saw no reason not to develop a similar faction to strengthen her own position. It was not surprising that she took the initiative and allied herself with the powerful Beaufort clan and became especially close to its leading lights, Suffolk and Somerset. With Gloucester out of the way they made an apparently unbeatable team. Unfortunately, by adopting such a partisan approach Margaret inevitably made enemies of other parties and thereby increased the tensions and rivalries at court. York perceived what was happening early on, and in time he was to become an implacable and potentially dangerous enemy—it has to be remembered that through his Mortimer relations he had a good claim on the throne and in his own right was a powerful and wealthy magnate.

Against that background the French king decided to make a fresh move to restore his position. During the prevarications over Maine and Anjou, Charles VII had patched up his quarrel with the Duke of Burgundy and had begun rebuilding his forces for an assault on Normandy. He was also helped by a piece of maladroit behavior by Somerset. As part of the peace settlement England had always hoped that Duke Francis of Brittany would be a key ally, but he was now in the Valois camp, although his brother Gilles, a childhood friend of Henry VI, remained solidly pro-English. To rectify that state of affairs Gilles was apprehended by his brother on Charles's orders and kept prisoner in various fortresses. This provocation provided Somerset with the excuse to intervene, and in March 1449 he sanctioned an attack on the important border town and fortress of Fougères by a force commanded by François de Surienne, a mercenary captain from Aragon who had been in alliance with the English since 1435. The raid was successful—Somerset made sure that he benefited from the plunder gained by de Surienne—but negotiations for Gilles's release foundered largely because Somerset refused to allow Charles VII to play any part in the proceedings on the grounds that Duke Francis was an English vassal. This refusal to negotiate gave the French the opportunity they had been seeking, and on July 31, Charles VII declared war.

Suddenly, Suffolk's peace policies began unraveling. Throughout the diplomatic talks he had based his tactics on securing a long-term peace through the secession of Maine and Anjou and the alliance with the House of Anjou, but there were two drawbacks: First, Charles VII did not fall in with the idea that a two-year truce should be translated into a long-term peace agreement, and secondly, Somerset had not bargained for the Breton equation. It was bad enough that Duke Francis had thrown in his lot with Charles, but the last straw was provided by the events involving his brother Gilles and the unjustified seizure of Fougères. This reckless behavior gave Charles VII his casus belli and allowed him to begin pushing the English out of Normandy.

It helped the French cause that the English forces in Normandy were hopelessly dislocated. Lack of funds had reduced their capabilities, and there was a serious shortage of manpower that Somerset had been unable to redress. Unlike York he was not an experienced soldier, and it showed in the disposition and direction of his defenses. By then, Charles had three armies at his disposal and was able to attack Normandy on different fronts—with his forces attacking through central Normandy to threaten Coutances, St. Lô, and Fougères, while the Burgundians attacked from the east and the Bretons invaded the Cotentin peninsula. However, these daring moves left the French forces divided and overstretched, and a better commander than Somerset could have taken advantage of the situation, but one other factor intruded. By then, the majority of the population no longer wanted English rule and tended to welcome the invading armies. In some places, the opposition was negligible and resistance quickly crumbled, with the townspeople simply opening the gates to the invading French armies. When Rouen fell in October, the inhabitants rebelled and forced the garrison to withdraw. One by one the major centers fell—Verneuil, Pont de l'Arche, Lisieux, Carenan, and Beauvais. On Christmas Day, there was a telling blow with the capture of Harfleur where the great adventure had begun three decades earlier. Slowly but surely the English were being squeezed out of their possessions, and triumphs like Agincourt were but a distant memory

In an attempt to shore up the defenses, a new English field force was hurriedly put together as 1449 came to an end, but Normandy was already a lost cause. Some idea of the disaffection and lack of morale can be found in an ugly incident during the first week of the new year (1450) when Bishop Adam Moleyns, the keeper of the privy seal, a key official in conducting the king's business matters, traveled down to Portsmouth to pay the new army as its soldiers assembled for embarkation to France. The men were in a rebellious mood, and when Moleyns, a Suffolk appointee, arrived, he was accused of betraying Normandy and was promptly hacked to death by the angry mob. With the deterioration of the situation in Normandy the only ports available to Somerset were Caen and Cherbourg, and it was to secure those that the new force, commanded by Sir Thomas Kyriell, was dispatched across the Channel in the middle of March. It was to no avail. As the English force, mainly archers, made their ponderous way down the Cotentin peninsula, Kyriell, a relatively unknown soldier, was completely outclassed by his opposite number, the Constable de Richemont, at Formigny on April 15, 1450, the biggest military setback to hit the English in many years. Within the next four months Caen surrendered, followed by Falaise and Cherbourg in August, and English rule in Normandy was at an end. All that was left of Henry V's empire was Calais and the holdings in Gascony, which would go the same way as Normandy within the next three years.

This was a disaster. "We have not now a foot of land in Normandy," wrote the clerk James Gresham to his master John Paston, a long-established and well-connected landowner in Norfolk (the letters provide an intriguing picture of English life in this period), and the dismay was echoed elsewhere. The search was started for a scapegoat; the English people had taken a great deal of pride in Henry V's achievement in winning the crown of France, and fingers started pointing at Suffolk as the chief villain. As Bishop Moleyn lay dying in Portsmouth, he had already implicated Suffolk as the architect of the decision to hand over Maine and Anjou to the French, or so the rumors insisted. Even if the report had not been true, Suffolk's growing power and influence at court also spoke against him at a time when he was under suspicion of self-aggrandizement. When he announced the betrothal of his eldest son John de la Pole to the seven-year-old Lady Margaret Beaufort, Somerset's sister and a granddaughter of John of Gaunt, it seemed that he was attempting to strengthen his own position if there was ever a disputed succession. He tried desperately to shore up his position by declaring his loyalty to the crown and condemning the "odious and horrid language" contained in the rumors about his role in creating the debacle in France, but it was to no avail. On January 22 parliament decided to act against him, and although Suffolk defended himself by reminding the Commons of his past services to king and country, four days later he was indicted for treason and corrupt practices. As the long rambling Bill of Impeachment made clear, the worst offenses came from Suffolk's agreement to cede Maine and Anjou and from his misuse of funds and other corrupt practices to maintain his position, all at the king's expense.

These were serious charges and backed by seemingly solid evidence; when the bill was produced on February 7, Suffolk was sent to the Tower of London as much for his own protection as for anything else, because the indictment had increased tensions and "the people were in doubt and fear of what should befall." It also put Henry in a difficult position. He had been excluded from any culpability in the loss of Normandy—not so his wife, who was widely blamed for what had happened—but he had to decide what to do with Suffolk, his favorite and his mainstay at court. Either he could punish him by allowing the legal procedure to continue, or he could declare the proceedings illegal. If he took the latter course, he would cause a crisis; if he allowed Suffolk to be impeached, his friend would certainly face execution. Faced by an impossible set of choices, Henry exercised his prerogative to deal with the matter himself, and on March 17, in front of an assembly of lords, Suffolk was summoned into the king's presence. Called upon to answer the charges, Suffolk denied them utterly and submitted himself to the king's will. Henry's response was to dismiss the charges of treason but to find him culpable of the secondary charges and to punish him by five years' banishment, the sentence to begin on May 1. This Henry did of his own volition, without taking advice from the Lords and overruling the wishes of the Commons, who had brought the charges in the first place.

It was not a popular decision, and when it was announced it roused the people of London to fury. Suffolk was lucky to get out of the capital intact—a mob attacked him as he attempted to enter his residence at St. Giles, and he was forced to beat an ignominious retreat to his estates at Wingfield in Suffolk. There, in his last days in England, he wrote a pitiful letter to his son expressing his conviction in his innocence and enjoining the young man to remain loyal to his sovereign lord the king. Together with his spirited defense of his innocence, the document shows Suffolk in a reasonably good light as the faithful servant done down by events outside his control, but, ironically, the fact that he had escaped indictment and punishment sealed his fate. On April 30 he sailed into exile from Ipswich carrying with him the king's letter of safe conduct, but it was not enough to protect him. Somewhere in the Dover straits his ship was intercepted by a small flotilla which included *Nicholas of the Tower*, a Royal ship. A boarding party apprehended Suffolk, the letters of safe conduct were ignored, and with the words "Welcome, traitor!" he was promptly hacked to death and thrown overboard.

The grisly corpse lay on the beach for several days until the sheriff of Kent ordered it removed and buried at Wingfield. No evidence was ever discovered about the perpetrators of the lynching, but it is inconceivable that those involved acted independently. Where then did the guilt lie? The king was an unlikely suspect: Henry's close affinity to Suffolk ruled him out of the equation. For the same reason Margaret had no reason to have one of her closest associates killed, and she was prostrated by grief when the news broke and kept herself in her room for three days. York is a possible suspect. He had no love for Suffolk and resented his authority as well as the decision to send him to Ireland. With his wealth and his contacts he would certainly have had the wherewithal to pay sailors to intercept Suffolk's ship and then murder him. Whatever else, in the wider realm of England there was no grief shown for a man who had come to be known in a contemporary mock office or dirge for the dead by the nickname of "jackanapes":

> Pray for this duke's soul that it may come to bliss,
> And let never such another come after this!
> His interjectors blessed may they be!
> And grant them for their deed to reign with angles,
> And for Jack Nape's soul, Placebo and Dirige [the opening words of the funeral mass].

Suffolk's death might have been a subject for mirth in an outburst of popular lyrics celebrating his demise, but the manner of his death and the reasons for it provided evidence of a wider malaise. The loss of Normandy, the growing dissatisfaction with the weakness of the government, and the country's burgeoning financial insecurity all combined to give the impression that public order was deteriorating and that the king and his council could do nothing to stop the rot.

10

THE GATHERING STORM

he shock of Suffolk's death had scarcely died down when the southeast of England was rocked by a popular uprising led by a shadowy figure called Jack Cade, who used a number of aliases including "John Amend-all" and, more provocatively, "John Mortimer." By using the Duke of York's maternal family name, Cade was clearly giving his approval to any claims York might have had on the English throne. (These were considerable as his lineage descended from Edward III through both parents: His father, Richard, Earl of Cambridge, was the son of Edward's fourth son, Edmund of Langley, first Duke of York, and his mother, Anne Mortimer, was the great-granddaughter of Edward's second son, Lionel of Antwerp, Duke of Clarence.) Cade's rebellion came in an atmosphere of gathering crisis. Normandy was about to be lost, the fight to save France had been massively expensive, the costs outrunning the available finance; the Royal court was in debt, it cost $48,000 a year to run yet its income was only $10,000 (in today's prices, respectively, $25 million and $5 million), and there were strong suspicions that those close to the king had used their positions at court to better themselves financially. As yet there was no personal criticism of Henry; he was after all England's anointed king, but it was apparent that he was not in control and that things were in danger of falling apart. The people of Kent understood all this. They could see the state of the soldiers returning from France as they passed through the Channel ports; most had no money or possessions and resorted to beggary or lives of crime to make good of their losses.

Coming on top of a succession of French attacks on Kentish ports, there was a growing feeling of discontent within the county, and this was aggravated by an unwise comment made by James Fiennes, Lord Saye and Sele, a leading member of the council. Following Suffolk's murder, he was reported to have said that the people of Kent were to blame for the assassination of Suffolk and that the county should be turned into "a wild forest" by way of reprisal. It did not take long for rumors to grow that Kent was about to be punished on the queen's orders to avenge her murdered lover Suffolk. Soon men were looking to their weapons and making plans to resist the expected attack. Unlike the earlier Peasants' Revolt, Cade's uprising was well organized and was led by a number of respectable gentlemen, mainly from Kent but also from Essex, Surrey, and Sussex, who were not prepared to go like sheep to the slaughter.

The flashpoint came during the Whitsun weekend—the Christian festival of Pentecost—with a huge gathering at Ashford attended by 3,000 armed men from all over the Weald of Kent. Led by Cade, they made their way to Blackheath on the southeastern outskirts of London, where they set up camp and published their grievances on June 1. It was a lengthy manifesto, but its demands were summarized in five main points, namely, that the king "has had false counsel, for his lands are lost, his merchandise is lost, his commons destroyed, the sea is lost, France is lost, himself so poor that he may not [pay] for his meat nor drink." As had happened before, and as would happen again in England's history while the monarch remained the ultimate ruler of the country, the grievances were not directed at the king himself but at his closest circle of misguided advisers, "the traitors that be about him," who had benefited from their positions at court and had been responsible for the loss of France. These people had to be punished, the king had to be forced to resume control of all his lands, and Suffolk's supporters had to be removed from the council. There were also demands for the redress of various financial grievances and for the punishment of anyone connected to the Duke of Gloucester's death. There was nothing treasonable about these demands; most of Cade's followers were reasonable and intelligent men who were intent on making a serious political point; they were not the unruly and unfocussed mob led by Wat Tyler. But as happened all too often during his reign, Henry mismanaged the crisis.

Having dissolved the parliament, which the had been sitting at Leicester, Henry and a large armed retinue returned to London on June 13, stopping in Clerkenwell, where the king agreed to send an embassy, including John Kemp, the Archbishop of York, to meet with Cade and to discover the reasons for his discontent. Even at this stage all might have been well and Cade's followers could have been pacified, but Henry was persuaded by his advisers to take military action to put down the rising. The manifesto was rejected out of hand and forces were deployed to restore order at Blackheath. On June 18, the Royalist army, numbering some 20,000, moved on the rebel camp, but they arrived only to find that Cade had already stolen a march on them by ordering his people to withdraw toward Sevenoaks. This left Henry in a quandary. He could not allow his will to be flouted by a commoner, but to pursue Cade would entail a violent confrontation with his own subjects, something he was reluctant to do. Eventually, his supporters persuaded him that he should personally lead his army in pursuit of the rebels, the reasoning being that Cade's supporters would probably melt away at the sight of the approaching Royalist forces—if they confronted the king in the field their actions could be construed as treason.

That plan might have worked. Cade was by no means certain that he would receive additional support, and his followers had already made it clear that they did not want a fight with the king. A sudden move on Sevenoaks by the numerically superior Royalist army could have nipped the revolt in the bud, but at the last moment the disastrous decision was taken to divide Henry's forces. The larger part was ordered to remain at Blackheath to provide protection for Henry, who was thought by the queen to be in danger, while a smaller force set off in pursuit of Cade's men. Led by Sir Humphrey Stafford of Grafton, a kinsman of the Duke of Buckingham, the Royalists came across the rebels in wooded country between Bromley and Sevenoaks and were soon involved in fierce fighting that lasted for over two hours. Many of Cade's supporters were experienced and well-armed former soldiers who had fought in France, and although some of their number were killed in the fighting, they inflicted a serious defeat on the Royalist forces. Stafford was cut down and killed together with his brother William, and the survivors scattered in panic. When the news of the defeat reached the king's camp, Henry ordered the remainder of his army to march to avenge the setback, but the men who had remained with him at Blackheath ignored his order. This was mutiny: Far from showing any inclination to obey Henry's orders, the men shouted that they would finish Cade's work for him and demanded the arrest of "the traitors about the king."

Faced with this obduracy, Henry panicked and retired to Greenwich, where he heeded Margaret's bidding and made his way to the safety of Kenilworth Castle in Warwickshire. Before leaving London he ordered the arrest of Lord Saye, who was detained in the Tower—as much for his own protection as for any mark of displeasure—while Saye's son-in-law William Crowmer, the Lord Sheriff of Kent, was incarcerated in the Fleet prison. Prudently the rest of the council joined Saye in the comparative safety of the Tower. Far from nipping the rebellion in the bud, as it was supposed to have done, Stafford's expedition and its defeat had destroyed any remaining belief in the king's good intentions. It also fanned the violence that spread into East Anglia and also toward the West Country, where there was further loss of life. At the end of June, William Ayscough, Bishop of Salisbury, was dragged out of Edington Church in

Wiltshire and hacked to death by his congregation. Five years earlier he had officiated at Henry's marriage to Margaret, but the fact that he was the king's confessor condemned him—he was held to be one of the "traitors" who had failed to prevent the king from acting wrongly. A few days later, Cade rode back into London with his supporters, who were still promising that they had sufficient "wit and wisdom for to have guiding or put in guiding all England." This time, though, there was none of the subservience that had accompanied his earlier ride on the capital. Cade wore a crown of blue velvet and a gilt headpiece, and on his feet could be seen the gilded spurs of a knight, probably taken from Humphrey Stafford's dead body. Ahead of him strode his squire carrying a huge sword as if he were a conquering king and not the Irish soldier of fortune that he was. However, his appearance clearly impressed the people of London, who clamored for him and his followers to be admitted. On July 2, the drawbridge on London Bridge was lowered so that Cade and his followers could enter the city in triumph.

The mood turned ugly the next day. Cade had a reputation for being able to keep his followers under control, but Stafford's attack had enraged the men of Kent and Henry's absence from the city encouraged a mood of revenge. Their targets were Saye and Crowmer, who were dragged from their prisons for hasty trials and equally rapid execution. Saye was taken to the Guildhall, where he attempted to argue that he should be tried by his peers, but he was promptly found guilty, taken to Cheapside, and beheaded. A similar fate faced Crowmer, who was removed to Mile End, where he and other followers met a similar fate. As happens so often with mob frenzy, the blood-letting raised temperatures, and soon Cade's followers were out of control. Several houses, including that of Philip Malpas, an alderman and one of Henry's supporters, were ransacked and looted.

This outrage led to a scuffle with a Royalist force from the Tower led by Captain Matthew Gough, who was killed in the street fighting that followed and that also accounted for the deaths of around 200 innocent citizens caught up in the violence. Finally the rebels were driven out of the city by the remnants of Gough's force and order was restored, allowing the Archbishop of York to reopen negotiations with Cade inside St. Margaret's Church at Southwark. In a compromise deal, Cade handed over his petition, and in return he and his followers received free pardons on condition that they returned peaceably to their homes. Fatally for Cade, his pardon was given in the name of John Mortimer. The majority of his supporters accepted their good fortune and quit Southwark, but Cade and a rump of his hard-line followers attacked Queenborough Castle on the Isle of Sheppey in an attempt to get booty to pay for their rebellion.

Retribution was not long in coming. Cade's pardon was revoked and he was hunted down in the name of "Jack Cade" by forces led by Alexander Iden, the Sheriff of Kent. A fortnight later, on July 15, Cade was run to ground in a garden in Heathfield in Sussex, where he fought bravely to save himself but was overwhelmed by superior numbers. Badly wounded, he was taken back to London to face inevitable execution, but he died on the way. Even so, revenge was insisted upon: His body was beheaded and quartered, and, according to Benet, "afterwards his head was placed on London Bridge, although he had not appeared before a court of law and had been condemned not according to the law but according to the king's wishes." Later in the year, eight of his followers were executed at Canterbury, and a further 26 went to their deaths at Rochester. Showing the desire for revenge that he had originally displayed against Gloucester's family and that is strangely at odds with his piety and humility, Henry personally attended each execution.

Cade's rebellion achieved absolutely nothing. None of the points made in his manifesto and petitions were ever met; the court party was left untouched by what had happened, and Henry himself seems to have been unmoved by the violent events of the summer of 1450. He was able to return to his capital, but behind the apparent normality he came back to a changed situation. For a short term, the governance of his kingdom had broken down, and he had exacerbated the problem by leaving London to its own devices. Nothing had been done to address the main grievances raised by Cade and his followers, and Henry had shown himself to be weak and indecisive when he should have used a firm but fair hand to deal with the rapidly deteriorating situation. Cade's rebels were not seeking to destroy the authority of the crown; they wanted to strengthen it by removing the evil advisers. Instead of negotiating with them as Richard II had done in similar circumstances, Henry had alienated the protestors further by using extreme violence against them. Not only had this demonstrated his weakness as a king, but in the longer term, it was a clear example of his incapacity to govern the country.

Immediately on returning to the capital, Henry compounded this failing by appointing Somerset as Constable of England, a curious promotion for a man who had been responsible for the run of defeats that had led to England's expulsion from France. This was a doubly dangerous appointment because it heightened the existing rivalry with York and brought into the open the two men's rival claims to the throne. Five years into his marriage, Henry was still childless and there was no heir. As Henry's uncles were all dead and had not left heirs, this left only two contenders to the throne—York and Somerset. York had a claim through both of his parents, but it was weakened by the fact that he was descended from John of Gaunt's younger brother Edmund. Somerset was also descended from John of Gaunt, but that claim had been negated by Henry IV's decision to disqualify the Beaufort family by act of parliament in 1407. Long disguised, that family rivalry was about to become more open and more bitter, leading eventually to open warfare.

Throughout the Cade rebellion there had been rumors that York was implicated in some way, but it seems unlikely. Despite his dislike of the court party and his claims to the throne, he was still loyal to Henry, and at that stage there was no evidence that he had ambitions to be declared heir-presumptive. That being said, he had taken a proprietary interest in what was happening. Not only was he a powerful and wealthy magnate in his own right, but he possessed a sense of noblesse oblige. He would have been aware of his heritage and the part played at court by other Royal princes such as Bedford and Gloucester in protecting Henry's fragile throne. In that role, he had also acted as the King's Lieutenant in France and Ireland, and as a member of the nobility he must have been aware of the problems that existed at court. In September he decided to act, fearing perhaps that his position might come under threat from Somerset or that the court party might take preemptive measures against him by declaring him a traitor. He was able to make this move through a clause in his letters of appointment that permitted him to return to England in time of any national emergency. Before leaving Ireland "with great bobaunce [ostentation] and inordinate people," he made his position clear in a series of open letters addressed to the king in which he reaffirmed his loyalty to the throne and announced his intention to defend himself against any false accusation and to help punish those "traitors" who were working against the king's best interests. When the king instructed a deputation to intercept and arrest York, Benet recorded that the rebels insisted that they had a sound cause—namely the protection of the king and the destruction of his advisers:

> The duke [York] replied, commending himself to the king's good grace and saying he had never rebelled against the king and would obey him always. He asserted that his uprising had been directed against those who betrayed the king and the kingdom of England and that he was not against the king and desired nothing but the good of England. He wished to tell the king of those who were encompassing the destruction of his two kingdoms, that is to say, of England and France. And these men were Edmund, Duke of Somerset, who had been responsible for the shameful loss of all Normandy and John Kemp, the archbishop of York, who was a cardinal and chancellor of England.

Having landed at Beaumaris in Anglesey, York made for his castle at Ludlow in the Welsh marshes to gather support, and with a force of around 4,000 men, marched on London. Thoroughly alarmed, the council tried to have him stopped before he reached the capital, but on September 29, York arrived at Westminster where Henry had taken refuge in his apartments. Undaunted, York forced his way into the Royal presence and having reaffirmed his loyalty told the king that he had to reform the way in which he governed England by ridding himself of his advisers and ending the corruption at court.

Henry was alarmed by the treatment meted out to him and he had every right to feel that way. York had protested his loyalty, but there had already been manifestations of public support for him as many people regarded him as a redeemer who would clean up the court and bring justice to the country. With that in mind, Henry had to act carefully. He realized that he had to appease York, but he could not give in to all his demands, otherwise he would have lost what little authority he still possessed. In a compromise he agreed that there had to be changes but that they would be decided by a new council that would include York, who then withdrew to his castle at Fotheringhay to await the opening of the new parliament on November 6. It was packed with his supporters; the Speaker Sir William Oldhall was a Yorkist who acted as York's chamberlain, and under his direction, the parliament produced a number of bills addressing the country's difficulties and pressing the need for reform. Principal among these was a petition of resumption that named those advisers whom the Commons wanted to be removed from court and provided for the return of Crown lands gifted by the king to his favorites during his reign.

All this was happening against a tense background in London, where the retinues of the leading figures paraded through the streets turning the capital into an armed camp. In one incident Somerset almost lost his life to an armed mob and was saved only by the intervention of Thomas Courtenay, the Earl of Devon and Steward of the Duchy of Cornwall. In an attempt to save his new favorite by getting him out of the country, Henry appointed Somerset Captain of Calais, a powerful position that York coveted, but this was not enough to calm the heightened tensions. When parliament reassembled after the Christmas recess, Somerset's name headed a list of 29 recalcitrant courtiers whom the Commons wanted to be removed for "misbehaving about your Royal person and in other places." Forced to act, Henry suspended those named and had Somerset confined in the Tower, although he was quickly released on Queen Margaret's orders and allowed to resume his place at court.

By then York's brief period of preeminence was already waning. Although his moves to reform the court had been broadly welcomed and implemented by the Commons, he lacked support among his own kind. The reason for this dis-affection was partly territorial. His lands were scattered throughout England, and unlike other great magnates like the Earls of Northumberland and Westmorland, he lacked a single, unified territorial power-base. Partly, it was caused by fear of civil strife—the attack on Somerset was a reminder of the enmity between these two powerful magnates that could quite easily degenerate into civil war. Partly, too, it was dynastic—the very fact that York had a sub-merged claim on the throne made him a potential enemy because most of the courtiers under attack owed their positions to Henry's patronage and were unlikely to support a man who wanted to change the system. Toward the end of the parliamentary session that reopened early in the following year, a member of the Commons, Thomas Yonge (or Young), attempted to have York named as the heir-presumptive, but the move failed, and for his pains Yonge was thrown into the Tower. As a result Henry promptly dissolved parliament, which had at least won concessions on finance and the grant of lands as well as the suspension of the named favorites. However, none of this strengthened York's own position, and with nothing to detain him in London, York left for his estates at Ludlow, to go into effective internal exile. Remaining in London would only have reminded him and others of his lack of standing among his fellow magnates and the failure of his attempt to make a decisive inroad into court politics.

Like Cade, who had supported similar demands, York had failed to reform the court, other than to have the grievances aired in public. He had taken con-siderable risks by returning from Ireland and announcing his criticism of what had been taking place at court. His contempt for Somerset was also in the open, and as his rival continued to enjoy the king's support and was now the leader of the court party in succession to Suffolk, it was clear to everyone that York's own position had been weakened. Apart from the Duke of Norfolk, York had received little support from the nobility, and already there were moves to oust Oldhall from his leadership of the Commons. On the other side, his enemies in the court party were united, and Somerset, now firmly implanted as the queen's favorite, had good personal reasons to want to hang on to his power and authority. There was another difference between the two men: money. Unlike York, Somerset did not enjoy inherited wealth and needed lucrative Royal patronage, including the post at Calais, to retain his public position. In other words, cupidity played a major part in fueling Somerset's ambitions: He needed to maintain his Royal connections in order to prosper. That was a powerful incentive and helps to explain his tenacity in hanging on to power.

From a purely political viewpoint, following his rapid emergence and faster disappearance from the scene, York was now on the sidelines, and his interven-tion had failed to change anything, leaving him to lick his wounds far away from London. He had also made an enemy of the king, who had come to believe that

York was not acting in the best interests of the kingdom but was merely pursuing a personal vendetta against Somerset in order to further his own ambitions. To a certain extent York had been hobbled by his very public declaration of allegiance to the king. Having stated that his quarrel was not with Henry but with those who surrounded him, he could hardly have accelerated his protest into a rebellion as that would have smacked of betrayal. It is also likely that he realized that any attempt at pushing his claims would have failed to attract sufficient support from his fellow magnates, who did not want to see any change in the country's power structure. York's one opportunity had come when he arrived in London with a large number of armed men for the opening of parliament. Had he used force at that moment, he could have pressed his claims and unseated Henry, but at that stage in his life York was not prepared to move into treasonable territory by usurping the crown. It was bad enough that he was already feared and distrusted by his fellow nobles, without giving them solid grounds for believing that he was only interested in furthering his own aspirations.

And yet, York's position was not entirely hopeless. Despite being virtually exiled from court—he was not able to make any contact with the king—he had not been punished in any way, his forces had not been disarmed, and he still retained his wealth and his authority. The king's relatively mild response meant that York was still a potent force who could bide his time for an opportunity to reassert his influence. His chance came sooner than he might have expected. In September the following year a dispute broke out between the Earl of Devon and Lord Bonville of Chewton and Shute over the disputed possession of the post of the Steward of the Duchy of Cornwall. Bonville, who had served in Gascony, was close to the court party and was allied with James Butler, the Earl of Wiltshire, while Devon, for the time being, was close to York. At the end of the summer the disagreement between the two men erupted into open warfare when the Earl of Devon took a sizable armed force across the county of Somerset and defeated Wiltshire's men at Lackham near Bath. He then marched back to Taunton to besiege Bonville's forces who were taking shelter in the castle. It was at that point that York appeared on the scene together with an armed retinue of 2,000 men to force Devon and Bonville to come to terms.

It was an extraordinary incident. Four private armies were in the field, one (Devon's) had inflicted a defeat on another (Wiltshire's), while York had entered the fray to prevent the conflict from spreading. The peace-broker (York) might have had the ulterior motive of forcing a confrontation with Somerset in whose lands the confrontation had taken place, but the episode gives a good idea of the underlying tensions that existed in England at the time. Here were private armies taking the law into their own hands without giving any thought to the king's authority and behaving in a way that disrupted the natural order. In an attempt to settle the issue and to regain his position, Henry summoned all the parties to Coventry, where Wiltshire and Bonville were ordered to be confined in their castles for a month. Henry was outraged by the incident, which he regarded not as an intervention to preserve law and order but as a further example of York's intransigence and ambition. The king's supremacy had been challenged, but there was nothing he could do to gain any redress. When York and Devon received the king's summons they simply ignored it. Following the display of armed force in the West Country this refusal to obey a Royal command showed how deep the estrangement between the king and one of the country's most powerful noblemen was. Henry had allowed himself to become so weak that his magnates were able to ignore Royal authority and act with impunity. Two months later the existing tensions were exacerbated when Oldhall was forced to take sanctuary in the Royal Chapel of St. Martin-le-Grand to escape an indictment of high treason, a move that clearly threatened York's position. (Founded in 1068 by William the Conqueror this collegiate church reserved the right of sanctuary, the right for an individual to be safe from arrest, which was recognized in English law until the seventeenth century.)

Faced by this turn of events, York realized he had to take matters into his own hands and could not allow events to overtake him. On January 9, 1452, after what seems to have been a lengthy period of deliberation, he issued a public statement of loyalty to the king in which he claimed that his good name was being traduced by "enemies, adversaries and evil-willers" who were attempting to turn the king against him. In the same manifesto, he asked the king to send three lords to Ludlow so that he could protest his loyalty on the sacrament. It was to no avail. The attempt at appeasement was ignored in London, and on February 3, York announced his intention to arraign Somerset and bring him to trial, if necessary by using force, on the charges of losing France and of subverting the court by abusing his own position. To underline the seriousness of his intentions, York began mobilizing his men and sent out letters to the principal towns in the East Midlands asking for support in the way of arms, money, and manpower. A move of that kind could not be kept secret for long, and so it proved: Both Colchester and Oxford were loyal to the king and forwarded York's letters to the court. Henry heeded the advice given to him, notably by his wife and Somerset, and moved swiftly. Having summoned his loyal nobles to "rebuke and chastise" York, he led his forces to Northampton on February 16, after giving orders that the gates of London be closed against the rebels. At the same time, backed by Devon and Lord Cobham who had supported him in the quarrel with Bonville, York set off to London with his army, gathering men to his

cause as he progressed, and arrived at Kingston Bridge only to be refused entry
to the capital. The sight of Londoners setting up defenses convinced York that
he could not take the city by storm, and so he set off in a southeasterly direction
and set up camp on Dartford Heath.

By then the king had received intelligence that York had arrived in the
London area, and having taken the advice of the principal nobility who had
answered his summons for armed support—including the Duke of Buckingham
and the Earls of Salisbury and Warwick—he decided to head back to the capital.
On February 27 the Royalist army crossed London and two days later halted at
Blackheath, where Cade had drawn up his rebels in 1450. The two armies were
now three miles apart and a battle seemed inevitable. York had drawn up his
forces in three formations known as "battles" with his men in the center and
Devon's and Cobham's on either flank. He also possessed a number of modern
artillery pieces, and seven ships lay in the Thames to the north to provide him
with food, supplies, and ammunition. Contemporary reports are unclear about
the exact size of the rival forces—some say that each was around 20,000—but
given the lack of support from the nobility who had mostly flocked to the king's
side, it is probable that York's force was smaller. Although some towns in East
Anglia had answered his call for assistance and had demonstrated in his favor,
they had not been able to send many men to swell the Yorkist ranks. That
absence of popular support and the failure of the nobility to side with him were
blows to York's cause, and with neither side keen to fight the way was open for
a compromise. On March 2, a Royal delegation including the Bishops of
Winchester and Ely and the Earls of Salisbury and Warwick arrived in York's
camp to broker an agreement that would end the confrontation. York must have
known that he was in a weak position as his army was not strong enough to take
on the Royalists with any confidence of winning; he realized that his show of
force could be construed as treason, and although he lacked allies, he was determined to get something from the negotiations. When the Royalist delegation
told him that his position was hopeless and that he had no option but to compromise, York agreed to renew his loyalty to Henry provided that Somerset was
arrested and punished. The deputation returned to the Royalist camp, where
York's demands were discussed and accepted. Thinking that he had scored a victory, York then rode over to the king's tent on Blackheath only to find Somerset
in Henry's company—the attempt at arresting him had apparently been thwarted
by the queen's intervention, and his brazen presence at the king's side showed
that he was once more back in Royal favor.

A furious row then broke out as York reiterated his claims, but there was little he could do to redress the situation. Not only was Somerset still at liberty and

predominant in the king's camp, but with only 40 of his retainers accompanying him to Blackheath, York was virtually a prisoner. That latter point was given added edge when he was forced to return to London with the court, riding ahead as if he were under arrest, and made to swear a solemn oath of allegiance to Henry at the high altar of St. Paul's Cathedral. In it he swore that he would obey the king's commands and would never again raise a body of armed men in any attempt to use violence against the king's person. Having made his vow in front of a huge congregation—another sign of obeisance—he was allowed to return to Ludlow, once more in exile from the court. Yet again his influence had waned and his armed intervention had achieved nothing except to alienate him even further from the source of power. The court party retained their supremacy, and Somerset's own position was strengthened by the promotion of key allies such as John Tiptoft, recently created Earl of Worcester, who was appointed treasurer, and the Earl of Wiltshire, who became the King's Lieutenant in Ireland in succession to York. Nothing had changed, and Henry felt so emboldened by the heady experience of being in the ascendant that he announced that he would emulate his father and take an army to France to attack and defeat the forces of Charles VII. On January 26, 1452, the first steps were taken to raise the funds and to provide the ships "for our crossing into our kingdom of France, which, God willing we are disposed and determined to undertake with the greatest diligence and expedition." However, nothing came of the king's plans as that summer Henry was required to make a number of Royal progressions through England in order to show the Royal presence and also to mete out justice in areas where disaffection and unrest had degenerated into public demonstrations against the authority. Some of them were violent. Amid rumors that Cade was still alive, there were disturbances in Kent in the first week of May, and in Shropshire a number of men declared their intention of putting York on the throne. This perambulation was one of the longest of Henry's reign. It took him as far west as Exeter and north to Coventry by way of the Severn valley and the Welsh marshes, but pointedly he did not meet York while passing through Ludlow, preferring to spend the night in the local Carmelite religious house.

That same year, 1452, the English position in France was on the point of collapse. Instead of attacking Calais, as might have been expected, the French switched their operations to Gascony, where the English had had a presence for over 300 years. In May 1451, a French force of 7,000 soldiers moved into the offensive to threaten the fortresses on the Gironde estuary; Bourg was taken, followed by the capture of Bordeaux on June 12, and everywhere English interests started collapsing. Not only were the French winning battles and regaining lost territory, but they had superior weapons, mainly artillery, which they used to good effect. They also had good leaders in the Count of Dunois and Jean Bureau, who acted as master of artillery, and, more importantly, they had the renewed self-confidence of those accustomed to winning. To great dismay the whole Duchy of Aquitaine, the inheritance of Queen Eleanor, fell into French hands at the end of August. Not that Charles VII was made universally welcome. The area had been in English hands for so long that sometimes the French were greeted as invaders and potential oppressors rather than as liberators; by the same token, the loss was keenly felt in England as Gascony had been a home away from home for several generations of Englishmen.

Attempts were made to win back Bordeaux by an army under one of England's best soldiers, the fiery Earl of Shrewsbury, who had won a huge reputation in France for the speed and aggression of his attacks, but his efforts were in vain. Despite entering Bordeaux in October 1452, his expedition was doomed to failure, largely due to the accuracy and power of the French artillery, and within a year the duchy was back in French hands. The last engagement was the successful siege of Castillon in July 1453, when the French master gunner Jean Bureau made good use of his artillery to rout the English forces that had been sent to raise the siege. The defeat virtually ended the Hundred Years' War— Charles VII reentered Bordeaux in triumph three months later—and there was to be no more serious fighting between the two sides for the rest of the century.

II

York's Protectorate: The First Battle of St. Albans

*I*n the spring of 1453, the queen became pregnant and the news proved to be a great boost to Henry's fortunes. After seven years of marriage and the recent bout of internal turbulence involving York and the court party, there was now a good chance that the birth of an heir would settle Henry VI's reign by solving the issue of the Royal succession. There was also a subtle strengthening of Henry's personal allegiances. Early in the previous year his half-brothers, Edmund and Jasper Tudor, became members of the Royal entourage and were ennobled respectively as the Earl of Richmond and the Earl of Pembroke. As these titles had once belonged to Henry's uncles Bedford and Gloucester, it was a clear sign of Royal favor. To cement that relationship, the brothers were given custody of Lady Margaret Beaufort, daughter of the old Duke of Somerset (the present duke, Edmund, was her brother) and previously the intended bride of Suffolk's son John de la Pole. Still a girl, the intention was that she should now marry Richmond, and the wedding duly took place in October 1455 when she was still only 12 years of age, at the time the earliest legal age for sexual intercourse. From this union sprang the Tudor dynasty of kings and queens when she gave birth to her only child Henry two years later. (It was a terrible experience as Lady Margaret was still immature; she never conceived again.) In return for the patronage Richmond became a loyal supporter of the Crown, protecting Henry's interests in Wales from his residence at Lamphrey in Pembrokeshire.

For Henry, though, the real prize was the subjugation of York, who had been condemned to the political wilderness. His armed intervention had been crushed, he had been personally humiliated, and his power and authority had been diminished. As a result, England was at peace and, just as importantly, Henry had demonstrated that he possessed the will to rule as king, an important consideration given his previous vacillations. At the same time, the court party was still supreme, with Somerset's position not only strengthened but seemingly impregnable. York's standing had also been weakened by the punishment of many of his lesser supporters during Henry's perambulation of England in the late summer and autumn of the previous year. One of the judicial sessions had been held in Ludlow, a Yorkist stronghold. According to one contemporary account the accused, all Yorkist supporters, were ordered to appear before the king naked and with nooses tied loosely around their necks. Given Henry's well-known prudish tendencies, however, this display of public nudity seems an unlikely embellishment. Nevertheless, these judicial commissions of oyer and terminer (writs for empowering the king's judges to hear cases of treason and other similar felonies) did much to stamp the king's authority on England and to reinforce his authority in the aftermath of York's attempt to intervene and influence events.

Henry's perambulation for 1453 began in Greenwich in the first weeks of January, and his journey took him to Windsor, Eltham, Barking, Norwich, Thetford, Sudbury, Berkhamsted, High Wycombe, and Reading before returning to Greenwich in July. There he found that he had to deal with an outbreak of dissension between two of England's most powerful families—the Nevilles, Earls of Westmorland, and their great rivals the Percys, Earls of Northumberland. Both held lands along the border with Scotland and both had made advantageous marriages that had strengthened their positions. Ralph Neville, the first earl, had married Joan Beaufort, a daughter of John of Gaunt (it was his second marriage), and their son Richard had become Earl of Salisbury following his marriage to the widow of the holder of the title who had been killed in France in 1428. His son, also called Richard, married Anne Beauchamp, daughter of Henry VI's former tutor, and that matrimonial alliance gave him his father-in-law's title, Earl of Warwick. History would remember him as "Warwick the King-maker." The fact that his father's sister Cecily was married to York should have made him a natural Yorkist supporter, but during the recent confrontation with the Crown, young Warwick had remained neutral. Henry's foolhardy behavior, especially his strong attachment to Somerset, was to change all that.

Early in 1453 Warwick became involved in a dispute with Somerset over the possession of matrimonial lands in south Wales—Warwick's father-in-law had married Isabel Despenser, widow of Richard Beauchamp, Earl of Worcester, and on her death her lands had been divided between the Warwick and Worcester families. For reasons that are vague but that were disastrous for his reign, Henry had put the Despenser lands in the custody of Somerset. As they had been held by Warwick since 1450, this was bound to cause offense and, not unnaturally, Warwick took steps to hold onto his possessions. A strong garrison was placed in Cardiff as Warwick built up an army to protect his interests and to use force if Somerset decided to move against him. Once again rival magnates were taking the law into their own hands as open warfare between the two factions seemed inevitable. At that stage, Henry should have recognized the danger and should have taken steps to defuse Warwick's anger. Instead, he simply fueled the controversy. When the council met at Sheen at the end of July. it ordered Warwick to comply with the king's wishes by handing over his Welsh possessions to Somerset. To add further insult, Somerset attended the council meeting but Warwick was not there to present his case. An armed struggle now seemed inevitable, and to compound the problem news arrived of an outbreak of rivalries between the Nevilles and the Percys in the north. Thomas Percy, Lord Egremont and brother of the Earl of Northumberland, had a long-standing disagreement with Sir John Neville, son of the Earl of Salisbury, over land, and this had rumbled on throughout the year despite the king's summonses to both men to appear before the council to answer for their breaches of the king's peace. In the middle of July, Henry appointed a commission of oyer and terminer to settle the issue, but before it set out, he was forced to deal with the confrontation between Warwick and Somerset in south Wales, which appeared at the time to be much more inflammatory.

At the end of the month, Henry left London and headed west into Dorset, where he stopped at the old Royal hunting lodge at Clarendon to the east of Salisbury. While he was there, he suffered a complete mental collapse that left him, according to Benet's chronicle, "so lacking in understanding and memory and so incapable that he was neither able to walk upon his feet nor to lift up his head, nor well to move himself from the place where he was seated." The reason for the breakdown and the cause of the illness are difficult to ascertain. There are no eyewitness accounts of the king's condition at the moment when he lost his reason, but it was obvious that the onset of this psychotic illness was disastrous for Henry. What we do know is that the king lapsed into a catatonic state that lasted for 18 months and that during this period he was insensible to what was happening to him. To all intents and purposes he was lost to the world, suffering from a condition that John Whetamstede, Abbot of St. Albans, characterized as leaving him completely impotent: "A disease and disorder of such a sort overcame the King that he lost his wits and memory for a time, and nearly all his body was so uncoordinated and out of control that he could neither walk nor hold his head up, nor easily move from where he sat."

The reasons for this sudden mental collapse have been much discussed, and from this distance in time, it is more or less impossible to provide a reasonable diagnosis. It could have been genetic. His mother was a Valois, and her father, Charles VI of France, suffered from periodic fits of mental instability, all of which were recorded and provide hard evidence of the manias that affected him during his lifetime. But there were differences. During Henry's madness, he was quiescent and withdrew from normal life; unable to communicate with those around him, he had to be looked after by his retainers and was almost childlike in his behavior. By way of contrast, his maternal grandfather was violent and manic in his periods of ill health; he would become extremely violent, foaming at the mouth and behaving more like a beast than a man. Henry was spared that kind of hypermanic behavior, and although one account says that he was "smitten with a frenzy," it adds that he simply lost his "wit and reason."

Contemporaneous events could also have provided the tipping point that produced the English king's mental collapse. While he was at Clarendon, he received the news of the disastrous defeat at Castillon, and this confirmation of the final loss of his French possessions could have unmanned him and produced the mental collapse. That was certainly the view of John Paston, a person who wrote of the king receiving a "sudden and thoughtless fright," and it could be that the shock was provided by the news from France. Never a mentally robust person, a person who constantly changed and rechanged his mind to the detriment of good governance, Henry was weak-willed and indecisive; coming on top of York's "rebellion" and the trouble caused by the Nevilles and the Percys, the defeat of his armies in France might have been the last straw. The medical treatment meted out to him cannot have helped and perhaps even made matters worse. He was put under the general care of John Arundel, the warden of the hospital of St. Mary of Bethlehem, who had studied mental illness and who came up with a variety of cures including laxatives, gargles, potions, poultices, bleedings, and cauterization to expel "corrupt humours" from his body. None of those no doubt well-intentioned cures worked, and recourse to exorcism to remove evil spirits fell on equally stony ground. Henry had taken leave of his senses and there were no remedies, a situation that left his supporters to do the best they could to paper over the incident and find some means of running England while the king was, so to speak, absent without leave.

For the first few months of his collapse, the governance of England was in the hands of the council, but they could rule only in Henry's name and lacked the ultimate authority of kingship. There was also the problem of the succession.

Until Margaret gave birth, there was no single accepted heir and there were lingering fears that the rivalry between York and Somerset could yet ignite a civil war. No one would have forgotten the fact that Charles VI's mental collapses had ushered in a period of internecine fighting between the different factions at the French court, and it was only too possible that there could be a similar outcome in England. Even when Margaret did give birth, to a boy, on October 13, the signs were still ominous. He was named Edward after his father's favorite saint, Edward the Confessor, and the news of his birth was greeted with acclaim throughout the land except in the one place where it mattered most—the Royal palace at Windsor. While the rest of the country rejoiced at the news of the young prince's birth, Henry remained in a daze, unaware that a son had been born to him and displaying none of the emotions normally expected of a new father.

There was more than the cementing of family relationships to consider in the ceremony of presenting the prince to his father: Until Henry formally acknowledged Edward as his son—a regonized necessity before legislation could be passed to confirm the succession—the council could neither determine the succession nor take any steps to confirm the legality of the boy's position. As a result, the country remained in a dangerous state of flux. The birth of Prince Edward and the king's incapacity affected both York and Somerset. Without Henry's protection, the latter was now in a vulnerable position at court, while the birth of a male heir had dented the former's claims to the throne. At the prince's christening, which followed later in the month in Westminster Abbey, Somerset was named as a sponsor, but that did little to strengthen his position as the honor sparked a malicious rumor that Edward was not Henry's son at all but the issue of an adulterous relationship between Somerset and Queen Margaret. This was followed by equally scandalous stories that Edward was a changeling who had been smuggled into the palace so that everyone would believe that Margaret had given birth to an heir. As for the king, if he had lost his mind, what could he possibly know about it and what could he have done to prevent it?

The birth and christening of the prince brought into sharp focus the need for the country to have a sound form of governance both to protect the body politic and to end the uncertainty caused by the king's mental breakdown. Unrest was still being fomented in the north by the Nevilles and the Percys, who were unwilling to end their feud and happily ignored letters from the council ordering them to bring their supporters to heel and to settle their differences. Instead of paying any heed to the summonses, the two families continued to take the law into their own hands, and by the middle of August, their rivalries had degenerated into violence when a force of Percys, led by Egremont, ambushed a party of Nevilles as they made their way from a family wedding back to their home at Sheriff Hutton near York. The brawl took place on Heworth Moor and quickly sprawled over into the nearby countryside; no one was killed, but the fact that over 700 Percy retainers and assorted thugs could behave in this way was a clear sign that the Royal writ did not run as far as Yorkshire and that the kingdom was in danger of spiraling out of control.

In an attempt to retain order, the council managed to maintain a semblance of normalcy in its regular business meetings, but there were too many rumors about the king's madness to keep up the pretense forever. To begin with, the council attempted to sideline York from their deliberations, but the birth of an heir had removed his status as a potential heir-presumptive and, by the beginning of November 1453, York was in London with a large retinue to protect his interests. From the outset, he showed that he had no intention of making concessions or of cooperating with Somerset. Norfolk, his old crony and close ally, reasserted the familiar claim that Somerset was guilty of losing the territories in France and condemned him for his vanity in presuming "over-great authority in this realm." It had the desired effect, and on November 23, Somerset was arrested and imprisoned in the Tower of London. This was a direct challenge to Margaret's authority, and she responded in a style that typified her robust attitude regarding the need to hold on to power. Toward the end of January 1454, she made a spirited attempt to affirm her son's rights and her own claim to be his regent on the grounds that she was in the strongest position to make the necessary state appointments.

It was a bold attempt to reassert herself and her position at court, but by attempting "to have the whole rule of this land," she had overreached herself. All along, she had counted on gaining the support of those magnates who still entertained suspicions about York's real motives, but her arrogant bid to become regent in her husband's place caused great offense. Following Margaret's intervention, power began to slip inexorably back toward the Yorkist faction, and on February 13, the council agreed to nominate York as the king's lieutenant to enable a new parliament to be called and to permit him to preside over it. All the while, tensions were mounting in London as the various magnates looked to protect their positions by bringing in large numbers of armed retainers, amid persistent rumors that Somerset was using a network of spies to attempt to influence matters and take over control of the country. Once again civil war seemed inevitable—one of the largest of the private armies was under the command of Warwick, now firmly in the Yorkist camp. On March 22, John Kemp, the Chancellor and Archbishop of Canterbury, suddenly died, and his passing meant that Henry's condition could no longer be kept secret, as the replacement for the see of Canterbury could be authorized only under the king's jurisdiction. Faced by the very real danger that the queen or Somerset, or, more likely the two of them working in tandem, might seize power, the council decided to act. Once again they made a formal visit to Henry to ascertain his mental state, and in the words of Benet's chronicle they "perceived that if the king did not recover, England would soon be ruined under the government of the Duke of Somerset. So the noblemen of the kingdom sent for the Duke of York." Five days after Kemp's death York was invested as the Protector and Defender of the Realm, thereby resurrecting an office similar to the one that had been occupied by his uncle Gloucester during the king's minority.

As things stood, York could have exploited the unexpected chance that had been presented to him to rescue himself from political oblivion. Although the remaining members of the council remained as a powerful counterweight, York was still in a position in which he could exert his authority over them by getting his own people into key appointments. Salisbury, his brother-in-law, was appointed chancellor; a close relation, Thomas Bourchier (his sister's brother-in-law), became Archbishop of Canterbury, and he himself took over the captaincy of Calais in place of the disgraced Somerset. At the same time, he ordered Margaret to be removed to Windsor, where she was held in conditions that amounted to open arrest. York confounded the fears of his enemies by emerging as a fair and conscientious protector who took his duties seriously and behaved with remarkable moderation. During the 18 months of his rule, his most notable achievement was to reduce expenditure at court and to cut back the size of the Royal household. He also managed to resolve the dispute in the north of England with a show of force in the summer of 1454, but the decisive moment came when Egremont, now in alliance with the ambitious and unstable Duke of Exeter, fell into the hands of Sir Thomas Neville, Salisbury's younger son, following a pitched battle between the two factions at Stamford Bridge near York in November. Arraigned for disturbing the peace, Egremont and Exeter were fined heavily and consigned to house arrest in their respective residences. To add to the complications, Exeter had his own Royal pretensions, being the grandson of Elizabeth of Lancaster, daughter of John of Gaunt and sister of Henry IV.

It could be said that York had little option but to rule within the limits of the conditions of the protectorate. Despite his alliance with Warwick and Salisbury, many of the great nobles still distrusted him—they refused to back his demand to try Somerset for treason—and he faced a hostile parliament. The terms of his office were also ambiguous: He held it until Edward came of age, which would have given him at least 14 years as protector, and he was still subordinate to the person of King Henry. Given time, York might have resolved those hindrances and taken advantage of his sudden and unexpected elevation, but before he could strengthen his position or benefit from it, Henry suddenly recovered his senses. The amazing transformation took place on Christmas Day 1454, when the king was suddenly restored as if he were a man waking from a long and deep sleep. Unlike the first occasion, when Henry had been presented with his son and failed to recognize him, on this occasion the king's recovery allowed him to acknowledge Prince Edward as his own and thereby ensure the succession. Inevitably, given the duration of the king's illness, the recovery was not complete or lasting, and according to contemporary evidence there were numerous occasions in the years to come when it was suggested that Henry was not the man he had been before his mental collapse.

However, the king had wit enough to preserve his own position. On December 30, York presided over his last meeting of the council that effectively dissolved his authority, and within a month he faced once more the political oblivion he had occupied before the king's madness. Henry moved swiftly to undo many of the decisions made during the protectorate. The Duke of Exeter was removed from house arrest, Salisbury was dismissed as chancellor and replaced by Archbishop Bourchier, John Tiptoft the Earl of Worcester was replaced as treasurer by the Earl of Wiltshire, and most tellingly of all, Somerset was freed from the Tower and restored to his position as Captain of Calais. All those sudden changes told York everything he needed to know about where the king's sympathies lay and where his position stood. Once again he had been sidelined, and once again Somerset and his allies were in the ascendant. Following the council meeting in March, York left London and returned to his estates, as did his allies Salisbury and Warwick. Within weeks of their departure, the chronicler Benet reported that "Somerset was plotting the destruction of York. He offered advice to the King, saying that the Duke of York wished to depose the King and rule England himself—which was manifestly false."

The stage was now set for confrontation, and once again Henry bungled the situation by producing fresh provocations. Having already humiliated York by reversing decisions taken during the protectorate, Henry decided to act against him once and for all. On April 21, 1455, a meeting of the council was summoned to take place in Leicester, the Midlands town in the Lancastrian heartlands. Its main purpose was to discuss the safety of the king's person, but as neither York nor Salisbury had been invited to the meeting and both had been ordered to disband their retinues on pain of being arraigned as traitors, they took it to mean that their own positions were under threat. Sensing a trap of the kind that had been laid for Gloucester eight years earlier, York, Salisbury, and Warwick started making their own military preparations by raising an armed force that would eventually number 3,000 men. By then, York realized he was a marked man and that he had to protect himself against Somerset, who was back in Royal favor and still enjoyed the powerful support of the queen. York's allies were also under renewed threat. The release of Exeter, a key Percy confederate, convinced Warwick that he had to take action to preserve the Nevilles' fortunes, and, likewise, Salisbury's abrupt dismissal was as clear an indication as any that he had no future under Lancastrian rule. With both sides feeling threatened—this time Henry seems to have believed the queen's warnings that York coveted the throne—civil war between the House of Lancaster and the House of York suddenly became unavoidable. On the one side stood Richard of York and his allies Salisbury and Warwick; on the other, was the king and the king's party composed of the Dukes of Somerset and Buckingham, the Earls of Northumberland, Wiltshire, and Devon, and Lords Clifford and Dudley, two prominent soldiers who had been recruited by the queen to join the Lancastrian cause.

Under the military conventions of the day, there was still time to negotiate before resorting to a war that would involve Englishmen fighting against Englishmen, cousin against cousin, and in one case, father-in-law (Salisbury) against former son-in-law (Worcester). The Yorkists took full advantage of the custom by sending a letter in reply to the king's demands, protesting their loyalty, complaining about their omission from the council, and demanding the extirpation of the traitors who surrounded the king. But time was running out. By the time the missive reached Henry, he had left London with his supporters and their armed retinues, numbering some 2,000 men, but at that stage he seems to have believed that York would hold to his solemn undertaking never again to take up arms against him. It was not until he received the letter from York that Henry realized the full implications of what was happening and took steps to increase the size of the forces available to him. On May 21, the king's retinue left London for Leicester, stopping for the night at Watford, but they were destined to get no further than St. Albans. At the same time, York halted at Ware, 15 miles to the north. Once again, there were last-minute attempts to reach a compromise. York sent his confessor, William Willeflete, to the king's camp at Watford bearing a second letter in which he reaffirmed his loyalty and demanded the arrest of Somerset. However, neither side was prepared to yield any ground as both felt that they were in the right.

The failure to find any common ground made violence inevitable, and the small abbey town of St. Albans was destined to be the scene of the first battle of the conflict known to history as the Wars of the Roses. At dawn on the morning of May 22, both sides were in full battle order, the Yorkists in the fields to the east of St. Albans, the Royalist Lancastrian forces in the town itself, having taken up position along St Peter's Street and Holywell Hill. In a last-minute change of plan, Somerset was replaced by Buckingham as the field commander of the king's army and the vanguard was under the direction of Lord Clifford, a veteran of the recent fighting in France and a powerful northern landowner used to dealing with the Scots. The Lancastrians had set up barriers around the unwalled town, but these were no obstacles for the heavily armed and armored Yorkist forces that had been drawn up in three "battles" or divisions under the command of York, Salisbury, and Warwick. Fighting commenced at around ten o'clock in the morning and lasted little more than an hour. Unusually for a battle of this period, the main struggle took place in the town itself and involved some close-quarter hacking and stabbing in the confined streets that was bloody and intensive. The first attack was made along the ground occupied by the present-day Hatfield Road and Victoria Street, but the king's forces held off this assault and it took the intervention of Warwick with his archers to break the Royalist resolve.

Henry had taken up his own position in the marketplace wearing full armor. Standing below the Royal standard, he presented an easy target to the archers who had been instructed by Warwick to concentrate on those guarding the king. The abbot of St. Albans was a horrified spectator, and his chronicle describes the streets of the town being "full of dead corpses" as Warwick's men fought their way toward the Royalist positions. As the lines began to thin under the arrow shower, heavily armored knights and men-at-arms broke into St. Peter's Square to complete the bloody execution. They knew what had to be done as they cut and slashed their way through the barricades: Common foot soldiers were generally spared, but those of any rank could expect no mercy. One of the first to fall was Somerset, who was overwhelmed and cut down near the Castle Inn—he saw the sign too late to remember that a soothsayer had warned him that a castle would be the cause of his doom. It is possible that his killer was Warwick himself. Northumberland, too, was hacked down in the streets of St. Albans, as was Clifford, and, all told, around 100 men, mostly Royalists, died with them. Henry received an arrow wound in the neck and, bleeding profusely, was persuaded to take refuge in a nearby tanner's house. There he was eventually approached by the Yorkist leaders, who knelt before him and pledged their allegiance to him. "And when the king perceived this," recorded Benet, "he was greatly cheered." Later he was taken to the abbey, where the leading commanders and the king spent the night before returning to London.

As a battle, St. Albans occupies a minor place in British military history, but its effects were long lasting. Great magnates had taken up arms against an anointed king and had created their own armies to enforce their will on the country's governance. In so doing, they had executed men loyal to the king—Henry was appalled by the news of Somerset's death, regarding it an illegal act—and the resulting enmity left lasting scars. Northumberland's death deepened the existing divisions between the Nevilles and the Percys, and Clifford's son vowed that his father's death would not remain unavenged. In the shocked aftermath of the battle, men stood and stared at the havoc they had created in the narrow streets of the small market town, where the abbot reported sights that law-abiding people should not have seen: "Here you saw a man with his brains dashed out, here one with a broken arm, another with his throat cut, a fourth with a pierced chest . . ." For those who had managed to get away from the Yorkists, there was flight; to York's credit there was no pursuit, but for some, there was disgrace. Sir Philip Wentworth, the king's Standard-Bearer, had, according to Paston, "cast it [the standard] down and fled. My Lord Norfolk says he shall be hanged therefore, and so he is worthy." In fact, Wentworth survived to fight another day, only to be executed later in the conflict.

Viewed dispassionately as a military action, St. Albans was little more than a street brawl with heavy weapons. Once the Yorkists had broken the Royalist lines and occupied the marketplace, known enemies, some of them great magnates, were singled out and dispatched with brutal ease. Others received debilitating wounds—Buckingham was wounded in the neck by an arrow, and Somerset's heir, the Earl of Dorset, had to be carried away in a cart, unable to walk. As the fighting died down, the people of St. Albans suffered the usual pillaging that follows any battle of this kind, and the surrounding countryside was also subjected to violence by rampaging gangs of Yorkist troops. On that score, it was not very different from similar military actions of that period, but there was a good deal more significance to the battle than the triumph of arms by one side. The fighting in the streets of St. Albans was also a bloody coup. As a result of the Yorkist intervention, the court party had been crushed, albeit temporarily, and its principal figurehead, Somerset, had been killed. This was exactly what York wanted—he counted Somerset a traitor and regarded him as a bitter rival whose baleful influence at court had resulted in the creation of wrongheaded policies. All along, that had been his complaint, and now he had the satisfaction of knowing that his great rival had been permanently removed from the scene. Furthermore, the king was now under the control of the Yorkist faction, and the following day, Henry was escorted back to London. With a symbolism that could not have been misunderstood by anyone watching, the king rode between York and Salisbury while Warwick rode ahead carrying the sword of state. The mystique of kingship remained intact, but it was self-evident that Henry was firmly in the hands of those who had defeated him.

On May 25, the celebration of the Feast of Pentecost, Henry appeared in St. Paul's Cathedral wearing his crown as a sign to his people that he remained their anointed king, but the pageantry was all for show. The reality was rather different. Immediately after winning control, the Yorkists started claiming the main offices of state—York became Constable of England, Warwick was appointed Captain of Calais, and Henry Bourchier, the chancellor's brother, was appointed treasurer in place of Wiltshire, who had been forced into hiding, having fled the field dressed as a monk, or as *Gregory's Chronicle* unkindly put it, he had "fought mainly with his heels for he was frightened of losing his beauty." At the same time, parliament was summoned and Henry was moved out of the London area to Hertford castle, where he took up residence with the queen. When parliament opened on July 9, it was packed with Yorkist supporters and its business was dominated by the need to restore normalcy in the wake of the fighting at St. Albans. Oaths of allegiance to the king were renewed and legislation was introduced to justify the actions taken by the Yorkists, who claimed that they had been forced to intervene in order to redress the "great tyranny and injustice to the people." Somerset and two minor associates were blamed for the disorder, and pardons were issued for everyone else, as if the Battle of St. Albans had been an aberration and not a turning point. At the same time Gloucester's reputation was rehabilitated, and an act was passed revoking most of the grants of land and money made by the king to his favorites during the first part of his reign. York was now in full control of the governance of England, and his paramount position was confirmed in November when a further meeting of parliament appointed him once more Protector and Defender of the Realm. As the Dijon chronicle concluded its musings, "the said Duke of York will now be without contradiction the first after the king and will have the government of all. God give him the grace to carry out his tasks well and have pity on the souls of sinners. Amen."

The conditions of York's office were similar to those he had accepted at the end of 1453 and the reasons for the appointment were the same. His new standing was also timely. Henry had succumbed once more to a mental breakdown—probably as a result of his wound and the trauma of battle—and was deemed to be incapable of ruling his country. The king's illness gave York the upper hand, but as he had done during the first protectorate, he was careful to rule through the council and was conscious of the limitations of his position. He was right to be so circumspect. For all that he enjoyed the support of Salisbury and Warwick, his power base was narrow and he was still viewed with misgiving by his fellow magnates, who could not rid themselves of the suspicion that he had ambitions to win the crown. York also had made many enemies, not least the sons of the men who had been slaughtered at St. Albans. Then there was the queen: Margaret of Anjou had been horrified by the death of Somerset, and although exiled from London, she set about strengthening the court party that was still in existence. Henry Beaufort, Somerset's son and the new duke, pledged his allegiance to the queen, as did his brother Edmund and Henry Cecil, the new Earl of Northumberland. Other prominent supporters included the Tudor Earls of Richmond and Pembroke, the Earl of Wiltshire, and Clifford's son, who gained the nickname "Black-faced Clifford" on account of his undisguised desire to avenge his father's death. The enmity seems also to have been personal: The queen now regarded York as a threat not just to her husband but also to the future well-being of her two-year-old son, Prince Edward. Although an uneasy peace had returned to the realm, there was to be no easy dissipation of the underlying tensions that had plunged England into the crisis that had challenged Henry's capacity to rule. All over England there was a sense of foreboding that was compounded in no small measure by the fact that violence had broken out and that the mounting disorders presaged worse times ahead. The apprehension was captured in an address to the king written by John Hardyng, the author of a contemporary verse chronicle that was written between 1440 and 1457 and was later revised to give it a slant toward the House of York:

> In your realm there are no justices of the peace that dare take the responsibility to suppress the quarrellers. Such is the extent of the sickness that has taken hold that they will not recognise the rioting or the fighting so common now throughout your people. This I dread fearfully, that from these riots shall more mischief arise, and from the sores unhealed a scab will form, so large that nothing may restrain its growth. Wherefore, good lord, if you will give me leave, I would say this to your excellency: withstand misrule and violence.

Hardynge's imagery is instructive and neatly sums up the sense of apprehension that had gripped the country: The English body politic was ailing, the wound was growing, and it needed urgent healing to stop it from plummeting to terminal decline.

12

A Great and Strong-laboured Woman

nce again, within a few months of York's second protectorate, Henry VI
confounded everyone by regaining his sanity. He was sufficiently recovered to return to the throne and reassert his authority. On February 25,
1456, he appeared in parliament and according to Benet, "in front of the King
the Duke [York] resigned his office and left Parliament before the session was
over." In fact, York seems to have been aware of the development and fully
expected to be dismissed: two weeks earlier he had arrived back in London with
Warwick, each man accompanied by a large armed retinue in a show of force
designed to protect and reinforce their positions. It was a sensible precaution;
otherwise, as John Paston noted at the time, the king might have ordered their
arrest. This time, though, Henry thought it preferable to keep York on friendly
terms; he remained on the council and was confirmed in possession of the
lieutenancy of Ireland, while Warwick was permitted to retain the captaincy of
Calais. This latter appointment had the double advantage of keeping Warwick
happy and making sure that he remained out of the country. Instead of appointing a lieutenant to deputize for him, as was the usual custom, Warwick decided
to take up residence in Calais, although it was not until April that he was able to
come to an agreement with the local Staple merchants about the payment of
wages owed to the garrison. (The Company of the Staple, or Staplers, had been
established in 1345 to regulate and manage the lucrative wool trade and
effectively ruled Calais.)

At the same time, an opportunity arose to get York out of London when
King James II of Scotland broke his truce by sending raiding parties into the

north of England. Emboldened by the new Burgundian alliance that had come about through James II's marriage to Mary, daughter of the Burgundian Duke of Gueldres in 1449, the Scots had used the connection to reequip their army with modern siege artillery and muskets. Although these were still relatively primitive, the possession of great guns gave an advantage to those who possessed them, and James had already made use of them to cow his old enemies the Douglas family into submission in the previous year. Following the razing of key strongholds at Abercorn in Fife and Threave in Kirkcudbrightshire by the king's artillery, the young Earl of Douglas (James Douglas, the 9th earl) had fled south into England to seek shelter with York. (He had good reason to fear the Scottish king as James II had stabbed his father to death in 1452.) When requests for his return were ignored, James led an army into Northumberland, and to compound the insult, he claimed that York was the rightful king of England and would do well to assert his rights. At first it was thought that Henry might lead an army north to deal with the threat, but sending York instead was too good an opportunity to miss as it removed him from London and kept him out of further mischief. As it turned out, York's arrival in Durham persuaded the Scots to retire, and for the time being, that put an end to the danger of invasion from the north. Four years later, the Scottish king's enthusiasm for artillery was to be his undoing. Hoping to lay siege to the castle of Roxburgh and wrest it from English hands, James led an army complete with "cartis of war" to surround the castle and to test its walls with his new weapons. When the siege began, James supervised the positioning and laying of each of the siege guns, and when Mary of Gueldres arrived on August 3, 1460, he ordered a cannonade to be fired. Unfortunately, one of the weapons exploded and a piece of iron smashed into the king's thigh, killing him. Undaunted, his widow ordered the siege to continue and the castle was pounded into submission.

At the time of Henry VI's return to sanity, the English king made it clear that he wanted to remain on good terms with York and hoped that he would be allowed to play a leading role on the council. From a purely pragmatic point of view, this made sense. The king's capacity to govern was still in question—the mental instability could return at any time—and despite York's earlier violent behavior in raising a rebellion, he had displayed good sense and confidence while acting as Protector. However, there was now a new and much more potent force at court in the shape of Margaret of Anjou, who emerged after Somerset's removal as the main focus of the opposition to York. There had not always been such bitter enmity between them. Earlier in the queen's reign, she had given lavish presents to York and his wife Cecily, and they had remained on reasonable terms, in spite of the quarrel with her favorite, Somerset. The birth of the

Crown Prince changed all that, and she came to regard York not just as a menace to herself and her husband but also as a serious threat to her son's succession. As Benet put it, the king might have received York and Warwick graciously but the queen "loathed them both." Her fears were exacerbated by his use of force against the crown, first at Blackheath and then more seriously at St. Albans. Here was a man, York, who had resorted to violence to get his way and might do so again. It had also not escaped her notice that during York's two protectorates, he had attempted to limit the size of her household and to cut back her finances. As Margaret could no longer count on her husband's complete support to maintain the dignity of the Crown due to his intermittent madness, she had to secure her position by exerting her own authority within the court. Even though York had been dismissed from his protectorate, Margaret continued to regard him as an implacable enemy, and in the summer of 1456 she started taking steps to ensure the safety of herself, her husband, and her infant son.

In August she removed the family to her castle at Tutbury and established the court at Coventry and Kenilworth in the Midlands, taking with her a large number of artillery pieces from the Tower. The move from the capital was more than symbolic. From the outset of her reign, Margaret had not been popular in London—she shared with Suffolk the blame for the loss of Anjou and Maine and the collapse of English power in France—and she came to regard the city as pro-Yorkist. In fact, throughout the conflict, the capital remained largely aloof from events and the ruling merchant companies resisted the temptation to take sides. However, the queen did not feel safe in London and preferred to move her court to the Midlands, where she could feel secure in the Lancastrian heartlands. Once there, she was surrounded by close allies and powerful courtiers: To the north in Lancashire was the chamberlain of the household, Lord Stanley; to the east in Leicestershire was Viscount Beauchamp; Lord Welles was a key Somerset ally in Lincolnshire; in Staffordshire were the Earl of Shrewsbury and the Duke of Buckingham; and to the southwest, in Gloucestershire, was Ralph Butler, Lord Sudeley, a veteran of the French wars who had served the king both as treasurer and household chamberlain. Wales was held by the Tudors, and in the West Country the Earl of Devon transferred his affections once more by allying himself with the queen's party, joining forces with the Duke of Exeter and the Earl of Wiltshire. At the beginning of October, Margaret's position was strengthened further when the Bourchier brothers were dismissed, and in their place William Waynefleet, Bishop of Winchester, became chancellor and the Earl of Shrewsbury was appointed treasurer. Both were adherents of Margaret's court party. Small wonder that in the Paston correspondence John Bocking wrote to his master Sir John Fastolff describing the queen as "a great and strong-labored woman, for she spares no pain to sue her things to an intent and conclusion to her power."

It was a curious time for the country. England was not in a state of war, but tension was never far below the surface of everyday life. There was trouble in London, with riots taking place in Lombard Street against Italian merchants who were thought to be undermining the wool market in Flanders. The odium was compounded by gossip that the Italians had been given preferential treatment as a result of the patronage of the court party and were favored by Queen Margaret. There were also persistent rumors that there had been further fighting between the king and his enemies, and, in addition to the invasion threat posed by the Scots, there was an outbreak of violence in Wales where Sir Walter Devereux, a Yorkist ally, crossed the border to attack the town of Hereford in August. Having taken it and made the mayor prisoner, he tried and hanged a number of innocent men before taking his retinue back into Wales, where he seized the castles of Carmarthen and Aberystwyth. Both were nominally possessions of the Duke of York as Constable, but at the time they were garrisoned by Somerset supporters who had refused to hand them over to their liege lord's sworn enemy. To complicate matters, the castles had also been granted by the king to the Earl of Richmond, who suddenly found himself imprisoned by Devereux. In his defense, Devereux insisted that he was acting with parliamentary authority—the return of both castles had been demanded from Somerset earlier in the year—but he overstepped his authority by taking the castles by force. Even if he did not act with the complicity of York, he was a known supporter and it was not difficult to believe that the action was part of a wider plot against the king. Anarchy was overtaking the country, and neither Henry nor his wife was capable of doing anything to retrieve the situation.

Having removed the court from London to Coventry where she had surrounded herself with Lancastrian supporters, Margaret set about promoting the concept of the Crown Prince being the rightful focus of Royalist support. Although she had no constitutional right to rule England, she was able to work within the framework of Royal power and, her husband being incapacitated, used her son's name and authority to make appointments. More than any other instance, one episode makes clear her growing preeminence and the sharp decline of her husband's reputation. On the Feast of the Exaltation of the Cross in September 1457, she entered Coventry where she was greeted by a pageant featuring representations of prophets, patron saints, and nine conquerors, one of which represented her in the form of St. Margaret slaying a dragon. Of the king, there was no mention, and the records show that increasingly he played little part in public life, leaving the compiler of the *English Chronicle* to mourn that "the realm of England was out of all governance . . . for the king was simple and led by covetous council, and owed more than he was worth." Though Henry had regained his sanity, he was a changed man. Always religious-minded and devout, he now spent long hours in prayer and devotion and seemed to need more sleep than other men.

There were more problems in the summer of 1457, when a French fleet commanded by Pierre de Brézé, the Grand Seneschal of Normandy, raided the Kent coast and set fire to the port of Sandwich. At the time, Margaret had been attempting to enter into a new treaty with Charles VII for military support and had used Brézé, a former admirer, as a go-between. Hardly surprisingly when the details became known, there were rumors that she either had instigated the raid or had ordered Brézé to carry it out. Neither was true, but in the overheated atmosphere there were always those who were ready to believe the slanderers. No one thought to place any blame on Warwick, who had been building up his strength in Calais and had used his great wealth to create a personal fleet of ten warships that he had used to attack the French in the Channel. Lacking funds from England, he simply took matters into his own hands and encouraged his captains to engage in what amounted to acts of piracy. Warwick's exploits endeared him to the merchants of London, who had seen their trade decline during Henry's reign, and inevitably his popularity rubbed off on the Yorkist cause. He was able to move freely between Calais and London, and during this period he opened up channels of communication both with the French court and with the Duke of Burgundy. Warwick's largesse, a result of his huge personal wealth, also helped—he visited London regularly and was lavish in his entertainment— and as a result, he turned into the acceptable face of the opposition to the king, becoming in Waurin's words "the prince whom they held in the highest esteem and on whom they placed the greatest faith and reliance." That popularity came at a price. By the end of 1456, he had been more or less excluded from power, and at the council meeting held in Coventry in the autumn, he and York, alone of the members, were required to swear oaths of allegiance.

In the late summer of 1457, Henry appeared to have entered a short period of relative sanity and returned to London, but even then he spent most of the winter in seclusion in abbeys at Reading, Abingdon, and Chertsey. Council meetings were still being held, but all too often they turned into armed camps, with the Yorkists and the queen's party bringing with them large retinues of armed men to protect them. In an attempt at reconciliation, Henry demanded that York and his supporters should endow a chantry (the singing of mass) at St. Albans to atone for the deaths during the fighting in the town and that the families of Somerset, Northumberland, and Clifford be given financial compensation for their losses at the same battle. However, the gloss was taken off this well-meant action when it became clear that Henry had agreed to it only after young Clifford had arrived in London at the head of a large armed force to demand that he receive compensation for the loss of his father.

Warwick provided the first flashpoint when he used his powerful position at Calais to flout Royal authority—not only did the garrison contain one of the largest English armies, but Warwick continued to use his warships in piratical raids on foreign fleets. In May 1458, his captains attacked a Castilian fleet and followed it up with an even more audacious attack on the ships of the Hanse League as they passed through the Channel. This was in direct violation of a truce two years earlier with this commercial entente that embraced the important north German and Baltic trading ports. Not unnaturally, their representatives made a vigorous complaint to Henry about Warwick's outrageous behavior. Largely at the instigation of the queen, who saw a chance to rid herself of a troublesome opponent, the council summoned Warwick to appear before them to account for his behavior. Undaunted, Warwick set out across the Channel with an armed retinue and marched into London, where his many supporters took to the streets to demonstrate their allegiance. Unfortunately, their actions turned violent, and there were clashes between Warwick's supporters and forces sent into the capital by the queen to restore order.

By then neither side was interested in making any attempts at reconciliation and both began planning for an uncertain future. At the end of the year, the queen's party started hoarding arms, including the provision of 500 pikes and a similar number of lead-coated clubs for the protection of those around the king against "certain misruled and seditious persons." Three new cannons were also ordered from John Judde, the master of ordinance, who assured the king that they would be able to break down the walls of any castle that dared to oppose him. This was followed in May 1459 by the removal from the Tower of 3,000 bows and sheaves of arrows. At the same time, the court moved back to Kenilworth and Coventry, where a meeting of the council was summoned to take place on June 24. Fearing for their personal safety, York, Salisbury, and Warwick refused to attend and were duly indicted as the Lancastrian magnates prepared their forces for action. The Yorkists, too, were making preparations. York, Salisbury, and Warwick all had well-armed and experienced retinues, but they were scattered over the country and it would take time for them to assemble at Ludlow, where York waited with his sons Edward, Earl of March, and Edmund, Earl of Rutland. The Calais garrison that included a force of 600 experienced soldiers under the command of Sir Andrew Trollope, Master Porter of Calais, and "a very subtle man of war," arrived in Kent and, having entered London on

September 21, headed north; at the same time, Salisbury's forces left Middleham in Yorkshire and marched across the Pennines toward the Yorkist heartlands. The news reached the queen in Cheshire while she was recruiting men for her army, and her supporters decided to send a force under the command of Lord Audley, a trusted Lancastrian supporter, to intercept Salisbury while the Royal family took shelter in Eccleshall Castle. It was a sensible move, as the Yorkist forces were still fractured and the Lancastrians outnumbered them two to one.

The two forces duly collided on the barren rolling countryside of Blore Heath near Market Drayton. Finding his way blocked by the Lancastrian forces when he spotted their banners and standards behind the crest of a ridge, Salisbury deployed his forces on rising ground to the east of Hempmill Brook, where his left flank was protected by woods and his right was guarded by a line of supply wagons. It was a good defensive position, as Audley's foot soldiers and cavalry would have to contend with the rising ground that had become sodden and heavy following days of wet weather and they would be forced to negotiate the high sides of the strong-flowing Hempmill Brook. As the Yorkists' forces got into position there was the customary attempt at negotiation, but this ended when Audley refused Salisbury free passage, and the trumpets were sounded for battle. First into action were Audley's knights and men-at-arms, who attacked across the brook, where they came under heavy fire from Salisbury's archers who, according to Waurin, "began to shoot so intensely that it was frightful, and so violently that everything in range suffered." With the Lancastrians unable to make any progress and falling under the sustained fire of Salisbury's battle-hardened archers, the Yorkist knights and men-at-arms, many of them veterans from the wars in France, counterattacked and began slaughtering their floundering opponents. A second Lancastrian assault met the same fate, and all was lost when Audley was killed leading a third charge that like its predecessors was beaten back with huge loss of life.

Realizing that the battle was lost, men began fleeing for their lives and were hotly pursued by Salisbury's men, who quickly showed that they were not prepared to give any quarter. Around 2,000 Lancastrians died on the battlefield, others while being pursued, and, according to local legend, the waters of Hempmill Brook ran red with blood for three days after the fighting. It was a massive victory but it was not decisive. The bulk of the Royalist army was encamped at Eccleshall, ten miles away, and Salisbury still had to get his forces to Ludlow and safety. He was also pained by the fact that his two sons Sir John and Sir Thomas Neville, Warwick's brothers, had been taken prisoner while pursuing the enemy and faced an uncertain future. Realizing that he had no option but to press on, Salisbury set out that same night—the battle had lasted the better part of the afternoon—and left behind some artillery pieces in the care of a friendly Augustinian friar who agreed to make use of them to give the impression that the Yorkist forces were still on Blore Heath. The ruse worked, and when the Royalist forces arrived the next morning, they found the area empty. Today the main road from Market Drayton to Newcastle under Lyme crosses the site of the battle on privately owned farmland. A cross, erected in 1765, is supposed to mark the spot where Audley fell, and a more recent stone marks the site of the Lancastrian positions. There are other memorials. Legend has it that Margaret of Anjou watched the battle from the spire of St. Mary's Church in nearby Mucklestone, before fleeing upon realizing that Audley was being defeated. It is said that she employed a blacksmith, William Skelhorn, to reverse the shoes on her horse to disguise the route of her escape, but this seems unlikely as she was probably with the rest of her forces at Eccleshall. Nevertheless, the anvil from the smithy stands in the churchyard at Mucklestone to commemorate what would have been an inspired escape.

Salisbury made good progress and arrived at Ludlow, followed shortly thereafter by Warwick and his men. All told, they had about 25,000 under their command—exact numbers are impossible to compute—but they were vastly outnumbered by the Royalists, who had anything from 40,000 to 60,000 available to them. There were other differences. Whereas the Royalists had the support of a large number of leading magnates including Buckingham, Northumberland, Shrewsbury, Devon, Wiltshire, and Beaumont, the Yorkists numbered only themselves and had failed to attract any sizable aristocratic support. Slowly the Yorkists began to move south toward Worcester, hoping to swing eastward toward London, but they found their road blocked by the larger Royalist army that was drawn up in battle order with the king's standard flying. This placed York in a quandary, for all along he had insisted that his quarrel was not with Henry but with his evil advisors, yet here was the king himself bearing his Royal banner and leading his own army to crush opponents who were now regarded as traitors and rebels. To buy time, York led his men back into Worcester, where he took mass in the cathedral and swore oaths of loyalty to the king that were then written on vellum and dispatched to the Royalist camp. Either they never reached Henry or they were intercepted by Margaret, because the gesture was ignored out of hand. The only response was the offer of a pardon to all the rebel earls bar Salisbury, presumably because he had been responsible for the bloodshed at Blore Heath.

Sensing that his position had been weakened by the strength of the Royalist army opposing him, York decided to pull back toward Ludlow and his own territory, partly to defend it against the forthcoming onslaught but primarily because he had no other realistic tactical option open to him. So began the long retreat through Kidderminster and on through Ledbury and Leominster with the Royalists in pursuit. At Ludford Bridge over the River Terne, York decided to make a stand south of the town on October 12. The fields were fortified with carts and cannon "set before the battles," and according to Gregory, York's men built a "great deep ditch fortified with guns, carts and stakes." Despite the solidity of the position and the fact that York was fighting on home territory, things were already looking bad for him. For a start, morale was low. Not only was his army numerically smaller and the men were probably tired after the long retreat, but also many of them were dismayed to find themselves about to take part in a battle against the king. It was one thing to fight on behalf of their liege lords in their quarrels with other magnates, but it was quite another to take up arms against an anointed monarch. To engage in that kind of activity was treason and, to the medieval mind it was also sacrilege, a sin that put at risk not only their lives but also their mortal souls. And it was all too evident that the king was present in the opposing army: Across the meadows the Royal standard could be seen flying as evening gave way to nightfall. In vain the earls sent another message protesting their loyalty to the king and cataloguing the "the great and lamentable complaints of your poor, true subjects, of robberies, ravishments, extortions, oppressions, riots, unlawful assemblies, wrongful imprisonments universally throughout every part of your realm." Henry had no need to take any heed of the protestations; he held the upper hand and his supporters knew it.

Some time during the night, York's position was weakened further when Trollope decided to defect to the Royalist camp, taking with him his experienced troops. He had served in France under Henry V, and although committed to Warwick, he could not bring himself to lead his men into action against his former commander's son and successor, the rightful king of England. Others followed suit, overawed by the size of Henry's army and the sight of his fluttering standards. York tried to halt the rot by spreading rumors that Henry had died, but the ploy came to nothing when it became all too evident that the king was still at the head of his army. A council of war was then held to judge the situation, and during the meeting it must have become abundantly clear to all the participants that their men would not fight and that even if they did, the result would be their complete annihilation at the hands of the superior Royalist army. All the rebel earls were brave and experienced men, but they were also hardheaded realists who understood the weakness of their position and the crazy reality of leading a small and demoralized force against the might of Henry's army. According to the account found in the Rolls of Parliament, "about midnight they stole away out of the field, under color they would have refreshed them[selves] awhile in the town of Ludlow; leaving their Standards and Banners in their battle directly against the field, [they] fled out of the town unarmed, with few persons, into Wales." Once out in the open countryside they split into two groups: York and Rutland made their way to Ireland through Wales, while Salisbury, Warwick, and March rode westward into Devon, where they managed to hire a small ship to cross the Channel and eventually return to Calais. When dawn broke the following day the Yorkist lines were still intact but there was no sign of the leaders.

The easy victory at Ludford Bridge was regarded by the Royalists as just revenge for Blore Heath. Not only had they seen off the Yorkist forces without striking a blow, but the opposition leadership had fled for their lives. True, York was in Dublin, where he enjoyed powerful local support, and Warwick and Salisbury were seemingly impregnable in Calais, but their cause had still suffered a grievous blow. Coming on top of earlier occasions when York had failed to impose himself on the king's will, the flight from his heartlands left him a lesser person, and it could be said that he never fully recovered from the decline.

Having seen off the Yorkist threat, Henry and his forces returned in triumph to Coventry, where a meeting of parliament was summoned for November 20. It was packed with the queen's supporters and in time came to be known as the "Parliament of Devils" as its main business was to deal with the Yorkist rebels and it quickly became apparent that they would see no mercy. A Bill of Attainder was produced on the opening day in which York and his main associates— Salisbury, Warwick, March, Rutland, the Bourchier brothers, Oldhall, and others—were declared traitors and their lands, honors, and titles were sentenced to forfeiture. Attainders and the sentence of attainting were reserved for members of the nobility found guilty of treason. It involved the forfeiture of title, bloodline, land, and fortune and for men like York and Warwick, it was a savage sentence. They had been stripped of all their offices, their estates and their incomes had been placed in the hands of receivers, their children had been disinherited, and, as a result, their families had been effectively ruined. For those who supported the king, it was a just outcome, as they believed that those who had been found guilty were also guilty of treason; but many more thought that the punishment was excessive and matched the retribution that had been handed down to the Duke of Gloucester in the previous decade.

The loss of possessions and honor was not the end of the matter. In return, the spoils were spread among Lancastrian supporters, and so it came about that York's fears were fully justified. His lands, name, and titles had been destroyed by his enemies. Somerset was declared Captain of Calais, but he could accept that appointment in name only as Warwick and his allies refused to hand over possession of the town to him. At the same time, Wiltshire was promoted to the lieutenancy of Ireland, but, again, that was in name only as the Irish parliament had promptly declared their support for York and supplied him with a retinue of archers. Even so, nominal decapitation and disinheritance were brutal sentences and York and his allies had paid dearly for their attempt to extricate the king from the queen's followers at court. From Calais, they issued the usual manifesto declaring their loyalty to the king and condemning their enemies at court for their misfortune, but it was only bravado.

As it proved to be impossible for Henry to lay hands on York in Dublin—before long the Irish parliament had passed legislation stating that any attempt on the lieutenant's life would be treated as treason—he turned his attention to Warwick in Calais. Somerset was determined to take possession of the colony: Not only would it give him considerable temporal powers—as "Christendom's finest captaincy" it provided wealth and a large standing garrison—but it had also belonged earlier to his father. Trollope's desertion at Ludford Bridge also suggested that Warwick might not be as secure as he thought himself to be and there might be an opportunity to convince others to turn against him. With Margaret's support, Somerset took an armed retinue across the Channel in December and demanded to be admitted into Calais so that he could take up his position. Unsurprisingly, the gates were closed against him and the garrison remained loyal to Warwick, leaving Somerset with no option but to retreat. To underline his superiority, at the beginning of 1460 Warwick then ordered an impudent raid on Sandwich to attack his rival's forces, and the raid, led by Sir John Dynham, brought about a spectacular coup by capturing Richard Woodville, Lord Rivers. He had been commissioned by the queen to lead a relief expedition to assist Somerset, but while he was asleep with his wife Jacquetta (the widow of the Duke of Bedford whom he had married in 1436, causing a huge scandal as she came from the nobility and he was of lower rank, being a Northamptonshire squire), Dynham's men captured them and took them back to Calais together with their son Anthony. Once they were safely inside the town, Rivers was hauled before the earls and given a sound dressing-down, not just because he supported the queen, but also because he was a man of humble birth who owed his nobility to his wife's position.

Along with Rivers, almost 300 Royalist troops went into captivity, and the daring sortie sparked fears of a French invasion. These were well grounded as Warwick had continued his dealings with Burgundy, who announced that he was entering into a new truce with the Yorkist faction.

Undeterred, Somerset raised a new army that included the professional soldiers under Trollope's command. Having arrived on French soil they captured the nearby, subsidiary castle at Guines within the Calais Pale, which gave them a base and a means of continuing operations against the main Calais garrison. Desultory fighting continued throughout the spring of 1460, but Somerset was unable to make any progress, and if anything, Warwick held all the advantages. A fresh relief expedition was mounted under John Touchet, the new Lord Audley, son of the Lancastrian leader killed at Blore Heath, but this too was a failure and young Audley was taken prisoner. Shortly afterward, he transferred his sympathies to the Yorkist cause. At the same time, the men inside Calais had not been idle. Building on the grievances that had been extant since Cade's rebellion ten years earlier, they magnified their propaganda campaign by sending letters and manifestos to possible supporters explaining the reasons for their disaffection and listing the problems that existed at Henry's court: the influence of the queen's party, the profligacy, the jobbery and corruption, the loss of France, and the enrichment of those who had the queen's ear. At the same time, they presented themselves as reformers and the preservers of good governance, men who were prepared to defend the birthrights of all loyal and decent Englishmen. All the while, they repeated the message that their loyalty to the king's person remained paramount and that their sole quarrel was with those who gave bad advice and turned Henry away from his rightful duties.

Their words fell on willing ears for the winter of 1459–1460 was one of huge discontent throughout England. The Yorkist uprising had unsettled people and there was a real sense of grievance against the court that was exacerbated by the decline in the economy. By taking Calais out of the financial equation, Warwick had forced the council to place an embargo on the wool trade, and this had made life difficult for England's wool traders, especially those living in London, where there was open hostility toward the court—another good reason for it continuing to be located in the Midlands. There were also fears of invasion, either by the French or by the Yorkists, or indeed both, and military preparations continued with the king's Master of Ordnance, John Judde, undertaking a nationwide survey of the state of the country's defenses. It did him no good personally: While returning to London before Christmas he was murdered by Yorkist sympathizers near St. Albans. The council issued new commissions of oyer and terminer to arrest known Yorkist supporters, heightening fears that a civil war was in the offing. All over England, men considered their options as they took heed of the message coming out of Calais. The Yorkists might have lost the advantage at Ludford Bridge, but against the odds they were slowly regaining support for their cause. In the spring, the people of Kent sent a message to Warwick and his fellow earls, "beseeching them that they would in all haste possible come and succour them from their enemies, promising that they would assist them with all their power."

In his role as propagandist, Warwick proved to be a masterful and persuasive influence, and he was also a good role model for York's son, Edward of March, who had decided to throw in his lot with the Calais garrison rather than follow his father and brother to Dublin. It turned out to be a sensible decision. Still a young man—he was only 17 during that first winter in Calais—Edward was free to follow his own pursuits and to learn from his powerful mentors. From the Staple merchants he became versed in commerce, and from taking part in the skirmishes against Somerset's forces he gained his first experience of fighting. A big man, well over six feet tall, he was open and affable in personality and according to a contemporary description, was of "a gentle nature and cheerful aspect." Edward was also something of a womanizer who was not above seducing other men's wives, or as Dominic Mancini, a visiting Italian diplomat, shrewdly put it in his account of his time in London, "he [Edward] pursued with no discrimination the married and the unmarried, the noble and the lowly." One of the ironies of William Paston's letter describing the scolding of Lord Rivers is that four years later, Edward was to be so besotted by his victim's daughter Elizabeth Woodville, that he would end up marrying her, despite being the daughter of a man he had "rated" for being a mere squire. By then, England had been plunged into its first civil war.

13

CIVIL WAR

S ome time in March 1460, a ship carrying Warwick slipped out of Calais
and made its way down the Channel before heading north for Waterford,
Ireland. Following the disastrous rout at Ludford Bridge and Warwick's
and York's imposed exiles in Ireland and Calais, respectively, they agreed to hold
a council of war to decide their next move. The fact that Warwick enjoyed command of the seas meant that he was able to travel unhindered and unobserved,
although by then, rumors were sweeping through England that both men were
intent on retrieving their positions. There is no record of what took place during
their meeting, but as it was followed a few months later by the invasion of
England, the two men must have agreed to a plan that would see the Calais
garrison cross to England to occupy Kent and London before York landed in the
north to rally support in his heartlands and in Wales.

From Yorkist spies in England they knew the extent of the people's discontent in Kent and realized that they could count on the support of a county that
had already suffered under Henry's rule in the wake of the Cade rebellion nine
years earlier. What was said about York's actual position with regard to the crown
is not clear, the party line seeming to be that they wanted to bring Henry under
their control and to reform his court but to stop short of actually deposing him.
Before the invasion took place, they increased their propaganda campaign especially in Kent, where they were already assured a warm welcome; later, Edward
of March recalled that when Warwick returned to Calais from Ireland he
brought with him "the greatest joy and consolation earthly." Their campaign
was given an added stimulus when the Royalist fleet under the command of the
Duke of Exeter failed to intercept Warwick during his return voyage and, worse,
its crews began voicing Yorkist sympathies. It was now a question not merely of
whether an invasion would take place but of when it would actually happen.

On June 26, Warwick and his supporters finally made their move, crossing over the Channel and landing at Sandwich with a force of some 2,000 men under the tactical command of experienced soldiers such as Dynham, Sir John Wenlock, and William Neville, Lord Fauconberg, Warwick's uncle. Wenlock was one of the most intriguing personalities of the period: A Bedfordshire landowner, he had served Margaret of Anjou and had fought for Henry VI at the First Battle of St. Albans, but his growing friendship with Warwick encouraged him to transfer his loyalties to the Yorkists. (As we shall see, it was not the only occasion when he changed sets.) The invaders received a warm welcome not just from the people of Sandwich but also from the inhabitants of the other Cinque Ports (a confederation of five channel ports: Hastings, Romney, Hythe, Dover, and Sandwich). From the coast, they made their way to Canterbury to receive the blessing of the archbishop, Thomas Bourchier, who had decided to forsake the queen's party and throw in his lot with Warwick's faction.

After leaving Canterbury, Warwick and his retinue made their way to London by way of Rochester and Dartford, and as they rode through Kent, they picked up more supporters. Inside the capital there was an anxious debate about what should be done when Warwick arrived. Initially, the authorities wanted to close the gates against the rebels and sent a message to that effect, but such was Warwick's influence among the mercantile community that the decision was overturned and on July 2 the Yorkist army entered the city in triumph. As for the Royalist garrison that was in the hands of several eminent Lancastrians including Lord Hungerford (whose grandfather had been an executor of Henry V's will), they wisely took refuge in the Tower under the protection of Lord Scales, an experienced veteran of the wars in France. From his secure position, Scales was able to deploy his artillery. However, despite firing his weapons as the Yorkists entered the city, he succeeded only in killing people in the streets and setting fire to their houses with "wildfire," a highly combustible substance similar to napalm. The following day, Warwick summoned a convocation in St. Paul's Cathedral where the leaders of the revolt swore solemn oaths on the cross of Canterbury declaring their loyalty to the king and repeating their threat to end the misrule of the country and punish those responsible for it. They also insisted that they wanted the accusations against them to be lifted and to have their good reputations restored.

The arrival of the Yorkists in London threw the Royalists into a quandary, because they had anticipated that the invasion would come from Ireland through Wales and they were unwilling to make any move that might compromise their position in the northwest. Warwick made up their minds for them by moving the bulk of his forces north towards Coventry. On July 5, Fauconberg left London at the head of an army of some 10,000 men, followed by another force under

Warwick, leaving Salisbury to lay siege to the Tower. Progress was slow due to the size of the armies involved and to the poor weather conditions, it being an unseasonably wet summer. To Henry's credit, he did not flunk the challenge facing him and refused to go into hiding in the Isle of Ely in the depths of the Fens as had been suggested by his supporters. Instead he rejected that advice and calmly donned his armor, setting out at the head of his army to confront those who were challenging his Royal authority.

The two armies met in open country on July 10, outside Northampton between Delapre Abbey and the village of Hardingstone. The Royalist army had been the first to arrive and had used the opportunity to dig a series of defensive ditches guarded by staked fences and several cannon. The army was drawn up in three battles with the swollen waters of the River Nene behind them, rain was falling heavily, and Buckingham the senior Lancastrian commander was keen to get his smaller force into action as soon as possible and certainly within hours of the arrival of the Yorkist army. Warwick, on the other hand, preferred to take his time as his men had been on the march for several hours and they were footsore and soaking wet. However, the armies had to go through the formalities of parley and negotiation before any blow could be struck. This turned out to be a long-winded business as Warwick did his best to gain permission to be allowed to address the king directly. First he sent a delegation consisting of Richard Beauchamp, the Bishop of Salisbury, and other clerics with a request for the king to hear the Yorkists' complaints, but this was dismissed out of hand. Standing beside the king, Buckingham simply retorted that if Warwick came into the king's presence he would be killed and, for good measure, added that the bishop was not a man of God but a man of war and would have to face the consequences of supporting the Yorkist cause. Further attempts were made by York's supporters to arrange a meeting between the king and Warwick, but by early afternoon, these too had failed and a battle became inevitable.

Warwick had drawn up his army in the traditional manner: three formations known as battles commanded by himself in the center, Fauconberg on the left, and March on the right. Before giving the order to advance, Warwick made it clear that his army was to be selective in its killing when it engaged the opposition, "that no people should lay hand upon the king nor on the common people, but only on the lords, knights and squires." Shortly after 2 PM, he ordered the trumpets to sound and the Yorkist army moved slowly forward to engage their well-defended opponents. At this point in the battle, even before the men got to sword point, the Royalists were as good as beaten. Not only had the rain made their cannon useless, but before the battle began, March had received a message from his direct opponent on the king's right, Lord Grey of Ruthin, that he would change sides and allow the Yorkist left to advance into his ranks. Grey was a wealthy and rapacious landowner who had answered the queen's call for support and had played a leading role in her party. For reasons that are shadowy but may have involved a quarrel over property—his father had engaged in similar disputes with Owen Glendower earlier in the century—he decided to switch his allegiance to the Yorkists. Three years later, he received his thanks when he was appointed treasurer. To the horrified astonishment of the Royalist forces, Grey's men pushed over the defenses and started helping the advancing Yorkists climb over the barricades. What had been a secure defensive system became a deathtrap; once inside the trench system March's men started cutting down their opponents, and as panic set in, the survivors did their best to get out of the killing ground. Many were drowned in the Nene as they tried to cross it. The actual combat phase of the battle lasted little more than half an hour, and as had happened at St. Albans, the final stages were marked by the butchery of anyone wearing the armor and colors of the nobility. Among the estimated 400 casualties were Buckingham, Shrewsbury, and Lords Egremont and Beaumont, the latter being Constable of England. The king was quickly apprehended and led away from the battlefield to the safety of his tent, where Warwick, Fauconberg, and March greeted him and asked for his forgiveness, all the while protesting their loyalty to his person.

No doubt they were being sincere. All the records from the period insist that they were acting in the king's best interests as "true liegemen," but the fact remains that they were the masters of the field and that Henry was in their hands and powerless to act. The one person capable of saving him was his wife, who had spent the day at nearby Eccleshall Castle waiting for the outcome of the fighting, but she was while there it had quickly become apparent that her cause was hopeless. She had lost the support of the Royalist forces including four of its leading commanders, and, in the wake of the battle, others made good their escape or in some cases switched sides and threw in their lot with the Royalists. Suddenly Margaret and her son were in danger of being apprehended or worse, and she had to act quickly. With a small retinue, she set off for Harlech Castle in Wales, the seat of her step-brother-in-law Jasper Tudor, Earl of Pembroke. Her escape was not without incident. At one point, one of servants, John Cleger, tried to rob her and she only managed to escape his clutches thanks to the intervention of a young attendant who led her to the safety of Harlech. Even then, she was not completely secure, and Pembroke took her north to the castle at Denbigh in the Vale of Clwyd, deep in the heart of Lancastrian territory. There she was joined by Exeter and set about rallying support among those magnates who remained loyal to her and the king. For the rest of the year, she remained in the security of north Wales, where Pembroke began recruiting reinforcements for the Royalists in the name of the infant Prince of Wales.

Meanwhile, the king had been taken back to London, where Salisbury had succeeded in ending the resistance of the Tower's garrison by starving them into submission and using heavy cannon to break down the outer defenses. Scales, who had expected to hold out until a Royalist army reached London, tried to escape but was recognized as he attempted to get into a boat and was murdered by an angry mob. The end of the siege marked the final defeat of the extant Royalist forces, and when Henry arrived in London on July 10, he was truly in the hands of the Yorkists. With a rapidity and decisiveness conferred by their positions as victors, the Yorkists set about making their own appointments to the principal offices of state—Warwick rewarded his brother George Neville, Bishop of Exeter, with the position of chancellor, and Thomas Bourchier was made treasurer. Parliament was summoned with the intention of canceling the Acts of Attainder, and the Duchess of York was released from her house arrest to return to London, where she took up residence first at Sir John Fastolff's house in Southwark and then at Baynard's Castle, her husband's townhouse on the Thames.

All along, York had been party to the plans of the Calais earls, but his entrance into the proceedings is clouded in some mystery. There was never any doubt that he would return to England or that he would time his journey to coincide with the reopening of parliament in October, but it is not clear if he had pretensions to seize the throne before he set out. At any rate, he left Dublin in the first week of September, some two months after the Battle of Northampton, and landed at Chester on September 9. From there he set out for London, and at some stage in his leisurely progress south, he had his arms emblazoned with the Royal arms and trumpeters announced his progress as he made his way toward the capital. His timing was also immaculate. Unwilling to meet his coconspirators in advance, he arrived in London on October 10, three days after parliament had assembled, and from the outset, he made it clear that he was a changed man. York had no intention of taking up his old position as protector; this time he wanted the crown and the manner of his arrival made that intention perfectly clear. Gone was any false humility, and in the words of the Abbot of St. Albans who was an eyewitness, in its place was "great pomp and splendour, and no little exaltation of spirit" as trumpets sounded and York's drawn sword of state was carried aloft before him as he made his way to Westminster:

> And there entering the palace he went straight through the great hall until he came to the usual room, where the king, with the commons, was accustomed to

hold his parliament. And coming there he walked straight on until he came to the king's throne, upon the covering or cushion of laying his hand, in this very act like a man about to take possession of his right, he held it upon it for a short time. But at length withdrawing it, he turned to the people standing quietly under the canopy of Royal state, he looked eagerly for their applause.

None came. By making the symbolic gesture of laying his hand on the empty throne, York was staking his claim to the crown of England and he fully expected to receive the backing of those present. But instead of acclaim, there was an embarrassed silence that York had to break by announcing that he challenged the right of Henry to rule the country and that he intended to be crowned king at the month's end. His argument carried strength—through his mother, he was descended from Edward III's second son and was senior to Henry, who descended from the third son—but the claim was made in the wrong place and at the wrong time. While it is true that his supporters had won a great victory over the Royalists at Northampton and had Henry in their power, it is also true that they had predicated their success on remaining loyal to the king's person. Given the sacred nature of sworn fealty to an anointed king, they could hardly break their word without forfeiting their honor. As a result, history did not repeat itself: Sixty years earlier, in 1399, Henry Bolingbroke had returned to England and had dissimulated to his supporters before grabbing the throne in similar circumstances. However, this time there was to be no repetition, either because the magnates did not support York wholeheartedly or because they were unwilling to unseat Henry, for all that he had shown himself to be a feckless ruler. Either way, having defied and challenged Henry on five earlier occasions, when the main chance of winning the throne had come tantalizingly close, York was unable to grasp it and was left with his dreams unfulfilled.

Thomas Bourchier, the Archbishop of Canterbury, broke the spell by suggesting that York should place his claim before the king as the highest authority in the country, but this only brought the angry retort, "I do not recall that I know anyone within the kingdom whom it would not befit to come sooner to me and see me rather than I should go and visit him." Despite those hot words, York did do as the archbishop suggested and confronted Henry in his chamber. Under the circumstances, the king was surprisingly calm: He refuted the claim and suggested that it should be taken to the Lords for their consideration. "My father was king; his father was king; I have worn the crown for forty years from the cradle," he told the assembled peers. "You have all sworn fealty to me as your sovereign, and your fathers did the like to my fathers. How then can my right be disputed?" What followed next was like a child's game of pass-the-parcel as each

section of the establishment did their best to avoid coming to any decision to respond to York's demand to succeed to the throne. On October 16, York presented his claim in writing and handed it to the chancellor, the Bishop of Exeter, who then passed it to the Lords. The Parliament Roll that describes what took place recorded that the Lords hedged their bets by replying: "In as much as every person high and low, suing to this high Court of Parliament, of right must be heard, and his desire and petition understand that the said writing should be read and heard, not to be answered without the King's commandment for so much as the matter is so, and of so great weight and poise . . ." Unable to find a solution, the Lords passed the claim to the king's justices, but they too refused to come to any conclusion, arguing that "the matter was so high and touched the king's estate and regalie, which is above the law and passed their learning, whereof they durst not enter into any communication thereof . . ."

Forced to fall back on their own devices, the Lords debated the issue again, this time in closed session, and rather than reach any definitive conclusion, they produced a list of objections that pointed out the impossibility of accepting York's claim. First and foremost, the Lancastrian line had produced three kings since 1399, all had been anointed, with all the mystical and religious connotations surrounding the ceremony, and the nobility, including York, had sworn oaths of allegiance to all three of those monarchs. Any change to the status quo would invalidate all legislation passed in their reigns, and that would cause chaos. There was also a question of interpretation: York was basing his claim on his mother's line to the Duke of Clarence, Edward III's second surviving son, and this was thought to be an innovation as previously his descent had been traced from his father's line—the Earl of Cambridge—back to Edmund of Langley, Edward III's fourth son. The result of their deliberations was a compromise— the passing of an Act of Accord that kept Henry as king but passed the succession to York and his heirs. On November 8, York was proclaimed heir to the throne and once again he became Protector of England; the lords swore allegiance to him, and he swore allegiance to Henry.

Despite the fact that his claim had not been accepted and, indeed, had caused a great deal of dismay among his own supporters, York was in a stronger position than he could possibly have anticipated before he made his dramatic intervention earlier in the year. His enemies at court had been defeated and scattered, the sentences on him had been lifted, and even though it was highly improbable that he would sit on the English throne, that right would pass to his son Edward of March. The result helped to calm the passions that had been running high in London in the wake of York's announcement of his claim. It also restored a degree of equanimity in his relationship with Warwick, who had not been best pleased by his coconspirator's sudden and intemperate announcement. He had already made his displeasure felt when the two men met at Westminster shortly after York had made his initial claim, using "hard words" to castigate his ally for his recklessness in making the bid. Warwick was in a difficult position. He could have supported York's bid and may even have hinted that he would do so when the two men had met earlier in Ireland, but at the end of the successful crushing of the Royalists at Northampton, he had renewed his oaths of allegiance to Henry, as had Salisbury and March. Having done so, any move against Henry would have been treasonable.

One other party was left dissatisfied with the outcome—Margaret of Anjou, who saw her son Edward disinherited from what she considered his rightful legacy. Not being the kind of person to accept such an unwelcome turnaround without protest, she immediately started planning to confront and defeat the family that had usurped her son. Immediately upon hearing the news from London, she began summoning her supporters and their armed retainers to create a new army, and she pointedly ignored demands from her husband to return to London. Among those she counted on were her natural supporters, Somerset, Pembroke, Northumberland, Devon, and Wiltshire, and with them came a number of experienced captains, all of whom promised to bring armed retinues to the gathering place at Pontefract Castle in Yorkshire, where they would be well placed to lay waste the lands of York and Salisbury. According to Gregory, "all these people were gathered and conveyed so privily that they were whole in number of 15,000 ere any man would believe it." Once again the country was hovering on the brink of a fresh round of civil strife, but this time there was a subtle difference. With the passing of the Act of Accord, the struggle had become dynastic. Margaret was fighting for her son's right to succeed to the throne of England, and York would be forced to respond to defend his own family's claim to be the king's rightful heirs. As for Henry, he had been sidelined and his own future would depend on the outcome of the next round of internecine fighting.

Margaret had taken one other step to strengthen her position. From north Wales she had sailed to Dumfries in southwest Scotland, and during the new year, she was ensconced in nearby Lincluden Abbey with the queen dowager Mary of Gueldres, the recently widowed queen of James II. Together with the young heir James III, a boy of nine, the two queens spent almost a fortnight discussing ways in which Scotland could offer military support to the Lancastrian cause. Money was out of the question as Scotland was never a wealthy country, but men and arms would be made available to Margaret. There was a price: In return for Scottish help, the strategically important east-coast port town of Berwick-on-Tweed would be ceded to the Scots and Prince Edward would marry one of Mary of Gueldres's daughters. Protected by a force of Scottish soldiers led by the Earl of Angus, who had been promised that his men would be paid by way of booty gained in England, Margaret set out across the border in the middle of January 1461 to join up with her forces in Yorkshire.

By then, the news of the Lancastrians' preparations could not be kept secret, and shortly before Christmas, York left London for the north with Salisbury and Rutland, taking with them a force of around 5,000 soldiers. After encountering some of Somerset's men near Worksop in Nottinghamshire, they made for York's castle at Sandal near Wakefield, where they spent Christmas in comfort and safety. Their plan was to sit tight while March built up his forces in the Yorkist heartlands in Staffordshire, Shropshire, and Herefordshire, but for some reason York decided to do battle with the Lancastrian forces that had been building in strength ten miles away at Pontefract. Why he took this uncharacteristically rash course is far from clear. Perhaps he felt sufficiently secure and had underestimated the size of the opposing forces—later there were suggestions of treachery, with accusations that the Lancastrians had disguised some of their men as Yorkists in the colors of Warwick. Perhaps he felt under threat and needed to act to safeguard his position. During the Christmastide period, a local truce had been arranged to run until the Feast of Epiphany (January 6), but this had not stopped the Lancastrians from attacking Yorkist soldiers, whose appearance outside the castle seemed to suggest that food was in short supply within Sandal and that York would be unable to hold out for very much longer. In other words, the Yorkists thought that those opposing them were smaller in number than they really were, while the Lancastrians knew that they held the upper hand and that the garrison inside Sandal Castle had to forage for food and fuel.

Whatever the reason for York's decision, it proved to be a costly mistake. On December 30, a force led by Somerset appeared outside Sandal Castle and York and Salisbury led their men out to attack it. They were not to know that on the advice of the professional soldier Andrew Trollope, two flanking battles led by Wiltshire and Lord Roos, a veteran of the French wars, had been concealed in nearby woodland awaiting their opportunity to join the fray. At first the Yorkists seemed to have the upper hand as they joined battle on the open ground of Wakefield Green, south of the River Calder, but, too late, they realized they were in a trap when a fresh attack came in from the flanks. What happened next on that freezing cold and darkening winter's day was all too typical of combat of the period. Ordinary foot soldiers were spared and allowed to leave the battlefield, but for the nobility, there was no mercy. York was dragged from his horse and killed, as was his son Rutland, who was intercepted by Lord Clifford as he attempted to escape. Clifford's words as he dispatched the 17-year-old boy have the authentic ring of a civil war: "By God's blood, thy father slew mine! So will I slay the accursed blood of York!" Others cut down included Salisbury's son, Thomas Neville, a son of Lord Bourchier, and a sizable number of Yorkist knights. Exact numbers are difficult to compute, but Benet claims that after the battle, Wakefield Green was thick with corpses; many men who survived the fighting but were wounded died later in the intense cold. It was a bad defeat for the Yorkist cause. One of those taken prisoner was Salisbury, who was led off to Pontefract Castle where he was promptly executed. It was an ugly end for one of England's most powerful magnates, but his life was probably forfeit anyway and it left his son Warwick the most powerful man in England. Then in an equally repulsive piece of spite, Clifford took Salisbury's head together with the decapitated heads of York and Rutland that had been retrieved from the battlefield and had them placed on spikes above the Micklegate Bar in York. To add further insult, a paper crown was placed on York's head to mock his pretensions to the throne of England.

This unexpected victory at Wakefield returned the initiative to the Lancastrians. They had defeated a Yorkist force and killed two of the faction's leading personalities; they also had superior numbers at their disposal and, bolstered by their Scottish allies, were in a good position to march on London, where Warwick was nervously trying to gather up reinforcements from Essex and East Anglia. At the same time, March was busily building up his forces at Ludlow in his family's home territory, where he was joined by local Yorkist landowners and supporters such as Sir William Herbert, Sir John Wenlock, and Sir Walter Devereux, all tried and tested soldiers. His immediate instinct would have been to march north to avenge his father or to return to London through Gloucestershire, but when he received information regarding the whereabouts of a large Lancastrian army led by the Earls of Pembroke and Wiltshire that was making its way through the Midlands to join Queen Margaret, he decided to engage it first. It was a good decision. March's force included a large number of English and Welsh archers, they were ably led by experienced soldiers, and he and his supporters would be fighting to defend their own territory. Against them the Lancastrian force was about the same size, around 4,000 men, but many of them were French, Breton, and Irish mercenaries whose professionalism and loyalty to the cause were dubious. One other factor gave Edward hope: When the two armies met at Mortimer's Cross between Ludlow and Leominster on February 2, Candlemas Day, they were confronted by a curious meteorological phenomenon called parhelion or mock sun that appears in winter skies when light refracted through ice crystals in the atmosphere produces an apparition that suggests several suns rising through the frosty air. To the terrified Yorkist soldiers, it seemed to be a terrible portent, but Edward took advantage of the imposing spectacle and the awe it created by declaring: "Beeth of good comfort, and dreadeth not. This is a good sign, for these three suns betoken the Father, the Son and the Holy Ghost, and therefore let us have a good heart, and in the name of Almighty God go we against our enemies." At that, his men sank to their knees in prayer in preparation for the ensuing battle, heartened by the apparition of "the sun in splendour," a vision so marvelous that Edward later used its imagery for one of his family badges.

Edward had drawn up his army between rising ground and the nearby River Lugg to the south of Wigmore Castle. They were arrayed in their usual three battle formations with the archers in front, ready to meet the Lancastrian attack from the west as Pembroke's forces started advancing across the frozen ground toward the Yorkist lines. As they did so, Edward's archers went into action firing heavy volleys at the advancing foot soldiers, most of whom lacked suitable protection from the arrow storm. As the Lancastrian lines began to thin out under the onslaught, Edward ordered his right flank to charge and the shape of the battle began to change. Slowly but inevitably, the Lancastrian lines began to collapse and the advancing Yorkists were able to wrap them up against the banks of the River Lugg. The end was not long in coming. In common with many other battles fought during this period, the actual details of the fighting are scarce, but it seems that the combat phase lasted about half an hour and ended in the rout of Pembroke's forces. Soon men were running or riding for their lives, hotly pursued by the Yorkist knights who kept up the pursuit as far as Hereford. The battle was known as Mortimer's Cross and it produced the bloodiest fighting of the war to date: Unlike previous battles at which the common soldiers were spared and the knights slaughtered, Edward's men did not hold back in their hour of victory. Some 4,000 Lancastrians were supposed to have been killed on that cold winter's day in the Yorkist heartlands. Most of them were Welshmen in Pembroke's service.

Those who managed to escape included Pembroke and Wiltshire, but it was not the end of the bloodletting. Among those taken prisoner was old Owen Tudor, husband of Queen Katharine and father to Pembroke, but even his Royal connections and his venerable age could not save him. He was stepfather to Henry VI, albeit never having had any official role in the boy's upbringing, and Edward was intent on avenging his own father who had fallen at Wakefield. Tudor was sentenced to die along with a number of other captured Lancastrian knights, but, according to *Gregory's Chronicle*, the old man did not fully realize that he was about to meet his end until he saw the actual ax and his doublet was ripped off prior to his execution in the marketplace at Hereford. "Then he said: 'That head shall lie on the stock that was wont to lie on Queen Katherine's lap,' and put his heart and mind wholly unto God and fully meekly took his death."

The execution of prisoners was commonplace throughout the conflict and they followed a pattern that is all too familiar in civil wars. Fathers' deaths were avenged by sons and vice versa, and the opposing families rarely lost an opportunity to take revenge on men who had killed their own people in earlier battles or skirmishes. Being Pembroke's father, Tudor's life was probably forfeit, but his execution was also a reprisal for the deaths and executions at Wakefield. Suddenly the war was getting more barbaric as opponents brought personal animus with them onto the battlefield.

The conflict was also spreading and involving greater numbers of soldiers. More were killed at Mortimer's Cross than had fallen at the three earlier battles combined, and across England there was growing fear about the size of the armies that were marching and countermarching across the length and breadth of the country to do battle. Of particular concern to many people was the creation of the huge Lancastrian army in the north of England that contained large numbers of Scots among its number and that would soon be making its way south. To most Englishmen, the Scots were a barbaric northern race known only for their depredations in raiding into the northern English Marches; they were an alien species, unknown and unknowable, violent and undisciplined, and although the English knew little about them, what they did know made them mightily afraid:

> The duke [York] being thus removed from this world, the northmen, being sensible that the only impediment was now withdrawn, and that there was no one now who would care to resist their inroads, again swept onwards like a whirlwind from the north, and in the impulse of their fury attempted to over-run the whole of England. At this period too, fancying that every thing tended to insure them freedom from molestation, paupers and beggars flocked forth from those quarters in infinite numbers, just like so many mice rushing forth from their holes, and universally devoted themselves to spoil and rapine, without regard of place or person. For, besides the vast quantities of property which they collected outside, they also irreverently rushed, in their unbridled and frantic rage, into churches and other sanctuaries of God, and most nefariously plundered them of their chalices, books and vestment, and, unutterable crime! Broke open the pixes in which were kept the body of Christ and shook out the sacred elements therefrom. When the priests and the other faithful of Christ in any way offered to make resistance, like so many abandoned wretches as they were, they cruelly slaughtered them in the very churches and churchyard.

That description appeared in a document known as the *Croyland* (or Crowland) *Chronicle*, the single most important source for the period. It exists in several parts or "continuations," written for the years between 656 and 1486, and the originator was supposed to be Ingulph (or Ingulf), abbot of the Benedictine Abbey of Croyland in Lincolnshire and secretary to William the Conqueror. He died in 1109 and the work was subsequently found to be a forgery, but the Second Continuation that covers the years 1459 to 1486 is a reasonably reliable guide to the reigns of Edward IV and Richard III. A marginal note describes the author as a doctor of canon law and a member of the Royal council who took part in an embassy to Burgundy in 1471; this was probably Bishop John Russell, who served as keeper of the privy seal to Edward IV and chancellor to Richard III. As a senior Royal servant, his eyewitness accounts of key events clearly gave him an authority that makes the chronicle both absorbing and credible.

Although in this case, the Croyland chronicler exaggerated the extent of the violence unleashed by the Scots, he reflected the growing concerns of many people who feared that they would be caught up in the fighting. And they had good reason to feel that way. Large numbers of men in Margaret's army, mainly the Scots, were not receiving any pay, and as they made their way southward through England they were counting on plunder to give them some compensation for their service. As happens so often in civil conflicts of this kind, the fighting between the rival houses of York and Lancaster turned the world upside down, with normally law-abiding sober young men becoming foul-mouthed soldiers who felt no shame in plundering, pillaging, and raping.

14

The Battle Continues

ortimer's Cross was a declaration: In battle, both sides would now fight to the last man to press home their advantage and there would be little sympathy for those on the losing side. As the Lancastrian army made its way south through the East Midlands heading toward London, it left behind a huge amount of destruction as soldiers made sure that they had food and shelter and that their horses received forage and water, whatever the cost to the local population. While Queen Margaret's army was making its southern progression, Warwick had assembled his forces and on February 12 had marched north out of London to meet the opposition, taking with him the captive king. With the structure imposed by the main north–south routes in middle England, it was unavoidable perhaps that the two rival armies would clash once again in the vicinity of the town of St. Albans. By this stage, the Yorkists had attracted additional numbers of the nobility to their ranks, and the Dukes of Norfolk and Suffolk, the Earl of Arundel, and Lords Bourchier and Bonville rode with Warwick. Warwick also had the assistance of a number of veteran soldiers from the French wars, notably Sir Thomas Kyriell, commander of the English forces at Formigny ten years earlier, as well as 500 Burgundian mercenaries, the majority of them archers. However, a lack of urgency in the Yorkist planning meant that March's army was still slowly making its way from the west, picking up supporters as it moved through Gloucestershire.

Both armies were more or less evenly matched. Gregory claims that Warwick had 100,000 under his command, but this was a gross exaggeration and it is probable that he only had ten percent of that number. The Lancastrian army was under Somerset's control, and those who accompanied him all owed their loyalty to the queen and represented the flower of England's aristocracy—Exeter, Devon, Shrewsbury, and Northumberland. Also riding with them were Lords Clifford and Roos, both powerful Lancastrian supporters, and the army also had the expertise of the professional soldier Trollope, who commanded the vanguard. One of the problems faced by Somerset was the undisciplined Scottish contingent. As they moved further south, the Scots began to worry about the distance that was growing between them and their homeland, not least because after a time they were weighed down with plunder. Showing more concern for their well-being than for the claims of the Lancastrian cause, they began slipping away and headed back north as the main part of the army approached St. Albans.

As Warwick approached St. Albans from the south, he had little clear idea of the opposition's dispositions: Instead of making toward Ware and Waltham, the Lancastrian army had moved further west and was heading toward Dunstable. To counter the move, Warwick decided in the first instance to deploy some of his men, mainly archers, in defensive positions inside St. Albans, while the main bulk of his army was spread out to the north along a four-mile stretch of road that led to Normansland Common. Having arrived earlier than the opposition army, Warwick used his time to good effect by constructing defenses that included caltraps, specially constructed nets made of cord and arrayed with sharpened points laid on the ground to deter cavalry. Warwick's army was also defended by pavises, wooden barricades with spikes, and had a limited number of artillery pieces; some of his Burgundians were equipped with primitive matchlock handguns, similar to the harquebus, which fired lead pellets and in some cases iron arrows. It was the first time that weapons of this kind had been seen in England. Warwick's tactics were guided by a number of circumstances— his lack of accurate intelligence, the composition of his army, many of whom were raw and frightened recruits, and the requirement to protect St. Albans from attack. This latter need was paramount in his mind as the town guarded the route to London, but by splitting his forces and deploying them over a large swath of ground, he ran the risk of overstretching his army and leaving its defenses spread out over uncertain ground. Not knowing the exact whereabouts of the Lancastrian forces also hindered him, and, as it turned out, he was surprised by their next move. From Dunstable, Somerset had taken his forces eastward along the old Roman road, Watling Street, and this change of direction meant that they approached St. Albans from the west with the River Ver on their right flank. As they had marched by night—an unusual maneuver in those days—they took the Yorkist archers by surprise and, in the first phase of the battle on February 17, were able to enter the town through the gate on Fishpool Street and press on over the Tonman Ditch.

As dawn began to break, the Yorkists quickly regrouped and unleashed heavy fire on the attacking force from their positions in the Market Place inside the town. The concentrated fire forced the Lancastrians to retreat across the river, where they regrouped and held a council of war to decide their next move. It was at this point in the battle that Trollope used his military experience to good effect. Having discovered from his scouts that Catherine Street was unguarded, he ordered a pincer movement to outflank the defenders who had grouped in St. Peter's Street. This was effected by the vanguard, with one group entering Fishpool Street while another skirted the Tonman Ditch along Branch Road, Verulam Road, Folly Lane, and Catherine Street. Both forces then entered St. Peter's Street to outflank and outnumber the Yorkists, who had no option but to begin withdrawing to the north toward the bulk of their army on Bernard's Heath. Despite encountering fierce resistance, Trollope's inspired move allowed the Lancastrians to overrun the town center following fierce hand-to-hand fighting in the narrow streets. Both sides suffered heavy casualties.

While Trollope's vanguard was engaged with the Yorkist archers, the rest of the Lancastrian force moved round the town and began attacking Warwick's scattered ranks on Bernard's Heath, where his brother, Lord Montague, was attempting to realign his defensive positions to meet the new threat. Eventually he got his men into a rough-and-ready defensive posture along the Harpenden and Sandridge roads, but already the battle was slipping out of his hands. The carefully positioned caltraps and pervises failed to halt the Lancastrian cavalry, and as snow began swirling, from the surrounding higher ground the artillery and handguns began to malfunction. Some refused to fire because the powder had become damp, while others misfired or exploded, killing the gunners. As Montague's division came under heavy attack he sent a desperate message to his commander requesting help, but there was an unexplained delay and Warwick received intelligence about the attack on his brother's outnumbered forces too late. There was then a further delay as Warwick attempted to bring his horsemen to the rescue, but this took time and time was not on the Yorkists' side. Even at that stage, Warwick's intervention could have been decisive, but the narrow lanes and high hedgerows hindered his progress, and by the time he reached a position known as Dead Woman's Hill, Montague had been captured and the survivors were beginning to stream away from the field as darkness fell. With little option but retreat, Warwick rallied those around him and set off westward for Chipping Norton, where he hoped to meet up with March. Around 1,000 lay dead on the field, most of them Yorkists, but unlike earlier battles, they were mainly archers and men-at-arms. The only nobleman of any note killed was the commander of the Lancastrian cavalry, Sir John Grey of Groby, who left a strikingly attractive widow, Elizabeth Woodville, the daughter of Lord Rivers and his wife Jacquetta. Within three years she would be destined to play a decisive role in the fortunes of the Yorkist cause.

Throughout the battle, Trollope, who handled his men well and grasped the advantage when it was presented to him, had outwitted Warwick. His pincer movement unseated the Yorkists in St. Albans and allowed him to bring the full weight of his attack onto Montague's smaller division strung out to the north of the town. Treachery also played a part in the Lancastrian victory. Inevitably, in a civil conflict of this kind where some loyalties will always be of the fair-weather variety, there were men who were only interested in themselves and were prepared to play fast and loose with their allegiances to superior commanders. One such was Henry Lovelace, steward of Warwick's household, who started the day in the Yorkist camp and ended it by serving the Lancastrian cause. His story is all too typical of this kind of behavior. Earlier in the conflict Lovelace had enjoyed Warwick's patronage and, being an experienced soldier, had been given command of the Yorkist vanguard. At Wakefield, he had been taken prisoner and was about to be executed when Queen Margaret decided to spare him if he changed his allegiance. This he did in return for a promise that he would be made Earl of Kent, and as a result of changing sides he and his men were part of the Lancastrian force that marched south. At Luton, either through treachery or as part of a grander design, which only he knew, he changed sides once more and rejoined the Yorkist forces. It was not his last about-turn. As it became clear that Montague was unable to withstand Trollope's attack, Lovelace cannily crossed back to the Lancastrian side, leaving a huge hole in the Yorkist defenses. As a hired hand Lovelace had no particular loyalties other than a need to better himself at the expense of the highest bidder, not unlike the earlier turncoat at Northampton, Lord Grey of Ruthin, who had used the conflict to further his own ends.

With the Lancastrians masters of the field the way was now open to march on London, but first the victorious commanders had to deal with the aftermath of battle. Astonishingly, Henry was found sitting under an oak tree from where he had watched the battle and its outcome, laughing and singing all the while, according to a report to the French court. He was under the personal guard of Lord Bonville and Sir Thomas Kyriell. Both were men of honor who had been charged by Warwick with carrying out the task of ensuring the king's safety during the battle and both had carried it out without demur. Under the circumstances, they had good reason to believe that their lives were not in jeopardy, but they too faced the rough justice prevalent at the time. On the following day after a number of leading Lancastrian captains, including Trollope, had been knighted by the seven-year-old Prince of Wales, Bonville and Kyriell were dragged in front of the court. Before the king could say anything—earlier he had promised to save their lives—Margaret turned to her son and asked what should be done with the two men; "Let them have their heads taken off," was the boy's cool reply, to which Bonville angrily responded: "May God destroy those who taught thee this manner of speech!" Both were taken outside and beheaded without further ado.

For the people of London the news of the Lancastrian victory at St. Albans was the worst possible outcome for them. It was from the capital that Warwick had taken his armies north, and as he was a firm favorite with the merchant community, they feared that Margaret would now take her revenge. To offset the danger, the Lord Mayor wrote an ingratiating letter to the king and queen insisting that he had remained loyal and begging them not to bring their army into the capital. By way of reply, Margaret sent a delegation consisting of the Duchesses of Bedford and Buckingham to reassure the people of London that she had no intention of occupying their city and that for the time being, they were safe. This opened the way for the king and queen to return to their capital, a move that the mayor and his aldermen were prepared to support, even though it would be unpopular with the bulk of the citizens. Years of misrule had put the House of Lancaster out of favor, and Margaret was especially disliked on account of her open disdain for London and its people. (Being French did not help her cause either.) At the same time, the Londoners were afraid of what might happen in the immediate future and certainly did not want armed troops entering their city. Some Lancastrian forces had already made their way toward London and were demanding entrance, a move that so alarmed Cicely, the Dowager Duchess of York, that she sent her younger sons to France to be put under the protection of Duke Philip of Burgundy.

All this indecisiveness sealed the Lancastrians' fate. If they had marched on London immediately, they would have had no difficulty securing the Tower with its strategic assets, and in so doing they would have prevented Warwick from returning to a city he regarded as a vital power base. The queen's protracted negotiations prevented any quick solution. While the parley was being strung out, Warwick had joined up with March and their forces were rapidly advancing on London. That changed everything. Rather than encourage a new battle with fresh forces and at a time when their own army had been weakened by the Scottish desertions, the Lancastrians decided to pull back toward Dunstable as a preamble to returning to their main area of support in the Midlands. While the move probably reassured the people of London, it also passed the advantage back to the Yorkists. March and Warwick now had London at their mercy, and when they made their move into the capital they were greeted with an acclaim the chronicler Robert Fabyan described as a prelude to greater things to come:

> And upon the Thursday [March 27, 1461] following the Earls of March and Warwick with a great power of men, but few of name, entered into the City of London, the which was of the citizens joyously received, and upon the Sunday following the said earl caused to be mustered his people in St John's Field, where unto that host were proclaimed and shewed certain articles and points that King Henry had offended in, whereupon it was demanded of the said people whether the said Henry were worthy to reign as king any longer or no. Whereunto the people cried hugely and said Nay, Nay. And after it was asked of them whether they would have the Earl of March for their king and they cried with one voice, Yea, Yea.

This time the Yorkists were taking no chances. Fabyan's chronicle makes it clear that the people of London were only too happy to accept Edward of March as their king—in stark contrast to the way they had greeted his father's claims in the previous year. Fear of the Lancastrians was one reason, a general despair following the years of misrule was another; but the main factor was that March offered the means of changing a system of government that had fallen into disrepute and that many people wanted to be changed. In that respect, Edward offered a fresh start. With the strategic situation now balanced in the Yorkists' favor, they had to act decisively. At St. Albans they had lost their control over Henry and had returned the advantage to his supporters; if they were to enjoy any legitimacy with the people of England, they needed their own king and with the security of his family's claims to the throne, Edward fit the bill perfectly. It was also important that the steps taken to achieve their goal were open and aboveboard and that precedents were followed so that as many people as possible understood the symbolism of making Edward king.

Behind Fabyan's description of Londoners hailing Edward as king, the Yorkists had in fact acted quickly, smoothly, and, more importantly, according to precedent, to create the conditions whereby Edward could be crowned king of England. The whole progression was brilliantly stage-managed. The meeting referred to by Fabyan took place on Sunday, March 1, at St. John's Fields and was addressed by Bishop George Neville, who assured the crowd that Edward had a rightful claim to the throne. If that was what the people wanted, then it was legitimate to hail him as king. Their acclamation allowed the news to be carried to York's London residence, and the following day, Neville's articles were formally proclaimed. On March 3, having ascertained that they had the people behind them, a Yorkist council met at Baynard's Castle and made the final administrative arrangements to offer the throne to Edward. Among those present were Warwick, Norfolk, the Archbishop of Canterbury, the Bishops of Salisbury and Exeter, and "many others unnamed." Later in the year, in November 1461, Edward's first parliament confirmed Edward's legitimate inheritance of the crown in a petition that stated that he was the rightful king and Henry VI had been a Lancastrian usurper who had plunged the realm into "unrest, inward war and trouble, unrighteousness, shedding and effusion of innocent blood, abusion of the laws, partiality, riot, extortion, murder, rape and vicious living."

The next stage was to crown Edward of March as King Edward IV. A formal coronation would have to wait until later as Edward wanted first to defeat Henry in a decisive battle, the *Croyland Chronicle* noting that "he would not at present allow himself to be crowned, but immediately, like unto Gideon or another of the judges, acting faithfully in the Lord, girded himself with the sword of battle." Even so, despite those sentiments in which the chronicler handily crossed the Bible with the sword, it was essential that Edward should be acclaimed as king in front of his people. On March 4, after hearing mass in St. Paul's he was led to Westminster Hall, where he took his oath as the king of England and, having donned a purple robe—a symbol of royalty—entered the abbey. There he sat on the throne and, with St. Edward the Confessor's scepter in hand, asserted his right as king. Offerings were made at the high altar, *Te Deum* was sung, and as Fabyan summed up the proceedings, "thus took this noble prince possession of this realm of England." The problem was that Henry was still alive, as was his son the Prince of Wales, and the Lancastrians still had a formidable army in the field. Edward had based his claim not as a usurper but as the rightful king by descent from Edward III and by right of the succession made legitimate by the Act of Accord that named York or his descendants the rightful heirs to the throne. However, the harsh reality of the situation was that Edward had only become king through the support of powerful magnates, particularly the Nevilles, and because he had contrived to seize control of London with all its wealth and assets. Before he could be really safe in his position, he would have to deal with the Lancastrian succession either by killing Henry and his son or by driving them into exile.

Edward began his putative reign with a positive outlook and firmness of purpose that was typical of his personality. Realizing that he had to crush the Lancastrians, who still enjoyed the support of the majority of England's great noble houses, he issued proclamations calling on all Englishmen to accept him as king and forbidding them to offer support to Henry. Those who submitted to him would be pardoned, while prices were put on the heads of a list of

Lancastrian soldiers whose lives were now forfeit. These included Trollope (for his desertion at Ludford) and the sons of the Duke of Exeter (thought to have executed Salisbury after Wakefield). His next step was to raise additional funds to pay for the raising of a new army that would march north to take on the Royalist army. The majority of the new recruits came from the Welsh Marches and East Anglia, both regions where Yorkist support was strong. A week after Edward's swearing-in, the first contingents left London under Fauconberg's command, followed two days later, on March 13, by the main force led by the king and Norfolk. The new king was in no hurry, because he counted on raising additional support as his army passed through the Midlands where Warwick was already engaged in the task of recruiting men aged between 16 and 60.

While the Yorkists were consolidating their power base, the Lancastrian forces had been regrouping outside the city of York, where Queen Margaret began rallying support for Henry and the Prince of Wales. In Wales itself, her support remained strong, with the fortresses of Carreg Cennen, Denbigh, Harlech, and Pembroke for the time being still under the control of Jasper Tudor. A request sent to Mary of Gueldres resulted in the dispatch south of a fresh force of Scots, and appeals for men locally brought in new recruits from the north. While accurate figures are impossible to assess, there is general agreement that the Lancastrians had the larger army, one contemporary account claiming that it numbered 30,000 knights and foot soldiers. What is certain is that Henry still retained the support of the bulk of the nobility, 19 peers to Edward's 8; among them were Somerset, Exeter, Northumberland, Devon, the newly ennobled Sir Andrew Trollope, and Lords FitzHugh, Hungerford, Beaumont, Dacre of Gilsland, Roos, and Clifford. Their plan was to keep the Royal family safe within the walls of York while they confronted the smaller Yorkist army that had reached Pontefract by March 27. Between them, the rival armies had mustered around 50,000 or 60,000 men, the largest show of force ever seen in England, and the battle they were about to fight was destined to be the bloodiest encounter of the entire civil war. It was fought on March 29, a bitterly cold Palm Sunday with snow showers blowing down from the north, and the fighting itself was equally sharp and to the point.

The first blows were in fact struck two days earlier when a Yorkist forward detachment clashed with a Lancastrian force led by Clifford while attempting to seize a crossing over the River Aire at Ferrybridge. Finding the bridge destroyed, Lord Fitzwalter, a veteran of Mortimer's Cross, ordered his men to repair it but failed to guard the working parties, allowing Clifford to make an undetected attack. In a short and bitterly contested action, the Yorkists were driven back and their commander was killed. In response, Edward ordered his vanguard under

Fauconberg to ford the river at Castleford about four miles upstream. This move allowed the Yorkists to outflank Clifford, who was felled by an arrow in his neck as his men fled northward into Dintingdale Valley. The destruction of this holding force allowed Edward's army to cross the Aire and to approach their opponents, who were drawn up in a line on the ridge 100 feet above them with the village of Towton behind them to the north and the flooded waters of Cock Beck, a tributary of the Aire, on their right flank. As the senior commander, Somerset commanded the center, with Northumberland and Trollope on his right and Devon and Dacre on his left. Both sides spent a bitterly cold night in the open with fresh snow blown in on the biting wind, and although there were the usual attempts at negotiation, with Henry pleading that no battle should be fought on such a holy day, everyone on the plateau knew that they were about to face a hard fight when night gave way to a gray dawn. There was still some concern in the Yorkist camp that Norfolk had not yet arrived and was reported to be at least ten miles away, but Edward was determined to force the issue and fight, come what may.

During the night, the wind had backed to the south, and this gave the Yorkists a priceless advantage. When their archers commenced firing at around 10 AM, they had the wind behind them and the arrows fell on their opponents more or less unseen amid the snow flurries. At the same time, the Lancastrian archers had to fire their weapons into the wind and the extreme weather conditions made it impossible for them to gauge distances. Stung by the ferocity of the Yorkist attack, Somerset gave the order to advance, and Trollope's vanguard charged downhill into the Yorkist left flank, scattering the horses. If Northumberland had attacked the right flank simultaneously, the Yorkist lines would have broken, but this failed to happen and the battle in the center degenerated into a grim slugging match in which quarter was neither given nor expected. It was an ugly business, with men stabbing and hacking their opponents to death over a period of several hours using swords, axes, halberds, and assorted blades; the ferocity of the fighting left the snow bloodstained, a fact that later gave the area the name of Bloody Meadow. Amid the melee, it was impossible for either side to see if they had gained the advantage, and it was not until the coming of dusk that the Lancastrian lines fell back to the west, where they found themselves trapped in the steep-sided gully of the Cock that was "not very broad but of great deepness." Those who could not cross the swollen waters were drowned or were simply hacked to death where they stood. At this crucial stage, with hundreds lying dead on the battlefield, Norfolk's men arrived and their appearance put fresh heart into the Yorkists and brought dismay to the Lancastrians, who began falling away as best they could from the place of slaughter. As the Yorkist horse gave chase, men were cut down as they fled toward York, and the final casualty list, as estimated by Edward's heralds, was put at 28,000, probably an overestimate but indicative of the slaughter that had undoubtedly taken place that day. After the battle, Warwick's brother George Neville, Bishop of Exeter, wrote, deploring the loss of life in what was fast becoming an increasingly savage and wasteful civil war:

> In this battle eleven lords of the enemy fell, including the Earl of Devon, the Earl of Northumberland, Lord Clifford and Neville with some cavaliers and from what we hear from persons worthy of confidence, some 28,000 perished on one side and the other. O miserable and luckless race and powerful people, would you have no spark of pity for our own blood, of which we have lost so much of fine quality by the civil war, even if you had no compassion for the French!
>
> If it had been fought under some capable and experienced captain against the Turks, the enemies of the Christian name, it would have been a great stroke and blow. But to tell the truth, owing to these civil discords, our riches are beginning to give out, and we are shedding our own blood copiously among ourselves . . .

Towton was not only the bloodiest battle fought in the England up until that date; it also broke Lancastrian power north of the Trent River. Devon is listed among the dead in Neville's letter, but he was in fact found among the wounded in York and was promptly beheaded. A similar fate befell Wiltshire, who was taken prisoner a few days later in Cumberland and taken to Newcastle for execution—having managed to escape unharmed from earlier battles, his luck had finally ran out. Among the prominent Lancastrian dead were Northumberland and Trollope, two of the best soldiers on either side, and in the shocked aftermath of the fighting, a total of 42 Lancastrian knights were put to death on the battlefield. For Edward it was a crushing victory over his rival, but it was not a complete success as there were still two kings of England—Henry, his wife, and his son had been able to escape from the shambles. They had spent the day in York awaiting the outcome, and as the first survivors reached the city bringing with them news of the disaster, they fled north toward Scotland, stopping briefly at Newcastle and then at Wark Castle, where they narrowly escaped falling into Yorkist hands. Only the intervention of forces loyal to Northumberland allowed the Royal party to make their way to Berwick, where they waited for the necessary passes to allow them to stay in Scotland.

In fact, the turnabout in the Lancastrian fortunes was an acute embarrassment to Mary of Gueldres, who was effectively ruling Scotland during her son's minority. Although she had entered into a treaty with the Lancastrians, largely at the bidding of the influential Bishop James Kennedy of St. Andrews, her uncle was the Duke of Burgundy, and through his friendship with Warwick, he largely supported the Yorkist claims to the English throne. If Mary offered any further military support to Henry and Margaret it would damage his attempts to forge a close relationship with Edward. Fortunately, Mary was alert to the problem and found a way out of it by offering asylum to Henry's party but declining to provide any further military assistance to them in the immediate future. To begin with, Henry was housed in a convent in Kirkcudbright, while his wife and son were given apartments in the Royal palace at Linlithgow to the west of Edinburgh, but it was a parlous existence. Although they were joined by prominent supporters including the Dukes of Somerset and Exeter, Lord Roos, and Sir John Fortescue, the exiled court lacked funds and had to borrow money from the Scottish court. That did not stop Margaret from plotting to regain her position. Her son Prince Edward was betrothed to James II's sister Margaret Stewart, and in return the earlier agreement to cede Berwick was made public, much to the fury of King Edward, who demanded that the Lancastrian couple and their son should be returned to England "without delay."

That failure to capture Henry and Margaret after the victory at Towton was to prove an expensive lapse: As long as they lived, they provided a focus for their supporters and Edward's position could not be totally secure. However, those were problems for the future, and in the days following his victory, Edward was able to bask in his victory. For the first time, his opponents' military power had been shattered, and when he entered York in triumph on Easter Monday, he was met by cheering crowds. One of his first acts was to order the removal of his father's and brother's heads and to replace them with those of his defeated enemies. Edward remained in the north of England until the beginning of May, when he returned to London leaving Fauconberg and Montague in charge of his forces. On his return to London he was given a rapturous welcome, and his coronation as King Edward IV followed shortly thereafter, on June 28, with a sonorous ceremony in Westminster Abbey. Earlier he created 33 new Knights of the Bath and rewarded those who had served him well during the campaign against Henry—Fauconberg became Earl of Kent, and his powerful brother Warwick was confirmed as Captain of Calais and created Warden of the East and West Marches, charged with guarding the border with Scotland. Other Neville relatives were also put into positions of power and authority. George Neville was reaffirmed as chancellor and Edward's younger brothers were ennobled, George as Duke of Clarence and Richard as Duke of Gloucester. To the people of England, the new king also had words of encouragement, promising to end Lancastrian oppression and to redress "the very decay of merchandise wherein rested the prosperity of the subjects." It augured well, and an unknown letter writer reflected the general mood, describing the country's reaction to the coronation in ecstatic terms: "The entire kingdom keeps holiday for the event, which seems a boon from above."

The reality was rather different as Edward still had a number of difficulties to overcome before his position could be properly secured. In addition to the continuing presence of the rival king and his entourage on the other side of the border in Scotland, the Yorkists still had to contend with parts of England in which support for the Lancastrians remained strong. These were surprisingly widespread—large parts of the north and west, Wales, and the Marches. There was also the danger of interference from outside, particularly from France, where Louis XI had become king in succession to Charles VII and showed worrying signs of wanting to capitalize on England's internal problems by threatening to support Henry. For that reason, Edward had to impose his authority on the country quickly and effectively because any setback, however minor, would have disastrous effects for the new regime. To cement his position, he needed to muster support, not just among the relatively small number of nobles who had backed him during the campaign, but also among those whose had been on the Lancastrian side and might be willing to accept the new circumstances. Factionalism had been an unsettling influence during Henry's reign, and Edward made it clear that he represented a new beginning and a fresh opportunity to unite the kingdom. Obviously, in those unsettled times, there were those who found it prudent to change their allegiance, and Edward assisted the process by explaining that he was prepared to show clemency to those who were prepared to trim their beliefs. Among those restored to Royal favor was Lord Rivers, who had been closely involved with Henry's affairs and had been mercilessly "rated" by Edward and Warwick during his period of captivity in Calais a year earlier.

It was also necessary to restore good governance after the years of Lancastrian misrule. From the outset Edward was determined that his court should be solvent, and although he was not averse to enjoying life's luxuries, he managed to ensure that he paid his way, mainly by raising funds from the nobility through a system known as "benevolences." He also proved to be a better manager of the crown estates by introducing realistic rents and clamping down on corrupt practices. Taxes were raised only to pay for military operations, and he introduced a new office, the chamber, which became the principal conduit for Royal funds, thereby bypassing the exchequer and allowing the king to have greater control over his own finances. Other measures aimed at restoring confidence included the Acts of Resumption that revoked many of the grants and awards made by Henry. He even considered closing down Eton College.

One of the first acts of his first parliament was to revoke all grants made to it since its foundation, and in 1463 he applied for a papal bull authorizing the college's abolition. Four years later he relented and Eton was spared, but elsewhere in Windsor, he was responsible for building a new chapel dedicated to St. George, a magnificent Gothic building that became his greatest memorial.

Some idea of the parlous nature of the early years of Edward's reign can be seen in his unquiet relationship with the north of England, which very quickly became a focus for Lancastrian disaffection. The first sign of trouble came in June 1461, when an army of Scots and Lancastrian supporters laid siege to Carlisle and had to be dislodged by forces led by the newly ennobled Earl of Kent. Another raid was mounted the following month when a party including Henry VI rode south and reached Brancepeth in south Durham before being forced to retire by local volunteer soldiers led by the Archbishop of York. It was not the end of Edward's problems. To all intents and purposes the whole of Northumberland answered to the Percys, and key fortresses including Alnwick and Dunstanborough remained in the family's hands. It was a measure of the difficulties facing Edward that he had to allow Sir Ralph Percy, Northumberland's brother, to retain power in the area even though he was hardly a natural ally—his father had been killed at St. Albans and his brother at Towton, both fighting on the Lancastrian side. Wales was also a problem. The castles at Pembroke, Harlech, and Denbigh were all in Lancastrian hands, and it was not until October that a measure of control was restored when forces led by the Earl of Pembroke were defeated at Twt Hill near Caernarvon. Amongst those captured was Pembroke's four-year-old nephew Henry Tudor, who was placed in the hands of Sir William Herbert, Edward's principal ally in Wales. With Sir Walter Devereux, Herbert quickly set about consolidating the Yorkist position in the principality: Pembroke Castle fell in September, followed by Denbigh and Carreg Cennen the following spring. Only Harlech continued to hold out, but Pembroke's defeat proved to be a severe blow to Queen Margaret's hopes of retaining Lancastrian support in Wales.

15

WARWICK, MAKER AND
BREAKER OF KINGS

On becoming King of England, Edward IV presented a noble picture to the rest of the world. Standing six feet three inches tall, he was a big, well-made man who was well aware of the effect he had on people. Although a surviving, anonymous portrait shows a beefy face and small eyes, Sir James Strangeways, the first speaker of Edward IV's parliament, addressed the new king in terms that were complimentary to his looks and made a point of referring to "the beauty of personage that it hath pleased Almighty God to send you." He also dressed well, another attribute that made him a pleasing personality and added to his personal reputation as a genial and open soul. Sir Thomas More, who knew him, described him as "a goodly personage and very princely to behold, of heart courageous, politic in counsel." Additionally, there is evidence to suggest that Edward was not above using his personal charm to get his own way, particularly in securing loans and gifts from wealthy merchants in London. A corollary was that he could appear lazy and vainglorious and had a tendency to overindulge, not least as far as women were concerned, a fact noted many years later by an Italian correspondent, Dominic Mancini:

> Moreover, it was said that he had been most insolent to numerous women after he had seduced them, for as soon as he had satisfied his lust he abandoned the ladies much against their will, to other courtiers. He pursued with no discrimination the married and unmarried, the noble and lowly. However, he took none by force. He overcame all by money and promises, and, having conquered them, he dismissed them.

Edward was fond of saying that he always had three concubines—one the merriest, another the wiliest, and the third the holiest—but the identity of all his many mistresses remains a mystery, although his numerous affairs are well attested. Only two names are remembered—Elizabeth Lucy, daughter of a Hampshire squire, and Elizabeth Shore (also called Jane), a goldsmith's wife in whom, according to More, Edward "took special pleasure." The first mistress bore the king an illegitimate son, Arthur Plantagenet, and the second remained a lifelong friend. More left a charming portrait of Mrs. Shore, praising her for her beauty and pleasant behavior: "For a proper wit had she and could both read well and write, merry in company, ready and quick of answer, neither mute nor full of babble."

The matter of Edward's marital status is one of the great mysteries in an otherwise transparent life. With his looks and his easy personality, he was a good catch, and early in his reign his advisors considered the possibility of entering him into a strategic marriage. One possibility was Mary of Gueldres, James II's widow, as it was thought that a Scottish marriage would be advantageous, as would the relationship to her kinsman the Duke of Burgundy, but her sudden death in 1463 put an end to that idea. Another option was the 12-year-old Princess Isabella, the Infanta of Castile, who eventually married Ferdinand of Aragon, but Warwick favored a French alliance and entered into negotiations with Louis for the hand of his sister-in-law Lady Bona of Savoy, who was renowned for her good looks. This would have been a useful match, but, by the time that the latter proposal was being negotiated in the summer of 1464, Edward astonished everyone by suddenly announcing that he had already married in secret. His new wife was Elizabeth Woodville (or Wydeville), the eldest daughter of Lord Rivers (from his marriage with Jacquetta of Bedford) and the widow of Sir John Grey of Groby, a prominent Lancastrian who was killed at the Second Battle of St. Albans. It was a curious match. For all that Elizabeth was considered a great beauty, she was four years older than Edward, she had two sons by Grey, and, more to the point, she was a commoner whose only Royal connections had been as a lady-in-waiting to Margaret of Anjou. The king made the announcement on September 14 at a meeting of the council, and it caused a sensation. Kings were not supposed marry commoners, and if they did, they were certainly not to do it in secret.

In fact, Edward's new wife came from a thoroughly respectable Northamptonshire family, and her mother Jacquetta had been married to the Duke of Bedford, brother to Henry V. In the eyes of the nobility, the Woodvilles might have been upstarts who had formed useful marriage alliances to better themselves, but in their own way, they were a well-established, respectable family, as was Elizabeth's first husband, who lived at Groby Castle near Leicester. Edward and Elizabeth married in secret on May 1, at Grafton near the family home at Stony Stratford, and astonishingly they managed to keep the relationship a secret for a while. The reasons for Edward's infatuation were much pondered over at the time and gave rise to many wild theories, the most common being that Elizabeth had refused to have a physical relationship with the king unless he married her. That was certainly possible. Elizabeth Woodville was a respectable widow with a reputation to maintain, and she refused to be just another of the king's conquests to be bedded and discarded. She must also have understood the strength of the king's passion for her because a ploy of demanding marriage in return for sex could have been a dangerous game. There were also rumors that Elizabeth had used sorcery or witchcraft to beguile Edward into marrying her. The day before their marriage was one of the witches' four Sabbaths, and local tradition had it that the couple was betrothed under an oak tree, thought to be a place where witches worshipped. Her mother was also thought to be involved in the sorcery, and several years later a neighbor made the astonishing accusation that Jacquetta had been implicated in a plot to have her daughter married to the king by using a black magic spell involving small leaden figures. Whatever the reasons for the king's infatuation and his secret marriage, it was considered shocking enough to be recorded in minute detail in Fabyan's diaries:

> In such pass time, in most secret manner, upon the first day of May, King Edward spoused Elizabeth, late the wife of Sir John Grey, knight, which before time was slain at Towton or York field [it was in fact at the second St. Albans], which spousals were solemnised early in the morning at a town named Grafton, near Stony Stratford; at which marriage was no persons present but the spouse, spousess, the Duchess of Bedford her mother, the priest, two gentle-women, and a young man to help the priest sing. After which spousals ended, he went to bed and tarried thereupon three or four hours, and after departed and rode again to Stony Stratford, and came in manner as though he had been on hunting, and there went to bed again.

Perhaps the best reasoning regarding the marriage is supplied by Gregory, who noted simply, "now take heed what love may do for love will not cast no fault nor peril in nothing." As Queen Elizabeth, she was presented to the court on Michaelmas Day and was led into the abbey chapel at Reading by Clarence, her new brother-in-law, and by Warwick, the most powerful man in the kingdom. The ceremonial augured well—the *Worcester Chronicle* recorded that she was "honoured as queen by the lords and all the people"—but within weeks of her arrival, the new queen had started causing resentment by seeking preferential treatment for her many relatives. Elizabeth had 12 brothers and sisters, and in quick succession, she started arranging advantageous marriages for them and influencing her husband to provide them lucrative sinecures. This was precisely the kind of behavior that had bedeviled Henry's court, but Elizabeth was wildly ambitious and had her husband in such thrall that Edward found it impossible to refuse her requests.

Within a month of the Royal marriage announcement, her sister Margaret had been betrothed to Thomas Maltravers, the heir of the Earl of Arundel, and, according to the evidence of the *Worcester Chronicle*, there was a steady progression of matches involving Woodvilles to powerful families: Her 20-year-old brother John was married off to the elderly Duchess of Norfolk, "a diabolical marriage" to "a slip of a girl about eighty years old" who had already survived three marriages (she was in fact in her 60s and survived her young husband by 14 years); another sister was paired off with the Duke of Buckingham, "to the secret displeasure of the Earl of Warwick"; while other sisters found themselves in matches with the heir of the Earl of Exeter and the heir of the Earl of Kent (now Anthony Grey of Ruthin; Fauconberg, the previous holder of the title, had died). Finally, in October the following year, Thomas Grey, the queen's son from her first marriage, was put down to marry Lady Anne Holland, heiress of the Duke of Exeter, "the king's niece, to the great and secret displeasure of the Earl of Warwick, for a marriage was previously bespoken between the said Lady Anne and the son of the Earl of Northumberland, the Earl of Warwick's brother [previously Montague]." Patronage was also forthcoming: Warwick's uncle Lord Mountjoy was relieved of his post as treasurer and replaced by Rivers, now created an earl, again "to the secret displeasure of the Earl of Warwick and the magnates of England."

Warwick had good reason to feel discomfited. Not only were these dynastic marriages disliked on account of the Woodvilles' social standing, or lack thereof, but the all-powerful Nevilles felt threatened by the sudden emergence of a new faction at court. While there was a certain amount of snobbishness in the reaction—Mancini alleged that the Woodville family was "detested by the nobles because they were advanced beyond those who excelled them in breeding and wisdom"—the main reason for the disapproval was power play. Once again, a rival faction was being created, this time to threaten the Nevilles. For Warwick, the emergence of the Woodvilles at court was doubly frustrating. First, it threatened his own position as the principal power-broker in England; second, it allowed the creation of a new set of alliances in a family that had been firm supporters of the Lancastrians; third, the Woodvilles made it clear that they did not agree with all of Warwick's policies, especially his plan to seek an alliance with Louis in preference to Burgundy. (The revelation of the Woodville alliance meant that there was no future in the plan to marry Edward to the Savoy princess.) All this was very galling for Warwick, who had spent the first three years of Edward's reign securing the northern border and virtually ending the Percys' power in Northumberland, all to the king's benefit.

Since moving to Scotland, Henry VI had become part hostage, part pawn, a man who lived in a twilight zone between his wife and son and his remaining supporters. But even though he was personally powerless, he was still a focus for Lancastrian hopes, and despite the attainder that had been passed by Edward ending his kingship, he still thought of himself as the anointed king of England. Others also found him useful. The Scots harbored hopes of gaining an advantage over England, but so faction-ridden was the Scottish court and so poor the country that it was impossible to imagine that they would be able to offer any substantial support by way of funds or manpower. Finding herself isolated at the Scottish court, Margaret then decided to look to France for backing and crossed over to Brittany during Easter 1462, carrying with her a promise from her husband to hand over Calais in return for armed support from her French cousin. At Touraine, Louis reluctantly agreed to the terms, but his help was halfhearted and consisted of a small force of 800 soldiers under the command of Margaret's old friend Pierre de Brézé, the former seneschal of Normandy and Poitou. With them, Margaret returned to Scotland to pick up her husband and Somerset, and their forces sailed down the coast to land near Bamburgh. Although the main northern fortresses of Alnwick and Bamburgh were occupied, the onset of winter forced her to withdraw and most of her fleet was wrecked. She and her husband managed to get back to Berwick with de Brézé, but the survivors of the shipwrecks were washed ashore near Lindisfarne, where they were set upon and massacred by Yorkist forces.

Nevertheless, the French incursion had thoroughly unsettled Edward, who moved north with a large army to meet the threat posed by the Scots. On reaching Durham, the king fell ill with measles, but Warwick took over command and set about besieging Dunstanburgh and Bamburgh. Both surrendered on Christmas Eve 1462, and Alnwick followed early in the new year. This restored the strategic advantage to Edward's forces, but the success was marred by an astonishing piece of bad judgment. An offer made by Somerset to change sides was accepted—he was created a knight of the bedchamber and given an annuity— and in a move that defies rational explanation, Sir Ralph Percy was allowed to remain in charge of the strongholds provided he swore allegiance to Edward. While this was typical of the king's generosity of spirit and conformed to his thinking that the kingdom had to be unified and old animosities healed, it was madness to offer an open hand to Somerset given his family's past history of support to the Lancastrian cause and his own close relationship to Margaret of Anjou. Equally, it made no sense at all to allow a Percy to control the main fortresses in Northumberland. Sir Ralph Percy had already broken an earlier agreement by opening the gates of Alnwick to a prominent Lancastrian, Sir William Tailboys, and within months, he repaid Edward's latest act of generosity by handing over Bamburgh, Dunstanburgh, and Alnwick to a joint force of Scots and French, thus restoring most of Northumberland to the Lancastrians. Once again, the Scots came over the border, this time in a full-scale invasion, and laid siege to the fortress at Norham, which stands a few miles inland from Berwick on the River Tweed.

In response to this new threat, Warwick and Montague rallied their forces and marched north. Outside York, the Scottish army was repulsed and the survivors fled north, hotly pursued by the Nevilles, who took their forces over the border into Scotland to harry the southern uplands, before a lack of supplies and reinforcements forced them to retire. The siege of Norham was lifted, and with support falling away from her, Margaret of Anjou escaped to Berwick, where a French ship took her and her son to Sluys and exile. Once in France, she established a small court at the chateau of Koeur-la-Petite near St Mihiel-sur-Bar on the River Meuse, close to Commercy, that belonged to her father. There Margaret and her supporters lived in what one courtier called "great poverty," unable to act without French support and waiting for events to unfold. As for Henry, he was taken back to Scotland, first to Edinburgh and then to St. Andrews, where he was placed under Bishop Kennedy's care and protection. The Lancastrian cause was dented further during the summer when Edward concluded a tripartite truce with Louis and the Duke of Burgundy before attempting to sign a separate treaty with the Scots.

There was some respite for the queen's party when Somerset changed sides once more. He had been treated well—the attainder against him had been lifted and he was appointed Captain of Newcastle—but he remained a Beaufort and his heart lay with the Lancastrian cause. Having raised a force that included Sir Ralph Percy and Lords Hungerford and Roos, he intercepted a force of Nevilles while it was moving north to Norham to meet the Scottish envoys who had been given safe conduct to conclude the treaty. During the fighting on Hedgeley Moor, some nine miles to the northwest of Alnwick on April 21, the Lancastrian left flank, commanded by Roos and Hungerford, was quickly broken and the affray became a one-sided business. Percy was killed and the remainder of the force retreated into the valley of the River Tyne, where they were trapped three weeks later in a narrow passage called the Linnels on the Devil's Water not far from the town of Hexham. (The battle site has been identified as lying between Linnels Bridge and Teasdale Fell.) Unable to deploy in battle order in the confines of the narrow ground, Somerset's men were crushed by the superior Yorkist forces on May 15. Those who escaped death on the battlefield were executed: Among them were Somerset, Roos, and Hungerford, who all paid the price for being on the losing side.

The collapse of the Northumberland fortresses followed the defeat— Alnwick and Dunstanburgh surrendered without a shot being fired, but the defenders at Bamburgh under Sir Ralph Grey, another Yorkist turncoat, attempted to hold out and the castle was battered into submission by "the great ordnance of England," heavy siege guns that were gradually coming into service at the time. Before ordering his gunners to open fire, Neville sent heralds to tell the garrison what awaited them if they continued to hold out, their words being recorded in the chronicles John Warkworth, Master of Peterhouse, Cambridge:

> The king, our most dread sovereign lord, specially desires to have this jewel whole and unbroken by artillery, particularly because it stands so close to his ancient enemies the Scots, and if you are the cause that great guns have to be fired against its walls, then it will cost you your head, and for every shot that has to be fired another head, down to the humblest person within the place.

The advice was ignored, and following a brief but heavy bombardment, Bamburgh opened its gates after Grey opened negotiations for its surrender. Much good it did him: He was dragged to Doncaster and immediately beheaded. Bamburgh produced the first and only set-piece siege of the civil wars and its fall was decisive: By midsummer, the Nevilles had crushed the power of the Percys in the north of England.

All effective Lancastrian resistance in England had now come to an end, and the Scots prudently entered a 15-year truce with Edward. As for the hapless Henry, he had taken refuge from the fighting in nearby Bywell Castle and was forced to go on the run, being sheltered in a number of safe houses in the north of England whose families remained loyal to his cause. All that was found of his presence was his crowned cap and some of his belongings that were taken into Montague's custody after the fighting in the Tyne valley. It was not until the following summer that Henry was eventually discovered while dining with pro-Lancastrian gentry at Waddington Hall near Clitheroe, the seat of Sir Richard Temple. Although Henry managed to escape, he was captured in the nearby Clitherwoods close to a ford over the River Ribble known today as Brungerley.

Taken south, he arrived in London on June 24 and was paraded through the streets as evidence of his capture before being lodged in apartments in the Tower, where he spent the next five years under guard. Although Lancastrian chroniclers alleged that he was cruelly treated during his confinement, the conditions seem to have been reasonably tolerable, and true to form, he spent much of the time in prayer and contemplation. The records show that he had the use of a priest for daily prayers and that he was given regular supplies of wine and velvet cloth for fresh clothes. According to the evidence of the Warkworth chronicles, Henry "was kept long time by two squires and two yeomen of the crown, and their men; and every man suffered to come and speak with him by licence of the keepers."

This turnaround strengthened Edward's position in that he now had full control over his opponent, but it came at the same time that he had caused dismay among this supporters by marrying Elizabeth Woodville and encouraging the rash of marriage alliances. It was especially galling to Warwick. Having pacified the north, the king's closest ally now found himself at loggerheads with Edward over the policy to be adopted with France. Although Warwick had been close to the Duke of Burgundy during his time in Calais, he favored entering into an alliance with Louis XI, whom he knew well and had come to like. Perhaps he was flattered by the French king's interest in him; he might also have boasted about his own influence over Edward at court, and during the course of several embassies during the 1460s, he was a constant promoter of a treaty of friendship with France. For Louis, this was an important perquisite for his own policies, as he was keen to break the power of the Dukes of Burgundy and Brittany and wanted to prevent England from entering into a separate treaty with the former. However, this is precisely what Edward was intent on doing.

Initially, Edward seems to have kept an open mind about his foreign policy. In May 1465, he appointed Warwick to confer with Louis, Duke Francis of Brittany, and Charles, Count of Charolais, the eldest son of the recently incapacitated Duke Philip of Burgundy, but the outbreak of fighting among all three in what became known as the War of the Public Weal prevented Warwick from making any progress. That window of opportunity closed as the Woodville faction, notably their leading light, Earl Rivers, began to exercise its influence at court. Edward now began to favor a treaty with the Burgundians, who were England's largest trading partners in the wool market. The following year, Charles of Charolais, a widower, put forward a proposal for the hand of Edward's sister, Margaret of York, while at the same time marrying the Duke of Clarence to his own daughter Mary. Neither proposal suited Warwick. There is contemporary evidence to suggest that he had formed an early and deep dislike for Charles, and he was opposed to the idea of the king's brother marrying into the house of Burgundy, as he entertained ambitions for Clarence to marry his daughter Isabel. Unfortunately for those dreams, Edward was opposed to such a match on the grounds of their consanguinity and he banned any further marriage negotiations. There was, of course, another reason for the king's opposition: The Duke of Clarence was his heir-presumptive, and at that stage in his life, Edward did not want to see his brother becoming allied to the powerful Nevilles. The king's fears were not without grounds: Warwick understood the authority that would accrue to him through the match at a time when he was forced to watch the Woodvilles making their own matrimonial alliances to powerful English magnates. Undeterred, Warwick entered into secret negotiations with Rome to obtain the necessary papal dispensation that would permit the marriage of his daughter to Clarence.

In the midst of this diplomatic activity, Edward tried to keep all sides guessing about his real intentions. In the spring of 1466, he signed a truce with Louis in which he agreed to keep out of the French king's hostilities with Brittany and Burgundy in return for a French promise not to support Margaret of Anjou. These agreements were signed, but neither side had any real intention of sticking to their conditions. At the same time, Edward made a private pledge of friendship with the Duke of Burgundy, who had been temporarily restored to health. Matters came to a head in June 1467, when a jousting tournament was arranged between the Duke of Burgundy's natural son, Antony, Bastard of Burgundy, and Anthony Woodville, Lord Scales, son of Earl Rivers. Both men were judged to be the foremost warriors of their age, and whoever won the tournament would be judged to be the champion of all Europe. Although jousting was not as fashionable as it had been in the previous century, the opportunity to witness a clash of arms between two leading exponents created a huge amount of excitement throughout England. Not only did it promise to be a spectacular event, but the tournament also seemed to be a harbinger of a new period of peace and prosperity. Henry VI was confined in the Tower, Edward was secure on his throne and had taken a wife, albeit one who was not universally popular, and that same year, the king gave notice that his court was solvent and that he could finally live off his own means. As it turned out, through no one's fault, the tournament was a nonevent. On the first day there was only one joust on horseback, and the second day's session with battle-axes reached no conclusion. Events were then suddenly stopped when a messenger arrived from the Burgundian court announcing the death of Duke Philip and forcing the Bastard to return home immediately.

Despite the unsatisfactory conclusion, the tournament had achieved its underlying aim of continuing the diplomatic discussions between the courts of England and Burgundy. In the week before the tournament, the Bastard and his retinue had enjoyed the hospitality of the court and had attended the opening of parliament. While the Bastard was being entertained, he did everything possible to reinforce the idea that the proposed marriage between Charolais and Margaret of York would pave the way for a lasting alliance between England and Burgundy. The Bastard was also able to witness firsthand Edward's determination to be his own man and to take steps to curb the power of the Nevilles. One of the notable absentees from London during the Bastard's visit was George Neville, now Archbishop of York, who had announced that he had no intention of being in the capital at a time when the king was entertaining representatives from Burgundy. As he also served as chancellor, this was a snub to the king, who probably also knew that Neville was busily scheming in Rome for a cardinal's hat and, against Royal wishes, was working hard to gain the necessary dispensation to allow his niece to marry Clarence. Within the week, the king took his revenge. Neville was removed from his position and replaced by Robert Stillington, the ambitious and time-serving Bishop of Bath and Wells who had risen from obscurity and had the dubious distinction of only visiting his see once during 26 years in office. Not only was the removal of Neville a slap in the face for his brother Warwick, who was in France at the time, but also it was a very public humiliation conducted in person by the king. On his return to London, Warwick brought with him a French delegation, who were treated politely but distantly and their embassy achieved nothing. To add insult, Edward insisted on entering into a treaty with the Duke of Brittany in which he agreed to support him in the event of attack by supplying 3,000 archers.

Both moves cemented the king's determination to have his own way in directing foreign policy, and the change of chancellor was a telling snub to the Nevilles as Stillington was simply a nonentity who had been chosen because he would cause little trouble. The way was now open for the king to conclude his alliance with Charles, the new Duke of Burgundy, and although he came out of the negotiations a poorer man—he was outbid in the settlement of the dowry and found himself having to find 200,000 gold crowns—the wedding with Margaret of York took place on July 3, 1468, at Damme in Flanders.

Against all of Warwick's wishes, Edward had now completed his steps in a diplomatic dance that brought England into partnership with two countries that were already in alliance against France. Once more the long shadow cast by the years of warfare with England's greatest enemy influenced the way an English king decided to forge his foreign policy. It was a classic maneuver that would have been understood by any of Edward's Plantagenet forebears: Take advantage of the enmity of France's enemies, both internal and external, by entering into compacts with them and then prepare for war. Not that Edward had any serious intention of attacking France in 1468: He would assist his new allies only in the event of any offensive action, but war with England's old enemy remained a possibility for the distant future.

Such a course of action brought obvious risks: As Louis became aware of Edward's hostility, he gave more thought to supporting the Lancastrian cause. The French king's immediate response was to fund an insurrection in Wales led by Jasper Tudor, who aimed to encourage the Welsh to rise up for the Prince of Wales and to make contact with the garrison in Harlech Castle that was still in Lancastrian hands. In July, he landed in west Wales and initially enjoyed some success in raising numbers of men to his colors—to get some idea of the extent of Tudor's achievement, he arrived with only 50 men and had to rely on his name and standing to encourage others to join him. It was a gallant attempt but Tudor's luck did not last. Yorkist forces led by Lord Herbert and his brother, Sir Richard Herbert, marched into Wales and crushed Tudor's army near Denbigh, which had previously been burned to the ground. The defeat forced the garrison inside Harlech to surrender on August 14, and Tudor was fortunate to make good his escape disguised as a peasant. It was a shattering blow for a man who prided himself on the strength of his support in Wales, and to make matters worse, the title granted to him by Henry VI was lost when a grateful Edward made Lord Herbert the new Earl of Pembroke. Once again, from the king's point of view, he had made a shrewd move. Herbert came from a long-established Welsh family and was one of the first men from his background to make an impact on the English court. He was an absolute Yorkist loyalist, known as "the king's lock-master" for Wales, and early on had forged an alliance with the Woodvilles when his son was married to Mary, one of the queen's sisters. Forceful and ambitious, the new Earl of Pembroke came to govern Wales almost as a viceroy, and he quickly acquired properties in England, becoming a powerful and wealthy magnate in his own right. However, the very traits that made him attractive and useful to Edward also brought him into conflict with Warwick, who was dismayed by his elevation as Earl of Pembroke. History seemed to be repeating itself with the creation of opposing factions at court, one loyal to the king consisting of the Woodvilles, including Pembroke, the other, the Nevilles, increasingly disenchanted with a group whom they considered to be upstarts and Edward's wrongheaded and avaricious advisers.

There is no single reason why Warwick's disillusionment with Edward led him to take action against him. It seems to have been due to a steady accumulation of setbacks, disappointments, and rebuffs that produced a realization that he was no longer supreme at court but just one of several people on whom the king relied. His influence had been challenged over the country's foreign policy, and Edward had not accepted his advice about alliances and marriages. At court, he had witnessed the inexorable rise to power of the Woodville family and had seen men like Herbert being promoted from relative obscurity to positions of power and authority. For Warwick, this was intolerable: He was a Neville, one of the wealthiest and most influential families in England; he had devoted much of his life to supporting the Yorkist cause and had seen his father and brother killed fighting for Richard of York and his son Edward. At the same time his attempt to marry his daughters to Edward's brothers had been thwarted, and his family had been further humiliated by the firing of his brother George Neville. Warwick still appeared at court and had been reconciled to Edward during a meeting of council when the king celebrated Christmas at Coventry, but that display of friendship was a ruse. During the summer and autumn of 1468, the man who is known to history as Warwick, the King-maker, was clearly disaffected and considering how he could retrieve his position.

Fatally for all concerned, it was at about this time that Warwick entered into a close relationship with Clarence, the king's brother. Like Edward, Duke George was a strapping, well-built, good-looking young man who had inherited his family's driving ambition and sense of place in the world. At his seat at Tutbury in Staffordshire he maintained a huge household, grander and more lavish than his brother's court, with around 400 servants. Although he received generous funding from the public purse, the creation of such an extravagant lifestyle meant that a good marriage to a wealthy heiress had become central to his plans, hence his willingness to fall in with the idea that he should marry Warwick's daughter. By 1468, he had been made aware of the secret negotiations with the papal *Curia* to gain a dispensation and was prepared to disobey his brother's wishes if Rome should find in Warwick's favor. Although Clarence had received generous reward simply for being a Royal duke—he was granted huge estates and received an income as lord lieutenant of Ireland—he felt that he had little influence at court and he became that dangerous creature, a jealous prince of the realm who had no distinctive public role, who entertained ambitions to become a power in the land.

The emergence of the Warwick–Clarence partnership came at the same time as fresh outbreaks of pro-Lancastrian sympathies—in the early summer of 1468, there was a rash of scares about Lancastrian plots to overturn the regime and to return Henry VI to the throne. Most of these involved the exposure of letters to known supporters that had been written by Margaret of Anjou. Among the most serious concerned a shoemaker called Cornelius who, according to the *Worcester Chronicle*, was arrested in London and after spending three days in the Tower "was tortured by burning in the feet until he confessed many things." Under the stress—the feet-burning was followed up with his flesh being stripped by red-hot pincers—Cornelius accused a number of conspirators who were also tortured. One of them was John Hawkins, a servant of Lord Wenlock, Warwick's associate in Calais, who implicated Sir Thomas Cook, a wealthy London merchant. The accused was lucky to escape with his life but was ruined financially on being forced to pay a huge fine after being found guilty of misprision of treason (being privy to treasonable activities but failing to report them). The case caused a good deal of bitterness in London when it became clear that the Woodvilles had been involved in the persecution. Earlier, Cook had refused to sell a tapestry to the Dowager Duchess of Bedford at the low selling price she demanded, and following his punishment, Queen Elizabeth insisted on imposing the ancient right of Queen's Gold which permitted her to take a further sum of money from Cook's estate. This was followed by the arrest of three suspected Lancastrian sympathizers, Henry Courtenay, brother of the attainted Earl of Devon, Thomas Hungerford, whose father had been executed after the Battle of Hexham, and John de Vere, 13th Earl of Oxford and Warwick's brother-in-law. All were accused of conspiring with Margaret of Anjou. Oxford was quickly released, but Courtenay and Hungerford were arraigned before a commission of oyer and terminer headed by Gloucester and were sentenced to traitors' deaths in Salisbury the following year. (Oxford was doubly fortunate as his father, the 12th earl, had been executed as a traitor six years earlier.)

The spy scares and the treatment of Cook all helped to fuel an atmosphere of fear and general ill will and increased the belief that trouble was brewing on a grand scale. *The Great Chronicle of London* recorded that "many murmurous tales ran in the city atween the Earl of Warwick and the queen's blood," and Warkworth's chronicle claimed that the country was in turmoil over a number of issues, namely bad governance and high taxes, and, as a result, people were "full glad to have a change." In fact, taxation had not been heavy during Edward's reign, but the disaffection seems to have been compounded by the general unhappiness with the Woodville faction at court and the favors that had been bestowed on them. At the same time, Royalist agents reported that whenever Warwick appeared in London, the people greeted him with cries of "Warwick! Warwick!" and the same point was made in the *Great Chronicle*. It also repeated a scurrilous story about a man called Woodhouse who managed to get into the king's presence wearing a strange outfit consisting of a short coat and thigh-length boots and carrying a long marsh pole. When Edward asked why he was dressed in that fashion, Woodhouse replied, "Upon my faith, Sir, I have passed through many countries [counties] of your realm and in places that I have passed the Rivers have been so high that I could scarcely scrape through them, but as I was fain to search the depth with this long staff." The chronicler claimed that the king understood exactly what Woodhouse meant and made light of the reference to the power wielded by Earl Rivers, but added that the incident "was an ill prenostication as ye shall shortly hear after."

16

DECLINE AND FALL

hen it came to pursuing his own ambitions, Warwick was nothing if not a great deceiver, and it is doubtful that Edward had any inkling about the earl's treasonable plans until he actually put them into practice. In the spring of 1469, Warwick acted as if the spirit of reconciliation was still alive, and he did nothing to stir up any suspicions at court, mainly by using his immense wealth to maintain his popularity. *The Great Chronicle of London* noted that Warwick continued behaving in the same expansive way with which he had always marked his time in the capital and through which he had won so many admirers: "Every tavern was full of his meat, for that had any acquaintance in that house, he should have as much sodden [boiled] and roast [meat] as he might carry on a long dagger . . ." It was not just in London that Warwick was cementing his public position. In April, he represented Edward at a meeting with Louis held at St. Omer; the following month he was present at a Garter ceremony at Windsor when the order was conferred on the new Duke of Burgundy. Everything seemed so normal that in the middle of June, Edward saw no reason to be concerned when his advisers encouraged him to undertake a pilgrimage to the shrine of Our Lady of Walsingham in East Anglia, taking with him Gloucester, Rivers, Scales, and other members of the Woodville family. It was the worst thing the king could have done, for already trouble was brewing in the north of England and these eruptions proved to be a harbinger for a fresh round of civil conflict.

The first outbreak of trouble had occurred in Yorkshire in April when a number of disturbances centered on a malcontent calling himself Robin of Redesdale or Robin Mend-All; according to Warkworth, this was the name adopted by Sir John Conyers of Hornby, a cousin by marriage of Warwick's.

(Robin was a catchall name for any popular people's hero.) At the same time, there was another separate flare-up in the East Riding led by another mysterious figure styled Robin of Holderness, who was probably a member of the Percy family as the main complaint voiced by him and his followers was the restoration of that family to the Northumberland earldom, currently in the hands of the Nevilles. Only one name has ever been posited, that of Robert Hillyard of Winstead, or even his son, another Robert, but that connection has never been proved. Whatever his real identity, Robin of Holderness's revolt was speedily and efficiently quelled by forces led by John Neville, the new Earl of Northumberland. Unfortunately, the same outcome was not the case with the other Robin. Although Neville managed to break up their meetings, Conyers's supporters dispersed and regrouped across the Pennines in Lancashire. From there, they returned to Yorkshire in May and began moving south with a force estimated by Warkworth at 20,000, "a mighty insurrection of the commons." The number was probably significantly smaller and most of them were Nevilles or Neville retainers and tenants. Warwick's nephew Sir Henry FitzHugh, son of Lord FitzHugh, was with them, as were sundry other distant relatives. Others joined Conyers for a variety of related reasons, not least dislike of taxation, lingering support for Henry VI, and a general dissatisfaction with Edward's government of the country.

The news reached the king's entourage while they were staying at Croyland Abbey, and Edward decided to ride in person to deal with the uprising. At the end of June, he made his way to Fotheringhay Castle in Yorkshire, where he stopped and waited for his main forces to arrive. These were slow in assembling, and it quickly became apparent to the king that his summonses for recruits were being ignored or that they were only being acted on with great reluctance. Despite calls to the main towns in the English midlands to supply men, it was proving difficult to raise the necessary forces, while from the north came alarming stories of the size and strength of Robin of Redesdale's armed host. With the situation deteriorating, Edward sent his Woodville relations to the safety of East Anglia and withdrew to Nottingham to wait for Welsh reinforcements that had been promised by William Herbert, Earl of Pembroke. It must have been clear to the king by then that Warwick was in some way implicated in the crisis, as he did not make any overt move against him nor had he offered any military support. On July 9, Edward wrote to Warwick, Clarence, and the Archbishop of Canterbury demanding that they give some sign of their loyalty by proving that they were not disposed to act treasonably. There was no response.

By then, having purchased the necessary dispensation in Rome, Warwick had decided that his daughter Isabel should marry Clarence without further ado, and the wedding party had crossed to Calais on July 4, taking with them the Archbishop of Canterbury and the Earl of Oxford. A week later, the ceremony took place in some haste and with little pomp; then Warwick decided to show his hand. From Calais, he issued a declaration that allied him and his brother to the petitions put out by Robin of Redesdale and his supporters. It was a document Richard II or Henry VI would have recognized and understood, and, as it echoed the grievances uttered by the northern rebels, it is easy to see that the national unrest in 1469 had been engineered by Warwick and his supporters. Their intention was to save the king from "the deceiving covetous rule and guiding of certain seducious persons," namely Rivers, Scales, Pembroke, and Devon, who had "caused our said sovereign lord and his realm to fall in great poverty of misery, disturbing the ministration of the laws, only intending to their own promotion and enriching." It also contained an ominous reminder of the fates of earlier kings—Edward II, Richard II, and Henry VI—who had excluded princes of the blood Royal from their council and had surrounded themselves with favorites whose only concern was self-advancement. To correct that imbalance, Warwick promised reform at court including the punishment of the "seducious person" and called on his supporters to meet with him and his army at Canterbury on July 16.

As had happened when he marched on the capital to put Edward on the throne, Warwick received a warm welcome from the local people when he crossed over to Kent. The enthusiasm continued as he marched on London through Canterbury, attracting recruits as he and his supporters made their way through the English countryside. When the force approached London, the city administration found itself in a dilemma about which faction to support, but Warwick's long-standing popularity in London ensured that the gates were opened to him and he was even given a gift of money, as much to make sure his army behaved well as to help his cause. From the capital, the Warwick faction moved north toward Coventry, where they hoped to meet up with the northern rebels. While this was happening, Edward did nothing except to remain at Nottingham and to see how events unfolded. He did not have long to wait. On July 25, Pembroke arrived at Banbury from the west, bringing with him a powerful force of foot soldiers. With him was another force led by Lord Humphrey Stafford of Southwick, who had been appointed Earl of Devon following the attainder of Thomas Courtenay the 14th earl. However, for reasons that are unclear but seem to have had something to do with precedence in the lodging arrangements, both men quarreled and Devon led his men off to separate billets. The disagreement had dreadful consequences. All of the Royalist archers were in Devon's force, and that left Pembroke in a weakened position that the approaching rebels were happy to exploit. The next morning Robin of Redesdale's men fell on the Royalist army at Edgecote Hill to the northeast of Banbury, close to the River Cherwell. In the early stages as the two sides battled for possession of the river crossing, Pembroke's Welsh soldiers fought bravely enough but they were outnumbered and, without archers, they were easy prey to the well-armed northerners. The tipping point came when a fresh force of Warwick's supporters approached Edgecote Hill; realizing that this was the vanguard of Warwick's army, most of the Royalists fled from the field. It was a crushing victory for the Nevilles and they exploited it to the full. Pembroke and his brother Sir Richard Herbert were taken to Northampton where, without trial, Warwick ordered them to be beheaded even though he had no legal or moral justification other than a desire for vengeance.

The news of the defeat reached Edward as he made his way from Nottingham to Northampton, and, while Edward spent the night at Olney, the Archbishop of Canterbury apprehended him. From there, he was taken into custody at Warwick Castle, while Warwick continued his self-appointed task of bringing the king's advisers to heel. Rivers and Sir John Woodville were soon rounded up while hiding in Somerset and both men were executed outside Coventry on August 12, again without trial. A week later, a similar fate awaited Humphrey Stafford after he was captured in Bridgewater and executed on the spot. Warwick was triumphant everywhere. He had secured a military victory over the Royalist army, the king was in his custody, and he had carried out his threat to extirpate many of the Woodvilles and the Herberts. And yet, in his hour of triumph, Warwick was painfully shackled. Like York before him, he had no broad support among the magnates, many of whom suspected his motives; there was the constant fear of a Lancastrian revival, and, shorn of any source of funds and authority, he was unable to extend the anticipated patronage to his followers. There was also the question of what to do with the king, who remained the country's anointed sovereign. Warwick dared not execute Edward and replace him with Clarence; that would have been treason and would lose him all support. And so Warwick attempted to rule the country through the right of a captive king, an experiment that depended on Edward complying with the fiction that he still exercised the ultimate authority.

Fortunately, Edward played along with the pretense and behaved impeccably throughout his confinement, even when for his own security he was sent to Middleham Castle in Yorkshire. He must have realized that time was on his side and that neither Warwick nor Clarence would be able to change the status quo without deposing him. Some of the problems facing Warwick soon became apparent. There was unrest in London and there were outbreaks of local trouble in Gloucestershire, Lancashire, and Yorkshire, but the principal danger remained the threat that Henry VI's supporters would take advantage of the unrest to mount a new campaign on the usurped king's behalf. If that was Warwick's fear, he did not have long to wait. In August, two northern landowners Sir Humphrey Neville of Brancepeth and his brother Charles raised the Lancastrian standard and appealed for support in Westmoreland and Northumberland. The threatened revolt was given little or no support locally, but Warwick was sufficiently alarmed by it to raise forces and march north to deal with the trouble. Under normal circumstances, people would have rallied when he summoned men to join him, but these were not ordinary times and his requests were simply ignored. Many potential supporters had ridden with Robin of Redesdale, they had seen their demands made good by the summary executions of the king's favorites, but they were puzzled by Edward's captivity and Warwick's role in it. Their message was clear and simple—they would not march north unless they did it with the legal and moral authority of the king. With no option but to turn to Edward for help, Warwick had him released, and when the king appeared in front of his people at York on September 10, he was met with acclaim. As a result, Warwick got his army and they quickly dealt with the two Neville brothers, who were brought to York and executed in the king's presence at the end of September.

This reversal in Edward's fortunes gave him the opportunity to restore his position, and he took it. From York, he summoned magnates who he knew were loyal to him—his brother Gloucester, his brother-in-law Suffolk, and a posse of earls including Arundel, Northumberland, and Essex. With them, he rode back to London and entered into the capital in triumph in mid-October. Now that he was at liberty and had surrounded himself with his closest allies, Edward was relatively safe and Warwick's attempt at ruling through a puppet king was over. As the Croyland chronicler recorded, a fragile peace had returned to the country:

> In the end, a great council of all the peers of the kingdom was summoned and on a certain day, which had been previously named there appeared in the great chamber of parliament, the Duke of Clarence, the Earl of Warwick, and the rest of their confederates; upon which, peace and entire oblivion of all grievances upon both sides was agreed to. Still, however, there probably remained on the one side, deeply seated in his mind the injuries he had received and the contempt which had been shown to majesty, and on the other: "A mind too conscious of a daring deed."

In fact, Edward decided to allow the recent events to be forgotten, and initially he took a mollifying approach to Warwick and Clarence. His policy boded well for reconciliation, but some things could not be forgotten, and Sir John Paston (II) was probably nearer the truth of the matter when he noted: "The King himself has good language of the Lords of Clarence and Warwick, and of my Lords of York and Oxford, saying they be his best friends; but his household men have other language, so what shall hastily fall I cannot say." One mistake would have consequences in the not-too-distant future. In an attempt to keep the north of England quiet following the recent eruption of revolts, the earldom of Northumberland was restored to the Percys, a move that meant that the current holder, John Neville, had to surrender the title. By way of compensation, he was promoted as the Marquess of Montague—an earlier title of his had been Lord Montague—and his son was created Duke of Bedford with the promise of marriage to the king's eldest daughter Elizabeth. It seemed to be a magnanimous settlement that should have pleased both families, but the move did not appease Neville, who claimed that he had been given "a magpie's nest," that is, a title without the means of maintaining it. What should have been a valued promotion was seen as an insult.

His brother felt even more aggrieved. Although Warwick had succeeded in getting rid of the Herberts and some of the Woodvilles, Edward was still king and his own position at court had not changed since the period before his rebellion. Politically, Warwick was isolated and he lacked the broad level of support needed to maintain a successful bid to curb the king's power, but, far from hindering him, those drawbacks only persuaded him to continue scheming. In the first quarter of 1470, there was a rash of fresh disturbances in Lincolnshire involving a territorial dispute between Sir Thomas Burgh of Gainsburgh, Edward's master of horse, and his neighbor Lord Welles, a second cousin of Warwick. With his son Sir Robert and another knight, Sir Thomas Dymmock, Welles attacked Burgh's manor and destroyed much of his property. This was a common enough occurrence in England at the time, but it was also one that challenged Royal authority. Fearing that he was losing ground and had to reestablish his position—both men involved in the quarrel had connections with the court—Edward decided to intervene by riding north with an armed force. His action provided Warwick with the opportunity he had been seeking.

When Welles and Dymmock were ordered to travel to London to explain their actions, the former's son, Sir Robert Welles, raised a fresh rebellion after summoning the men of Lincolnshire to attend him fully armed at Ranby Hawe on March 7. The summons also carried the names of Warwick and Clarence, although this detail was as yet unknown to the king, who had received offers of military support from both men. As Edward moved north, he received further news of fresh disturbances in Yorkshire, but, buoyed by the expectation that he would soon be receiving assistance from his major allies, he continued his journey, showing a determination and sense of purpose that had been lacking the previous year. Five days after Sir Robert Welles had issued his summons, the Royalist army fell on the rebels at Empingham, five miles to the west of Stamford. Before going into action, Edward showed that he meant business when Lord Welles and Sir Thomas Dymmock were brought before the army and summarily executed despite the earlier promise of a pardon. The battle itself was over in minutes. Edward possessed a large artillery train that he used to good effect against the poorly led and inexperienced men of Lincolnshire, who quickly fled from the field when they came under fire. So rapid was their flight that in their haste, many cast away their clothing, and as a result the battle gained the name of Losecoat Field. When the news of the defeat reached Yorkshire, the threatened revolt failed to materialize and Edward was left master of the field.

His triumph also revealed the extent of Warwick and Clarence's treachery. Contemporary accounts of the uprising show that many of Welles's men had advanced into the battle shouting "Clarence!" and "Warwick!" and on the field a casket belonging to Sir Robert Welles was recovered which, according to an anonymous contemporary chronicler, was full of "many marvellous bills, containing matter of the great seduction, and the very subversion of the king and the common weal of all this land, with the most abominable treason that ever were seen or attempted." This gave Edward all the evidence he needed. Welles and other leaders of the revolt were captured at Grantham, and having confessed that Warwick and Clarence were "partners and chief provokers of all their treasons," were promptly beheaded. The king's next move was to dispatch his herald to summon Warwick and Clarence to attend him or face due punishment. In reply, the rebels demanded safe conduct and a pardon, but having seen his friendship betrayed, Edward was in no mood to offer reconciliation and condemned both men as "rebels and traitors."

This time the king realized that he had to take firm action to safeguard his position, and he also knew that he now enjoyed military superiority. The Dukes of Norfolk and Suffolk had ridden to his assistance, as had the Earl of Worcester, and according to Sir John Paston (II), when Edward rode north toward Doncaster never before had England seen "so many goodly men, and so well arrayed." By then, Warwick and Clarence could see that their rebellion had ended in disaster and that, shorn of support, they had no option but to get out of England as quickly as possible. Having summoned their families, including Isabel of Clarence, who was in the ninth month of pregnancy, they managed to get to Dartmouth, where they took ship for Calais. Earlier, Warwick had attempted to gain possession of his warship the *Trinity* in Southampton but had been beaten off by a force led by Anthony Rivers, the new Earl Rivers. There was further disappointment when the acting captain of the garrison, Sir John Wenlock, now ennobled as Lord Wenlock, obeyed Edward's instructions to the letter and refused to let them enter the harbor. Wenlock had always been close to Warwick, but on this occasion he decided to obey the king's orders, and even when Isabel went into labor, he would not yield. She survived the incident, but unhappily the baby was stillborn.

As the Duke of Burgundy also refused to allow Warwick to land in any port in Flanders, the rebels were forced to set sail for Honfleur, which they reached during the first week of May following an inconclusive battle with Royalist ships under the command of Lord John Howard, the treasurer of the king's household. The rebels' arrival in France changed everything. For some time, Louis XI had harbored hopes of effecting an alliance between Warwick, whom he liked personally, and Margaret of Anjou, whose Lancastrian cause he supported. Warwick's unexpected appearance in France gave him the opportunity to put those hopes into practice. If he succeeded in persuading Warwick to change sides, it would make good his promise to support Margaret and put her husband back on the throne; in return, Henry VI, by then surely a grateful ally, would provide Louis with military assistance for an attack on the Duke of Burgundy. From the outset, Louis knew that it would not be easy to bring the two parties together. Although Warwick needed French financial and military support if he was going to return to England and confront Edward with any hope of effecting a change of regime, he was hardly going to help restore the House of Lancaster when his original plan was to place the Yorkist Clarence on the throne. Margaret, too, would be difficult to placate: Warwick was the power behind the king who had unseated her husband and had been a senior commander in the Royalist army that had forced her and her family into exile. But Louis was a master in the arts of intrigue, and he played a skilful cat-and-mouse game to convince Warwick and Margaret that their best hopes of achieving their ambitions lay in uniting in common cause.

His first step was to meet the two parties at Amboise on the Loire, each one meeting him separately and privately so that he could put forward his case and secure some form of common ground. On June 8, the first meeting took place with Warwick, and, faced with no viable alternatives, the English magnate agreed to an alliance with Margaret on condition that Louis supply him with funds and a suitable force of armed soldiers. In return, England would then assist Louis in his planned offensive against Burgundy. As anticipated, the meeting with Margaret was not as agreeable. She found the idea of an alliance with such a man abhorrent, for not only had Warwick driven her from the kingdom but he had also "dared to defame her reputation as a woman by diverse false and malicious slanders." (As other Yorkists had done, Warwick had questioned the paternity of Margaret's son Prince Edward.) These were the words of a woman scorned, but Louis persevered by bluntly telling her that Warwick was her last and best hope of retrieving the English throne for her son. The French king must have made a persuasive case, for although it was reported that Margaret remained obdurate, she eventually conceded that she would meet Warwick in the middle of July when the court met at Angers. This, too, proved to be a difficult occasion. Warwick showed his deference by going down on bended knee, and Margaret demonstrated her haughtiness by making him stay in that position for a quarter of an hour, but agreement was eventually reached whereby the two former enemies were reconciled. Edward, Prince of Wales, was betrothed to Warwick's younger daughter, and in return Warwick would invade England.

This gave each consenting party roughly what they wanted. With French help, Warwick would invade England and restore the House of Lancaster, and in return his daughter Anne would marry Prince Edward, who would eventually succeed to the throne. As it was painfully obvious that Henry VI would be in no state to rule the country, Warwick would hold the regency of England until the Prince of Wales was old enough to succeed. Louis used his money and his persuasive skills to gain a key ally to help him in the forthcoming campaign against Burgundy, and Margaret would live to see her husband's line restored to the throne of England. Only Clarence had lost out. He had placed his faith in Warwick as the best means of winning the English throne, he had betrayed his brother, and now he could only look on while a rival from the House of Lancaster was promoted ahead of him. Ten days later, Anne and Edward were betrothed in Angers Cathedral—consanguinity through descent from John of Gaunt meant that they needed a dispensation from the pope before they could marry—and Warwick pressed ahead with his invasion plans. Although he had little trouble assembling his army, he did not enjoy command of the sea, as French ports were under constant blockade by English and Burgundian warships. Ironically, many of these had once been under his command.

The preparations could not be kept secret and Edward soon knew what was afoot, but during that summer his attention was diverted when he received intelligence about a new Neville-inspired rebellion in the north of England led by Lord Henry FitzHugh of Ravensworth, one of Warwick's brothers-in-law. Remembering what had happened in 1469 when he wavered, and the successful policy a year later when he had marched to crush the rebels, Edward decided to deal with the uprising himself. Placing his trust in Howard's fleet to guard the Channel while he was away from London, he gathered an army and marched north to York, where he found that FitzHugh's rebellion had fizzled out and its leader had fled into Scotland. As a result, Edward set out to return to London on September 7, and stopped in the Midlands, where he expected to be supported by another army commanded by Warwick's brother Montague. By then, Warwick was also on the move. A freak late summer storm had scattered the English and Burgundian ships and by chance had given his fleet of 60 ships a favorable wind to cross the Channel unopposed. With him went Clarence, the Earl of Oxford, and Jasper Tudor, who hoped to raise forces in Wales and reclaim his old title of Earl of Pembroke, and, shortly after they arrived in the west of England, they were joined by the Earl of Shrewsbury and Lord Stanley. Their message was familiar: They had arrived in England to end the misrule of Edward IV and to restore Henry VI to the throne as the rightful king of England.

Edward had miscalculated by leaving his southern flank exposed, and he was to pay for the mistake by losing his throne. As Warwick marched north, people started flocking to his ranks; at the same time, they began melting away from the king's side. Edward had never enjoyed much support in the north, where Lancastrian sympathies were always strong, and in other parts of England there was a sudden and dramatic slump in his own standing. It was also the case that Warwick was well liked and that his arrival encouraged Lancastrian magnates to renew their support for the cause by declaring their hand; as happened so often in these civil wars, the mere display of success was frequently sufficient to encourage people to declare their allegiance or change their minds. With support quickly ebbing away, Edward was hit by a major catastrophe as he waited the arrival of Montague and his army of 6,000 from the north. Still smarting from the perceived insult of losing the Northumberland earldom, Montague suddenly decided to throw in his lot with his brother Warwick.

Montague's defection was decisive because it placed the king between a hammer and the anvil. While he rode down from the north with Montague behind him, Warwick was coming up from the south and the king was caught in the middle. Realizing that he lacked sufficient force to take on either army, let alone both of them, Edward followed the line of least resistance and fled east across Lincolnshire to the port of Lynn, where he and his small band of followers managed to find two Dutch ships that took him into exile in Burgundian territory. With the king went Gloucester, Earl Rivers, and Lord Hastings, a loyal courtier who had started his career as chamberlain of the Royal household in 1461, and who had played a leading role in negotiating the marriage of Edward's sister to Duke Charles of Burgundy (as Charolais had become following the death of his father). On arrival in Burgundy, Edward hoped that his brother-in-law would lend him assistance, but Duke Charles had decided to play a waiting game to see if Warwick would keep his promise to Louis. Faced by this inaction,

Edward and his small court settled in Bruges, where they received help and support from Louis, Lord of Gruthuyse, a personal friend who had acted as the Burgundian ambassador to England. For the king, it was a shocking turn of events. Only three weeks had passed between Warwick's arrival and his own flight to the continent, and in that short time, his support had evaporated, just as it had done in 1469. Faced by his enemies' numerical superiority, Edward's only choice had been to quit England, as he probably realized that his fate would be very different if he fell into Warwick's hands. The king-maker had proved that clemency was not a preference when it came to dealing with defeated enemies.

While Edward bided his time in the Low Country, Warwick set about making good the promises he had made to Margaret in Angers. Having sent Sir Geoffrey Gate and the Bishop of Winchester ahead of him to liberate Henry VI from his lodgings in the Tower—the imprisoned king was reported to be "amazed" at the turn of events—Warwick rode into London on October 6, together with Shrewsbury and Stanley, and all greeted Henry as their lawful king. They found that Henry was poorly dressed—"not worshipfully arrayed as a prince and not so cleanly kept as should seem such a prince"—and Warwick ordered that he be given a blue velvet robe before being paraded through the streets on his way to new quarters at the Bishop of London's palace near St. Paul's cathedral. Here the crown was replaced on his head, but it is hard, to say if Henry understood what was happening to him. The chronicler Georges Chastellain supplied a graphic description of the comatose state in which the king found himself following five years of captivity: "a stuffed wool sack lifted by its ears, a shadow on the wall, bandied about as in a game of blind man's buff . . . submissive and mute, like a crowned calf."

Such a man was putty in Warwick's hands, and no sooner had the news of Edward's flight been made known than Warwick issued a statement that the previous king had been deposed and Henry had been restored to the throne in a move that was known henceforth as "his readeption to Royal power." One by one prominent Lancastrians began emerging from internal or external exile, while, at the same time, their Yorkist opponents went into hiding, adopted low profiles, or sought sanctuary in religious houses. Queen Elizabeth (Woodville) was given succor in Westminster Abbey, where she was provided with lodgings by Abbot Thomas Milling and later gave birth to her first son, another Prince Edward. Both Edward IV and his brother Gloucester were attainted, but there was no unnecessary bloodletting and the most prominent Yorkist to be executed was the reviled John Tiptoft, Earl of Worcester, brother-in-law to Warwick and a renowned Latin scholar who had entered Edward's circle early in the reign and was highly regarded at court. However, he was also a sadist who devised new and horrible ways of putting people to death, using methods that brought him the nickname, "the butcher of England." Huge crowds attended his execution, and the fear of a lynching led to a brief overnight postponement with Worcester being placed in the Fleet prison for his own safety. The next day he was led to Tower Hill, where he met his end with calm dignity, claiming that he was simply protecting the state. He was the only prominent Yorkist supporter to be punished in this way.

On October 13, the day before Worcester's execution, Henry was paraded through the streets of London and taken to St. Paul's with the cheers of the crowd ringing in his ears. His restoration was proving to be popular, and Warwick also shared in the feel-good factor that accompanied Henry's return to office. To strengthen his own position, Warwick claimed the office of Great Chamberlain of England and reclaimed his position as Captain of Calais; he was also recognized as Lieutenant and Protector of the Realm, while Clarence was reappointed Lieutenant of Ireland. Parliament met on November 26, to confirm Henry as king of England and to name his successors as his son Prince Edward and, failing him and his heirs, the Duke of Clarence. At the same time, Edward and his line were disinherited and attainted, while Lancastrian magnates had their titles and lands restored to them. Among them was Jasper Tudor, who once more became Earl of Pembroke; one of his first actions was to ride to Hereford to release his nephew Henry Tudor from the custody of Lady Herbert. And yet, despite the feeling expressed by Rous that Warwick had "all England at his leading," his position was still not entirely secure. Lack of money and authority made it impossible for him to reward those who had supported him, and there was still a feeling in Lancastrian circles that despite his recent actions, he remained a dangerous enemy who might one day make a personal bid for the throne. Clarence, too, was a problem, and this would get worse as soon as Margaret and her son Edward returned to England to make the Lancastrian hold on the throne a reality. For all that he had played a leading role in the readeption, he was still the exiled king's brother and could easily change his mind and allegiance once again.

However, the most pressing problem facing Warwick in the short term was the need to repay Louis by preparing a force to fight in France against the Burgundians. Warwick tried to be as good as his word and promised to raise a force of up to 10,000 archers, and at the beginning of 1471, he ordered the Calais garrison to begin offensive operations against the Burgundians, who were already under attack by French forces in Picardy. Having lost his patience with these tardy moves and in a move designed to put additional pressure on Warwick, Louis had ended the truce with Burgundy and declared war in December 1470. Perversely, the outbreak of hostilities concentrated Duke Charles's mind and helped alter his attitude to Edward. From being an embarrassing guest in Bruges, the exiled English king once more became a key player, and, following a meeting at the beginning of 1471, he was promised the necessary funds to return to England and ships were prepared for his use on the island of Walcheren. Slowly and in great secrecy a small invasion fleet began to assemble at Flushing, with ships being supplied both by the Burgundians and by the Hanse League in return for lucrative trading rights should Edward return to the English throne. A propaganda war had also been started. During the winter months, the exiled king had used his time well by making contact with Clarence and other potential supporters in England, notably Henry Percy, a potential supporter, to whom he had already restored the earldom of Northumberland.

However, time was not on his side. On December 13, Henry VI's son Prince Edward had married Anne Neville at Amboise and preparations were begun for the couple and Margaret of Anjou to return to England. Once they were back in England, they would make a formidable party who seemed to have everything on their side: Edward was 17 and ambitious to be king, Henry would surely offer no resistance to the idea that he should abdicate in favor of his son, the Lancastrian magnates had shown their hands, and the combined strength of the forces available to them would have been more substantial than anything Edward IV could raise at that time. But, disastrously for the Lancastrian cause, Margaret delayed her departure from France. They spent Christmas in Paris, and the early weeks of 1471 were passed waiting for Warwick to cross to France to accompany her and her party for their return to England. However, while she fretted, Warwick started prevaricating, claiming that shortage of funds prevented him from making the journey. Even when Margaret did get to Dieppe, bad weather caused further delays, and it was not until the last week of March that she was able to leave Harfleur for the short Channel crossing. By then it was too late: England was about to face a fresh round of civil conflict as the two rival kings vied for the control of their country.

17

THE RECOVERY OF ENGLAND

Throughout the winter of 1470–1471, Edward had been plotting and making preparations for a return to England, but his plans were always in danger of being thwarted by the fact that Warwick's fleet controlled the Channel. True to form, the master intriguer had found the funds for keeping the ships at sea by encouraging his shipmasters under the command of his kinsman the Bastard of Fauconberg (the illegitimate son of Lord Fauconberg, hence his title) to engage in piracy against Spanish and Burgundian ships and to use the proceeds to fund their operations. To cross the Channel or to approach the southern English coast, Edward's small invasion fleet would need either luck or excellent seamanship to avoid their clutches.

The bad weather that had hindered Margaret's preparations could also have prevented Edward from putting to sea, but on the contrary, the uncertain conditions helped him. During the February storms that kept the English and French ships in port, there was a brief and unexpected lull when the gales subsided, providing a welcome window of opportunity. Edward decided to risk everything on a crossing of the North Sea to allow him to land in East Anglia, where he had powerful allies including the dukes of Norfolk and Suffolk. On March 11, 1471, his small invasion fleet of 36 vessels led by the flagship *Antony* put out of Flushing, and following a choppy overnight crossing, the king's party made landfall at Cromer, where they found scant welcome. The coast had been secured by forces led by the Earl of Oxford, and the Duke of Norfolk was nowhere to be seen as he had been taken into custody by Warwick as a precautionary measure. Because it would have been foolhardy to attempt a landing—the Yorkist army consisted of only 1,200 men—Edward decided to push further north toward the coast of Yorkshire. Once again the weather was against him and the little fleet was scattered over a wide area, but two days later, on March 14, the *Antony* arrived at Ravenspur in the estuary of the River Humber and the first members of Edward's party went ashore to be joined by the rest of the force the following day. This time, the omens were better. Ravenspur had seen an earlier claimant to the English throne: Henry Bolingbroke had arrived at the selfsame spot 72 years earlier on his way to unseat Richard II.

Fortunately there is a detailed account of the events that followed the landfall in Yorkshire—a document known as the *Arrivall of Edward IV*—that was created at the time of the actual events. Written by one of the Royal courtiers who was present throughout the operation—identified by many as Nicholas Harpisfield, clerk to the Signet—it is a detailed but partisan summary of the events as they unfolded. The narrative provides a realistic picture of the difficulties facing the king as he took his first steps to reclaiming his throne. By landing in Yorkshire, Edward might have been following, albeit unconsciously, Henry IV's successful example, but he was deep in enemy territory. Despite its name, Yorkshire was Lancastrian country and there was little local support for the king's party. Bands of armed men were rumored to be gathering to halt the king's progress, and when the Royal party approached Hull, the gates were closed firmly against them. Nearby, Beverley provided a warmer welcome and Edward was allowed to enter York, but only after he agreed to leave his army outside the city walls. It also helped that he had borrowed Bolingbroke's ruse of professing that he was not seeking to return to the throne but only wanted to reclaim his dukedom and the rights and property that went with it. Although Edward's promise soothed local anxieties and he was able to continue to his family's castle at Sandal near Wakefield, the author of the *Arrivall* conceded that, "as to the folks of the country there came but right few to him, or almost none." Edward's one stroke of luck was that Montague failed to act against him as he passed by Pontefract Castle and that the Earl of Northumberland also did nothing to stop his progress. While Percy did not make any move to lend physical assistance to Edward—to have done so would have betrayed the Lancastrian dead of Towton, many of whom were Yorkshire men—he "did the king a right good and notable service" by doing nothing. For Edward and his party, the decision to restore the Northumberland earldom to the Percys was now paying a useful, if unlooked-for, dividend. Had either Montague or Northumberland acted to arrest Edward while he moved through Yorkshire, the king's cause would have been stopped before it began.

By then, Warwick had received news of Edward's return and immediately sent out summonses for military support, only to find that some magnates, notably Shrewsbury and Pembroke, were waiting for Queen Margaret to show her hand. According to the *Arrivall*, where this help was not forthcoming Warwick "straightly charged them to come forth on pain of death," but even that grim warning was not enough to encourage people to take up arms. One potential supporter, Lord Stanley, received the summons but preferred to ignore it as he was involved in a private feud with the Harrington family over possession of their castle at Hornby in Lancashire. Nevertheless, Warwick had to act decisively if he wanted to protect his position. Leaving his brother George Neville, Archbishop of York, in charge of affairs in London, he took his army north to Coventry, where he hoped to meet up with his main supporters, Clarence and Oxford, who had already sent out summonses to their own people, in the southwest and East Anglia, respectively. Meanwhile, finding himself unhindered in Yorkshire, Edward continued marching south toward Nottingham and Leicester, and as he passed through middle England, his support began to grow. More importantly, his brother Clarence was weighing his options and had started taking soundings about Warwick's ability to counter the invasion.

By the end of March, the strategic position still favored Warwick even though there were doubts about how much support would be given to him. Edward was in Nottingham gathering his forces, but to the north, he faced Montague; in front of him, Warwick occupied Coventry; and on the flanks were the armies of Clarence and Oxford. A coordinated attack at this point would have had dire consequences for the outcome of his invasion, but Edward was aware of the danger and was determined to act quickly to retain the initiative. Instead of waiting for more followers to rally to his cause, he marched his army toward Coventry, where Warwick responded by staying within the city's walls, refusing all challenges to give battle. Even when Edward proposed a general pardon to avoid bloodshed, Warwick spurned the offer and simply sat tight to await the response from the main Lancastrian magnates. It was not a good move. Far from enjoying unqualified support, he was still regarded with great suspicion on account of his decision to change sides, and men with long-held family links to the Lancastrian cause such as Edmund Beaufort, the attainted Duke of Somerset, and John Courtenay, the heir to the Devon dukedom, preferred to await the arrival of Queen Margaret and her son before taking up arms. Their refusal to act made Warwick anxious about the strength of his own position, and eventually his refusal to offer battle to Edward led to his undoing.

Clarence, always a fair-weather friend, had finally decided that his best interests lay in throwing his lot in with his brother. Ever since Henry VI had been returned to the throne, Clarence had been gradually sidelined, and he had everything to gain and nothing to lose by changing sides once again. Supporting Warwick had only strengthened the claims to the throne of Henry's son, and Clarence's own position not only was precarious but garnered him nothing but the contempt of the Lancastrian court. Clarence was also under family pressure from his mother and his sisters as well as from other prominent Yorkist supporters, and allied to Warwick's incapacity to act, this burden was too much for him to bear. Never a particularly stable character, from an early age Clarence had been overwhelmed by his own ambition, hence his decision to betray his brother and join Henry VI; having seen his hopes thwarted by the Lancastrians, he was equally hasty to switch allegiances again once it became apparent that there was little chance of him succeeding to the throne.

This was a man who could not trust himself from one day's end to the next. When Gloucester visited him on April 2 to persuade him to change sides, his mind was easily made up, and on the following day, the three Yorkist brothers met at Edward's camp at Banbury where they were reconciled. Edward promised to restore Clarence's estates, while Clarence offered the support of his not inconsiderable army, and there was "right kind and loving language betwixt them." Together the brothers led their army back to Coventry and offered a final challenge to Warwick, who not unnaturally refused to give battle once he saw the size of the force ranged against him. Once again, he decided to wait behind the city's walls to see what would happen because, by then, he knew that Queen Margaret was about to leave France for England and that her arrival would bring in the wavering Lancastrian support.

Warwick's obfuscation left Edward in a quandary. While he wanted to defeat his powerful rival and erstwhile ally, he could not afford to mount a lengthy siege of Coventry. Not only was the town well defended while his own army was running short of supplies, but he feared being caught between Montague's and Oxford's armies. There had already been a brief skirmish between his forces and a Lancastrian army led by Exeter and Oxford. Believing that his best option lay in a bold move, on April 5, Edward decided to march on London. Not only would this provide him with a power base, but it would bring Henry VI into his hands, thereby preventing Warwick from exercising his influence in a place that had always supported him in the past.

When the king's intentions became clear, Mayor John Stockton was thrown into a panic, as he knew about Queen Margaret's arrival and had already been contacted by Warwick warning him not to support Edward. Choosing sides proved to be such an awkward task that, wisely, he decided to take to his bed until the crisis was over. His removal allowed Neville to take control of the city; the archbishop decided to parade Henry through the streets as a means of drumming up support, but instead of encouraging resistance, the ploy rebounded badly on him. Far from looking like an all-powerful monarch, Henry cut a sorry figure as he rode with his retinue through the streets wearing a plain blue robe "as though he had no more to change with." Not for the first time in his life, Henry regarded the event with a vacant expression as if he were not part of it but a mere spectator. The *Great Chronicle* noted that Neville had to lead his charge by the hand and that the king looked "more liker a play than the showing of a prince to win men's hearts, for by this means he lost many and won none or right few." Political realism also played a part in what happened next. The city council decided not to resist Edward because they claimed they lacked the military means to do so and that resistance would only create unacceptable casualties; besides, they were anxious to avoid the destruction of property and, if possible, to recoup the loans they had made to the king in happier times. Phillip de Commynes was in London at the time; he noted the council's decision and added one more reason why Edward was being offered this unequivocal support:

> As I have been since informed, there were three things especially which contributed to his reception into London. The first was, the persons who were in the sanctuaries [Yorkists], and the birth of a young prince [Edward of York], of whom the queen was there brought to bed. The next was, the great debts which he owed in the town, which obliged all the tradesmen who were his creditors to appear for him. The third was, that the ladies of quality, and rich citizens' wives with whom he had formerly intrigued, forced their husbands and relations to declare themselves on his side.

Once again, Edward was being helped by actions from his past—perhaps the only time in his life when his amorous nature stood him in good stead—and he continued his advance from Coventry, arriving in the capital on April 11, in time to celebrate Good Friday. His first step was to go to St. Paul's to offer thanks for his restoration and to secure the person of Henry VI, who embraced him with the words, "My cousin of York, you are very welcome. I know that in your hands I will not be in danger." Together with Neville and other Lancastrian supporters, he was then placed in the Tower while Edward made his way to Westminster to be reunited, first with his Crown and then with his wife Elizabeth, who presented to him their son in the abbey sanctuary. The following day, Good Friday was duly celebrated, but with Warwick now approaching London from the north, there was little time to tarry. Having installed his wife and family in the safety of the Tower, Edward led his army north out of the capital toward Barnet, where his advance guard collided with Warwick's forward scouts during the afternoon of

April 12 and drove them out of town. By then, night was falling and both armies had to maneuver in darkness, a difficult procedure given their respective sizes— Warwick's army was around 15,000 strong, while Edward had 10,000 men under his command.

Confronting one another's forces in darkness created other problems for the field commanders. Warwick drew up his forces in the traditional three battles on a ridge to the north of Barnet straddling the present-day highways—Oxford on the right flank, Montague in the center, and Exeter on the left—but in the darkness, the forces were misaligned with the result that they overlapped each other on the flanks. (For his part, Edward was in the center, while Gloucester commanded the vanguard on the right and Hastings was on the left.) The confusion was compounded by Warwick's decision to order a night bombardment of the Yorkist lines. While this produced a great deal of sound and fury, the firing was ineffective due to the proximity of both armies and the fact that the gunners were unable to see the opposition in order to gauge the shot. On the overlapping flanks, they simply overshot and caused no damage. The bombardment also produced a huge amount of smoke that combined with the early morning mist to make the battlefield impenetrable when dawn began to break. Despite the uncertainty, showing his usual sense of purpose, Edward decided to attack at first light. According to the *Arrivall*, he "committed his cause and quarrel to Almighty God, advanced banners, did blow up trumpets, and set upon them, first with shot, and, then and soon, they joined and came to hand strokes."

The first action was on the Yorkist left where Hastings's men came under sustained arrow fire and faltered. Taking his chance, Oxford ordered his men to charge—his division overlapped Hastings's force—and using the advantage of the slope, they attacked the Yorkist lines slashing and battering until their opponents ran from the field. In this kind of bitter close-quarter fighting, there was very little room for delicacy of touch. Men were pressed hard up against each other, and death could come from sword point or from the bludgeon of the poleax, a fearsome weapon that incorporated a blade for hacking, a hammer for cracking open armor, and a hook for pulling knights from their horses. Once a man fell injured, he stood little chance of regaining his feet and was usually smashed where he lay. Gradually, the "hand-strokes" began to make their mark and Hastings's men started to fall back on Barnet with their opponents in hot pursuit. Only a desire to exchange slaughter for pillaging prevented a greater rout, and Oxford was hard-pressed to prevent his men becoming a rabble; others simply continued the pursuit south beyond Barnet as the terrified Yorkists tried to make their way back to London and safety. Luckily for Edward, the fog prevented his and Gloucester's men from witnessing the collapse of the Yorkist left flank.

Similar scenes of carnage were being enacted on the Yorkist right flank, where Gloucester had charged Exeter and was attempting to roll up his position. The misalignment of the two positions meant that he failed to make contact in his initial charge, but the mistake allowed him to engage in a flanking attack on Warwick's position that was already under attack from Edward's forces in the center. As the Lancastrian line on the left began to buckle under the strain of the attack, the position of both armies began to change and they found themselves fighting along a north–south axis in a depression, aptly enough known as Dead Man's Bottom. In the mist and confusion, the battle lost all coherence as men simply struck out at those who were closest to them. The change of the original alignment was to have one more consequence and it decided the fate of the battle. Having rallied around 800 of his men in Barnet, Oxford led them back to the field, but by the time they returned, they found themselves facing not the remnants of Hastings's flank but Montague's men in the center. Both were allies, but Oxford's men were wearing the de Vere livery of the star with streamers that, in the bad light, looked remarkably like Edward's badge of the sun in splendor. Mistaking them for the enemy, the Lancastrian troops opened fire with their guns and Oxford's men ran from the field shouting "Treason! Treason!" Not many escaped as many of Warwick's men thought that their erstwhile allies had changed sides, and they were rapidly dispatched in the mistaken belief that they were now fighting for Edward.

In the midst of the mayhem, Edward kept his head and launched his reserves into the melee in Dead Man's Bottom. That decided the issue. Montague was chopped down and killed, and confusion and panic quickly overtook the Lancastrian soldiers who started fleeing from the field in a disorganized rout, ignoring Warwick's pleas to withstand one last charge. Now on foot, Warwick, too, joined the fleeing soldiers and tried to make his way to Wrotham Wood where he had tethered his horse. Although Edward had given orders that Warwick was to be taken alive, the king's words were not enough to save him. Amid the carnage, he was recognized by a group of Yorkist foot soldiers, surrounded, knocked to the ground, and quickly dispatched. As news of his death spread through the ranks, any remaining resistance crumbled, and after three hours of intense fighting, the field belonged to Edward. It was scarcely daybreak yet over 1,000 Lancastrians had been killed and about half that number of Yorkists were dead. The most prominent casualties were Warwick and Montague, whose bodies were taken to London and put on public display to prevent any rumors that they had survived and would return to the fray. Others made good their escape. Exeter was horribly wounded and left for dead but survived to spend the next four years in the Tower. Oxford managed to escape to

Scotland and was followed there by Viscount Beaumont. On Edward's side, the casualties were smaller but they included some illustrious names: Lord Saye and Sele (a fellow exile in Bruges), Lord Cromwell (Humphrey Bourchier, son of Henry Bourchier, Earl of Essex, and nephew of Thomas Bourchier, Archbishop of Canterbury), and Sir William Blount, the heir of Lord Mountjoy. As happens in any civil war, there were turncoats on both sides. Also fighting in the Lancastrian army were two of the Paston brothers (confusingly, both called John, II and III), who had switched their allegiance from the Yorkists in order to regain Caister from the Duke of Norwich. The price of getting the necessary patronage from the Earl of Oxford was their presence in his ranks at Barnet; now they faced ruin and perhaps the forfeiture of their lives. As John (II) aptly wrote to his mother in the aftermath of the battle, "the world, I assure you, is right queasy."

The Pastons' one hope was that all was not completely lost and that the arrival of Queen Margaret in the west country on April 16 would quickly restore the balance of power. She and her retinue were at Cerne Abbey when they received the news of Warwick's defeat and death at Barnet, and although she was "right heavy and sorry," she was persuaded not to give up her cause. Somerset was given command of her forces that included a strong contingent provided by Devon, and from Wales came intelligence that Jasper Tudor was busily raising forces, and the survivors from Barnet were slowly trickling westward to join him. The trick would be to preserve the Lancastrian field army and to avoid immediate battle with Edward until there was a reasonable chance of raising sufficient forces with which to beat him. Accordingly, Somerset gave orders for his men to retire toward Exeter before heading north in the direction of Bristol and the Severn valley, where they hoped to meet up with the Welsh contingent. If they managed to get further north, there was a good chance that they would also receive reinforcement from Cheshire and Lancashire in the shape of much-needed archers. Despite the hangover from Barnet, there was still sufficient optimism that the cause was not lost and that Edward could still be defeated, provided that there was no military engagement in the immediate future.

The king, too, had been preparing for the next round. After the battle, he retired to London, where his first task was to remuster his soldiers, as was customary, had retired to their homes. On April 23, he celebrated the feast of St. George with a Garter ceremony at Windsor and then set off westward, taking with him some 3,000 men together with a large artillery train. By then, artillery pieces were becoming more effective even though they remained unwieldy and were difficult to transport—most were constructed by shrinking iron hoops around iron staves on the barrel principle. Primitive handguns were also in use, although these were often more dangerous to the user than to the intended target. Edward had no option but to move quickly. He needed to crush the Lancastrians before they raised additional support from the regions and were in a position to threaten London. From his intelligence network of spies, he had a good understanding of his opponents' movements and from the outset could work out that they were making for the Severn valley. On April 24, he left Windsor and pushed on to Malmesbury, where he received information that the Lancastrian vanguard was advancing toward Chipping Sodbury on the road from Bristol and appeared to be on the point of offering battle. Edward hoped that the issue could be settled then and there, but on deploying his army on Sodbury Hill, he quickly understood that he had been outwitted. The vanguard was a ruse; instead, the bulk of Somerset's forces was making for Gloucester and its important crossing over the Severn.

This unexpected move gave the Lancastrians a sudden advantage, but the weather was against them. The beginning of May was unseasonably hot, and Somerset's men had to march 36 miles through what the *Arrivall* described as "foul country, all in lanes and strong ways betwixt woods without any good refreshing." At the same time, Edward's men had the benefit of the higher ground, marching along the western escarpment of the Cotswold ridge. They were also helped by the fact that Edward had sent messages to Sir Richard Beauchamp, the governor of Gloucester, forbidding him to open his gates to Somerset's army and ordering him to deny them the use of the bridges. Beauchamp kept his word, and as a result the Lancastrians had to push north toward the nearest crossing at Tewkesbury, which they reached late in the day on May 3 following a forced march of 24 miles. At the same time, Edward had passed Cheltenham, and by the same evening, his army was only three miles away. His men, too, were exhausted, having marched a similar distance in the blinding heat, and rations were running low, but having reached their enemy, battle was inevitable. As night drew on, they took what little rest they could and made preparations for the battle that would follow when dawn broke. If Edward wanted to prevent Margaret from joining forces with Jasper Tudor, he knew that battle had to be joined the following day and that he had to win it.

On Saturday, May 4, it seemed that the Lancastrians held the advantages. They were drawn up to the south of Tewkesbury with the River Avon behind them and the Severn to the west, and they occupied the high ground that looked down on what the *Arrivall* described as "evil lanes and deep dykes, so many hedges, trees and bushes, that it was hard to approach them near, and come to hand." The army was drawn up with Somerset and Sir Edmund Beaufort on the right flank; the center was commanded by the elderly Lord Wenlock, a veteran of the First Battle of St. Albans, where he had fought on the Lancastrian side, and also of Towton, where he had fought on the Yorkist side; Devon was on the left. Against them, to the south, Edward held the center, with Gloucester on his left and Hastings on his right. Astutely, Edward took the precaution of deploying a small force of 200 mounted spearmen in the woods to the left of his army; they were to clear the ground of any enemy who broke through the left flank or to be used as a mobile reserve to exploit any advantage gained by the main force. Having "committed his cause and quarrel to Almighty God, to our most blessed lady his mother, Virgin Mary, the glorious martyr Saint George and all the saints," Edward ordered his archers and gunners to open a "right-a-sharp" fire that had a devastating effect on the opposition.

Unnerved by the ferocity of the assault, Somerset ordered his men to advance toward Edward's left flank. At first, they made good progress as their intentions were masked by the roughness of the terrain, but as they clashed with Gloucester's lines, two things happened to stall their progress. If the attack was to have any chance it depended on Wenlock's battle moving forward at the same time to engage Edward's men in the center, but for reasons that are unclear, the men in the center remained static, their banners blowing in the breeze on the "marvellous strong ground." The lack of any support allowed Edward to extend his line to help stem the Lancastrian attack, and at this point, the 200 hidden horsemen joined the battle from the woods on the left, riding with couched lances into the Lancastrians' exposed flanks. As a result, Somerset's men were now outnumbered and outmaneuvered.

It was not the end but the beginning of the end. After half an hour's fierce close-quarter combat, Somerset's men were in disarray as they were pushed inexorably into narrow ground by the River Avon, which later received the grim appellation, "Bloody Meadow." Some fled the field, riding as hard as they could to get away from the slaughter, while a handful made their way back to the center to continue the fight. Among the latter was Somerset, whose blood was up not just on account of the fighting but because he had been badly let down by Wenlock. In the words of the Victorian antiquarian and battlefield visitor Richard Brooke, "Lord Wenlock not having advanced to the support of the first line, but remaining stationary, contrary to the expectations of Somerset, the latter, in a rage, rode up to him, reviled him, and beat his brains out with an axe." The incident was recorded by Warkworth and is an apt, if extreme, demonstration of the way to deal with a divisional commander who has failed on the battlefield. Rumors abounded that Wenlock had survived the incident and that another body had been buried in his place, but he was never heard of again and he remains one of an infamous band who served on both sides, having changed sides first from the Lancastrians to the Yorkists and then back to the Lancastrians.

Although the readjustment of the Lancastrian lines brought some much-needed shape to the battle, the advantage had now swung to Edward's forces in the center. The king seized the opportunity presented to him and, leading by example, took his men forward to engage the remains of the Lancastrian defensive lines. This was a horrible phase of the battle, with men standing within reach of each other, stabbing with swords and hacking with battle-axes, until the front gave way and men started running from the field as best they could, with Yorkist mounted men and foot soldiers pursuing them. Most attempted to get back into the safety of Tewkesbury or took refuge in the abbey, but others were trapped by the Severn and cut down by its banks. With the Lancastrian field army destroyed, the slaughter began in earnest. The most prominent casualty was Prince Edward, who was recognized by his surcoat emblazoned with the arms of England, and was summarily hacked to death. Also slain in the last stages of the fighting were Devon and Somerset's brother John Beaufort. Those who had fled to the abbey for safety soon discovered that it was no sanctuary. A force led by Edward, Clarence, and Gloucester arrived outside its gates, swords in hands, and demanded that the abbot hand over those who were sheltering under his roof. He pleaded in vain that holy ground was being polluted; the king and his brothers demanded the expulsion of their enemies, and the abbot had to comply. Among those who became prisoners was Somerset, who was given a quick trial by Gloucester and Norfolk the next day and summarily beheaded in the marketplace in Tewkesbury. Another dozen prominent Lancastrian knights received similar treatment, largely because they had proved themselves to be obdurate supporters of Queen Margaret and had broken previous promises to keep the peace. As for the queen, who probably watched the battle from the tower of the abbey, she was apprehended three days later in a religious house near Malvern and taken to London.

The victory at Tewkesbury left Edward in complete control of England. Henry's son and heir was dead, thereby ending the Lancastrian succession, his mother was in custody, the execution of Somerset and the death of his brother extinguished the Beaufort male line, the power of the Nevilles had been broken at Barnet, and leading Lancastrians such as Northumberland had been bullied or bought into submission. All that remained was the melancholy figure of Henry VI in London, imprisoned and to all intents and purposes out of his mind, and the more threatening figure of Jasper Tudor, who was still at large with his young nephew, Henry of Richmond, who wisely took the opportunity to go into exile in France. His mother Margaret Beaufort had been a prominent Lancastrian, but having seen her son removed from England, she threw in her lot with the Yorkists by marrying Edward's steward, Lord Thomas Stanley. They were all that remained of the once mighty house of Lancaster that had suddenly disappeared from history.

Edward's return to London on May 21 was the high-water mark of his reign, and he entered his capital with all due pomp and ceremony, according to the Croyland chronicler, "ordering his standards to be unfurled and borne before him." In his retinue rode his brothers and the Dukes of Norfolk, Suffolk, and Buckingham, "together with other nobles, knights, esquires and a host of horsemen larger than had ever been seen before." Those who had supported the king, notably those who had resisted Fauconberg's demands to enter the city, were rewarded with knighthoods. Also present was a litter carrying Margaret of Anjou, who was subjected to the taunts and derision of an angry crowd. Her presence spelled doom for her husband. Not only was Henry VI no longer needed, but also his continued presence in the capital acted as a focus for unrest; as long as he lived, there would always be the possibility of civil war, and so he had to die. On the king's orders, he was assassinated that very night, and it is highly probable that Gloucester was involved. That was the view of Warkworth and Commynes, and even if the king's brother did not actually carry out the deed, he was probably in the Tower when Henry met his end. No one believed the account put out by the *Arrivall* that Henry had died a natural death "of pure displeasure and melancholy" caused by his son's death and the defeat of his cause. The point of view voiced by the Milanese ambassador was more realistic: Henry had been killed because Edward had "chosen to crush the seed." (When his body was exhumed in 1911, his skull was found to have been smashed, indicating sharp blows to the head.) His body was displayed in public in the streets of London so that all could see that he was indeed dead. Later, he was interred at Chertsey Abbey in Surrey.

As for his wife, whose ambitions had largely been responsible for the civil wars that had marred his reign, she was kept in the Tower and remained in English custody for four years until Louis XI had her ransomed and returned to France. By then, as a childless widow, she no longer presented a threat to the Yorkists and could hardly be used as a focus for disaffection from what remained of the Lancastrian cause. Little is known about the last years of her life. On her return to France, she was housed first in a chateau near Angers and finally at Dampierre near Saumur, where she died on August 25, 1482. History was not kind to her, and because the winning side wrote the first accounts, she was represented as a cold, domineering, and ambitious woman whose machinations plunged the country into years of internecine conflict. While it is true that she demonstrated a hard and aggressive approach to winning power and then held on to it, especially as far as her son was concerned, she was also influenced by events. The best that can be said about her is that she found herself encumbered by a weak-willed and passive husband, and to protect her own position, as well as that of her family, she had to show resilience and fortitude. In that respect, she was a victim of circumstances who had to be a "great and strong-laboured woman"—the Pastons' accurate, if somewhat unkind description—in order to survive.

With Henry's death and the ascendancy of Edward of York, the civil wars between the rival houses were over. Everything now depended on the new order producing a period of stability and good governance after Henry VI's catastrophic reign. By defeating the Lancastrians so heavily and so decisively, Edward IV had reinforced his leadership abilities and had shown himself worthy to be a king. In contrast to Henry VI's weak and vacillating character, he had emerged as an energetic and courageous leader who was prepared to take risks and was happy to back his judgment with actions. By taking opportunities when they were presented to him, not least during Warwick's dithering behavior at Coventry, he was able to take the war to his opponents before they could unify their larger forces. At Barnet and Tewkesbury, he had exposed himself to danger in combat and displayed a boldness in leadership that inspired his men. From a military point of view, he had underscored many of the virtues of kingship, and in so doing, he had added greatly to his personal authority. That made him an attractive king; the next step would be to stamp his personality on the next years of his reign and provide England with a peaceful and stable form of governance.

18

MASTER OF HIS OWN KINGDOM

*A*s events would quickly demonstrate, the second period of Edward's kingship proved him to be in a much stronger position than he had ever been in the previous decade, and his second reign began with the Crown unexpectedly strong and more settled than it had been since the early years of Henry IV's rule. Edward's hold on power had been won on the battlefield—as it had been at the beginning of his reign—and his throne was virtually unassailable once it had been recovered in the summer of 1471. He did not have to look over his shoulder to see what Warwick might be plotting, his great rival the House of Lancaster was virtually extinct, he had destroyed his most potent enemies among the aristocracy, and he was well placed to stamp his own authority on his personal rule. Never one to deny the ostentatious and pleasure-loving side of his personality, Edward now gave free rein to his vanity by spending huge sums of money on improving his wardrobe and enriching his court so that he could look every inch the king. The Royal accounts for the second period of his reign confirm not just that Edward was also interested in wearing fine clothes but also that he was prepared to spend large amounts of money on setting new fashions. At Christmastide in 1482, he appeared at court "clad in a great variety of most costly garments, of quite a different cut to those which had usually been seen hitherto in our kingdom." Thanks to loans from well-wishers and fines imposed on his enemies, there was no shortage of cash to pay for all this luxury, and the wardrobe accounts for 1480 reveal that he possessed 26 gowns, doublets, or jackets, some of them made of cloth-of-gold, satin, and velvet and edged with ermine and sable. During the later years of his reign, he accumulated a huge amount of expensive plate and jewelry, and he was no shrinking violet when it came to demonstrating his personal wealth. As the Italian visitor Dominic Mancini recalled in his memoirs, Edward enjoyed the fact that his subjects took pleasure in his appearance and was not shy about making sure that he himself was seen by as many people as possible:

> Frequently he called to his side complete strangers, when he thought that they had come with the intention of addressing him or beholding him more closely. He was wont to show himself to those who wished to watch him, and he seized any opportunity that the occasion offered of revealing his fine stature more protractedly and more evidently to on-lookers. He was so genial in his greeting, that if he saw a newcomer bewildered at his appearance and Royal magnificence he would give him courage to speak by laying a kindly hand upon his shoulder.

However, for all the brilliance of his court and for all the charisma he brought to the throne, Edward still faced a number of potentially irksome domestic difficulties—for example, he had to decide how to handle the shallow and easily led Clarence. Far from being grateful that he had survived and was not being punished for his earlier treacherous behavior, the king's wayward brother was already showing signs of resentment. Instead of leading a quiet life, as might have been expected following his dealings with Warwick and the Lancastrians, Clarence showed little desire to accept his position and was soon in open disagreement with his siblings. However, Edward's most urgent need was to complete the pacification of the realm and to take the necessary steps to prevent any fresh outbreak of hostilities. Never a vindictive man—unlike Henry VI, who had condoned several needless executions—Edward was not interested in revenge. Instead, he instituted a two-pronged policy by sidelining potential enemies and by offering the hand of friendship to prominent supporters of Henry VI who he felt could be trusted. In a three-year period between 1472 and 1475, Edward rescinded 30 sentences and judiciously offered offices of state to men who had been in the employment of the previous regime.

There were also rewards for those who had supported him throughout the period when he had lost his crown and had to fight to regain it. Edward's friend and close ally Hastings was given the task of settling Calais together with Lord Howard, and they took with them an armed retinue to give weight to what they were prepared to offer—pardons for the captains and considerable sums of money to make sure that the garrison switched its loyalty to the new order. Many of Warwick's supporters accepted the pardons when they were offered to them, and the funds were used to pay the Lancastrian soldiers' wages, another sensible move considering the propensity of the Calais garrison to act independently and cause trouble. Edward was less lenient in Kent and Essex, where he was determined to make an example of those who had supported the Bastard of Fauconberg and in so doing to prevent any repetition of the unrest that had almost led to a fresh outbreak of civil conflict in a part of England notorious for its troublemaking. The main punishment was the imposition of heavy fines; Canterbury had its liberties taken away and had to repurchase them; these tactics helped swell the Royal coffers. Coventry, too, had to pay for its liberties to be restored as a result of its support for Warwick. It was a rough-and-ready system, and, even though it created a good deal of animosity, it avoided mass bloodshed—or, as the *Great Chronicle* put it, "such as were rich were hanged by the purse, and the other that were needy were hanged by the necks."

Alongside the punishments, there were pardons for prominent Lancastrians who were prepared to come into the Yorkist fold. Prominent among them were administrators who had given loyal service to Henry VI but were now prepared to trim their positions to the new order simply because there was no other option following the death of their patron and his only son. As soon as it became clear that there was going to be no viable opposition to Edward's rule, a number of leading Lancastrian supporters chose pragmatism and threw in their lot with the restored court. There were exceptions, the most notable being John de Vere, Earl of Oxford, and Jasper Tudor, together with his nephew Henry, who all stayed in exile. Exeter, too, remained in custody in the Tower, but for the most part, men were happy to engage with Edward and offer him their unstinting support. In turn, this allowed the king to develop Royal patronage and to construct a network of trusted professional retainers and bureaucrats who managed his affairs and those of the country in return for grants of money, land, and influence. Among those who benefited from Royal patronage were two lawyers, John Morton and Sir John Fortescue, who typified a new breed of bureaucrat that came to the fore during the second period of Edward's reign. Once the new reign began, they showed that they were prepared to switch loyalties to keep themselves in power and seem to have had little or no fixed allegiance to those who had given them preference early in their careers. Both Morton and Fortescue had served Queen Margaret and had suffered the privations of exile with her, yet when Edward offered them positions after his restoration, they were happy to accept the proposal. Morton, the son of a Dorset squire, had been educated at Cerne Abbey and had been destined for the church, but his secular career had progressed under the House of Lancaster. He played a role in the Parliament of Devils in 1459 that attempted to break the House of York and rose quickly in Lancastrian favor, yet by 1472 he was Master of the Rolls and was reported to be enjoying Edward's "secret trust and special favour." In later years, he became Archbishop of Canterbury and Chancellor of Oxford University, an extraordinary achievement for one who had been so close to the House of Lancaster and who had made no secret of his dislike for Edward IV; in 1483, in a letter to the Duke of Buckingham, he explained his ability to change sides seemingly at will:

> Surely, my lord, folly were it for me to lie, for I would swear the contrary your lordship would not, I ween, believe, but that if the world would have gone as I would have wished, King Henry's son had had the Crown and not King Edward. But after that God had ordered him to lose it, and King Edward to reign, I was never so mad that I would with a dead man strive against the quick.

The same kind of self-interest propelled Sir John Fortescue, who had been chancellor in exile to Henry VI. A lawyer of Lincoln's Inn, he had previously served as a member of parliament and Chief Justice of the King's Bench and had followed Queen Margaret into exile in Scotland in 1461. During that time, he had also written forcefully against Edward's claim to the throne, but the king was anxious to let bygones be bygones. Fortescue was the first eminent constitutional historian, and his monument is the treatise *On the Governance of England*, which analyses the political upheavals of the period and argues that the English form of government was superior to foreign forms of monarchy such as the French absolutist form. Fortescue prospered as a result of his decision in 1471 and happily transferred his loyalties to his new liege lord, King Edward IV; his estates in Gloucestershire were restored to him, and he lived out his life in prosperity and comfort.

The most prominent member of the king's circle of advisers was now Gloucester, Edward's closest affiliate and a devoted brother whose loyalty had never wavered. In contrast to Warwick and Clarence, Gloucester had cemented his allegiance to Edward through his deeds, and, as his most recent biographer has pointed out, the story of his career between 1468 and 1483 is one of unbroken service and fidelity to the Crown. Unlike Clarence, he did not change sides to gain any advantage, and he remained a loyal and diligent servant of his brother the king even during the difficult months of exile and the uncertain return to England when there was still much to do to cement Edward's cause. He remained loyal to the succession: When Edward proclaimed his oldest son Prince of Wales shortly after the restoration, Gloucester was the first to pledge allegiance to his nephew. In return, he was richly rewarded, as indeed he expected to be. Gloucester might have demonstrated exemplary dependability and devotion to duty, but he was also extremely acquisitive, and like many other men in his

position, he wanted to be rewarded so that he could enjoy the fruits of his success. As the youngest son in the Yorkist dynasty he had no settled inheritance, yet
he had to support his status as a Royal duke and one of the greatest men in the
land. During Edward's first reign, he had come to believe that he was being
shortchanged, one reason being that his brother the king had little in the way of
patronage to give him, but the second reign changed all that and the riches and
property that came his way altered the direction of Gloucester's life by turning
him into a rich and powerful magnate.

Following the crushing of the Nevilles, Edward decided to present the bulk
of their power base in the north to his younger brother. At the end of June,
Gloucester was granted the key Neville strongholds of Middleham and Sheriff
Hutton in Yorkshire and Penrith in Cumberland, and these acquisitions were
quickly followed by the award of the office of Chief Steward of the Duchy of
Lancaster, a post Warwick had previously held. As he was already Warden of the
West Marches, these new possessions gave Gloucester considerable temporal
power in the north, and he set about buttressing it by gaining other important
posts such as Sheriff of Cumberland, Constable of Bewcastle, and Custodian
of the Northern Forests, the latter post previously having been held by
Northumberland. The following year, he cemented his new position of authority in the north by marrying Anne, Warwick's youngest daughter and the widow
of the Lancastrian Prince Edward, who had been killed at Tewkesbury. To do
this, he had to risk papal displeasure as Anne was a cousin and he should have
sought a dispensation on an account of consanguinity, but Gloucester was determined to make the match and placed the girl and her mother in sanctuary in the
Convent of St. Martin-le-Grand in London while he pleaded his case before the
king and council. (Astonishingly, Anne appears to have been employed as a
kitchen maid at the time and may even have been secreted away in that guise by
Clarence in a vain attempt to prevent the marriage.) The match was opposed by
Clarence, who rightly believed that it would eat into his own authority—he was
married to Anne's sister Isabel and laid claim to the Beauchamp and Despenser
lands through her—but he was powerless to intervene. As a result, Gloucester
became one of the Neville heirs, laying claim to the Salisbury and Neville lands,
and, more importantly, through his marriage, he was able to present himself as
the true recipient of the loyalty and obedience that the Neville retinues normally
afforded their lord. In time, he came to claim the support of such influential
northern lords as FitzHugh, Greystock, Scrope, and Dacre, all of whom had at
one time thrown their weight behind Warwick. Even Northumberland gave
Gloucester his allegiance and entered into what was effectively a power-sharing
agreement that allowed both men to retain their positions in the north of

England. This was an important consideration, as Gloucester increasingly regarded the area as his power base by developing former seats of Neville authority, whereas the Percys were already one of the most dominant families in the same part of the world.

However, Gloucester's claims on the Neville inheritance were not as cut and dried as he would have liked them to be. As long as Warwick's widow Anne lived, the outcome of the inheritance should not have been an immediate issue. Although she was under what amounted to house arrest at Beaulieu Abbey in Hampshire, she was determined to protect her rights, but her continuing presence loomed over the issue and caused a huge amount of ill feeling between Clarence and Gloucester. The quarrel also produced a headache for Edward. From the outset, Clarence remained obdurate about his rights and behaved in a high-handed and intemperate manner that did not suit the weakness of his position. While he had been restored to the king's favor, he was still a man who had changed sides more than once and was guilty of betraying both his brother and his friend Warwick, but like many ambitious men, he paid little attention to what had happened in the past and thought only about what he could achieve in the future. In February 1472, Edward summoned his brothers to Sheen to debate the issue, but apart from some minor tinkering involving the partition of the Warwick estates and the granting of the title of Earl of Warwick to Clarence, the issue remained unresolved.

At the heart of the quarrel was the position of Warwick's widow, who was the heiress of Richard Beauchamp, Earl of Warwick, and Isabel Despenser, daughter of Thomas Despenser, Earl of Gloucester. At the same time, the rightful heir to her husband's Neville lands was George Neville, Duke of Bedford, the son of John Neville, the Marquess of Montague (her husband Warwick's brother), who had been killed at Barnet. To compound the difficulty, neither Clarence nor Gloucester wanted to gain the disputed lands by Royal grant as their security would not be completely guaranteed—if there were a change of policy or regime they might be attainted or forced to surrender them under an act of resumption. For that reason, both men were determined that the lands in question should be given to them under the law of inheritance, and neither was prepared to budge on that point.

Faced with a complicated and seemingly intractable problem, Edward chose the line of least resistance and produced a policy that suited both his brothers, but it proved to be a shady and squalid piece of legal chicanery. In May 1474, parliament passed an act that divided Warwick's inheritance between the two Royal dukes, and to circumvent the countess's legal claim, it was declared that the decision had been taken as if she "were now naturally dead." A second act followed early in the following year debarring Bedford or any of Montague's male heirs from laying claim to the Neville inheritance. This was carried through on the dubious grounds that Edward had been minded to attaint Montague for his treason in supporting Warwick during his recent rebellion but had been dissuaded by his brothers. As for the dispossessed Countess of Warwick, she was left bereft and penniless and was forced to live with Gloucester at his residence at Middleham Castle in Wensleydale. No one came out of the episode with any dignity. Clarence and Gloucester had shown themselves to be rapacious and unfeeling, and Edward had revealed a weak side. True, he had prevented a quarrel from spinning out of control into a new round of civil conflict, an important point given the country's recent history, but at the same time, he had ridden roughshod over the country's legal system by introducing a judgment that had no regard whatsoever for the laws of inheritance.

The squabble over the Warwick inheritance also coincided with two episodes that briefly threatened Edward's authority and that may have prompted him to seek an early and lasting solution to his brothers' quarrel. In April 1472, the king decided to act against George Neville, Archbishop of York, the one member of the Warwick faction who had been permitted to remain in a position of authority. Initially, Edward had had no immediate plans to punish him and could not remove him from his see without the pope's authority, but this worldly, acquisitive, and meddlesome priest was still a power in the land and remained a threat to the king's authority—as brother-in-law to the Earl of Oxford, his loyalty to the king might not have been absolute. Without giving any reasons, Edward had the archbishop arrested and sent into exile at Hammes Castle in the Calais Pale. Not content with ridding himself of the threat, Edward took possession of Neville's wealth and his revenues from the see of York, his household was broken up, and to add to the shame, the richly jeweled archbishopric miter was smashed into pieces to make a new crown for Edward. Few mourned Neville's passing—he died in 1476 without regaining his authority—and the Warkworth chronicle merely noted that "such goods as were gathered with sin, were lost with sorrow."

The second threat to the peace of the realm was more serious. After a short stay in Scotland, the Earl of Oxford had taken himself to France where he hoped to win the support of Louis XI. At the time, the French king had good reason to assist any action that might be taken against Edward and was already in negotiation with James III of Scotland to create a new anti-English alliance that would also involve bringing Oxford into the plot. In May 1473, Oxford attempted an armed landing in Essex but was forced to retreat and put to sea again, committing acts of piracy in the Channel throughout the summer. His next move was to land in Cornwall with Viscount Beauchamp (Oxford's companion in exile in Scotland) and seize St. Michael's Mount, a rocky offshore outcrop whose fortress was easily defended but needed continuous supply and resupply. It was also convenient to besiege and to cut off supplies, as Royalist forces proved by the end of the year. Faced by starvation and tempted by the offers of pardon, the soldiers in Oxford's garrison began to defect, and the episode ended with everyone, Oxford included, being offered Royal pardons. For his pains, Oxford was sent back across the Channel to join his brother-in-law in Hammes Castle, where he remained for the rest of Edward's reign. His attainted lands were passed to Gloucester, leaving the Dowager Countess, Oxford's mother, penniless and homeless. Placed in confinement in Stratford, she was forced to hand over her property and lands to Gloucester after he had petitioned parliament and threatened her with "heinous menace of loss of life." Although her son's attempt to raise a rebellion had failed to make any impression on the well-being of Edward's throne, it did leave an uneasy suspicion that both Neville and Oxford might be acting in collusion with Clarence against the king's best interests. Apart from rumors mentioned in the Pastons' correspondence about the involvement of Clarence in Oxford's plans, there is no firm evidence to support such a charge, but as matters were soon to show, it is clear that Edward had become highly suspicious of Clarence's intentions since the restoration. His unsteady and immoral brother was the only man in England who possessed sufficient authority, wealth, and opportunity to effect a change of rule, and Edward probably understood that.

The settlement of his brothers' quarrel over Warwick's possessions allowed Edward to turn his attention to the great matter of France and Burgundy. Despite the expulsion of English forces from the country, Edward still styled himself King of France, and on his arms were quartered the lilies with the leopards. It was still possible that he might be able to reassert English claims to the throne or at the very least reclaim some of the lost English territories in Normandy and Aquitaine. There was also a good deal of personal animus involved as Edward resented the hostility shown to him by Louis XI, who had supported the House of Lancaster and was still a source of mischief, as his recent dealings with the Earl of Oxford had demonstrated. However, Edward was also realist enough to understand that a war against France had the potential to be a ruinous expense on the English exchequer, and he realized that he could hardly attempt it without allies. The obvious candidate in this latter respect was the Duke of Burgundy, but Edward remembered the tardy treatment he had received from Duke Charles during his exile in Bruges, and he could not bring himself to rely solely on a fair-weather friend who offered his support only at the last minute and when he himself knew he could benefit from it. A more reliable option was Duke Francis

of Brittany, who, having no male heir, was forced to protect his interests by entering into foreign alliances. To offset French attempts to attack Brittany, Edward
dispatched 2,000 archers in April 1472, and this was followed by an embassy led
by Earl Rivers. The result was the signing of the Treaty of Chateaugiron on
September 11 that allowed the English to use Brittany as a springboard for the
invasion of France in return for territorial concessions and agreement for
English protection for the defense of the duchy during the military operations.

For Edward, the next stage was to withdraw his reservations about Burgundy
and to begin negotiations with Duke Charles, whose support would be essential
for any successful English invasion of France. The middleman was Louis, Lord
of Gruthuyse, Edward's host in Bruges who had been rewarded for his help by
being appointed Earl of Winchester, and a series of embassies made their way
across the Channel as part of a general diplomatic offensive. By then, Burgundy
was ready to resume hostilities against Louis XI, but he exerted a high price for
entering into an alliance with Edward and Duke Francis: If the operations were
successful, Burgundy would support Edward's claims to be crowned King of
France, but he expected to be rewarded with territory in Champagne and the
Somme that would allow him to achieve his ambition of linking his northern and
southern possessions. Having completed the diplomacy and laid military plans,
Edward then had to persuade parliament to find the money to pay for the adventure, and when the notion was discussed, it soon became clear that an attack on
France was not an attractive proposition. Edward countered by arguing that
control of northern France would reduce expenditure on the defense of the
Channel and that there were exciting possibilities for an expansion of trade.
Besides being a rightful expedition, it was necessary to punish Louis XI and to
reassert England's claims to his throne. In November 1472, parliament finally
agreed to grant a special tax of one-tenth of all incomes from land to pay for the
war, but as *The Great Chronicle of London* recorded, Edward still had to raise funds
by other means and was forced into the unseemly position of having to beg
or borrow contributions from his wealthier subjects, using whatever means came
to hand:

> It was reported that as he passed by a town in Suffolk and called before him
> among other a rich widow and frayned [asked] of her what her good will should
> be toward his great charge, and she liberally had granted to him £10, he thanked
> her and after took her till him and kissed her, the which kiss she accepted so
> kindly, that for that great bounty and kind deed, he should have £20 for his £10.

Not everyone was as delighted as the wealthy widow. Writing to her son
John (III), Margaret Paston lamented that the indulgences had impoverished

the entire country: "The king goes so near us in this country, both to poor and rich, that I wot not how we shall live if the world amend."

To keep all his options open, Duke Charles entered into a formal alliance with Edward on July 25, 1474, its terms being similar to those of the previous agreement, namely that Duke Charles would recognize Edward's claim to the French throne in return for substantial territorial compensation and for English military support against Louis XI. The agreement allowed Edward to start planning for an invasion in the following year, and he used the intervening period to reach an agreement with the Hanse League to end a long-standing dispute over commercial privileges and to prevent the eruption of a new naval war in the Channel. Diplomacy also kept Scotland in the English fold. Although James III had been in negotiation with Louis XI, the Scottish king was not keen to pick a fight with his English neighbors and was happy enough to enter into an agreement with them. Agreed in September 1473, the treaty would see his son, also James, marry Edward's daughter Cecily; this arrangement formed the basis of a truce that lasted until 1519. Five years after signing the agreement with Edward, the détente was strengthened in 1478 by the proposed marriage of James III's sister Margaret to Earl Rivers, Edward's brother-in-law, who had lost his wife a year earlier. But the match never happened, and by the end of the decade, optimism had given way to a renewal of enmity when Scots raiders started causing trouble along the border to break the truce, no doubt with the connivance of the Scottish authorities.

Having brokered an agreement with Burgundy and seen off the ever-present threat posed by the Scots, Edward was now in a position to proceed with his plans to invade France. The preparations were detailed and extensive. In December 1474, steps were taken to requisition the ships that would be necessary to transport the English army and their supplies across the Channel. The majority came from English ports, the Cinque Ports providing 57, but such was the demand that additional ships had to be hired from the Low Countries through the good offices of the Duke of Burgundy. Orders were also given for additional bows and sheaves of arrows as well as a well-equipped artillery train. Thirteen of the artillery pieces were huge siege guns armed with over 700 stone projectiles. The army consisted of over 11,500 armed men together with as many noncombatants in support, and if Commynes is to believed, it was the largest army ever assembled for a campaign in France, although he added the proviso that when they assembled, the "men seemed very inexperienced and unused to active service." Leading them were five dukes (including Clarence and Gloucester), three earls, one marquess, and a dozen barons, a contingent that represented the flower of the English aristocracy.

From the end of May, the huge army began assembling in Kent and the first elements crossed to Calais on June 20.

Everything now depended on Burgundy making a move, but when he met Edward at Calais, the English were disconcerted to discover that their main ally was accompanied only by a small personal retinue and not the sizable army they had expected. In the period before Edward's invasion, Burgundy had gone to war with the Swiss in order to add to his dukedom in Lorraine, the possession of which would have allowed him to unite his territories in Flanders and the Duchy of Burgundy. This placed Edward in a dreadful quandary. It was a massive risk to continue his advance into French territory without Burgundian support, yet to retire back across the Channel or to stay put in Calais would produce a huge loss of face, not to say the waste of the funds raised during the past months. He could hardly do nothing, but he was also uneasily aware that his forces were both inexperienced and badly balanced—there were too many archers and too few men-at-arms. It was also proving to be a wet and cold summer, and the campaign got off to the worst possible start when the English army, at Burgundy's suggestion, started moving southeastward toward Peronne on the Somme. When they arrived outside St. Quentin, they were met with sustained cannon fire and most of the advance guard was either killed or taken prisoner. The English were now deep in French territory, and Louis XI had started moving his army from its positions in Normandy, where it had expected Edward to land, toward Artois and Picardy. Far from striking any blow, the English were now in danger of being caught in a trap.

Faced by the impasse, Edward fell back on diplomacy. In fact, he had already paved the way for a negotiated settlement by sending the Garter Herald to the French court even before the "great enterprise" (as he called it) began. Ostensibly, the herald's task was to present Louis XI with Edward's official demand for the return of English territory and to make his claim on the French throne, but according to Commynes, who was present throughout, there was also a private discussion about the possibility of a settlement without going to war, provided that the approach was made by the French. And that was the eventual outcome. Louis did not want to engage in a potentially ruinous war with an adversary who had a large if untested army, and he realized that Edward, too, wished for an accommodation. Accordingly, following an exchange of envoys, the French king offered the opportunity of a meeting for peace negotiations. The two sides met near Amiens—Dr. Morton was amongst the English delegation— and a deal was quickly produced. In return for the payment of 75,000 French crowns ($320,000 in today's prices) and an annual tribute of 50,000 crowns ($212,000), the English army would be withdrawn as soon as was practical. Also included in the arrangement were a number of commercial agreements to allow greater mercantile freedom and a private understanding for continuing friendship that would be cemented by the marriage of the dauphin to Edward's daughter, Elizabeth of York.

Louis was keen to execute the plan before Burgundy could intervene once more in the process, and the English demands were accepted without demur. To give the whole proceedings a dignity that was missing from what was in reality a sordid commercial transaction, the English and French armies proceeded toward Amiens in full battle array. It was all for show, and so concerned was Louis to keep the peace that he produced lavish entertainment for the English soldiers, who immediately took advantage of the huge amounts of food and drink made available to them:

> The king [Louis XI] had ordered two large tables to be placed on each side of the street, at the entrance of the town gate, which were covered with a variety of good dishes of all sorts of food most proper to relish their wine, of which there was great plenty, and of the richest that France could produce; and abundance of servants to wait on them, but not a drop of water was drunk. At each of the tables the king had placed five or six boon companions, persons of rank and condition, to entertain those that had a mind to take a hearty glass. . . . Those English who were within sight of the gate, saw the entertainment, and there were persons appointed on purpose to take their horses by the bridles, and lead them to the tables where every man was treated handsomely as he came, in his turn, to their very great satisfaction.

Commynes also noted somewhat tartly that during the three days' spree, the English would be seen drunk in the streets as early as nine in the morning. Another account claimed that women were also made available to the English and "many a man was lost that fell to the lust of women, who were burnt by them [infected by venereal disease]; and their members rotted away and they died."

Against that unedifying backdrop—drunken behavior and sexual indulgence on the part of the English and a disdainful response from the French—the two kings finally met at Picquigny some three miles downriver on August 29. A bridge had been built across the Somme, and the French had taken the sensible precaution of including a palisade or barrier in the middle to allow discussion but keep the two sides apart. They wanted no repetition of the incident at Montereau where Duke John of Burgundy had been killed on a bridge during similar negotiations 56 years earlier. Agreement was quickly reached; this had been made easier by Louis's decision to offer bribes to Edward's advisers, all of whom left France with pensions and lavish gifts of silver bullion. According to

Commynes's evidence, the two kings were soon on amiable terms, with Edward addressing Louis "in quite good French," and the agreement known as the Treaty of Picquigny was quickly sealed. War had been averted, Edward returned from France with a healthy profit, few lives had been lost, but far from being the "honourable peace" claimed by the Croyland chronicler, the French expedition left a bitter memory in many minds, a belief that it was without honor and that somehow the English had been duped by getting drunk and accepting bribes. Louis, though, was well pleased with the outcome because he had avoided a costly war and had managed to uncouple Edward from Burgundy. "I have chased the English out of France more easily than my father did," he boasted, "for he had to drive them out with armies, while I have seen them off with venison and good French wine."

The real loser was Burgundy, who failed to help Edward because of his military commitments in Lorraine. By the end of the year he was still engaged in his ruinous war against the Swiss, and in so doing, he lost his life at the battle of Nancy on January 5, 1477. With his death, his line came to an end and his vast territorial holdings were divided between France and his daughter Mary and her husband Archduke Maximilian, son of the Holy Roman Emperor. Five years later, Mary of Burgundy had also died as a result of a fall from her horse, and in the same year, 1482, as a result of the Treaty of Arras, Louis XI was confirmed in possession of the duchy. The duke's death ended Edward's hopes of an alliance to challenge France and to make any fresh claim on the French throne. When Edward returned to England later in the summer, he faced criticism in some quarters for failing to wage a successful war against the French, and the feeling lingered that it was a dishonorable episode in the country's history. From Edward's point of view, the best that can be said of the "great enterprise" is that he came out of it with his hands clean and his reputation intact. He also brought final settlement to the problem posed by Margaret of Anjou, who was handed over to Louis XI on payment of a ransom and on condition that she renounce her claim to the English Crown and all her dower lands in England. With her removal, one more vestige of Lancastrian rule was ended; she lived on for another six years, but it was a pitiful existence as Louis forced her to give up all claims inherited from her father King René of Anjou and her mother Isabella of Lorraine.

19

GLORY AND
TRANQUILLITY

On his return to England, Edward was at the peak of his power. For the time being at least, he no longer had to worry about France, his finances were secure, and, with his main rivals killed or sidelined, his kingdom was at peace and he could afford to indulge himself and his family. The commercial strictions ended by the Treaty of Picquigny allowed English merchants to prosper once more, and there was a welcome expansion of trading with France especially in the cloth and wool markets that had stagnated during the recent civil wars. The king also freed himself from the financial dependency of parliament and was able to live of his own, a remarkable achievement and one that helped alleviate any lingering concern about the recent flawed operations in France. Another innovation was his decision to engage in trade himself, becoming a shrewd and successful venture capitalist with several successful import–export concerns under Royal control. Much of the enterprise was in the hands of his managers, but according to the Croyland chronicler, Edward was himself involved in trade and Royal ships were used to export wool, cloth, tin, and other products all to the advantage of the king's exchequer. A number of leading aldermen in London received knighthoods, and Edward was unusual in maintaining cordial relations with the merchant class. Coming after the profligacy and reckless expenditure of the House of Lancaster, Edward's good housekeeping and solid financial judgment helped make the years after 1475 something of a golden age in English history, a quiet period the Croyland chronicler was moved to describe as a time of "glory and tranquillity." Together with the king's French pensions and other revenues, continued the same chronicler, "all these particulars in the course of a very few years rendered him [Edward] an extremely wealthy prince."

He was also becoming increasingly vain and sensuous in his approach to life. During the meeting on the bridge at Picquigny, Commynes had expressed his surprise that Edward was becoming fat and had lost the youthful handsome features that had been much admired during his earlier years with Warwick in Calais. Greed and lack of exercise were the cause. According to Mancini, one of Edward's less pleasing failings was the use of an emetic during banquets so that he could gorge and regorge for the simple pleasure of eating and drinking as much as possible. Added to this was the continuing and well-attested interest he took in women. Writing later, Sir Thomas More complained that the king's "greedy appetite was insatiable, and everywhere all over the realm intolerable. For no woman was there anywhere, young or old, rich or poor, whom he set his eye upon . . . but without any fear of God, or respect of his honour, murmur or grudge of the world, he would importunely pursue his appetite and have her, to the great destruction of many a good woman." More was quoting the Duke of Buckingham in 1484, at a time when Edward's character was under attack, although as a very young boy at the time, the author was probably cognizant of the king's immoral behavior. Edward's principal mistress remained Jane Shore, who finally received an annulment of her marriage on account of her husband's impotence, an unusual and rarely used reason for ending a marriage relationship. She had the happy knack that not only had she captivated the king sexually but she made friends with him as well, and it proved to be a lifelong bond. More also makes the point that the king listened to her and there were occasions when she was able to intercede in his affairs: "Where the king took displeasure, she would mitigate and appease his mind; where men were out of favour, she would bring them into his grace." Not unnaturally, the situation did not please Queen Elizabeth, who was said to hate "that concubine whom the king her husband most loved," and she was also resentful of the role played by Hastings, whom she thought "secretly familiar with the king in wanton company." But the queen's displeasure over these antics did not keep Edward out of the marital bed—by 1480, the couple had ten children, two of whom died in infancy (Margaret and George).

The one blot on this otherwise settled landscape was Clarence. With Gloucester, he had accompanied his brother to France and had provided a well-armed retinue, but on his return to England, his behavior became increasingly erratic. In December 1476, his wife Isabel died in childbirth at Warwick Castle where her husband had assumed all the rights and properties of her father, the king-maker, and this left Clarence free to marry again. One suggestion was Burgundy's heiress Mary, but such a match would have caused all sorts of problems. Not only would it have strengthened Clarence's own position as a possible claimant for his brother's throne—if he remarried, his new wife was Edward's niece—but there was a further, though distant, Burgundian claim through Mary's grandmother Isabella, who was a granddaughter of John of Gaunt. Edward forbade the match on the grounds of consanguinity and common sense, and as a result of the king's ruling, the relationship between the brothers quickly deteriorated. Clarence seems not to have learned from his previous mistakes. Instead of standing behind his brother and supporting him as Gloucester had done, he spent too much of his time attacking the king and, from the scant evidence available, involving himself in plots against him, as "each began to look upon the other with no very fraternal eyes." The Croyland chronicler takes it further, alleging that the situation was exacerbated by "flatterers running to and fro, from the one side to the other, and carrying backwards and forwards the words which had fallen from the two brothers, even if they had been spoke in the most secret closet."

Two incidents combined to bring about Clarence's downfall, and it is clear from both of them that he was largely the author of his own misfortunes. In April 1477, he arranged for the abduction from her house in Somerset of Ankarette Twynho, a former lady-in-waiting in his household whom he suspected of poisoning his duchess Isabel by giving her "a venomous drink of ale mixed with poison." In a single day, she was taken to Warwick Castle, tried before the justices, indicted, and then summarily hanged along with an alleged accomplice called John Thursby. This was a disgraceful abuse of power and it was followed by another equally serious error of judgment. In the month following Twynho's lynching, an Oxford astronomer Dr. John Stacey was arrested for attempting to use magic against the king, and under torture, he implicated one Thomas Burdett, a Warwickshire landowner and a member of Clarence's household. A third man, Thomas Blake, was also arrested, and all three faced trial on charges of using necromancy to kill or "imagine the death" of the king and the Prince of Wales. During the trial, Blake was reprieved, but on May 20, Stacey and Burdett were taken to Tyburn and hanged, drawn, and quartered. Clarence was already implicated in that Burdett was in his employment, but instead of staying clear of the affair and keeping silent, he decided to intervene by making sure that the two condemned men's declarations of innocence were read aloud to the council. To make matters worse, Clarence arranged for the protest to be read out by John Goddard, a friar who had become notorious during the Readeption by preaching on Henry VI's absolute right to the throne. This act of lèse-majesté enraged Edward, who decided that enough was enough; Clarence was arrested in June and incarcerated in the Tower of London.

Clarence remained there until parliament convened on January 19, 1478, its main business being to arraign him on charges of high treason, the attainder being introduced by the king. This was a staged political trial—Clarence could not call witnesses and was only permitted to refute the charges made against him—but the king was determined that on this occasion, there should be no second chance for his foolish and wayward sibling. Edward did not stint himself in listing the accusations against his brother. Clarence, he said, was guilty of "heinous treasons," he had betrayed his loyalty to himself by whispering that Edward was a bastard (it was not the first occasion that he had made that allegation), he had committed a crime by hanging Ankarette Twynho, and he had presumed the innocence of Burdett who had committed treason. In short, Clarence was "incorrigible" and had committed "a much higher, much more malicious, more unnatural and loathely treason than at any time heretofore had been encompassed, purposed and transpired." Despite their closeness as brothers and for all that the king was generally minded to forgive his enemies, in this instance Clarence had tried Edward's patience so sorely that he deserved to be punished. It was a sorry business. Clarence was doomed before the trial began, and Edward was determined that on this occasion, there should be no second chance. As the Croyland chronicler makes clear, the charges against Clarence were vague and unsubstantiated, and when witnesses were produced they were present not to give impartial evidence but to add to the condemnation:

> The circumstances that happened in the ensuing parliament my mind quite shudders to enlarge upon, for then was to be witnessed a sad strife carried on before these two brethren of such high estate. For not a single person uttered a word against the duke, except the king; not one individual made answer to the king except the duke. Some parties were introduced, however, as to whom it was greatly doubted by many, whether they filled the office of accusers rather, or of witnesses: these two offices not being exactly suited to the same person in the same cause. The duke met all the charges made against him with a denial, and offered, if he could only obtain a hearing, to defend his cause with his own hand [by meeting his accusers in personal battle]. But why delay in using many words? Parliament, being of the opinion that the informations which they had heard were established, passed sentence upon him of condemnation, the same being pronounced by the mouth of Henry, Duke of Buckingham, who was appointed Seneschal [Constable] of England for the occasion.

Clarence was taken back to the Tower, and there he lay for ten days while Buckingham delayed the imposition of the death sentence. Being newly appointed as Constable of England, Buckingham was not anxious to rush the execution of a man who was after all the king's brother, and it was not until the Speaker of the Commons intervened to demand an immediate execution that he arranged for Clarence to be dispatched on February 18. To avoid unnecessary scandal, the imprudent duke was done to death privately within the Tower, and afterwards a legend grew that he escaped hanging or beheading—the normal method of execution—only to be drowned in a cask of sweet Malmsey wine. This explanation came to be accepted, although it is equally possible that Clarence was drowned while bathing in a tub, but whatever the method, the act was little more than judicial fratricide. The case against Clarence was largely trumped up and was pushed through parliament by the king, who used the kind of language that brooked no disagreement. In terms of natural justice, the treatment of Clarence was illegal and immoral, but in terms of realpolitik, Edward had been pushed into a corner. His brother had already sorely tried his patience by siding with Warwick and then by switching his allegiance when it suited his ambitions. Clarence was devious and untrustworthy, and it was highly probable that he continued to act duplicitously after the return from France with a view to pushing his claim on his brother's throne. Even though the execution of a brother leaves a stain on Edward's reputation, the situation had reached a point where he had to act against Clarence to ensure his own survival. Seen in that light, the wonder is not that Clarence was sentenced to death but that he managed to survive for so long: Most other European kings of the period would not have been so lenient and would have dealt with the threat much sooner than Edward did.

Hardly had the furor over Clarence died down than Edward was forced to deal with a new foreign policy crisis involving France and Burgundy. Duke Charles's death had reopened the whole question of where Edward's allegiances should lie. Following his détente with Louis XI and his acceptance of the French pensions and the offer of his daughter in marriage to the Dauphin, Edward was honor-bound to maintain the harmonious agreement that had been brokered at Picquigny, but the balance of power was immediately altered when French forces started moving into Picardy, Artois, and Burgundy to capitalize on the duke's death. This changed everything. Louis was now taking advantage of Burgundy's enfeeblement to add to his kingdom and, worse, the moves threatened English mercantile interests in Calais. There was also a domestic angle: The Dowager Duchess of Burgundy was Edward's sister, and she began pressing him for support by insisting that he had to find an English husband for her daughter. Had Clarence possessed a balanced personality and acted as a loyal brother, he would have suited the bill, but as he had enjoyed neither of those virtues Edward was left to solve the matter by diplomacy. On the one hand there was the traditional English distrust of France and the tendency to favor Burgundy; on the other were the substantial benefits gained by the Treaty of Picquigny and Edward's unwillingness to surrender them. It was a tricky problem and one that alarmed Sir John Paston (II), who wrote that it seemed to him "that all the world is quavering." In order to buy time, Edward reinforced the Calais garrison as a signal to Louis XI to stay away from the English possession and sent an embassy to France led by Dr. Morton and Sir John Donne, another trusted official who had given loyal service to the House of York. (A Welshman by birth, he had served in France and had been knighted after Tewkesbury. His links to the throne had been strengthened through his marriage to Hastings's sister Elizabeth.)

As a result of their negotiations, Louis agreed to extend and strengthen the terms of Picquigny, but these were little more than diplomatic niceties. At the same time, a halfhearted attempt was made to marry Rivers to Mary of Burgundy, but as Commynes tartly noted, this was hardly a serious offer as "Rivers was only a petty earl and she the greatest heiress of her time." (This was before her marriage to Archduke Maximilian.) The question of matches for his own children also occupied Edward's mind. All told, he had eight surviving children and was determined to make suitable marriages for them, both to strengthen his dynasty and to give England powerful allies. First and foremost, he had to settle his son Edward, Prince of Wales. One possibility was marriage to the Infanta Isabella, the heiress of Ferdinand of Aragon, but this came to nothing when a son and heir was born to the Spanish rulers in 1478, making the match less attractive. Other names that were discussed were Maximilian of Austria's sister and the daughter of the Duke of Milan. Edward was keen to pursue the latter as she came from a wealthy family, but as the Milanese ambassador reported to his master, the duke, that was ample reason for denying the match. In April 1479, the ambassador wrote a candid assessment of the situation in which he spoke of the "great quantity of money" that Edward would demand in a dowry and expressed his belief that he would do this as "one who tends to accumulate treasure." To balance his relationship with Louis, Edward then thought to marry Prince Edward to Anne of Brittany, the elder daughter and heiress of Duke Francis. The negotiations for this match were lengthy and complicated and involved the use of substitutes should any of the children die—Prince Richard was a first reserve for Edward—but nothing came of the discussions. Later, Richard would be affianced to Anne, the daughter of the Duke of Norfolk and heiress to her family's great Mowbray fortunes. The marriage actually took place in January 1478, when both partners were little more than six years old, but Anne died three years later when she was still a child. Under the law of inheritance, her fortune should have passed back to her family, but as Edward had already demonstrated in his dealings with the Warwick family, mere laws were not a bar when it came to enriching his own family. In January 1483, an act was passed by parliament that allowed Prince Richard and his heirs to inherit the Norfolk fortune, and should he die childless, the inheritance would pass to King Edward. Like the propensity for overindulgence at the dinner table, this greedy side of Edward's nature leaves a question mark over his later years, when acquisitiveness seemed to replace his earlier generous and open disposition.

Scotland, too, was proving once more to be a source of concern. The truce of 1474 remained intact and relations remained cordial, but James III had problems with his own people and these troubles impinged on his relations with England. During his minority, James had been more or less kidnapped by the powerful Boyd of Kilmarnock family, who kept him a prisoner in Edinburgh Castle, and he had managed to regain his liberty only at the time of his marriage to Princess Margaret of Denmark in 1469, a good match that brought Scotland possession of Orkney and Shetland. He also had to deal with the threat posed by John MacDonald, Lord of the Isles, and the exiled Earl of Douglas, with whom Edward IV had entered into an agreement in 1462. Under its terms, James III would have been unseated and Scotland would have been divided and partitioned, with MacDonald and Douglas ruling as English vassals. Then there was the "Auld Alliance" to consider, the military and political contract with the French throne that had come into being as a Scottis–French bulwark against Plantagenet aggression. Over the years it had changed complexion, sometimes being a diplomatic lever, at other times being a military alliance with soldiers from both countries lending assistance to the other in the perennial wars against the English. The Royal families of both countries were linked by marriage, another brick in the alliance, but by the reign of James III, there was an increasing need for the Scots to balance the French connection by keeping the peace with England.

Unusually in the Stewart succession, James III was actively interested in foreign affairs, and during his reign there emerged a new national self-confidence. Partly out of personal inclination and partly out of common sense—Berwick and Roxburgh had been restored—for the first time in many years the Scots wanted and needed a long and lasting peace with England. However, James, like Edward, was cursed by brothers he could not control. In his case, both his siblings had been imprisoned in Edinburgh Castle in 1479 on suspicion of treason, and the younger of the two, John, Earl of Mar, had died while in captivity, probably murdered on the king's orders. His brother, the headstrong Alexander, Duke of Albany, did not wait for the same fate to befall him and managed to escape to France, where he attempted to ingratiate himself with Louis XI and succeeded in getting a French wife, Anne de la Tour, daughter of the Count of

Boulogne and Auvergne. By then, Edward had decided to act against the Scots as a punishment for a resurgence of cross-border raids and also to dissuade James from lending any assistance to the French by invading England. Early in 1480, an embassy was sent to Scotland taking with it a list of impossible demands. These included the return of Berwick and Roxburgh, the pardoning of Douglas, and the handing over of Prince James, the eldest son and crown prince, to be educated in England, just as James I had been. Most humiliating of all, James would be required to pay homage to Edward as his liege lord. No king could accept those conditions and hope to survive, and James was no exception. As England started preparing for war, the Scots took the initiative in August when the Earl of Angus led a large raiding party into Northumberland and set fire to Bamburgh.

This incursion led Gloucester and Northumberland to call out their own forces for a retaliatory raid, but even at that late stage, James was keen to pull back from all-out war. In an attempt to find common ground, two heralds were sent to London in November, but they were angrily ignored as Edward and his council made preparations to invade Scotland with a land army of 7,000 soldiers and a sizable naval force to operate off the east and west coasts. Although Edward had threatened to lead the English forces in person, he failed to make any move during the summer of 1481, and all military activity was left in the hands of Gloucester, who contented himself with mounting a number of cross-border raids. Nor were the Scots idle. In September, their forces raided English territory again to burn and loot before withdrawing back into Scotland. At the same time, Gloucester began preparations for besieging Berwick, which became the main target when hostilities resumed the following year. The idea was to use English naval supremacy to block the seaward defenses and prevent the town and its garrison from being supplied from the sea, but largely due to the king's inaction, progress was slow. By the end of the summer, Edward was still in London, and when he finally did move, he failed to get any further than Nottingham. There were also reports that he was ailing in mind and body, and that he preferred his bed and home comforts, and to compound the general air of unease, the winter of 1481 had produced bitterly cold and wet weather. In an age when portents were often more potent than reality and when a king's ability to reign was measured by his personal capacity to impose his authority on the kingdom, these were worrying signs that things were amiss in Edward's life and that the country would suffer as a result.

A new campaign against the Scots was planned for the summer of 1482 under Gloucester's direction as Lieutenant of the North. With him, he had most of his brother's most trusted adherents. Lord Stanley, Steward of the Royal

Household, led a force from Lancashire and Cheshire, Northumberland was there with his northerners, the Woodville levies were under the command of the Marquess of Dorset, the queen's eldest son from her first marriage. Other notable lieutenants included Rivers and Sir Edward Woodville, both of whom were distinguished jousters, but the surprise element in Gloucester's force was provided by the Duke of Albany in his role of Scottish Warden of the West March. In Albany's personality there were many similarities with Clarence. Headstrong, pushy, a stranger to loyalty, he entertained ambitions to seize his brother's throne, and after discovering that Louis was not inclined to offer French help, he had tried his luck at Edward's court. There was no need for any persuasion. Edward's agents had already contacted him, and on June 11, 1482, the unscrupulous Albany entered into an agreement at Fotheringhay that would see him crowned as "Alexander of Scotland by the Gift of the King of England." In return he would hand back Berwick to the English, as well as other places on the border including Lochmaben, Eskdale, and Annandale; the alliance with the French would be ended; and Albany would acknowledge Edward as his feudal superior. To cement the new arrangement, he would get rid of his French wife "according to the laws of the Christian church" and marry Edward's daughter Cecily. Foolish and ruthless though Albany undoubtedly was, he must have realized that the agreement would never be accepted by the Scottish nobility, who would hardly allow such humiliating conditions to be imposed on them and the country. But having betrayed his brother James, Albany now had nothing left but to tie himself to Edward's plans.

The invasion began in earnest in July with the investment of Berwick under Lord Stanley while Gloucester took the bulk of the army into the Lothians toward Edinburgh. At the same time, James rallied his own forces, declaring that he would "defend the realm in honour and freedom, as his noble progenitors had done in times past." Having assembled his army on the Burgh Muir, Edinburgh's traditional mustering point, James led it south into Lauderdale, where his nobles finally decided to end their support for him in a dramatic and spectacular way. Led by the Earl of Angus, they demanded that the king rid himself of his favorites, most notably Robert Cochrane, a commoner, who had reformed the currency and had been promoted to the vacant earldom of Mar, a promotion that had angered the older and more venerable Scottish noble families. On being told that the Scottish nobles were like the mice in the fable who agreed that it was in their interests to hang a bell around the cat's neck but none was prepared to take any action, Angus is supposed to have proclaimed to his fellow conspirators, the Earls of Huntly, Lennox, and Buchan, that he would "bell the cat." He then promptly led the way and hanged Cochrane and the other favorites over the bridge at Lauder. Then, having accomplished their mission, the conspirators took the king into their custody and marched back to Edinburgh.

Forever after, Angus's nickname was "Bell the Cat" and the tale passed into Scottish folklore to become an accepted historical fact. While it is likely that there was an incident at Lauder involving the king, that account is not the whole story. From the English State papers it is clear that Gloucester invaded Scotland and quickly gained the upper hand; it is also true that Albany was treasonably implicated on the English side; James also had problems with his nobles, but the reality of the events in Scotland in the summer of 1482 is more prosaic. When Gloucester reached Edinburgh, James and his followers locked themselves in the impregnable castle and sat tight. To the frustration of the English, there was no pitched battle and the episode ended in compromise. Backed by the citizens of Edinburgh, who agreed to repay the marriage dowry due to Edward, James had his authority restored to him and was able to negotiate with Gloucester for a return to the status quo and the renewal of the earlier peace agreement, including the marriage of his son to Cecily. In return, Berwick would be surrendered, never to be returned to Scotland—it had changed hands 14 times since 1296—and a new truce between the two countries came into immediate effect.

As a result of his triumph, Gloucester was awarded palatinate authority in Cumberland and any Scottish territory in the West March of which he was Warden, moves that confirmed his pre-eminence among his peers. Even his brother was pleased with the outcome, writing to Pope Sixtus IV that Gloucester's "success is so proven that he alone would suffice to chastise the whole kingdom of Scotland." The other winner was Albany, who renounced his claim to the Scottish throne and was restored to his earlier position and authority within the country. Like Clarence, though, he did not know when to stop intriguing, and in his feline way, he kept his links to the English court open with the hope of one day being able to reforge the Fotheringhay agreement.

While Gloucester had benefited from the Scottish expedition, it had done little to help Edward, and the Croyland chronicler lamented the decision to pull out of the country without inflicting a decisive blow against the Scots. As he pointed out, barring the capture of Berwick, little had been gained in return for a great deal of effort and unnecessary expenditure: "This trifling, I really know not whether to call it gain or loss—for the safekeeping of Berwick each year swallows up ten thousand marks—at this period diminished the resources of the king and kingdom by more than a hundred thousand pounds." As ever, it was not the end of the matter. It is clear from the parliamentary records that Edward intended to reopen hostilities with James when the campaigning season began in the summer of 1483. He was also under pressure from Maximilian to support

Burgundy by invading France, and the conflict with Scotland provided a good excuse for keeping out of that particular quarrel. However, the end of the year also brought about a dramatic change of direction in the long-running saga of English, French, and Burgundian relations. Earlier in the year, Mary of Burgundy had died in a riding accident, and this unexpected event led to a détente with Louis who took advantage of the new situation by proposing a match between the Dauphin and Margaret, the baby daughter of Maximilian and Mary. This changed everything, and France and Burgundy agreed to the proposal in the Treaty of Arras, which was signed shortly before Christmas. Under its terms, the match was negotiated with the dowry being found from the lands of Artois and Burgundy. As Edward no longer brought anything to French interests, there was no need to keep the terms of the Treaty of Picquigny and the pension payments were stopped forthwith. A furious Edward briefly considered taking his revenge by going to war with France, but it was all fantasy: As long as he was contemplating further war with Scotland, it was impossible to fight on two fronts.

The sudden return to England of the unstable Albany at the beginning of the year rekindled hopes that the English would be able to renew hostilities on the northern front, but like much else in Edward's foreign policy at this stage of his reign, it is hard to avoid the impression that the king had lost his grip on affairs. The basic mistake he had made while pursuing his tripartite foreign policy was his failure to recognize that James III was unwilling to uphold the Auld Alliance by going to war with England at Louis's behest. Having entered into an agreement with the Scottish king six years earlier, Edward would have been better advised to maintain friendly relations at a time when there was no threat apart from the never-ending cross-border raids that were commonplace and could have been contained by Gloucester. Instead, he seems to have harked back to his earlier policy of wanting to crush the Scots and force their king to pay allegiance to him—that belief had first become an issue in 1463 when James III's mother had offered military support to Margaret of Anjou and the House of Lancaster. Twenty years later, it still rankled that the Scots had gone unpunished.

All in all, Edward's diplomatic efforts had achieved very little. To the king's displeasure, the Treaty of Arras had ended the fruitful relationship begun at Picquigny—the Croyland chronicler recorded that Edward "thought of nothing else but taking vengeance," for not only had he lost his pension, but there was no longer any chance of his daughter marrying the Dauphin. For a few wild days, Edward considered the possibility of building up his forces to invade France and went so far as to promise to send a force of archers to Brittany if Duke Francis decided to support him in France, but these were only the reactions of a disappointed man. Eventually, he decided on compromise and sent an embassy to the French court in February 1483 to negotiate a new truce. That left only the problem posed by Scotland, and contemporary accounts make it clear that throughout this period of his reign, Edward was determined to maintain an aggressive posture toward his northern neighbor. In this respect, he had been helped by the arrival of Albany, who was again living in England even though his brother James had been pleased to appoint him lieutenant governor. By February, the terms originally agreed at Fotheringhay had been renegotiated: Albany would lead an army into Scotland to depose James III, and then forces led by Gloucester and Northumberland would march into the country to lend him assistance. Once on the Scottish throne, Albany would terminate the Auld Alliance and adhere to the promises he had made at Fotheringhay the previous year. This would have two benefits: Edward would achieve his long-held dream of reducing Scotland to a vassal state, while the new dispensation would allow Scottish troops to be used in any invasion of France. However, everything hung on the lightweight Albany, who led the invasion force in the company of another disaffected nobleman, the Earl of Douglas, only to be heavily defeated at Lochmaben on July 22, 1484. That was the end of Albany's machinations: He fled to France, where he died the following year.

Unfortunately, Edward's problems with the shifting alliances of France and Scotland were mirrored by a sudden and growing discordance at court. Ever since the marriage to Queen Elizabeth, the Woodvilles had maintained and reinforced their preeminent position, much to the chagrin of the king's associates, who believed that they were being sidelined by powerful rivals who were far too close to the throne. At the beginning of 1483, the queen's brother Earl Rivers was the master of the Prince of Wales's household, his brother Sir Edward Woodville was poised to take command of the navy, and another brother, Lionel, was Bishop of Salisbury. In the next generation, the Marquess of Dorset was deputy governor of the Tower of London and enjoyed a close friendship with the king. All this alarmed the faction centered around Hastings, the Duke of Buckingham, and Lord Stanley, the steward of the Royal household, and the result was an alarming confrontation between the rival magnates. The main clash was between Rivers and Hastings, although the latter also entertained contempt for young Dorset. Both of the main protagonists were powerful men in their own right and both enjoyed strong links to the throne. As Anthony Woodville, Rivers had built up an international reputation as a jouster and had fought in the Yorkist army at Barnet and Tewkesbury. Soldiering came easily to him, but he was also an ascetic who wore a hair shirt and took an interest in the arts and literature. The Italian writer Mancini thought highly of him, claiming that "however much he prospered, he never harmed anyone, while doing good to man." But this was an overstatement. Rivers was as cunning and ruthless as any other English magnate of the period, and he was determined to crush Hastings's influence at court.

From the outset, Hastings had been a committed Yorkist—his father was a retainer to Edward's father the Duke of York, and he had risen rapidly in Royal favor, becoming a wealthy and substantial landowner. He had accompanied the king into exile and was a prominent supporter when he returned; crucially, he was rewarded by being granted the lieutenancy of Calais, which he received in 1471 in succession to Rivers, who had incurred the king's displeasure by planning to go on a crusade against the Moors in Portugal. At the same time, Hastings built up his power and authority in England, entrusting his office in Calais to his brother Ralph, and during the 1470s, in his role as lord chamberlain, he emerged as the king's main confidant.

There was also social animus between the factions. Although Hastings was a courtier who had made his way in life, the Woodvilles were still regarded as upstarts who owed their rise to the fact that they had married into the Royal family and had used their position to build up powerful alliances. That was the view taken by Mancini, who observed that "they were certainly detested by the nobles, because they, who were ignoble and newly made men, were advanced beyond those who far excelled them in breeding and wisdom." The enmity between the two men was conducted by means of a whispering campaign similar to the one that finally ruined the relationship between Edward and Clarence. Supporters spread smears that were readily believed, the most common being that at different times both Rivers and Hastings had attempted to betray Calais to Louis XI. Mancini records that the king "loved each of them" (Hastings and Rivers) and attempted to find a means of ending the feud, but the fact that it existed is a reminder of the clash of overmighty magnates that fueled much of the conflict in England during the reigns of Richard II, Henry IV, Henry V, Henry VI, and Edward IV. Sadly for the people of England, this propensity was to be the country's further undoing in the years that followed.

20

THE END OF INNOCENCE

*I*n general, with the exception of his uncertain foreign policy, the second period of Edward's reign had been a felicitous time for the king and his country, but it did not have long to run. Before Easter 1483, Edward fell ill and his condition rapidly deteriorated. He seems to have become unwell at the end of March, and he died at Westminster on April 9, three weeks before his 41st birthday. There is no specific evidence to suggest the cause of his death, although there was a good deal of contemporary speculation about why a man in his prime should have succumbed to a fatal illness. The Croyland chronicler contented himself with the bland thought that the king was "neither worn out with old age nor yet seized with any known kind of malady, the cure of which would not have appeared easy in the case of a person of more humble rank." Mancini suggested that Edward caught a chill while fishing with his courtiers, while Commynes offered two explanations, the first that the king died of apoplexy brought on by excess and the second that he fell victim to melancholia caused by the failure of his French policies and the realization that England no longer had any influence in France. There could, of course, have been a connection: If Edward had been downcast by the Treaty of Arras, he might have taken comfort in immoderate consumption of food and drink, and his incontinent appetite could have hastened the onset of a stroke. Both Mancini and the Croyland chronicler left ample evidence about Edward's corpulence and his tendency to overindulge. There were also hints about poisoning, and a later Tudor chronicler, Edward Hall, claimed that the illness was caused by a recurrence of malaria caught while the king was in France in 1475, the disease being prevalent in the Somme region.

Although in the greater scheme of things it does not matter how Edward died—his early death was the real problem—the most likely cause was a stroke caused by his excessive lifestyle. It is clear from all the contemporary accounts that Edward was overweight and increasingly self-indulgent, and as a result, as he got older he probably exercised rarely. His inability to lead the previous year's expedition into Scotland could be evidence of lack of fitness and general lethargy. That he lingered for a while suggests that he suffered a first stroke that left him incapacitated and then a second that was fatal. Whatever the cause of his death, Edward's funeral rites befitted his rank and his stature. For eight days, his embalmed body lay in state in St. Stephen's Chapel at Westminster before being carried into the abbey on April 17. On the following day, the funeral procession set out for the final resting place at Windsor. From Charing Cross, the body was born to Sion Abbey before being taken to St. George's Chapel, where it remained overnight. Following the funeral masses that were led by the Archbishop of York and the Bishops of Lincoln and Durham, Edward was delivered into the tomb he had ordered constructed eight years earlier. This was followed by the solemn Royal interment ceremony: After the burial, Edward's household threw their staves and badges of office into the grave and the leading members of the nobility made their own offerings to a king whom the Croyland chronicler eulogized as a good man:

> The prince, although in his day he was thought to have indulged his passions and desires too intemperately, was still, in religion, a most devout Catholic; a most unsparing enemy to all heretics, and a most loving encourager of wise and learned men, and of the clergy. He was also a most devout reverer of the Sacraments of the Church, and most sincerely repentant for all his sins. This is testified by those who were present on the occasion of his decease; to whom, and especially to those whom he left as executors of his last will, he declared in a distinct and catholic form, that it was his desire that, out of the chattels which he left behind him in such great abundance, satisfaction should be made, either fully, or on a composition made voluntarily, and without extortion on their part, to all those persons to whom he was, by contract extortion, fraud or any other mode, indebted. Such was the most beseeming end of this worldly prince, a better than which could not be hoped for or conceived, after the manifestation by him of so large a share of the frailties inherent to the lot of mankind.

All this was true, and laying aside the need for the chronicler to indulge in hagiography, it was a fair assessment of the man and the life he had led. Those sentiments were repeated by writers immediately after Edward's death, historians like Thomas More and Polydore Vergil who had access to men who had known the king or had lived through his reign. In later centuries, however, there was a radical reassessment. From being the fair-minded ruler portrayed in the

Croyland Chronicle, Edward was frequently painted as a cruel despot whose virtues were outweighed by his greed, laziness, and propensity for violence, the execution of his brother Clarence cited as a preeminent example of his blood-thirsty nature. In more recent times, there has been further reassessment to rebalance his reputation. Although criticism of his political judgment still exists, especially in his dealings with France and Burgundy and his misreading of the situation in Scotland, Edward emerges from the latest judgments in terms that his contemporaries would have recognized. The best that can be said about him is that he rescued England from the horrors of civil war and brought a much-needed stability to society and the economy after the haphazard years of Henry VI's reign. Through his capacity to bring order and a sense of direction to his country, he prepared the way for the Tudors to build on foundations that were more solid than anything that had existed previously. Also, from the evidence of those who knew him or observed his behavior, he seems to have possessed a well-rounded and likable personality, especially in his younger years, before he allowed the natural hunger of youth to turn into the greed and unrestrained personal appetite of his later middle years.

The second half of his reign was crowned by stability, and with no claimants to the throne worthy of the name, he enjoyed a security that had not existed since the years of Henry V. He wanted to build on that independence by enlarging his own fortune and freeing himself from the public purse, hence his obsession with dowries and his pensions from France and his involvement in trade. That made him a wealthy man and removed the financial problems that had bedeviled Henry VI and Richard II; it meant, too, that his subjects were not overburdened by taxation, another reason for his personal popularity during his reign. When Edward died, England was secure, stable, and relatively prosperous; the prestige of the monarchy had been restored; and he had brought peace to the country after the long years of bloody civil strife. The one thing that was missing from the picture was a settled succession, and that absence was to plunge the country into another period of bloodletting as, all too typically, the magnates with most to gain or lose struggled to gain the ascendancy during the period of uncertainty that followed Edward's death. At the time of the king's passing, the rift between Hastings and the Woodvilles had not been healed, and there was also the poten-tial for bad blood between Richard of Gloucester and the Woodvilles. With the king's moderating influence gone, there was a very real danger that there could be a power struggle over which court party controlled the heir to the throne, the 12-year-old Prince Edward.

On the face of it, though, there seemed to be little immediate concern. There had been minorities before and Prince Edward would soon reach his majority, the kingdom was settled, and at that stage the Crown Prince enjoyed the support of all his powerful close family relatives. Richard of Gloucester in particular was in a strong position. He was the dead king's brother, he was rich and influential in his own right, and he enjoyed massive support in the north of England. During his brother's lifetime, he had sworn an oath of loyalty to his nephew as successor, and, according to the Croyland chronicler, on Edward's death Gloucester summoned the northern magnates to "hold a solemn funeral ceremony" in which they reaffirmed their loyalty to the "the king's son; he himself swore first of all." Gloucester also reinforced his position by writing to the queen declaring his loyalty to her son. He also wrote in similar terms to the council, adding that he was well positioned to act as his nephew's protector, but the members were not ready to accept this offer. They preferred to establish a council of regency in which Gloucester would play a role but would be constrained by others. Their decision was mainly due to the influence of the Woodvilles, who were also busily protecting their own positions and had the support of influential men like Dr. Morton. While this jockeying for position was taking place, Prince Edward remained in Ludlow Castle under Rivers's protection, but the council wanted to bring the Crown Prince to London as quickly as possible so that he could be shown to the people and crowned king as early as May 4. Rivers agreed to do this and to bring with him a retinue of 2,000 armed soldiers to provide a lifeguard for the prince. For her part, the Queen proposed herself as regent, but this was quickly rejected. The one person in a position to control events was Hastings, who remained in London both to safeguard his own position and to keep the Woodville faction in check. His advice to Gloucester was that he should leave the north and return to the capital as quickly as possible with a suitable force of armed men. This would enable Gloucester to secure the Crown Prince and take any necessary action against the Woodvilles. Having Gloucester and his men in London would also help Hastings, who had made clear his dislike of "the entire kin of the queen" and was concerned that he might be outmaneuvered. His one compensation during these difficult days was a small but personal one: On Edward's death, Jane Shore had moved in with him, More noting tartly that "in the king's days, albeit he [Hastings] was sore enamoured upon her, yet he forbare her, either for reverence or for a certain friendly faithfulness."

Once again in the wake of a king's death and the absence of a mature successor, the battle lines were being drawn as the rival camps built up their strength and consolidated their positions. On the one side were the Woodvilles, who held the trump card in that Prince Edward remained in their possession and was on his way to London under the protection of Earl Rivers, one of the most powerful men in the kingdom. Dorset caught the mood of the moment when the council suggested that no further decisions should be made until Gloucester arrived in London. Far from agreeing with the proposal, Dorset's quick and self-important response reinforced a belief that his family was in the ascent and now had full control of the situation: "We are quite important enough to take decisions without the king's uncle and see that they are enforced." Soon Dorset was styling himself "half-brother to the king," as indeed he was, being Queen Elizabeth's son from her first marriage, but it was an unnecessary indulgence that only made the situation more tense than it need have been. There were also rumors that the Woodvilles had plundered the Royal exchequer and were preparing to take preemptive action to preserve their positions. Opposed to them was the faction now led de facto by Gloucester and supported by Hastings, as well as by Buckingham, who had no love for his Woodville in-laws—he was married to the queen's sister but always insisted that she came from a low-born family of interlopers. With the date of the coronation fast approaching, both parties had to act, and both had to be able to justify their actions if they were to have any hope of gaining the upper hand.

The news of the king's death had reached Ludlow on April 14, but it took a few days for Rivers to muster the armed retinue that he would take with him to his nephew's coronation in London. This was not just for his own protection but was a normal procedure when traveling with royalty; however, the creation of any large armed forces in fifteenth-century England was bound to be suspicious. It took longer for the news to get to Gloucester, but forewarned by Hastings, he acted more quickly and left York on April 23 with a retinue of 600 "gentlemen of the north" and their followers. By April 29 he had reached Northampton, where he received the news that Rivers and Prince Edward were nearby at Stony Stratford. Buckingham then came in with 300 supporters and the entire party spent the evening together. What happened when they met is a matter for conjecture, but the outcome was real enough. Having enjoyed what was reported as a convivial evening, Rivers was arrested at first light together with his half-brother Richard Grey and the head of the household, Thomas Vaughan. Ominously all three were sent north under close arrest to Pontefract deep in Gloucester's heartlands, and Rivers's forces were ordered to return to Ludlow. Gloucester and Buckingham claimed that they had acted in self-defense to preserve themselves and Prince Edward from traitors, but understandably, the news caused panic when it reached London as rumors spread that Gloucester meant to seize the crown just as his brother had done in 1461. To a certain extent, those fears were allayed by Hastings, who reminded the council that Gloucester had expressed his loyalty to the Crown Prince and that they had nothing to fear as "all should be well." Only the queen was unimpressed. She fled into sanctuary at

Westminster, taking with her Prince Richard, and when she was told of Hastings's words of comfort, she replied, "Ah, woe worth him, for he is one of them that labour to destroy me and my blood."

Initially, there was still little cause for alarm; there had been no preemptive executions or clash of arms between the rival factions as might have happened earlier. Gloucester continued his progress to London, and when he arrived in the capital, he went out of his way to treat the young prince, his nephew, with all due deference. At its next meeting on May 8, the council then appointed Gloucester Protector of England, the appointment to run until the king's coronation that was fixed for June 22. Unlike Humphrey of Gloucester in 1422, who had not received full powers in dealing with Henry VI, Richard was given the guardianship of the future king's person. The first step was to have Prince Edward lodged in the palace of the Bishop of London and then in the safety of the Tower. The Protector then set about strengthening his own position by sacking the chancellor Archbishop Rotherham, a friend of the queen, and replacing him with John Russell, Bishop of Lincoln and the supposed author of the second continuation of the *Croyland Chronicle*. At the same time, he began packing the council with his supporters. There were rewards for Buckingham, Northumberland, Stanley, Howard, and Hastings, who became Master of the Mint. The Croyland chronicler reported that the latter was "bursting with joy over this new world," and there is no reason to disbelieve the comment. Hastings had seen his rivals' power destroyed—Rivers was under arrest, the queen was in sanctuary, and the detested Dorset had wisely fled into exile in France, as had Sir Edward Woodville—and his friend Gloucester had achieved his wish to become the Lord Protector. Considering that prior to Edward's death Gloucester did not have any discernible quarrel with the Woodvilles, it had all turned out very satisfactorily for Hastings and Buckingham.

Crucially, Prince Edward was now in the hands of his uncle and his supporters, an important consideration when taking into account what happened next. On the surface, there was an air of normalcy in London. The coronation of Prince Edward had been fixed and planning for the event was in progress, the Woodville faction had been sidelined, and Gloucester had been confirmed in his new position, but already the Protector was thinking in grander terms than merely acting as his nephew's adviser. He now wanted the crown for himself. Just as no one knows when Henry Bolingbroke decided to make his bid for Richard II's crown, it is impossible to place a date on Gloucester's change of heart, but it seems unlikely that he coveted his brother's throne when he rode into London at the beginning of May. His earlier protestations of loyalty have to be taken at face value as evidence of what he really believed at the time, and for the rest of the month he went about his business normally, attending council meetings and talking to his close associates, especially Hastings and Buckingham. The fact that he moved Prince Edward to the Tower cannot be held against him as a suspicious move: It was a secure Royal residence and entirely suited to its purpose. True, he had to decide what to do with Rivers, Grey, and Vaughan, whom he had accused of treachery, but in his present position, he could not have them summarily executed, much as he might have wanted to do so. All the contemporary evidence from Croyland, Mancini, and other chroniclers accepts the state of normalcy that existed during those unreal days, yet for reasons that have a number of causes, Gloucester decided that he did not want to remain as Protector but preferred to reign as king in his own right by making a bid for the vacant throne.

Toward the end of the month, Gloucester attempted to persuade the queen to leave her sanctuary and to surrender her younger son, Prince Richard, in advance of the coronation, but the bid was rebuffed. Then, following a council meeting on June 9, Gloucester wrote an anxious letter to the city of York asking for military reinforcements to protect him against "the Queen, her blood, and their affinity which have intended and daily do intend to murder us and Our Cousin the Duke of Buckingham and the Old Royal Blood of this Realm." Similar letters were sent to the earls of Northumberland and Westmorland. Gloucester was clearly looking to protect himself from an uncertain future: He had come to London with a small force, had neutralized Rivers's retinue, yet was now seeking reinforcement from the north and from two of his closest regional allies. Once raised, the troops were to muster at Pontefract on June 18. This was not the response of someone trying to stay out of trouble but of someone desperate to protect his position, and as Gloucester's letters make clear, he expected the disruption to come from the queen and her allies. The flashpoint came four days later at a council meeting held at the Tower, ostensibly to discuss the forthcoming coronation but in reality to allow Gloucester to mount an audacious coup d'état.

Fittingly for what happened next, June 13 fell on a Friday, the conjunction of date and day being considered unlucky, and there were other portents. One of those attending the meeting was Lord Howard, the Yorkist loyalist who had fought at Towton and would later become Duke of Norfolk and Earl Marshal. He called at Jane Shore's house to accompany Hastings to the meeting, and while walking together along Tower Street, they met a priest who fell into conversation with Hastings only for Howard to complain that they must hurry as his friend had no need of a priest yet. More, who recorded the incident and enjoyed the benefit of hindsight, added that the tone of voice suggested that Howard meant "you shall have need of one soon." And so it proved. Gloucester arrived at nine o'clock in a good mood, but all that changed after he excused himself and returned at 10:30 wearing "a sour and angry countenance." In an outburst that shocked and surprised those present, he charged Hastings with conspiring with the queen and others to commit treason. Banging his fist on the table, he shouted "Treason!" and at this prearranged signal, armed men rushed into the room and apprehended Lord Stanley, Dr. Morton, and the recently sacked chancellor Archbishop Rotherham. The man most affected by this unexpected turn of events was Hastings, who was taken out to the green and instantly beheaded, the one kindness shown by Gloucester being the arrival of a priest to take his confession before execution. It was an extraordinary moment. Gloucester had moved with his usual speed and efficiency to deal with an alleged threat, but in so doing, he had acted like a tyrant. The wretched Hastings was given no trial, he was summarily executed on Gloucester's word and had not been presented with any opportunity to defend himself.

An act of that kind required forethought; it was not done on an impulse, and in any case, Gloucester was not normally a reckless man. Clearly, he had taken it into his head to rid himself of Hastings and in his usual clinical way had acted swiftly by arresting him and ordering the execution to be carried out as quickly as possible. As for his reasons, Mancini got close to the matter when he observed that Gloucester was simply protecting his back before he made a bid for the throne:

> Having got into his power all the blood royal of the land, yet he considered that his prospects were not sufficiently secure, without the removal or imprisonment of those who had been the closest friends of his brother, and were expected to be loyal to his brother's off-spring. In this class he thought to include Hastings, the king's chamberlain; Thomas Rotherham, whom shortly he had relieved of his office; and the Bishop of Ely [Dr. Morton]. Now Hastings had been from an early age a loyal companion of Edward, and an active soldier; while Thomas, though of humble origin, had become, thanks to his talent, a man of note with King Edward and had worked for many years in the Chancery. As for the Bishop of Ely, he was of great resource and daring, for he had been trained since King Henry's time; and being taken into Edward's favour after the annihilation of King Henry's party, he enjoyed great influence.

At the time, Gloucester accused Hastings of making association with "that sorceress [the queen] and others of her counsel, as Shore's wife, with her affinity," and while the allegation has never been fully disproved, there has never been any material evidence to support it. Given Hastings's contempt for the Woodville family, it is most unlikely that he would have changed sides in such a dramatic and damaging way unless it was done to preserve Prince Edward and better his own position. Gloucester was the brother of the king who had made Hastings's career, and contemporary evidence shows that he welcomed his friend's appointment as Protector and supported the idea of a settled succession. The only thing that could have made him reconsider his loyalty was if Gloucester had confided in him any plan to usurp the throne and needed to keep it confidential. But there is nothing to suggest that this happened. The most likely explanation is the one given by Mancini, namely that having taken the Prince of Wales into custody and having hobbled the Woodvilles, Gloucester had to remove his brother's loyal servant Hastings if he was to have any chance of seizing the throne. As the Italian recorded: "Thus fell Hastings, killed not by those enemies he had always feared [the Woodvilles] but by a friend whom he had never doubted." There seems to have been no personal animus in the quarrel, and everything points to the act being a savage preemptive strike by Gloucester. Following the execution, Hastings's wife (Katherine, daughter of Richard Neville, Earl of Salisbury) was permitted to keep her husband's fortune and the victim himself was buried in the place he had requested in his will, alongside Edward IV in St. George's Chapel, Windsor. As for the other "conspirators," they were eventually released and two of them, Stanley and Morton, were to be heard of again.

In the aftermath of the coup, Gloucester quickly set about consolidating his position. Following a show of armed force, the queen agreed to surrender Prince Richard first to Archbishop Bouchier and then into Gloucester's care at the Tower, where he joined his brother Edward. At the same time, Gloucester made arrangements for Clarence's son, the young Earl of Warwick, to be brought to London, where he was kept in similar confinement. (As an attainted son, he posed no immediate threat, but Gloucester knew that attainders could be reversed and that the young man had a distant claim on the throne through his Neville and Beaufort ancestry.) To put a stop to the Woodville's influence, orders were given for the immediate execution of Rivers, Grey, and Vaughan. These steps were necessary for Gloucester to protect his position, but he also needed to convince others that his actions were justified as punishment for treasonable activities. In the hours following Hastings's execution, a herald read a proclamation claiming that one of the key players in a plot against him had been Jane Shore, "with whom he [Hastings] lay nightly, and namely the night past before his death." As punishment, she was taken into custody and the following month was forced to do penance, walking through the streets of London with the traditional lighted taper as a symbol of her willingness to embrace God's light of forgiveness. As a punishment, it was a mixed success; Jane Shore looked so comely that the watching crowds, mainly men, were "more amorous of her body than curious of her soul."

More successful in Gloucester's propaganda campaign was the besmirching of his brother's reputation. Jane Shore's punishment had been part of the process—she was arraigned as a "common harlot" and not as the king's mistress—but there was also a more substantial attack, this time on the probity of the succession. On Sunday, June 22, Dr. Ralph Shaw (or Shaa), brother of the mayor of London, preached and published a sermon at St. Paul's Cross, next to the cathedral, claiming that Edward IV's marriage to Elizabeth Woodville was invalid because he had already been betrothed to Lady Eleanor Butler, a daughter of the Earl of Shrewsbury. Although she had died in 1468, she was alive at the time of the Woodville marriage and the "pre-contract" was still in existence, thereby making the king's match illegal. If that were true, then the Woodville marriage was invalid and the two princes were bastards and could not succeed to the throne, as Edward and Elizabeth were living together "sinfully and damnably in adultery, against the law of God and his Church." The message was clear: If Edward had been adulterously married to Elizabeth Woodville, only Gloucester had the right to succeed to the throne. Two days later, Buckingham repeated the allegation, and on June 25 he led a delegation of noblemen and aldermen to Baynard's Castle to ask Gloucester to accept the Crown on the grounds that he was the rightful heir, as Edward's marriage was made "privily and secretly, without reading of banns, in a private chamber, a profane place, and not openly in the face of the Church."

For good measure Shaw also claimed that both Edward and his brother Clarence were born illegitimate and only Gloucester was born within wedlock. Once again, it is difficult to ascertain the veracity of Shaw's sermonizing and Buckingham's use of it before making the offer to Gloucester—the allegation of Edward's illegitimacy had been used before and enjoyed a wide currency. However, the facts were incorporated in *Titulus Regius*, the document that was produced to affirm Gloucester's right to the throne. The story of the marriage to Lady Eleanor Butler was also given credence by Robert Stillington, Bishop of Bath and Wells, a curious character who had risen from obscurity to become Edward's chancellor, before being sacked in 1473 and sent to the Tower. He claimed to have married Edward and Lady Eleanor, and if that were so, it could explain why he received so much Royal patronage. Given the fact that Edward kept his marriage to Elizabeth Woodville a secret for so long, it was not impossible that he had entered into an earlier marriage compact with another woman and then needed to remove himself from it. It is probable that people did not believe the story at the time or did not know what to believe, but the rumor's importance lies not in its veracity or otherwise but in the fact that it provided Buckingham the chance to offer Gloucester the throne. It also gave Gloucester the opportunity to accept the proposal, albeit after much theatrical prevarication. That same day, June 25, Rivers, Grey, and Vaughan were executed at Pontefract and their bodies thrown into a common grave. The coup was complete and the following day Gloucester rode from Baynard's Castle to Westminster Hall, where he sat for the first time on the King's Bench and in the presence of the judiciary consented to execute justice according to the laws of the land as king of England. He would reign as King Richard III, ironically being presented with the opportunity to do what his father the Duke of York, another Richard, had failed to achieve in the same place in 1460.

The coronation took place on July 6 and it was a suitably grand occasion. Richard was dressed in a blue and gold doublet and a purple gown trimmed with ermine, and his wife, Queen Anne, was carried in a sumptuous litter with five ladies-in-waiting, the chief one being Lady Margaret Beaufort, whose husband, Lord Stanley, had been restored to Royal favor and would shortly become Constable of England. The coronation procession left the Tower and preceded to the Palace of Westminster accompanied by a huge retinue that included Buckingham, Norfolk (as Lord Howard had become), and Northumberland, together with a representative selection of the aristocracy, knights, and gentlemen. Stripped to the waist, the new king and queen were anointed with holy oil before the crowns were placed on their heads by a clearly reluctant Archbishop Bourchier. There followed a coronation banquet and everyone agreed that it had been a grand occasion, as well it might have been—the arrangements had already been made, albeit for the coronation of a different king.

It was significant that neither Prince Edward nor Prince Richard were present at the coronation. Being the king's nephews, it was expected that they would be in attendance, in spite of being exposed as the illegitimate sons of Edward IV. Being a "bastard" was not a crime in the middle ages, many kings and princes fathered children out of wedlock and made sure that they were cared for, and the title "Bastard" was used throughout Europe as a term of respect. On grounds of protocol, therefore, there was no reason why they should not have been present at Westminster during their uncle's coronation service. It would have been wiser had they been there because they had not been seen in public since their removal to the Tower and already there were rumors about their well-being. Mancini reported that his friend and colleague Dr. Argentine, the Royal physician, had attended to the princes and that Prince Edward had taken to daily confession and repentance "because he believed that death was facing him." Following the removal of Hastings, the one man who might have been in a position to save them, they were moved into the inner apartments of the Tower and were never seen again in public. Together with their uncle's usurpation of the throne, the fate of the princes in the Tower is one of the great mysteries of Gloucester's life. There is little doubt that they were killed on Richard III's orders—only he stood to gain by their execution for as long as they lived, his hold on the throne was not totally secure—but the exact timing and reasoning behind the act are open to question.

The most detailed version about "the dolorous end of those babes" is recounted in More's history, and while there are some inconsistencies in his account, it remains the most credible description of what might have happened, if it is accepted that Richard was ultimately responsible for the murders. He certainly had the motive. Shortly after his coronation, Richard took off on a peregrination around his new kingdom, a journey that took him through Reading and Oxford to Gloucester and thence on to Leicester and north to York. While he was journeying, it is possible that he decided that while the princes lived, they posed a threat to his succession and that he could never be totally secure. Fearing that his enemies might hatch a plot to rescue the two boys and use them as figureheads in a move to unseat him, there was no option but to get rid of them. According to More's version, a message was sent to Sir Robert Brackenbury, Constable of the Tower, ordering him to carry out the killing, but to his credit, this honest man refused to carry out the order. When the response reached Richard, he was at Warwick, and while there, he gave the commission to Sir James Tyrell, a reliable retainer who had been knighted for his services at Tewkesbury and could be trusted implicitly. Armed with the king's orders, Tyrell rode to London and ordered Brackenbury to give him the keys so that he could carry out the murder. This was left in the hands of Miles Forest, one of the princes' servants and "a fellow fleshed out in murder before-time," and John Dighton, "his own horse-keeper, a big broad, square, strong knave." More continues the story:

> Then, all the others being removed from them, this Miles Forest and John Dighton, about midnight (the silly [innocent] children lying in their beds) came into the chamber and suddenly lapped them up among their clothes, so bewrapped them and entangled them, keeping down by force the feather bed and pillows hard unto their mouths, that within a while, smothered and stifled, their breath failing, they gave up to God their innocent souls into the joys of heaven, leaving to the tormentors their bodies dead in the bed.

Tyrell was then summoned to view the scene, and the bodies were hastily buried "at the stair foot, meetly deep in the ground, under a great heap of stones." Much of what More recounted was based on secondhand and frequently dubious accounts, but one salient fact backs up his story: Two hundred years later, in 1674, workmen demolishing a stone staircase in the White Tower came across a wooden chest containing the bones of two male children. These were undoubtedly the remains of Prince Edward and Prince Richard, smothered to death on the orders of their uncle. In introducing his account, More makes much of the fact that his version is based on what he had heard "by such men and such means as me thinketh it were hard but it should be true," but despite that drawback, it remains the only evidence from that period. It also seems highly probable. Following his coronation, Richard decided that to remain safe he had to kill his nephews, who were taken from public view after Hastings's execution and were never again seen alive. While the killing of innocent children is considered to be especially repugnant, Richard was no stranger to violent execution, and behind him lay the examples of Henry IV, who had been implicated in Richard II's death, and Edward IV, who had connived at the execution of Henry VI. During this troubled period, violence was a fact of life and one that could be quite arbitrary. Richard had already acted impulsively and without thinking of the consequences when he usurped the throne, first killing his friend Hastings; it is more than probable that similar impulses guided him when he arranged for the summary execution of his nephews in the late summer of 1483.

The truth will never be known. All that can be stated is that the two princes disappeared from public view and were never seen again. It is possible that they died by other means—Buckingham has been associated with their murders, as have others such as Henry Tudor and Lady Margaret Beaufort—and it has also been debated that they died of natural causes, either from illness or from being killed, with or without intent, during a rescue bid. Those who support Richard's innocence argue that it was not in the king's nature to murder the children of a brother to whom he had promised his loyalty and that he had no need to eliminate them as they presented no immediate threat to the succession. Under the terms of *Titulus Regius*, Edward IV's marriage to Elizabeth Woodville was illegitimate, and if that were accepted, then the two sons were bastards and could not succeed to the throne. If Richard had wanted to prove his own innocence, he could have displayed the princes in public, but because he chose not to do so, by the autumn rumors were rife that the boys were dead. The best that can be said in Richard's defense is that while it is impossible to prove his guilt, his own innocence is "not proven," the verdict handed down in Scots law when neither guilt nor innocence can be proved beyond a shadow of reasonable doubt.

21

THE FINAL RECKONING

*A*fter going into exile with his uncle Jasper Tudor in 1471, Henry Tudor had led a checkered existence. Initially, the two men made their way from Tenby in Pembrokeshire to Brittany, where they were welcomed by Duke Francis II, but under pressure from Edward IV, the hospitality turned into an existence that amounted to little more than house arrest. The two refugees were separated, with Henry being kept a virtual prisoner at Largoet under the jurisdiction of Jean die Rieux, Marshal of Brittany, while his uncle was kept in separate custody at Vannes and in other locations. On one occasion, in 1476, Edward managed to persuade Duke Francis to hand Henry Tudor over to him in return for a cash payment, but the move was foiled when Lady Margaret Beaufort managed to warn her son of the danger facing him. When the transfer was due to take place at St. Malo, Henry Tudor feigned illness and was able to escape. Edward then encouraged Louis XI to secure custody of the two men and extradite them to England, but that bid also failed. That was the nadir of the relationship between Henry and the English king, and from that point onwards there was a steady improvement. Henry and his uncle lived under Duke Francis's protection at Vannes, and legal steps were taken by his mother to protect his English inheritance. Now back at court as the wife of Lord Stanley, Lady Margaret Beaufort used the last years of Edward's reign to rehabilitate her son and to attempt to bring him back to England, not as a potential enemy of the Crown but as the king's son-in-law. In June 1482, a deed was drawn up that would have seen Henry Tudor pardoned and permitted to return to England to inherit his mother's estates and to succeed his father as Earl of Richmond. The same settlement would have paved the way for a marriage between him and Edward's eldest daughter,

Princess Elizabeth of York. Had this match taken place before Edward's death, it would have changed everything by bringing Henry Tudor's own claims to the throne through his Beaufort ancestors into the open. As it was, Richard seems to have been unaware of the proposals, and on becoming king, he did nothing to deter Lady Margaret Beaufort from pursuing her attempts to bring her son back to England.

In the first weeks of Richard's reign, she had been minded to support the new king—as steward of the household, her husband enjoyed considerable influence at court and she had attended Queen Anne during Richard III's coronation—but she was unsettled by the continued detention of the two princes in the Tower and by the growing rumors that they had been murdered. She may even have been implicated in an unsuccessful plot to free the two boys in July. According to the *Great Chronicle*, four men organized the rescue attempt in connivance with Jasper and Henry Tudor, and that could have triggered Richard to order the boys' execution. Lady Margaret's concern for the boys' welfare also encouraged her to enter into a treasonable relationship with others who were plotting the new king's downfall. Among those involved was her kinsman Buckingham (she was first cousin to his mother and widow of his uncle, Sir Henry Stafford), who had become disenchanted, suddenly and dramatically, with his erstwhile friend Richard III and may even have coveted the throne himself. As a Beaufort and a great-grandson of Thomas of Woodstock, Edward III's youngest son, Buckingham possessed a distant claim, and he also enjoyed the wealth, lands, and prestige with which to back any bid. However, against that, he had no immediate motive to move against Richard, whom he had recently helped to put on the throne. He had supported him against the interests of his own relatives by marriage, the Woodvilles, and he had been amply rewarded, becoming the new king's principal adviser and a key member of his inner circle. What did he hope to gain by attacking his erstwhile ally, and what were the impulses that led him to be involved with a wider rebellion against the crown so soon after Richard's usurpation?

The answer lies in a number of factors that came together during the summer of 1483. While Richard III was making his perambulation around England, there was an outbreak of discontent in the southern counties with rumors of plots and counterplots involving disgruntled Lancastrians, former members of Edward IV's household, associates of the Woodvilles, and those who simply disliked the new king. Much of the upheaval was caused by the unknown fate of the Princes in the Tower and a growing belief that they had been murdered by their uncle. There was also lingering disapproval of the way in which Richard had seized the throne, and this was fanned by his brother's supporters, who would have preferred the succession to pass to Prince Edward. Although Buckingham was based outside London and within the south of England at his castle in Brecon on the Welsh border, he would have been aware of the mood of the country, and being a powerful magnate in his own right, he would have taken steps to decide what was best for his own interests. If anything were to happen to Richard and if he were to be toppled from the throne—by no means an impossibility in that uncertain age—Buckingham's own position as the king's closest ally could become untenable. It is possible that Buckingham decided to act because he wanted to protect himself and to strike a preemptive blow for those who were plotting to unseat the new king. He may even have believed that he had a legal claim to the throne— Sir Thomas More certainly thought so—but in view of what happened next, this seems unlikely.

While Buckingham was based at Brecon, he had the company of Dr. Morton, Bishop of Ely, who had been released from arrest in the Tower and transferred into his care. It was a fateful conjunction. Morton was a persuasive and perspicacious politician, wise in the ways of the world, cunning at heart, and according to More, "a man of great natural wit, very well learned and honourable in behaviour, lacking no wise ways to win favour." He had given loyal service to the House of Lancaster and had served Edward IV equally well. A natural bureaucrat, he was also an elder statesman who was able to judge what was best for the country and, just as important, to decide where his best interests lay. While staying with Buckingham, he was able to work on the younger and impressionable man and gradually convinced him to change his allegiance. To begin with, Buckingham swore his support for his friend King Richard, but Morton countered this with another and equally potent argument. He put forward the case that in the natural scheme of things, Henry VI's son should have become king, but as he was dead, Morton had decided to transfer his loyalty to Edward and "glad would have been if his son had succeeded him." He also reminded Buckingham that his own family had been solid Lancastrian supporters—his father and grandfather had given their lives to the cause—and this argument led on to the fact that the surviving member of that family was Buckingham's cousin, Henry Tudor. If this man, a near relative, were to marry Elizabeth of York, Edward's daughter, as his mother Lady Margaret Beaufort had already proposed, the resultant match would achieve the kind of unity and peace the country so badly needed.

Morton's intervention was wise on two counts: First, it removed any obligation on Buckingham's part to make a personal bid for the throne that might not have won widespread support, and second, it put him in the role of king-maker. Having won over Buckingham, Morton sent a message to Lady Margaret Beaufort, who had already been in secret contact with Edward IV's widow, Queen Elizabeth, to gain her support for the plan to put Henry Tudor on the throne on the condition that he married Princess Elizabeth. On receiving word from Morton, she then wrote to her son in Brittany to persuade him to raise a rebellion that would be led by Buckingham and supported by a confederation of old Lancastrian backers, Woodvilles, and others in the south and west of England who were disenchanted by the way in which Richard had seized the throne. That outline of what happened is confirmed both by More, who heard the story from Morton, and by the Croyland chronicler, who added his own personal belief that Edward IV had probably "died a violent death."

It is possible that Henry Tudor was not contacted immediately and might not have been apprised of the plans until later in the year; the dating in all the near-contemporary accounts is sketchy, but the facts remain that Buckingham was involved in a revolt against Richard in the autumn of 1483 and that Henry Tudor made an effort to launch an invasion in the southwest of England early in November to claim the throne. What is surprising about this revolt is that it enjoyed widespread support across the south of England and that it happened so soon after Richard's accession to the throne. It was not just Lancastrians and Woodvilles who were involved; many of those who joined the rebellion had everything to lose if it failed—establishment figures such as justices of the peace, sheriffs, minor landowners, and other well-established types who would normally have relied on Richard's patronage. That they should have rebelled against an anointed king in the months after his coronation shows how deeply Richard was loathed by such a large and influential section of his subjects. In this respect, the rebels' feelings may have been enflamed by the fact that Richard had built up his power base in the north of England and was regarded as a powerful northern magnate who had little interest in the needs of those living in the south of England.

However, the very disparate nature of the revolt and the lack of a strong central leadership proved to be its undoing. The only coordination was a vague plan to begin the uprising on October 18 (St. Luke's Day), but the men of Kent, always anxious to strike the first blow, took the initiative a week earlier than expected and marched on London, only to be repulsed by forces led by the Duke of Norfolk. This alerted Richard that trouble was brewing, and he was also helped by a lack of security in the rebel camp. On the day itself, the south of England experienced a number of uprisings in the main county towns as planned, but everything hinged on Buckingham being able to get his Welsh forces through the Forest of Dean to meet up with his followers coming up from the West Country. Almost immediately, the weather turned foul and it rained incessantly for over a week, the rivers Severn and Wye broke their banks, the surrounding countryside was flooded, and the hard going made it impossible for Buckingham to make any progress. He soon found that his Welsh soldiers were unwilling followers and that any enthusiasm they might have felt for the operation quickly melted away in the atrocious weather conditions. By the end of the month his army had more or less disintegrated, and Buckingham was forced to flee in disguise into Shropshire. His luck did not hold. Although he sought refuge at Wem with one of his retainers, one Ralph Banastre (or Bannister), there was a price on his head and it could not be resisted.

The news of Buckingham's revolt had deeply shocked Richard, who wrote to his chancellor Bishop Russell describing his erstwhile friend as "the most untrue creature living, whom with God's grace we shall not be long till we will be in that part and subdue his malice." Lured by the promised bounty, Banastre promptly betrayed Buckingham, who was taken to Salisbury and beheaded in the market-place on November 2, All Souls' Day. In vain, he tried to seek an audience with the king. Richard had no intention of making any exchanges with such an ungrateful wretch, and as happened so often during this violent period, Buckingham was promptly and savagely dispatched without further ado. In the weeks that followed his execution, many other supporters were rounded up and executed, among them Sir Thomas St. Leger, the husband of Richard's sister, Anne, whose pleas for clemency fell on deaf ears. His was an extraordinary betrayal that reveals the extent of the animus against Richard. Not only was he a Royal brother-in-law and a trusted courtier, but in 1471, Edward IV had permitted Anne to divorce her husband the Duke of Exeter in order to allow her to marry St. Leger, who was her lover.

Another casualty of the rebellion was Henry Tudor, who had left Brittany with high hopes and a sizable force, only to be caught up in the same storms that imperiled Buckingham's uprising. Although he made landfall first at Poole and then at Plymouth, the disastrous news of Buckingham's failed revolt and Richard's gathering strength in the West Country forced him to sail back across the Channel and return to winter quarters in Brittany. Also on the run were the Marquess of Dorset, whom Richard denounced as a seducer who had "many and sundry maids, widows and wives damnably and without shame devoured, deflowered and defiled," and Dr. Morton, who managed to escape to his diocese in Ely and then crossed the Channel to go into exile in Flanders. From there, he made contact again with Henry Tudor, who was slowly rebuilding his strength at Rennes, and it was there in the cathedral on Christmas Day that his followers knelt before him as a king-in-waiting.

Although Buckingham's revolt had not succeeded, it had brought Henry Tudor's claim into the open. From being a penniless and insignificant member of the House of Lancaster who was unknown to most English magnates (Buckingham was an exception), he now emerged as the main contender to restore the country's fortunes by ending Richard's reign and claiming the throne for himself and Elizabeth of York. All this was now known to Richard, who suddenly had to accept the fact that he faced a serious contender and that his hold on the throne had suddenly become extremely insecure. Due to good intelligence and the plotters' incompetence, he had been able to put down the first revolt without any difficulty, and most of its leaders had been punished or forced into exile, but even in that respect he caused further offense. Under the attainders, the defeated rebels had their property confiscated, and the Croyland chronicler had difficulty restraining his annoyance that the main beneficiaries were Richard's "northern adherents, whom he planted in every spot throughout his dominions, to the disgrace and loudly expressed sorrow of all people in the south who daily longed more and more for the return of their ancient rulers, rather than the tyranny of these people." Richard kept Christmas in great splendor at Westminster, but despite his ostentatious wealth and his hold on the throne, he was by then a worried man. As More makes clear, the strain was beginning to show:

> He [Richard] never had quiet in his mind, he never thought himself sure. Where he went abroad, his eyes whirled about, his body secretly armoured, his hand ever on his dagger, his countenance and manner like one always ready to strike back. He took ill rest an-nights; lay long waking and musing, sore wearied with care and watch; rather slumbered than slept, troubled with fearful dreams—suddenly started up, leapt out of his bed and ran about his chamber.

While there may be elements of poetic license or hindsight in More's description, Richard entered 1484 with many troubles on his mind. He had been badly shaken by the attempted revolt, not least by Buckingham's treachery and by the sudden emergence of Henry Tudor as a challenger to his authority. The former had betrayed him, while the latter had emerged from the shadows to threaten his hold on Royal power. No sooner had the year begun than

Richard had to contend with the terrible blow of his son's early death. Aged only ten, young Edward of Middleham died at the beginning of April, leaving Richard without any direct male heir, and it soon became apparent that his wife Anne was incapable of bearing further children. With few other close associates, the king turned increasingly to Stanley, who had played no part in the rebellion even though his wife Lady Margaret Beaufort had been implicated in it behind the scenes. Her standing and credibility had been damaged by her involvement, but she escaped being attainted on condition that her possessions were made over to her husband, who was also made responsible for her custody and future good behavior. For his loyalty and steadfastness in such difficult times, Stanley was appointed Constable of England in succession to Buckingham.

The first act of the new year was to hold a meeting of parliament that had been postponed since November 1483. It was the only parliament of Richard's reign, and its main business was to reinforce his claim to the throne and to punish those who had opposed it. Over 100 sentences were issued to punish those who had supported the recent rebellion, and, more important, the statute *Titulus Regius* was enacted by parliament to underline the right of Richard's hold on the throne. Central to its argument was the invalidity of Edward IV's marriage to Elizabeth Woodville and the consequent bastardization of their children, especially the crown prince. The document was an important element in strengthening Richard's grip on the throne: It presented him as the natural successor to a king whose reign had been blighted by his connection to the Woodville faction, who were opposed to the common good of the country and its people. As part of this move to prove himself the natural successor and a superior being to his brother, Richard also agreed to end the unpopular practice of seeking benevolences, and there were reforms in the land tenure system and in the criminal justice system regarding the right to bail. A College of Arms also came into being to regulate the granting of heraldic arms, and during the sitting of parliament, steps were taken to induce Queen Elizabeth and her daughters to come out of sanctuary in return for the "surety of their lives" and a promise that "they shall not suffer any hurt." Astonishingly, in spite of everything that had happened, she accepted. Not only had Richard usurped her son's right to the throne and had probably had him and his brother murdered, but the *Titulus Regius* document had effectively destroyed her husband's reputation.

In another attempt at atonement, in the summer of 1484, Richard arranged for the reburial at Windsor of the body of Henry VI, whom he was popularly supposed to have murdered following the final defeat of the House of Lancaster. A cult had grown up around the dead king at his resting place at Chertsey Abbey that was said to be the scene of several miracles, and this helped reinforce the idea that the murdered king was a saint. Understandably, as Richard was uneasy about the sanctification of an earlier Lancastrian king and his own role in his demise, he arranged for the body to be removed to the more dignified ambience of St. George's Chapel in Windsor, where it was interred to the south of the high altar. Other attempts at penitence on Richard's behalf included the expenditure of substantial sums of money on chantries and chapels in which masses would be sung for the souls of the dead. One grandiose plan foresaw the creation of a huge chantry with six altars at York Minster where 100 priests would sing mass in perpetuity around the clock; another grant was given to the Grey Friars at Richmond to sing 1,000 masses for the soul of his dead brother Edward. The Croyland chronicler complained that these "splendid and highly expensive feasts and entertainments" were arranged to "attract himself to the affection of the people," and there is much to support that conceit: Richard was clearly using these religious obligations to reinforce his right to the throne and to place himself in the best possible light.

Alas for all those fond hopes, 1484 was not a good year for the king. Not only did he have to endure the misery of his son's untimely death in April, but as the year progressed there were signs that his tenure on the English throne was becoming increasingly unpopular. It was now almost impossible to halt the growing rumors about the fate of the princes in the Tower, and it was taken for granted that in all probability they had been murdered on Richard's orders. For all that Richard attempted to salve his reputation through his grants and his benefices, his high-minded patronage failed to win over his subjects, and by the end of the year, his reputation was in tatters. As the year drew to a close, England was inundated with various proclamations and manifestos, all of them attacking Richard in one way or another. Very few of those manifestations have survived, but proof that they did exist is made clear from Richard's own musings on the subject. Not only did he instruct the authorities at York to take steps against anyone slandering him, but he made it clear that he himself was greatly concerned by the sudden outbreak of propaganda that was aimed at him by "seditious and evil disposed persons" who had been found to "sow seed of noise and slander against our person." In and of themselves, such outpourings of slanderous rhymes and angry accusations were not enough to threaten Richard's hold on the throne, but they were symptomatic of a wider malaise within the kingdom and a growing belief that he was not worthy of his crown.

Those feelings were quickened by the death of Edward of Middleham and by the realization that his wife Anne was unable to bear him further children. Although Richard attempted to settle the succession by passing it to Clarence's son Edward (at the time, still a prisoner in the Tower) and then to John de la Pole, the youthful Earl of Lincoln, son of his sister Elizabeth and the Duke of Suffolk, there was no denying the reality that he possessed no direct heir of Royal blood. That weakened him considerably. He needed a son, but his wife was incapable of giving him one; inevitably, his thoughts turned to finding a substitute who came from the right background and would be suitably fecund. His choice fell on his niece, Elizabeth of York. At Christmas, Richard cast caution aside and made it clear to his entire court that he meant to make the match even though his wife was still alive and Elizabeth was a blood relative. His behavior could not be ignored and it outraged the Croyland chronicler:

> Oh God! Why should we any longer dwell on this subject, multiplying our recital of things so distasteful, so numerous that they can hardly be reckoned, and so pernicious in their example, that we ought not as much suggest them to the minds of the perfidious. So too, with many other things which are not written in this book, and of which I grieve to speak; although the fact ought not to be concealed that, during this feast of the Nativity, far too much attention was given to dancing and gaiety, and vain changes of apparel given to Queen Anne and the Lady Elizabeth, the eldest daughter of the late king, being of similar colour and shape; a thing that caused the people to murmur and the nobles and prelates greatly to wonder thereat; while it was said by many that the king was bent, either on the anticipated death of the queen taking place, or else, by means of a divorce, for which he supposed he had quite sufficient grounds, on contracting a marriage with the said Elizabeth. For it appeared that in no other way could his kingly power be established, or the hopes of his rival be put an end to.

It was a high-risk policy, but Richard seems to have been sufficiently besotted by the idea to make no attempt to conceal his ambitions. Three months later, the issue was again tested when Anne died, leaving Richard free to marry his niece. This time there were substantial objections. His northern supporters disliked the idea of a match with the Woodville family, arguing that it would restore the prominence they had lost at the time of Edward IV's death, and there were religious objections to the marriage of an uncle to his niece. As a result, Richard was forced into making a public declaration repudiating his intentions. Not that his disavowal did Richard any good. Within days of his wife's death, rumors were

afoot that he had murdered her, and few believed that he had completely surrendered his earlier intention to marry his niece. Richard entered 1485 without a
wife, and suspicions were mounting both about his right to the throne and about
his capacity to hold on to it. He was also short of funds as Edward IV had left an
empty treasury, and in February, Richard was forced to seek loans from parliament. While these were not the same as the benevolences he had previously
outlawed, the request was unpopular and added to a belief that Richard had
squandered his brother's inheritance.

Meanwhile, Henry Tudor was slowly reinforcing his power base in
Brittany. His position had been strengthened by the escape of the Earl of
Oxford from Hammes Castle in the Calais pale and by the arrival of several
influential magnates including Jasper Tudor, the Earl of Devon, Richard Lord
Rivers (brother of the recently executed earl), and prelates such as the Bishop
of Exeter and Richard Fox, who later became Bishop of Winchester. By the
summer of 1484, his court in exile at Vannes consisted of some 500 supporters
and he entertained high hopes of reattempting an invasion of England before
the year was out. There was a scare for him during the summer while Duke
Francis was suffering a periodic fit of insanity. During the duke's incapacity,
Richard took the opportunity of attempting to bribe Brittany's corrupt treasurer Pierre Landais to surrender Henry Tudor, but the plot was foiled by the
intervention from Flanders of Dr. Morton. Having gone into exile in the wake
of Buckingham's revolt, he maintained contact with those opposed to Richard,
and it is likely that he received notice of the king's intentions from Lady
Margaret Beaufort, who, in turn, probably heard it from her husband Lord
Stanley. The intervention was decisive. Morton passed on the warning through
a trusted priest, Christopher Urswick, and Henry was able to leave Vannes and
cross over the border into France in September. By then, Louis XI had died,
and under the terms of the regency established for his son Charles VIII there
was an inclination to oppose Richard III, who was seen as a potential enemy
intent on reclaiming English interests in France. In this respect, Charles's elder
sister Anne de Beaujeu was particularly influential, and once Henry Tudor and
his supporters had arrived in Rouen, she agreed to provide the necessary
financial and military support for a fresh invasion of England. Backed by that
support and encouraged by the arrival of the Earl of Oxford, Henry Tudor
spent the rest of the year writing to potential supporters in England, condemning Richard as a "homicide and unabated tyrant," and in a telling move
he signed those letter H.R.—Henricus Rex.

Richard could not afford to await the outcome of events. As it became clear
that his succession could not be guaranteed, he issued a proclamation against

"divers rebels and traitors" and called on Commissioners of Array to provide the necessary forces for the defense of his kingdom. In raising an army, he was heavily reliant on three great allies—Lord Stanley, the Duke of Norfolk, and the Earl of Northumberland—and during the summer, he moved his power base north to Nottingham. Later, the historian Polydore Vergil claimed that Richard was "overwhelmed by pinching cares on every hand," but even though the king knew that he faced a challenge from Henry Tudor and supporters who were threatening "to do the most cruel murders, slaughters and robberies and dis-herisons that were ever seen in any Christian realm," he still believed that he had the military capacity to counter it. To begin with, he had numerical superiority over any forces that Henry would be able to muster, and despite the uncertain times, he still commanded obedience in his realm. It is possible that he mis-trusted Lord Stanley, who was busily mustering troops on the king's behalf, but to prevent any possibility of recidivism, he ordered Stanley's son Lord Strange to take his father's place at court. Even when news arrived that Henry Tudor and his supporters had arrived at Milford Haven in south Wales on August 7, the Croyland chronicler reported that "on hearing of their arrival, the king rejoiced, or at least seemed to rejoice, writing to his adherents in every quarter that now the long-wished-for day had arrived, for him to triumph with ease over so con-temptible a faction, and thenceforth benefit his subjects with the blessings of uninterrupted tranquillity."

His self-confidence was misplaced. By the beginning of the summer, Henry Tudor had managed to raise an army of some 3,000 men, including 1,500 French troops under the command of Philippe de Crevecoeur and a number of Scottish mercenaries commanded by Bernard Stuart (or Stewart), third Seigneur d'Aubigny, the captain of the Scots guard of the French kings. On August 1, the invasion fleet left the Seine and a week later arrived in south Wales, where Henry had been promised the support of a number of landowners, mainly from Pembrokeshire where his uncle still retained some influence. Support was slow in coming, and it was not until Henry reached the English towns on the Welsh Marches that his numbers began to swell. Everything hung on the Stanleys, who enjoyed considerable support in north Wales, but as yet they were not prepared to show their hand. Summoned to join Richard at Nottingham, Lord Stanley prevaricated by pleading illness, while his brother, Sir William Stanley, sent forces into the western borders without actually joining up with the invaders. Lord Stanley's son insisted that his father would remain loyal to the king, but all the while the family played a waiting game, biding their time to see what would befall the king. They were in a difficult position: All evidence points to them wanting to support Henry Tudor, Stanley's stepson, but at the same time they had to tread carefully as Lord Strange was a hostage in Richard's camp and it was by no means certain that the Tudor challenge would succeed. Astutely, Stanley took his forces of 6,000 men toward Atherstone to the southwest of Leicester so that he could claim that he was going either to join Richard or to be in a position to throw in his lot with the invaders.

Although it was taking undue time for Northumberland and Norfolk to rally their forces behind the king's cause, Richard had high hopes that his army would eventually number 12,000 soldiers and that they would all be in place by the third week of August. Against them, Henry Tudor had some 5,000 men. By the night of August 21 both armies and Stanley's shadowing forces were in the English Midlands and a battle was imminent. Richard's army was camped near Sutton Cheney, while Henry's smaller force spent the night to the west at Whitemoors, both close to the market town of Market Bosworth in Leicestershire. As contemporary accounts are sparse and in some cases contradictory, it is difficult to piece together the precise course of the battle and the disposition of the two forces, so much so that there is no commonly agreed narrative about what actually happened. Other sites have also been debated as the place where the battle actually took place, and the area around the village of Dadlington, some one and a half miles to the south, is considered to be a stronger candidate for the actual location due in part to the large number of human remains and weaponry discovered in the area.

What seems to have happened is this: In the early morning of August 23, Richard moved his army onto the high ground of Ambion Hill (or Ambien Hill, at 417 feet, no great height, but still a commanding physical presence in the generally flat landscape), and facing west, they took up position with the Duke of Norfolk's men spread out in a defensive column with artillery on both flanks. Behind them was Richard's main guard, and covering them was Northumberland's force ready to protect the flanks. For the advancing Lancastrian army, it must have been a daunting sight as they approached from the west. Not only were they outnumbered, but their opponents occupied the high ground. To face them, Oxford took up position with Sir Gilbert Talbot on the right southern flank and Sir John Savage to the left, with Henry taking command of a small mounted force to the rear. One other army was in the vicinity, and it would play a decisive role: The Stanleys, under the operational command of Sir William Stanley, were also close by, probably to the north on high ground covering the Shenton to Market Bosworth road. (It has also been claimed that they remained to the south, but this is unlikely as there was wet and marshy ground to the southwest of Ambion Hill. Known as "Redemore," it means "the place of the reedy marsh." Another theory is that the force was divided with Sir William to the north and Lord Stanley to the south, but this, too, would have put the latter behind the marshy ground, an unlikely eventuality.)

On the face of it, Henry Tudor's cause was not particularly hopeful. While he had an experienced subordinate field commander in the Earl of Oxford, he himself was untested in battle and the odds were stacked against him. To gain any advantage, he needed the support of the Stanleys, but even though the two parties had been in touch before the battle, Sir William sent a dusty reply that he would not make any precipitate move but would join battle at the appropriate moment. In the meantime, Henry and Oxford should put their forces in order and make the first move. They had little option but to follow that course of action. (When it became clear that the Stanleys were not going to intervene on the Yorkist side, Richard gave the order for Strange's immediate beheading, but in the confusion, the execution was not carried out.) The battle then began in earnest with Norfolk's archers firing on Oxford's lines, followed by a general advance down the slopes of Ambion Hill. To protect himself, Oxford shortened his line, and as a result Norfolk's advancing men slammed into a concentrated mass of men on the lower slopes. This was a hard-pounding slugging match with men engaged in fierce hand-to-hand combat as the two lines reeled under the shock of the first collision. Some of the impetus of Norfolk's charge had been countered by the cohesion of Oxford's concentrated defensive positions, but as the Yorkists pulled back to regroup for a further onslaught, they still held the initiative. Sensing the seriousness of their predicament, Henry Tudor made a move, not by joining battle but by riding with his retinue toward the Stanleys' lines to beg them to intervene on his side by attacking the Yorkist flanks. This proved to be the decisive moment of the battle.

Watching from his position on Ambion Hill, Richard noticed the move and recognized that he had a sudden chance to defeat his rival by charging and engaging Henry Tudor's smaller band of horsemen. The tactics were risky as it was an all-or-nothing attack, but Richard had noticed a gap opening up on Oxford's right flank between Talbot's position and the marshy ground. If this could be exploited and if he could engage Henry Tudor and kill him, the day would be his. With his mounted knights in support, Richard rode down the slope toward the opposition, and in the first stage the impetus of the charge seemed to work in the Yorkists' favor. Henry Tudor's standard-bearer, Sir William Brandon, was cut down, and the fighting degenerated into a succession of individual battles with Richard to the fore, cutting and hacking in his desperation to reach his rival and deliver a mortal blow. He was the more experienced soldier, and had he been able to engage Henry Tudor in combat the day would have turned out very differently. At that point, though, the Stanleys decided to intervene. Knowing that they would never be forgiven by Richard for not joining him and realizing that their own position would be in jeopardy if they were on the losing side, the Stanleys decided to throw in their lot with Henry Tudor and gave their men the order to charge Richard's flanks. The weight of their unexpected assault altered the balance of the battle and placed Richard and his followers in great danger. As the battle lines began to break up, Richard was unseated from his horse and he was quickly struck down by Welsh foot soldiers. Although he carried on fighting to the last, death came to him at the hands of anonymous billmen who hacked him down with their long blades, ripped off his crown—a circlet above his helmet—and dumped the blood-spattered body in the nearby marshy ground close to the modern village of Stoke Golding. Later, his body was stripped of its armor and it was taken on horseback to Newark, where it was put on display for two days to prove that the tyrant king was dead. To Richard III falls the melancholy distinction of being the only king of England to fall in battle since the Norman conquest.

The battle ended with the rout of the Yorkist army. Norfolk had been killed, as were many others in Richard's retinue, and Northumberland simply melted away with his men once the fighting was over, having decided to take no part in the battle from his position as the rear guard. According to Polydore Vergil, who left the only near-contemporary account of the battle (based on the evidence of those who had witnessed it), the winning side hailed Henry as their new king, and Lord Stanley cemented the moment by crowning his stepson with Richard's crown circlet, "which was found among the spoil in the field." After two hours of heavy and frequently confused pounding, the Battle of Bosworth Field was over. It had not so much been won by Henry Tudor as lost by Richard III, who was undone both by his impetuosity in leading the fateful cavalry charge and by the treasonable behavior of the Stanleys. At Bosworth Field, he finally came face to face with the harsh reality that he was king in name only and was about to pay the penalty of fighting without a sufficient number of trustworthy allies. "I will die King of England," he is supposed to have said in a last utterance. "I will not budge a foot." Those were brave words spoken by a man who did not lack courage or fortitude, but Richard was on his own when he was unhorsed and turned to face Henry Tudor's avenging foot soldiers. He had forced his way to his brother's throne by executing his main opponents and by probably ordering the killing of his two nephews, the princes in the Tower, and those facts could not be denied. In that respect, he was probably no worse than many of his Plantagenet predecessors, but in the last battle, to save his skin, the battle was lost by his lack of close associates and the treasonable behavior of those who should have supported him. Under the circumstances, it was probably neither more nor less than he deserved.

22

THE LAST AND MOST DOUBTFUL OF THE USURPERS

y a grim process of terminal elimination and the passing of the years, the least likely candidate of Edward III's entire lineage succeeded to the throne of England as King Henry VII, the founding father of the Tudor dynasty. By any standards, Henry Tudor, Earl of Richmond, was a rank outsider, and it was a combination of luck and circumstance that gave him his crown or at least allowed it to be placed on his head by his supporters in the wake of his fortuitous victory at Bosworth Field. His claim, if remote, was real enough: He owed it to his Beaufort ancestors, his mother Margaret Beaufort being the great-great-granddaughter of King Edward III and only daughter of John Beaufort, Duke of Somerset, son of John of Gaunt, Duke of Lancaster, through his liaison with Katherine Swynford. On the other hand, he was still something of an outsider and very few people of any rank in England had actually met him. His father Edmund Tudor was a commoner and died before he was born, his child-hood was interrupted by the fallout from the civil conflict, and he spent much of his time with guardians or in exile with his uncle Jasper Tudor. If Edward IV had not died so unseasonably and if his eldest son had been allowed to succeed him instead of being supplanted and probably murdered by his uncle Richard of Gloucester, Henry Tudor might have lived out his life as one of the lesser-known male members of the House of Lancaster, either in exile in France or in reduced circumstances in England. As the Yorkist line had been strengthened by Edward IV's control of the throne and the elimination of most of the possible rivals, the

Yorkist line could have survived and perhaps English history would have turned out very differently. If Edward had lived longer or if his sons had not disappeared, there is no reason to suppose that the House of York would not have maintained the Royal line for many years to come; within the country, they certainly had the support to do so.

Instead, Henry Tudor was crowned king, he proceeded to marry Elizabeth of York, sister of the murdered princes, and by that marriage alliance he reconciled the rival claims of the houses of York and Lancaster. The long years of internecine conflict were brought to an end, and the House of Tudor cemented its right to rule England by virtue of Henry VII's claim and his fortuitous victory over Richard III. Despite threats to the new king's succession and a series of rebellions against him, Henry VII was able to hold on to his crown and lived until 1509 when his son who reigned as Henry VIII succeeded him. Although the direct Tudor line eventually came to an end in 1603 with the death of Elizabeth I who was childless, the succession continued through Henry VII's daughter Margaret, who had been married off to James IV of Scotland. That same year, 1603, their great-grandson James VI of Scotland was crowned James I of England, thus beginning the process of uniting Scotland and England and forging the kingdom of Great Britain. (James VI had Tudor blood on both sides of his family. He was the son of Mary Queen of Scots from her marriage to Henry, Lord Darnley, the son of Matthew Stewart, Earl of Lennox and Lady Margaret Douglas, who was the daughter of Margaret Tudor from her marriage to Archibald Douglas, the 6th Earl of Douglas.) Although the Stewarts retained the Crown only until 1689 when James's grandson, James II (of England) and VII (of Scotland), went into exile, the latter's daughter Mary went on to rule jointly with her husband William of Orange. After their deaths, the succession passed to Sophia of Hanover, a granddaughter of James I and VI, and through the Act of Succession, her son succeeded to the throne in 1714 as King George I, thus retaining the Tudor bloodline. It was not a bad outcome for a man described (unfairly) as a Welsh adventurer who invaded England to win a throne—albeit from a usurping king—and had been fortunate to triumph at Bosworth Field where, to begin with, all the odds had been stacked against him.

The coronation of King Henry VII took place at Westminster on October 30, 1485, amid much solemnity and general rejoicing—his mother Lady Margaret Beaufort "wept marvellously" (as much in foreboding, according to Vergil, for she trembled at the precariousness of her son's position and remembered the privations of the past)—and the following year he carried out his intention to marry Elizabeth of York, having secured the necessary papal consent through the good offices of Dr. Morton, now serving his third king and shortly to become

Archbishop of Canterbury. Not having many family alliances in England, Henry VII had to create his inner circle from former Lancastrian supporters and erstwhile members of the court of Edward IV. There were rewards for those who had supported him while in exile and during his brief military campaign against Richard III. Jasper Tudor was created Duke of Bedford and was appointed Lieutenant of Calais. Later still, he would become Lord Lieutenant of Ireland and Earl Marshal of England; in 1491, four years before his death, he was married to Catherine Woodville, the widow of the executed Duke of Buckingham, although there were no children from the match.

There was also promotion for Henry VII's stepfather Lord Stanley, who was made Earl of Derby and continued as Constable of England in return for his timely intervention at Bosworth. His wife, the new king's mother, Lady Margaret Beaufort, became very influential indeed, being entrusted, among other things, with the safe custody of the ten-year-old Earl of Warwick, Clarence's eldest son and a possible claimant to the throne. Later, and perhaps ominously, the boy was moved into the Tower of London for safer keeping. Throughout her son's reign, Margaret Beaufort was a prominent figure at court, both as the king's mother and as one of his principal advisers and confidantes, in time becoming so powerful that she signed herself "Margaret R" and adopted the title "My Lady the King's mother," dressing in a manner that befitted her rank and person. During the Christmas celebrations in 1487, she caused some comment by appearing at court wearing a coronet and robes similar to those worn by her daughter-in-law. Oxford, too, emerged as a leading and trusted figure at court, becoming Henry's Great Chamberlain and High Admiral. His confiscated estates were restored to him, and he was installed as a Knight of the Garter. Another beneficiary of Royal patronage was Sir John Paston III, who became sheriff of Norfolk and Suffolk and later enjoyed a close relationship with Henry VII, being described in one of the letters from the king as "my right trusty and well beloved counsellor." Others who had helped Henry during the years in exile were also suitably rewarded; Dr. Morton was eventually appointed a cardinal, and Christopher Urswick became Dean of Windsor.

Conversely, there was little bloodletting among Richard's supporters and associates for the good reason that none of them represented a tangible threat and some of them could be useful to the new regime. Northumberland spent some time in confinement, hardly the reward he might have expected had he really offered Henry wholesome support at Bosworth Field. This lack of recompense to one England's greatest magnates raises the intriguing possibility that Northumberland had either not been prepared to engage his forces on the king's behalf in the first place or that Richard's precipitate charge took him by surprise and he was unable to intervene. Whatever his motives, he paid for his inaction with his life, being murdered four years later in York during a tax revolt in April 1489. The unrest had been created by parliament's need to raise funds for a possible English military intervention in Brittany, but Northumberland's murder was also ascribed to northern anger over his failure to support Richard III—there were several of the former king's followers in the crowd that lynched him. On the other hand, an equally prominent Ricardian and battlefield commander at Bosworth Field, Norfolk's son the Earl of Surrey, prospered and rose in Royal favor, in time becoming the king's lieutenant in the north.

Not surprisingly, given the dynastic turmoil of the earlier years, Henry was anxious to reinforce his claim to the throne not just through right of conquest but also by descent. One of the earliest tasks undertaken by his first parliament was to delete Richard III's *Titulus Regius* from the statute books and thereby to end the taint of his wife's illegitimacy. As for his new mother-in-law, Elizabeth Woodville, widow of Edward IV, she was not punished for her miscalculation in throwing in her lot with Richard III in the closing period of his reign. Initially, she was well treated and awarded a pension, but in 1487 these were canceled and she was lodged in modest apartments in Bermondsey Abbey where she died in 1492. (It is highly probable that Lady Margaret Beaufort, who could not afford to have the matriarch of the House of York as a rival at court, caused the turnaround in her fortunes.) The birth of a son, Prince Arthur, to the new Royal couple in September 1486 seemed to cement the Tudor succession and gave hope for the future, but Henry VII's reign was to be shaken by a number of serious challenges that showed that factionfighting and support for the Yorkist cause were not things of the past. The first incident took place the year after the new king's accession and involved Viscount Lovell, a former chamberlain of Richard III's household, and Sir Humphrey Stafford of Grafton, who proclaimed John de la Pole, the Earl of Lincoln, as the rightful heir to the throne, being the son and heir-presumptive of Richard III's sister Anne. The plot failed—Stafford was executed and Lovell managed to escape into exile in Burgundy together with Lincoln—but it provided the impetus for another attempt to challenge Henry the following year, in the spring of 1487.

This lamentable affair involved the use of a dupe called Lambert Simnel, who had been coached by a priest, Richard Simons, to impersonate the young Earl of Warwick, Clarence's eldest son. It was doomed from the outset. Simnel was the son of an Oxford carpenter and organ builder, and there was never any lasting likelihood that he would be mistaken for Clarence's son. Even so, he received considerable support from Yorkist loyalists. Lovell and Lincoln both backed his claim, and he was hailed as a genuine candidate by the Irish chancellor

Sir Thomas FitzGerald of Lackagh, a brother of the influential Earl of Kildare. Another powerful supporter was Edward IV's sister Margaret of Burgundy, who, according to Vergil, "pursued Henry with insatiable hatred and with fiery wrath never desisted from employing every scheme which might harm his as a representative of the hostile faction." Vergil added that in all probability Margaret did not believe that Simnel was the young Earl of Warwick, but the opportunity to strike a blow against the Tudor succession was too good to be missed: "Consequently, when she learnt of the new party which had recently risen against Henry, although she considered the basis of it to be false (as indeed it was), she not only promised assistance to the envoys, but took it upon herself to ally certain other English nobles to those already active in the new conspiracy. Furthermore, Francis Lord Lovell, who had crossed over the Flanders at this time, encouraged the woman to undertake more ambitious plans . . ."

To give some momentum and authority to his cause, Simons took the young man to Dublin, still a center of Yorkist support and intrigue under Kildare's governorship of the country. Following the demise of the Earl of Desmond, who had been executed by the Earl of Worcester in 1468, Kildare had become the dominant figure in Ireland, mainly by stabilizing the English Pale and forging links with leading Anglo-Irish and Gaelic families including the O'Neills of Tyrone. Seeing in Simnel an opportunity to restore Yorkist fortunes while increasing his own standing, Kildare lent his support to the young man, who was crowned and anointed as Edward VI by the Archbishop of Dublin in Christchurch Cathedral on Whit Sunday, May 24. This was followed by the arrival of Lovell and Lincoln together with an armed force of two thousand Swiss and German mercenaries supplied by Margaret of Burgundy and under the command of Colonel Martin Schwarz, an adventurer from Augsburg. Together with their Irish allies led by FitzGerald of Lackagh, they crossed over to England, landing at the Lancashire port of Furness on June 4 and then moving quickly inland. In an attempt to forestall the rebellion, Henry VII had ordered the real Earl of Warwick to be paraded in public in London, but there was never any likelihood that Simnel would gather much support or that his story would be believed. All that his main backers could hope for was that known Yorkist sympathizers would throw in their lot with them if Lincoln and Lovell managed to win an early victory with their mercenary army. In actuality, the anticipated backing in Yorkshire failed to materialize, and the only support came from small and insignificant retinues led by two influential northern landowners who were also cousins—Lord Scrope of Bolton and Lord Scrope of Masham, whose great-grandfather had been involved in the plot to unseat Henry V in 1415. Their forces besieged York, but lack of support meant that they were forced to give up the attempt. Neither cousin was punished, although both were admonished and Scrope of Bolton was forced to live within 22 miles of London to keep him apart from his northern supporters.

The Royalist military response to the invasion was led by the Earl of Oxford and strongly supported by the new Earl of Derby and his son Lord Strange. Northumberland, too, became involved by seizing York and securing it against any possibility that its pro-Yorkist inhabitants would support the rebellion. By mid-June, Lincoln's force had made its way down the Fosse Way and had reached Newark, where Oxford was waiting to the east of the River Trent close to the village of East Stoke. In common with the events at Bosworth, little is known about the actual fighting and its exact location, but it seems that Lincoln opened the battle early in the morning of June 16 with a determined attack on Oxford's forces, attempting to unsettle them before they had fully deployed. It was Lincoln's best chance of winning as not only was he outnumbered but also he had less reliable troops than those ranged against him. Although the Irish knights and Schwarz's *landsknecht* mercenaries fought bravely enough, the bulk of the foot soldiers were poorly armed Irish peasants who were quickly slaughtered by Oxford's archers and men-at-arms. Such as it was, the battle was over well before the main force led by Henry VII arrived on the field. During the fighting, Lincoln and FitzGerald of Lackagh were killed but Lovell made good his escape, last being seen riding his horse across the River Trent. He was never seen again, although a seated skeleton discovered two centuries later within the walls of his house at Minster Lovell in the Cotswolds could well have been his remains. Most of the mercenaries fought to the bitter end—that was their lot— but Simnel was taken prisoner. Instead of being executed, as might have been expected, his youth and lack of guile saved him and he ended his days working as a scullion in the Royal kitchens. Later, he was trained as a falconer and died in 1525.

The Battle of Stoke, as it came to be known, was the last pitched battle of the civil wars between the rival houses of York and Lancaster, but it did not still the undercurrents of rumor, bad feeling, and incipient rebellion that had underpinned English public life since the reign of Richard II. As a result, Henry VII could never relax his guard, and the threat of a Yorkist backlash, especially in the north, remained a real possibility throughout his reign. Even after Richard's death and allowing for impostors like Simnel, there were still members of the House of York who could lay claim to the throne of England and, if so minded, were more than capable of rallying support for their cause. Among them were Clarence's son Warwick and the brothers Edmund and Richard de la Pole, both of whom had a tenuous claim on the throne through Richard III's naming of their brother, the late Earl of Lincoln, as his heir-apparent. Both of the surviving de la Pole brothers lived into the following century and the reign of Henry VIII. Edmund was eventually executed in 1513, and Richard, known throughout Europe as "The White Rose," was killed fighting in Italy 12 years later. By then, the young Earl of Warwick had also been killed as a result of his involvement in a fresh plot centered on another impostor, Perkin Warbeck, who emerged from obscurity in 1491 and may have been a bastard son of Edward IV.

For the next six years, Warbeck managed to keep up the pretense that he was of Royal blood and had a rightful claim on the English throne, in his instance by pretending to be Prince Richard, the younger son of Edward IV, one of the princes in the Tower. Once again, the dupe was supported by Margaret of Burgundy, who believed, or allowed herself to believe, that this son of a Tournai merchant was none other than her long-dead nephew, and once again there was some support in Ireland when the young, well-dressed man suddenly turned up in Cork after traveling around Europe. On this occasion, though, Kildare had made his peace with King Henry and was not prepared to support another Yorkist claim on the English throne. Various attempts were made to land in England and to stir up Yorkist military support behind Warbeck, but nothing came of them. The most serious challenge came in 1495, but the plan was betrayed and Warbeck's English supporters were rounded up and executed. Among the plotters was Sir William Stanley, whose charge at Bosworth had changed the course of the battle in Henry Tudor's favor. In an attempt to save his life, he made a full confession, probably expecting leniency, but Henry could not afford to pardon someone who had acted treasonably against him, and despite his family's standing, Stanley was executed. The reasons for Stanley's ill-judged change of heart are unclear but probably centered on perceived personal dissatisfaction with the rewards he had received from the new king—he had entertained ambitions to be created Earl of Chester—but the family also had a long history of scheming and dissimulation. In 1459 he had been sentenced for supporting the Yorkists at Blore Heath, while his brother Lord Stanley had kept his forces out of the battle and was subsequently pardoned by Queen Margaret.

Warbeck also tried his luck at the court of King James IV of Scotland, who acknowledged his claim and married him off to a cousin, Katherine Gordon, the daughter of the Earl of Huntly. The Scots also mounted a number of raids into Northumberland in 1495, uncalled-for acts of aggression that broke a truce signed two years earlier, but following the intercession of Spain, James sensibly withdrew his support for Warbeck, whom he had styled "King Richard." This about-turn suited Henry VII, who wanted to keep his northern border secure, and in January 1502, a treaty of perpetual peace came into being that was concluded with the betrothal of James IV to the English king's daughter Margaret. The following year saw the wedding of "the Thistle with the Rose" in the Abbey Church of Holyrood in Edinburgh, an alliance that should have ensured (but did not) the end of fighting between the two countries. Shorn of Scots support, Warbeck returned to Ireland before landing in Cornwall in September 1497. Although he got as far as Taunton, Henry VII had forces waiting for him, and the impostor surrendered on being promised that he would not be punished. Imprisoned in the Tower of London, Warbeck came into contact with the real Earl of Warwick, and a plot was allegedly concocted between them to act in mutual support to overthrow the king. When this was uncovered, both were executed within days of each other. Warbeck was little more than a deluded, if clever, dupe who allowed the machinations of others to get the better of him, while Warwick was judicially killed for no other reason than he represented, as his father had done, a threat to the Royal succession at a time when Prince Arthur was about to marry Catherine of Aragon. With Warwick's death—he was beheaded on Tower Hill at the end of November 1499—the last direct male heir in the Yorkist line disappeared and there was to be no further serious or credible challenge to the rule of Henry VII.

Following Warwick's execution, the Spanish ambassador claimed that there "remained not a drop of doubtful Royal blood" in England, but it was not the end of the carnage. Warwick's sister, Margaret Countess of Salisbury, married Sir Richard Pole, whose mother was the half-sister of Lady Margaret Beaufort, and with him she bore five children, one of whom, Reginald, became Archbishop of Canterbury. Following her husband's death in 1505, she survived into the reign of Henry VIII, who called her "the saintliest woman in England," but the good relationship did not last. In 1538, another son, Henry Pole, Lord Montague, was involved in a plot against Henry VIII and sentenced to death. With him Henry Courtenay, the Marquess of Exeter and a grandson, through his mother Catherine of York, of Edward IV, was executed. Three years later, Henry VIII lost patience with the remaining Plantagenets and had the old Countess of Salisbury executed at the Tower. It was a shocking affair: Almost in her seventies, Margaret tried to run away after the executioner struck her back instead of her neck and had to be held down while her head was chopped from her body. With her death, the last of the direct bloodline of the Plantagenets was eliminated. For almost 350 years, the house had ruled England and much of France and Ireland and had attempted to impose its will on Scotland. For over a quarter of that period, during the final 108 years of their reign, the last six kings had struggled and fought to hold on to their thrones, only for an obscure claimant to end the line, "the last and most doubtful of the usurpers, a wanderer from the Welsh marches, a knight from nowhere who found the crown of England under a bush of thorn." After decades of intermittent civil war, the battle for supremacy between Lancaster and York was finally over and a new age of peace and prosperity beckoned.

Against that background and with Henry Tudor still regarded by many Yorkists as a usurper king, Tudor writers had a vested interest in reinforcing the legitimacy of his rule. Through their efforts, a picture gradually began to emerge that painted Henry VII as England's savior, the king who had settled the long years of bloodshed and disharmony and who had righted the wrongs of that past tumultuous age. In turn, this revisionism meant that the memory of Richard III had to be effectively besmirched. In John Rous's *History of the Kings of England* that appeared in 1491, the last of the Yorkist kings appeared not so much as a monarch but as an Antichrist and outcast. Not only was Richard III painted as a wicked man, but also he was portrayed physically as a monster, and so came into focus the familiar picture of Richard as a pinched little hunchback who was more than capable of committing an act of gross infanticide and other frightful acts of murder:

> He was small of stature, with a short face and unequal shoulders, the right higher and the left lower. He received his lord King Edward V blandly with embraces and kisses, and within about three months or a little more he killed him together with his brother. And Lady Anne, his queen, daughter of the Earl of Warwick, he poisoned. . . . And what was most detestable to God and all Englishmen, and indeed to all nations to whom it became known, he caused others to kill the holy man King Henry VI or, as many think, did so by his own hands.

Not only did Rous claim that Richard III was a misshapen villain, but he also took the opportunity to sanctify the hapless Henry VI who was the author of so many of England's misfortunes during the internecine wars and whose weak character was the cause of so many disasters. The theme was followed by other chroniclers of the period such as Richard Fabyan and was then taken up and enhanced by Vergil and Sir Thomas More. As a result, in the latter's history, Richard III is a mirror image of the portrait produced by Rous—"little of stature, ill-featured of limbs, his left shoulder much higher than the right . . . malicious, wrathful, envious and, from before his birth, ever forward." Winners always get the right to construct their own versions of what happened, and the Tudor account of events passed into English historiography as the solid truth. As a result, Richard was quickly transmogrified from man into monster, and the version coined by Rous and More was swallowed wholesale by Shakespeare to create an unforgettable dramatic character whose grotesque personality springs from an unnatural birth and a deformed body. In Shakespeare's rendering of events, audiences have to believe implicitly in Richard's inherent wickedness to understand why he dragged the kingdom down with him, but, of course, that necessary dramatic license cannot be the last word on the man.

It does not help Richard III's reputation that he spent so little time on the throne, a mere 26 months, or that his claim to it was so shaky. He also lacked that prerequisite of any king during the period—an heir who would be able to follow in his place should he die or be deposed, and he never made good that defect following the death of his only son. Those drawbacks left him exposed and his reputation open to attack. Add on the suspicion that he was a murderer who had arranged for the deaths of family members close to him—in the case of the princes whose protection was his duty—and it is not difficult to see why posterity has treated him badly. He also had the misfortune to be on the losing side at Bosworth, where his failure to be protected by close allies and the treachery of the Stanleys were his undoing. That was his real failing. Given time, he could have built up allegiances, especially in the north where he was liked and respected as Edward IV's lieutenant and enjoyed a strong following. As a Royal duke, he was a loyal subordinate, and perhaps that was the role that suited him best. When his brother died, following a short period of prevarication, Richard was presented with the opportunity of claiming the throne and he took it, choosing to reign as king and disdaining to be a mere protector. Clearly, he did not want to repeat the experience of Henry VI's uncle Bedford, who was little more than a caretaker, and he would have remembered, too, the example of his grandfather and namesake Richard of York, who touched the throne but failed to claim it. Being a protector was not sufficient for a man like Richard III; for him, it had to be all or nothing.

Unfortunately, taking that route led him into wrongdoing—the peremptory execution of Hastings and Rivers and his alleged complicity in the deaths of his nephews—and that revelation of ice in his heart lost him support. It was no worse than Henry IV's role in the disposal of Richard II, but that earlier usurper had the time to reconstruct his reputation that was denied to Richard III. So, this last of the Plantagenet kings remains an enigma, and given the outcome of the wars that ended with his death, that is perhaps predictable. In most respects, Richard III conformed to the class from which he sprang: He exploited the hereditary principle to get what he wanted and then acted ruthlessly in his own interests. But shorn of valid support, his violence of mind and action meant that when he fell, he fell mightily.

What of the others who survived the fight at Bosworth Field and became part of the Tudor inheritance? Most of those surrounding Henry VII had past allegiances to both York and Lancaster that had to be trimmed to match the new order. The fate awaiting some of them we already know. Death in a York scrimmage for Northumberland, whose true allegiance was a mystery known only to himself; death in bed for old Jasper Tudor, a good uncle who had remained true to his nephew throughout their wanderings in Europe. Surrey changed sides and succeeded his father as Duke of Norfolk in 1514; as Earl Marshal to Henry VIII, he became one the most important men in the kingdom and one of the most successful military commanders of his generation. Lincoln decided to pursue his own ends and paid for it with his life at Stoke. Having chosen the winning side at Bosworth, Sir William Stanley made the wrong move when he backed Perkin Warbeck and forfeited his life, but his brother, the Earl of Derby, survived until 1504 and on his death left a family that prospered to become one of England's great aristocratic lines. In time, it came to be said of them: "The Stanleys do not marry; they create alliances." His wife, the king's mother, also flourished and in turn became one of the country's major patrons of the arts and an important source of power at court. Although much of Lady Margaret Beaufort's life had been spent apart from her son, his accession to the throne introduced a new closeness, almost as if they had to make up for those lost years. Not only did she lavish affection on her "good and precious prince, king and only son," but she was installed as one of his principal lieutenants. Her official residence at Collyweston in Northamptonshire was transformed into a palace and became the seat of her power and authority. In 1499, she took a vow of chastity and lived as a nun, fasting regularly, scourging herself with a hair shirt, and tending to paupers in Collyweston's almshouse.

Sadly, she had the parent's misfortune to outlive her son, if only by a few months, dying on June 29, 1509, and was buried in Westminster Abbey. She had been one of the great figures of her age, a survivor in an uncertain world and one of the first influential female figures in English history. The other great female character from the period, Jane Shore, also lived into old age. In 1483, this beautiful former mistress of Edward IV remarried for the last time, this time to Thomas Lynam, King's Solicitor to Richard III, and she lived into the reign of Henry VIII, making a final and pathetic appearance in More's history as "lean, withered and dried up, nothing left but ravelled skin and hard bone."

Henry VII's daughter Margaret had a different fate. Her husband James IV was perhaps the most attractive of all the Stewart kings, and during his reign Scotland enjoyed something of a golden age. Having succeeded to the throne following his father's death in a fight with his nobility at Sauchieburn in 1488, James IV oversaw a period of relative calm, prosperity, and cultural advancement. In domestic affairs, he proved to be a true Renaissance prince, and he also developed his country's military power, especially its navy, causing the *Great Michael*, the largest warship of its day, to be built—the leviathan was 240 feet long, and its crew numbered 300 sailors with space for 120 gunners and 1,000 soldiers. However, the king's dabbling in military matters attracted a high price. In 1491, James IV had renewed the Auld Alliance treaty with France, but this was effectively canceled by his marriage to Margaret Tudor in 1503 and the resultant truce with England.

Both treaties were mutually incompatible should England and France ever go to war, and it was unfortunate that Henry VIII proved to be a bellicose king, anxious to pursue an aggressive foreign policy in Europe. In November 1511, he joined Pope Julius II's Holy League that combined the Papacy, Venice, Spain, and England in an alliance aimed at stifling French territorial ambitions in Italy, a move that put him on a collision course with the Scots. James delayed taking any action until the summer of 1513, but when he did, it proved to be a disastrous move. The fleet, including the *Great Michael*, was loaned to the French and an extended raid was made into England to force English soldiers to return home from France. James's popularity created a sizable force but it lacked gunners, the best being at sea with the fleet. Having crossed the border, his army was outmaneuvered by an English force led by the Earl of Surrey and was heavily defeated at the Battle of Flodden on September 9. During the fighting, James was killed together with a large number of nobles and members of his household; for the English it was a relatively tame victory, but for Scotland it was a disaster that affected the whole nation. In the aftermath, Margaret threw herself into an unwise marriage with Archibald Douglas, the Earl of Angus, and the country was soon caught up in an internecine conflict to win control of the childking, the future James V. Margaret died in 1541, but not before she had tired of Angus and married Henry Stewart, Lord Methuen—like her brother Henry VIII, she did not enjoy a particularly happy matrimonial history.

In many respects, Wales should have done well out of the new order. The coming of Henry Tudor to the throne seemed to fulfill the prediction of the bards who had prophesied that a Welshman would one day secure the Crown of Britain and that there would be a new age of freedom for the country. The birth of Prince Arthur and the choice of his name increased the sense of expectation— the legend of King Arthur is central to early Welsh poems such as *Y Gododdin* and *Marwnad Cynddylan* in which he is portrayed as a paragon—but the boy's early death at the age of 15 was deeply mourned as a disaster for those great hopes. There was some progress in the principality—during the reign of Henry VII, there was greater migration between Wales and England, with grants of land for those who had supported the Tudor cause—but this was balanced by an intensive incorporation of Wales into the English representative system, with 12 counties and 11 boroughs each providing one member to the English parliament. This suited the centralizing tendencies of Henry VIII, but it is fair to say that the Welsh did not gain as much from the Tudor connection as the Scots were later to reap from the Stewart nexus. Ireland was also transformed, under successive Tudor monarchs it benefited from the control of a central government and emerged as an integrated country under an English king. This Tudor conquest of Ireland turned the sixteenth century into a time of great violence, with a number of related internecine wars as the English pushed out the boundaries of the Pale to achieve full sovereignty throughout Ireland. During the fighting that began in 1547 and did not end until 1603, the country was brutally colonized and its Gaelic Irish aristocracy was either defeated or forced into negotiated settlements with the new English overlords.

The ending of Plantagenet rule and the arrival of the Tudor dynasty in 1485 were important punctuation marks in British history, for the civil wars in England had also affected events in Ireland, Scotland, and Wales as well as the wider world of European affairs. With the end of the dynastic conflict and the turmoil caused by the clash of rival magnates, a new age did eventually dawn; the Tudors proved to be businesslike, efficient, and capable rulers. It helped that they were solvent, and thanks to the income from the lands they inherited, successive kings and queens of the line were spared the financial indignities of their fifteenth-century predecessors. Henry VII began the process by ruthlessly acquiring land and money mainly by fining the nobility and increasing rents. Not only did his acquisition of wealth make him the richest king since the Norman conquest, but his methods also weakened the power of nobility. The Tudors also created a strong and centralized state that was governed not by all-powerful magnates but largely by capable professional men from middling backgrounds. Building on the foundations created by Edward IV, the Tudors were able to marry peace with prosperity, and in so doing to transform late medieval doctrine into modern forms of ruling the country; it is hardly surprising that they have been credited with building a stable order in England, so different from the reckless turmoil of the immediate past.

By then, much else was changing in the world and horizons were expanding. As the century ended, the Renaissance was given new impetus by the advent of printing and by the expansion overseas of European commercial and territorial interests, notably Spanish and Portuguese, to create the first of the great modern trading empires. In 1493, the two innovations went hand-in-hand to symbolize the dawning of the new age, as the world became a bigger place. When the Genoese adventurer Christopher Columbus returned from his voyage to the

Americas to announce his feat in sailing as far as Cuba and Hispaniola, the news was produced in a printed letter. Not only did this document propagate the story of his voyage and spark huge excitement, but Columbus's words encouraged volunteers to join his next expedition. New lands and new means of communicating the news: Overnight, accepted theories about world geography had to be rethought, and this transformation also encouraged the belief that a new age was dawning as other navigators such as Magellan and Vespucci joined the search. Seen from that wider perspective, the civil wars fought between the Lancastrians and the Yorkists seem to belong to an older and darker age, and the dynastic union ushered in by Henry VII brought fresh promise and new hope. It was both a beginning and an end.

APPENDIX: THE MAIN CHARACTERS

During the Wars of the Roses, the names of the nobility and other great families appear, disappear, and frequently reappear with bewildering regularity. If a nobleman was attainted or died without a male heir, his title could become extinct and later be resurrected by the monarch to reward another family for loyal service. (Confiscated titles reverted to the Crown and were frequently used in this way.) When that happened, the title would remain constant but the family name would differ. The following represent the principal titles in England, Ireland, and Scotland and the names of the people who held them. Also included are the names and identities of many of the leading players in the story.

ALBANY

(i) Robert Stewart, Earl of Fife and Menteith, Duke of Albany (1339–1420). Third son of King Robert II of Scotland. Ruled as Governor of Scotland while King James I was in English captivity. He was succeeded by his son Murdoch (c. 1362–1425). Another son, John (c. 1380–1424), through his second wife Muriella Keith, became Earl of Buchan and with the 4th Earl of Douglas led the Scottish forces in France. Both men were killed at the battle of Verneuil in 1424.

(ii) Alexander Stewart, Duke of Albany (c. 1456–1485). Younger son of King James II and brother of King James III, recognized by King Edward IV as king of Scotland by the Treaty of Fotheringhay in 1482. Died in exile three years later.

ANGUS

(i) George Douglas, 1st Earl of Angus (1380–1403). Brother of James, 2nd Earl of Douglas, and married to Mary Stewart, daughter of Robert III. Died of plague in England after being taken prisoner at Homildon Hill.

(ii) William Douglas, 2nd Earl of Angus (c. 1389–1437). Son of the above, Scottish Warden of the Middle March.

(iii) Archibald Douglas, 5th Earl of Angus, known as "Bell the Cat" (c. 1449–1513). Grandson of the above. An opponent of King James III and supporter of the Albany faction. His son and heir, the Master of Angus (1469–1513), was killed at the Battle of Flodden, and his grandson Archibald Douglas, 6th Earl of Angus (c. 1489–1557), married Margaret Tudor, the widow of King James IV.

ARUNDEL

(i) Richard FitzAlan, 4th Earl of Arundel (1346–1397). Naval commander and member of King Richard II's council. One of the five appellant lords who defeated Robert de Vere's forces at Radcot Bridge. Found guilty of treason and executed in 1397.

(ii) Thomas FitzAlan, Archbishop of Canterbury (1352–1414). Brother of the above. Made chancellor in 1386, but his association with the Lords Appellant led to his downfall when he was exiled in 1397. On the accession of Henry IV, he was recalled and served three terms as chancellor.

(iii) Thomas, 5th Earl of Arundel (1381–1415). Son of the 4th earl, he died of dysentery during the siege of Harfleur in 1415 without leaving an heir.

AUDLEY

(i) John Tuchet, 6th Lord Audley (d. 1490). Originally a Lancastrian supporter, he transferred his allegiance to Edward IV. Lord Treasurer in 1484.

(ii) James Tuchet, 7th Lord Audley (c. 1463–1497). Second son of the above. Yorkist supporter, raised rebellion in the west country against Henry VII in 1497, and executed as a traitor.

BEAUCHAMP: SEE WARWICK

BEAUFORT: SEE ALSO EXETER AND SOMERSET

(i) Lady Joan Beaufort (1376–1440). Daughter of John of Gaunt and Katherine Swynford. Married, secondly, to the Earl of Westmorland, by whom she had 12 children who survived.

(ii) Cardinal Henry Beaufort (d. 1447). Second son of John of Gaunt and Katherine Swynford. Appointed Bishop of Winchester, and later cardinal, he was one of the wealthiest men in England and a close associate of Henry V.

(iii) Lady Margaret Beaufort (1443–1509). Daughter of John Beaufort, Duke of Somerset, and Margaret Beauchamp of Bledsoe. Betrothed to John de la Pole, she eventually married Edmund Tudor in 1455, and from the union came Henry Tudor, who later reigned as Henry VII. She married, latterly, Lord Stanley.

BEAUMONT

Lord William Beaumont (d. 1508). Son of the Lancastrian Lord Beaumont killed at the Battle of Northampton in 1460. Fought at the battles of Towton and Barnet, and with the Earl of Oxford captured St. Michael's Mount in 1473. On the accession of Henry Tudor, his lands were restored, but Beaumont subsequently went mad and lived out his life as a guest of the Earl of Oxford, who also married his widow Elizabeth Scrope.

BEDFORD

(i) John, Duke of Bedford (1359–1435). Third son of Henry IV. Guardian of England during Henry V's expedition to France and subsequently Regent of France during the minority of Henry VI. He was married first to Anne of Burgundy, Duke Philip's sister, and secondly to Jacquetta of Luxembourg (1416–1472), daughter of Peter of Luxembourg, Count of Pol, who later married the 1st Earl Rivers.

(ii) Sir George Neville (d. 1483). Son of John Neville, the Marquess of Montague. A supporter of Edward IV in 1470, he married the king's eldest daughter Elizabeth and was elevated to the dukedom of Bedford. This was stripped from him in 1478 on the grounds that he could not support the estate.

BOLINGBROKE: SEE LANCASTER

BONVILLE

William Bonville, 1st Lord Bonville (d. 1461). West Country Lancastrian supporter who changed sides when his great rival the Earl of Devon switched his support from the Yorkists to the Lancastrians. Executed after the Second Battle of St. Albans.

BOURCHIER: SEE ALSO ESSEX

Cardinal Thomas Bourchier, Archbishop of Canterbury and Lord Chancellor (c. 1411–1486). Brother of Henry Bourchier, Earl of Essex. A leading prelate, he officiated at the coronations of Edward IV, Richard III, and Henry VII.

BUCHAN: SEE ALBANY

BUCKINGHAM

(i) Humphrey Stafford, 1st Duke of Buckingham (1402–1460). Captain of Calais and Constable of England, he commanded the Lancastrian forces at the First Battle of St. Albans in 1455 and was killed at the Battle of Northampton in 1460.

(ii) Henry Stafford, 2nd Duke of Buckingham (1455–1483). Grandson of the above and married to Katherine Woodville, sister of Queen Elizabeth. Originally supported Richard III's claim to the throne but rose against him and was executed in 1483.

BUTLER: SEE ORMOND, WILTSHIRE

CAMBRIDGE

Richard of Conisburgh, Earl of Cambridge (c. 1375–1415). Younger son of Edmund Duke of York and Isabella of Castile, thereby cousin to Henry V. Through his marriage to Anne Mortimer, sister to the (English) Earl of March, his heir was Richard, the future Duke of York. He was executed in 1415 following a plot to unseat Henry V.

CATESBY

Sir William Catesby (1450–1485). Member of Richard III's council and Speaker of the 1484 parliament. Executed after the Battle of Bosworth.

CHICHELE

Henry Chichele, Archbishop of Canterbury and founder of All Souls, Oxford (c. 1362–1443). A member of the council in 1410, he accompanied Henry V's expedition to France and was involved in the diplomatic negotiations with the Emperor Sigismund in 1416.

CLARENCE

(i) Thomas, Earl of Aumale and Duke of Clarence (1388–1421). Second son of Henry IV, he served as a soldier in France and was present at the siege of Harfleur. He was killed while leading the English army in a rash attack on the French at Baugé in 1421.

(ii) George Plantagenet, 3rd Duke of Clarence and Earl of Warwick through his marriage to Warwick the King-maker's daughter Isabel Neville (1449–1478). Younger brother of Edward IV, his father was Richard Duke of York and his mother was Cecily Neville, the daughter the 1st Earl of Westmorland. Rebelled against his brother in 1469 and 1470, involved in treasonable activities in 1473 and 1477, and finally judicially murdered on his brother's orders, possibly in a cask of Malmsey wine.

CLIFFORD

(i) Thomas Clifford, 8th Baron Clifford (1414–1455). Lancastrian field commander killed at the First Battle of St. Albans.

(ii) John Clifford, 9th Baron Clifford (1435–1461). Son of the above and nicknamed the "Butcher." According to legend, he killed York's second son, the Earl of Rutland, after the Battle of Wakefield. Killed at Towton.

COURTENAY: SEE DEVON

DACRE

(i) Humphrey Dacre, 1st Baron Dacre of Gilsland (d. 1485). Warden of the West March and Yorkist supporter.

(ii) Thomas Dacre, 2nd Baron Dacre of Gilsland (1467–1525). Son of the above. Supported Richard III but transferred his loyalty to Henry VII.

DERBY: SEE ALSO BOLINGBROKE

(i) Earl of Derby, one of the titles of Henry Bolingbroke, Duke of Hereford and later Henry IV.

(ii) Thomas Stanley, 2nd Lord Stanley and brother of Sir William Stanley whose intervention at Bosworth won the day for Henry Tudor (1435–1504). The husband of Margaret Beaufort, he was created Earl of Derby in 1485.

DESMOND

Thomas Fitzgerald, 8th Earl of Desmond (c. 1426–1468). Yorkist supporter, appointed deputy in Ireland by King Edward IV in 1463. Attainted and executed at Drogheda five years later.

DESPENSER

(i) Henry Despenser, soldier and Bishop of Norwich (1341–1406). Grandson of Hugh Despenser who was executed with his father the Earl of Winchester following the coup mounted by Queen Isabella and Roger Mortimer in 1326.

(ii) Thomas Despenser, Earl of Gloucester (1373–1400). Great-grandson of Hugh Despenser. Married Constance, daughter of Edmund Langley, Duke of York. Supporter of Richard II and lynched by a mob after an unsuccessful coup against Henry IV.

DEVEREUX

(i) Sir Walter Devereux (1411–1459). Prominent Herefordshire landowner, soldier, and retainer of Richard Duke of York. Together with William Herbert Earl of Pembroke he led a force into Wales to enforce York's authority.

(ii) Walter Devereux, 1st Baron Ferrers of Chartley (c. 1432–1485). Son of the above and brother-in-law of Pembroke. Member of Edward IV's inner circle of advisers.

DEVON

(i) Thomas Courtenay, 13th Earl of Devon (1414–1458). Supported the claims of Richard Duke of York in 1452 but switched allegiance to Queen Margaret of Anjou.

(ii) Thomas Courtenay, 14th Earl of Devon (1432–1461). Son of the above. Captured after Towton and executed.

(iii) Henry Courtenay (d. 1469). Brother of the above. The Devon lands were restored to him after Towton, but he was executed after plotting against Edward IV.

(iv) John Courtenay, styled Earl of Devon (d. 1471). Son of the 14th earl, commanded the rearguard of Queen Margaret's army at Tewkesbury, and was killed during the withdrawal.

(v) Edward Courtenay, 1st Earl of Devon, Third Creation (d. 1509). Heir male to the above. Attainted in 1484 and fled to join Henry Tudor in Brittany.

(vi) Henry Courtenay, Marquess of Exeter (c. 1498–1538) Grandson of the above and made marquess in 1525. Executed for treason against Henry VIII.

DORSET

(i) Thomas Grey, Marquess of Dorset (c. 1455–1501). Son of Queen Elizabeth Woodville by her first marriage to Sir John Grey of Groby, he fought for his stepfather Edward IV at Tewkesbury but later went into exile when Richard III assumed power.

(ii) Thomas Grey, 2nd Marquess of Dorset (1477–1530. Third son of the above. Like his father, never entirely trusted by Henry VII and imprisoned in the Tower. Rehabilitated by Henry VIII.

DOUGLAS

(i) James, 2nd Earl of Douglas (c. 1358–1388). Married Isabel, daughter of King Robert II of Scotland. Killed at the Battle of Otterburn in 1388, leaving no heir.

(ii) Archibald, Lord of Galloway and 3rd Earl of Douglas, known as the "Grim," bastard of the 1st Earl of Douglas (c. 1328–1400). Warden of the Scottish Western March.

(iii) Archibald, 4th Earl of Douglas and Duke of Touraine (c. 1369–1424). Known as the "Tineman" (loser). Married Margaret, daughter of King Robert III. Fought in France and was killed at the Battle of Verneuil in 1424.

(iv) Archibald, 5th Earl of Douglas (c. 1391–1439). In French service in the 1420s and Lieutenant of the Realm during the minority of King James II.

(v) James, 9th Earl of Douglas (1426–1488). Yorkist supporter, he was involved in the plans put forward by King Edward IV to crown the Duke of Albany as King Alexander of Scotland. An invasion of Scotland failed in 1484, and after being captured, Douglas spent the rest of his life in captivity at Lindores Abbey.

DUDLEY

John Sutton, 1st Baron Dudley (1400–1487). Lancastrian commander and Lieutenant of Ireland, 1428–1430. Following Henry VI's defeat at Northampton, he joined the Yorkist side and was appointed Constable of the Tower. Later supported both Richard III and Henry VII.

EGREMONT

Thomas Percy, 1st Baron Egremont (1422–1460). Son of the 2nd Earl of Northumberland and involved in the Percy–Neville land disputes in 1453. Killed at Northampton.

ERPINGHAM

Sir Thomas Erpingham (1357–1428). Served the households of John of Gaunt and Henry Bolingbroke. Commanded the English archers at Agincourt.

ESSEX

Henry Bourchier, 1st Earl of Essex (c. 1408–1483). Brother of Cardinal Bourchier. Married to the Duke of York's sister Isabel, he served under his brother-in-law in France and was appointed treasurer by Henry VI in 1455. He was on the Yorkist side at Northampton and served as Edward IV's treasurer between 1473 and 1483.

EXETER

(i) Sir John Holland, 1st Earl of Huntingdon and Duke of Exeter (c. 1352–1400). Half-brother to Richard II through the marriage of his mother Joan of Kent, the widow of the Black Prince, to Thomas Holland, Earl of Kent (c. 1315–1360). One of the conspirators against Henry IV. In January 1400, he was arrested and executed.

(ii) John Holland, 2nd Duke of Exeter (1395–1447). Son of the above, one of Henry V's ablest commanders, he distinguished himself at Agincourt and as a naval commander at Pontoise in 1419. Appointed Governor of Aquitaine, and his services were recognized by the restoration of the dukedom.

(iii) Henry Holland, 3rd Duke of Exeter (1430–1475). Son of the above and prominent Lancastrian supporter. Married to Edward IV's sister Anne, who divorced him in 1471 in order to marry her lover Sir Thomas St. Leger.

FASTOLF

Sir John Fastolf (d. 1459). English soldier and field commander in France, present at Harfleur and Agincourt. Later served under Bedford and was present at Verneuil. He retired from active service in 1435 and retired to Caister Castle in Norfolk. His legal representatives came from the Paston family.

FAUCONBERG

William Neville, Lord Fauconberg and later Earl of Kent (d. 1463). A younger son of the Earl of Westmorland and brother of the Earl of Salisbury, he commanded the Yorkist vanguard at Northampton and Towton and died in 1463. His illegitimate son Thomas Neville (d. 1471) was the Bastard of Fauconberg, a noted naval commander who raised a rebellion against Edward IV in 1471 and was executed for treason.

FIFE: SEE ALBANY

FITZALAN: SEE ARUNDEL

FITZGERALD: SEE ALSO DESMOND AND KILDARE

Sir Thomas FitzGerald of Lackagh (d. 1487). Younger brother of the Earl of Kildare and Lord deputy of Ireland. Killed at the Battle of Stoke during the Lambert Simnel rebellion.

FITZWALTER

(i) Walter Fitzwalter, 5th Baron FitzWalter (1400–1431). Yorkist supporter and field commander in France.
(ii) John Ratcliffe, 6th Baron FitzWalter (1452–1496). Grandson-in-law of the above. Yorkist supporter.

FORTESCUE

Sir John Fortescue (c. 1394–1476). Lord Chief Justice of the King's Bench and Lancastrian supporter. Pardoned by Edward IV and a member of his council. Author of *De Laudibus Legum Angliae* and *On the Governance of the Kingdom of England*.

GLOUCESTER

(i) Humphrey, Duke of Gloucester (1390–1447). Fourth son of Henry IV and brother of the Dukes of Clarence and Bedford. Married first Jacqueline of Hainault and secondly Eleanor Cobham.
(ii) Richard, Duke of Gloucester (1452–1485). Younger brother of Edward IV, whom he succeeded in 1483. Married to Anne Neville, daughter of Warwick the King-maker.

GREY OF RUTHIN: SEE ALSO KENT

Reginald, 3rd Lord Grey of Ruthin (c. 1362–1440). Landowner on the Welsh borders and in contention with Owen Glendower.

HASTINGS

(i) Lord William Hastings (c. 1430–1483). Yorkist supporter, married Katherine Neville, sister of Warwick the King-maker. Opponent of the Woodville faction and close associate of Edward IV. Charged with treason and executed on the orders of Richard III.

(ii) Sir Ralph Hastings (1440–1495). Younger brother of the above. Served Edward IV, Richard III, and Henry VII.

HERBERT: SEE PEMBROKE

HEREFORD: SEE LANCASTER

HOLLAND: SEE EXETER

HOWARD: SEE NORFOLK

HUNGERFORD

(i) Walter Hungerford, 1st Baron Hungerford (d. 1449). Speaker of the House of Commons in 1414 and steward of Henry V's household.

(ii) Robert Hungerford, 3rd Baron Hungerford (1428–1464). Grandson of the above. Lancastrian supporter and soldier, executed after the Battle of Hexham. His son, also Robert (1450–1469), was executed with Henry Courtenay in January 1469.

HUNTINGDON: SEE EXETER

KENT: SEE ALSO FAUCONBERG

(i) Edmund Grey, Earl of Kent (1416–1490). Son of Lord Grey of Ruthin and Catherine Percy, daughter of the 2nd Earl of Northumberland. Lord Treasurer 1463.

(ii) Anthony Grey 4th Duck of Exete (d. 1480). Son of the above, married to Eleanor Woodville, sister of Queen Elizabeth.

(iii) George Grey, 2nd Earl of Kent (d. 1503). Younger brother of the above and supporter of Richard III. Married, first, Anne Woodville, daughter of Earl Rivers, and, secondly, Catherine Herbert, daughter of the Earl of Pembroke.

KILDARE

(i) Thomas Fitzgerald, 7th Earl of Kildare (d. 1478). Yorkist supporter and the founder of the Kildare ascendancy in Irish politics.

(ii) Gerald Fitzgerald, 8th Earl of Kildare, known as Gearóid Mór (1456–1513). Governor of Ireland, he served five English kings and supported the claims of Lambert Simnel in 1487.

LANCASTER

(i) John of Gaunt, Duke of Lancaster (1340–1399). Third son of Edward III. Married first to Blanche of Lancaster, secondly to Constanza of Castile, and thirdly to his mistress Katherine Swynford. From Swynford came the Beaufort line.

(ii) Henry Bolingbroke, Earl of Derby and Duke of Hereford (1367–1413). Eldest son of the above and heir to the Duchy of Lancaster. One of the Lords Appellant, he was exiled by Richard II but returned in 1399 and claimed the throne as Henry IV.

(iii) Henry V, King of England (1387–1422). Eldest son of the above. Married Katherine Valois of France.

(iv) Henry VI, King of England (1421–1471). Son of the above. Married Margaret of Anjou.

(v) Edward of Lancaster, Prince of Wales (1452–1471). Son of the above. Married Anne Neville, daughter of Warwick the King-maker. Killed at Tewkesbury.

LINCOLN: SEE SUFFOLK (v)

LOVELL

Francis Lovell, 9th Baron and 1st Viscount Lovell (d. after 1487). Member of Richard III's council and Lord Chamberlain. Fought at Bosworth, escaped, and supported Lambert Simnel's claims to the throne. Disappeared after the Battle of Stoke.

MARCH (ENGLAND)

(i) Edmund Mortimer, 3rd Earl of March (d. 1381). Married Philippa, daughter of Lionel Duke of Clarence, second son of Edward III.

(ii) Roger Mortimer, 4th Earl of March and 7th Earl of Ulster (1373–1398). Son of the above, his brother Edmund married the daughter of Owen

Glendower and his sister Elizabeth was married to Sir Henry Percy, also known as "Hotspur." Heir presumptive to Richard II. Killed in Ireland at the Second Battle of Kells.

(iii) Edmund Mortimer, 5th Earl of March (1391–1425). Son of the above. Fought under Henry V in France and appointed Lieutenant in Ireland in 1421. Died childless, and title and estates passed to Richard, Duke of York.

MARCH (SCOTLAND)

George Dunbar, 3rd Earl of March (d. 1420). Succeeded to the title in 1371 and fought at Otterburn (Chevy Chase) in 1388. Defected to the English side in 1400 when the Duke of Rothesay refused to marry his daughter Elizabeth, preferring to marry into the Douglas family.

MONTAGUE: SEE ALSO NEVILLE, SALISBURY

Henry Pole, Lord Montague (d. 1538). Son of the Countess of Salisbury, executed for treason with Henry Courtenay, Marquess of Exeter.

MORTIMER: SEE MARCH (ENGLISH)

MORTON

John Morton, Bishop of Ely and Archbishop of Canterbury (1425–1500). Prominent churchman who served both Henry VI and Edward IV. Lord Chancellor under Henry VII.

MOWBRAY: SEE NORFOLK

NEVILLE: SEE ALSO FAUCONBERG, NORTHUMBERLAND, SALISBURY, WARWICK, WESTMORLAND

(i) Robert Neville, Bishop of Salisbury and Bishop of Durham (1404–1457). Younger son of the Earl of Westmorland and Joan Beaufort and brother of the Earl of Salisbury.

(ii) George Neville, Archbishop of York (1432–1476). Son of the Earl of Salisbury and brother of Warwick the King-maker. Created chancellor in 1460.

(iii) John Neville, Marquess of Montague (c. 1431–1471). Third son of the 5th Earl of Salisbury, he received the title of Earl of Northumberland in 1464 following the forfeiture of the Percy earldom and estates. Forced to relinquish the title in 1470 and named Marquess of Montague. Changed sides and fought against Edward IV; killed at the Battle of Barnet.

(iv) Cecily Neville, Duchess of York (1415–1495). Daughter of the Earl of Westmorland from his marriage to Joan Beaufort. Wife of Richard of York and mother of Edward IV.

(v) Anne Neville (1456–1485). Younger daughter of Warwick the King-maker and wife of the Duke of Gloucester, later Richard III. Later married Walter Blount, Lord Mountjoy.

NORFOLK

(i) Thomas Mowbray, Earl of Nottingham and 1st Duke of Norfolk (1366–1399). One of the five Lords Appellant who defeated de Vere at Radcot Bridge, he was appointed captain of Calais. On Richard II's orders, he arrested Gloucester and was probably responsible for his murder on the king's orders. He was banished for life when he and Bolingbroke accused one another of treason in 1398. His son Thomas Mowbray was Earl Marshal, who was executed for treason against Henry IV in 1405.

(ii) John Mowbray, 2nd Duke of Norfolk (1392–1432). Second surviving son of the above. His service to Henry in France led to the restoration of the dukedom and estates in 1425.

(iii) John Mowbray, 3rd Duke of Norfolk (1415–1461). Son of the above and a nephew of the Duke of York. Notable for securing the victory at Towton when his army arrived at a critical time to secure Edward IV's victory.

(iv) John Howard, Duke of Norfolk (c. 1430–1485). Served in France and fought at Towton. Created Duke of Norfolk and Earl Marshal in 1483. Killed fighting for Richard III at Bosworth and attainted.

(v) Thomas Howard, Earl of Surrey and Duke of Norfolk (1443–1524). Son of the above and supporter of Richard III. Entered the service of Henry VII and emerged as a leading soldier. Led the English army at the Battle of Flodden in 1513. Created Duke of Norfolk in 1514.

NORTHUMBERLAND

(i) Henry Percy, 1st Earl of Northumberland (1342–1408). Married to Margaret Neville, their son was Sir Henry Percy, also known as "Hotspur" (1364–1403), who was married to Elizabeth Mortimer, daughter of the 3rd Earl of March (English).

(ii) Henry Percy, 2nd Earl of Northumberland (1394–1455). Son of Hotspur, married to Eleanor Neville, younger daughter of the Earl of Westmorland and brother of the Earl of Salisbury.

(iii) Henry Percy, 3rd Earl of Northumberland (1421–1461). Son of the above. Lancastrian commander, killed at the Battle of Towton.

(iv) Henry Percy, 4th Earl of Northumberland (c. 1446–1489). Son of the above, supported Richard of Gloucester when he succeeded to the throne but played no part at Bosworth. Lynched in York in 1489.

NOTTINGHAM: SEE NORFOLK

ORMOND

(i) James Butler, 4th Earl of Ormond (1390–1452). Lancastrian Lord Lieutenant of Ireland. Maintained a 30-year feud with John Talbot, Earl of Shrewsbury.

(ii) James Butler, 1st Earl of Wiltshire and 5th Earl of Ormond (1420–1461). Son of the above, created Earl of Wiltshire in 1449. Appointed Lord Lieutenant in Ireland and served in Pembroke's army that was defeated at Mortimer's Cross. Executed for treason in 1461.

OXFORD

(i) Robert de Vere, 9th Earl of Oxford (1362–1392). Close associate and friend of Richard II, his appointment as Duke of Ireland in 1386 created a good deal of jealousy. In 1387, he raised an army on the king's behalf but was defeated by the Lords Appellant at Radcot Bridge and fled into exile.

(ii) John de Vere, 12th Earl of Oxford (1408–1462). Prominent Lancastrian supporter, executed with his son Aubrey for treason following his attempts to make contact with Margaret of Anjou's exiled court in Scotland.

(iii) John de Vere, 13th Earl of Oxford (1433–1513). Second son of the above. Prominent Lancastrian supporter, escaped to France after the Battle of Barnet in 1471. On the accession of Henry VII, he received the post of Great Chamberlain and was responsible for defeating a Yorkist revolt at the Battle of Stoke in 1487. Married first to Margaret Neville, sister of Warwick the King-maker, and secondly to Elizabeth Scrope, widow of Lord Beaumont.

PASTON

East Anglian family whose correspondence is one of the main primary sources for the period: John I (1421–1466), married to Margaret Mautby; John II

(1442–1479), son of the above, married to a daughter of Sir John Fastolff; John III (1444–1502), brother of the above, Sheriff of Norfolk and Suffolk.

PEMBROKE

(i) Jasper Tudor, Earl of Pembroke and Duke of Bedford (c. 1431–1495). Second son of Owen Tudor and Queen Katherine, Henry V's widow. Lancastrian field commander, he fought at the First Battle of St. Albans and at Mortimer's Cross. Supported his nephew Henry Tudor's claim to the throne and married Catherine Woodville, widow of the Duke of Buckingham.

(ii) William Herbert, Earl of Pembroke (1423–1469). Yorkist supporter and commander at Mortimer's Cross. Defeated and executed by Warwick the King-maker after the Battle of Banbury.

PERCY: SEE NORTHUMBERLAND

PLANTAGENET: SEE CLARENCE, MARCH (ENGLAND), YORK

POLE, DE LA: SEE SUFFOLK

RICHMOND

Edmund Tudor, Earl of Richmond (1430–1456). Son of Owen Tudor and Queen Katherine, widow of Henry V. Married to Lady Margaret Beaufort and father of Henry Tudor.

RIVERS

(i) Richard Woodville (or Wydeville), 1st Earl Rivers (d. 1469). He made his name and his fortune by marrying Jacquetta, the widow of the Duke of Bedford, and rose rapidly at court, becoming treasurer. Taken prisoner at the Battle of Edgecote in 1469, he was executed on Warwick's orders. His daughter Elizabeth married, secondly, Edward IV.

(ii) Anthony Woodville, Lord Scales and 2nd Earl Rivers (1442–1483). Eldest son of the above and married to Elizabeth, daughter of Lord Scales. A veteran of Towton and Barnet, he served as captain of Calais and on Edward IV's death was appointed guardian of the future Edward V. He was seized on the orders of Richard of Gloucester and executed in 1483.

ROOS

Thomas, 9th Lord Roos (d. 1464). Married to the sister of John Tiptoft, Earl of Worcester. Lancastrian supporter, executed after the Battle of Hexham. His daughter Eleanor married Robert Manners (d. 1495), a Yorkist supporter who succeeded to the title.

ROTHESAY

David Stewart, Duke of Rothesay (1378–1402). Eldest son of King Robert III of Scotland and nephew of the Duke of Albany. Betrothed to the daughter of the Scottish Earl of March, he married Marjory, daughter of the 3rd Earl of Douglas, in 1400. The decision prompted March to side with king Henry IV.

RUTLAND: SEE YORK

SALISBURY

(i) John Montague (or Montacute), 3rd Earl of Salisbury (c. 1350–1400). One of the members of the plot to assassinate Henry IV in 1400. Executed as a traitor.

(ii) Thomas Montague (or Montacute), 4th Earl of Salisbury (1388–1428). Son of the above and a leading field commander in France (victor at Cravant in 1423). Killed during the siege of Orleans.

(iii) Richard Neville, 5th Earl of Salisbury (1400–1460). Son of the Earl of Westmorland from his second marriage to Joan Beaufort and son-in-law of the above (he married the 4th earl's daughter Alice in 1421). His son was Warwick the King-maker. Executed following the Battle of Wakefield.

(iv) Margaret, Countess of Salisbury (1473–1571). Daughter of the Duke of Clarence and Isabel Neville. Married to Sir Richard Pole (no relation of the de la Pole family). Her son Henry was executed for treason against Henry VIII in 1538, and she followed him to the block in 1571.

SAYE AND SELE

James Fiennes, 1st Lord Saye and Sele (?–1450). Variously sheriff of Kent, Surrey, and Sussex, he later became warden of the Cinque Ports and was appointed treasurer to Henry IV. Lynched by the mob during Jack Cade's rebellion. His son William Fiennes, the second baron, was killed at Barnet.

SCALES

Lord Thomas Scales (c. 1399–1460). Soldier who served in France under Bedford and Fauconberg. Held the Tower of London for Henry VI in 1460, and after surrendering, he was murdered by boatmen while on his way to sanctuary. His title passed to the 2nd Earl Rivers following his marriage to Scales's daughter Elizabeth.

SCROPE OF BOLTON: SEE ALSO WILTSHIRE

John Scrope, 5th Lord Scrope of Bolton (1435–1498). Fought with Richard III at Bosworth and took part in the Lambert Simnel plot to unseat Henry VII.

SCROPE OF MASHAM

(i) Richard Scrope, Archbishop of York (c. 1350–1405). Third son of the 1st Lord Scrope of Masham. Executed following his support for Northumberland's rebellion against Henry IV in 1405.

(ii) Henry Scrope, 3rd Lord Scrope of Masham (c. 1376–1415). Married, secondly, to Joan Holland, widow of the 2nd Duke of York, and served Henry IV as treasurer. Executed in 1415 following the failure of his plot with the Earl of Cambridge to assassinate Henry V.

(iii) Henry Scrope, 6th Lord Scrope of Masham (1459–1493). Great-grandson of the above and cousin of the 5th Lord Scrope of Bolton, took part in the Lambert Simnel plot to unseat Henry IV.

SHREWSBURY

(i) John Talbot, 1st Earl of Shrewsbury (c. 1387–1453). Lancastrian field commander in France and three times lord lieutenant of Ireland. Killed at Battle of Castillon.

(ii) John Talbot, 2nd Earl of Shrewsbury (c. 1413–1460). Son of the above. Commanded the center of the Lancastrian army at Northampton, where he was killed.

(iii) John Talbot, 3rd Earl of Shrewsbury (d. 1461). Cousin of the above. Served with the Lancastrian army and was killed at Towton.

(iv) John Talbot, 4th Earl of Shrewsbury (d. 1473). Son of the above. Joined Warwick the King-maker's rebellion against Edward IV in 1470 but transferred his allegiance to the Yorkists. Fought at Barnet and Tewkesbury.

SOMERSET

(i) John Beaufort, Duke of Somerset (1404–1444). Son of John Beaufort, elder son of John of Gaunt. Served in French wars as captain-general. Married to Margaret Beauchamp, their only child was Lady Margaret Beaufort, the mother of King Henry VII.

(ii) Edmund Beaufort, 1st Duke of Somerset (c. 1406–1455). Brother of the above and favorite of King Henry VI. Killed at the First Battle of St. Albans.

(iii) Henry Beaufort, 2nd Duke of Somerset (1436–1464). Eldest son of the above and favorite of Queen Margaret of Anjou. Fought on the Lancastrian side in all of the major battles and was attainted in 1461. Killed fighting at the Battle of Hexham in 1464.

(iv) Edmund Beaufort, 3rd Duke of Somerset (1438–1471). Younger brother of the 1st duke and commander of the army of Queen Margaret of Anjou. Defeated at Tewkesbury and executed the following day. His brother John was killed during the battle.

STAFFORD: SEE BUCKINGHAM

STANLEY: SEE ALSO DERBY

Sir William Stanley (c. 1435–1495). Younger brother of Lord Stanley, the Earl of Derby, whose change of side at Bosworth gave the victory to Henry Tudor. Attainted and executed in 1495 following his involvement in the Perkin Warbeck plot.

SUFFOLK

(i) Michael de la Pole, 1st Earl of Suffolk (c. 1330–1389). Chancellor to Richard II, impeached and died in exile in Paris.

(ii) Michael de la Pole, 2nd Earl of Suffolk (c. 1367–1415). Son of the above, title restored by Henry IV. Died at the siege of Harfleur.

(iii) Michael de la Pole, 3rd Earl of Suffolk (c. 1395–1415. Son of the above, killed at Agincourt.

(iv) William de la Pole, 4th Earl and 1st Duke of Suffolk (1396–1450). Brother of the above and a leading member of Henry VI's council. Impeached and banished but executed by sailors en route to Burgundy.

(v) John de la Pole, 2nd Duke of Suffolk (1442–1491). Son of the above, married Elizabeth, sister of Edward IV. Their son, John de la Pole, Earl of Lincoln (c. 1460–1487), was named heir-presumptive to Richard III but died at Stoke leading a rebellion against Henry VII.

SURREY

Thomas Holland, 6th Earl of Kent and Duke of Surrey (c. 1374–1400). Son of Thomas Holland, 5th Earl of Kent, half-brother of Richard II. Leading supporter of Richard II in the struggle with the Lords Appellant. Lynched by the mob following an unsuccessful revolt against Henry IV.

TALBOT: SEE ALSO SHREWSBURY

Richard Talbot, Archbishop of Dublin (d. 1449). Brother of the Earl of Shrewsbury and prominent in the governance of Ireland as deputy lieutenant on three occasions.

TROLLOPE

Sir Andrew Trollope (d. 1461). Lancastrian soldier and master porter of Calais. Defected to Margaret of Anjou's camp before the Battle of Ludford Bridge. Killed at Towton.

TUDOR: SEE PEMBROKE, RICHMOND

ULSTER: SEE MARCH (ENGLISH)

VERE, DE: SEE OXFORD

WARWICK

(i) Thomas Beauchamp, 12th Earl of Warwick (1315–1401). Appointed governor to the young King Richard II in 1379. Joined the Lords Appellant and was present at the Battle of Radcot Bridge. Arrested in 1397, he escaped the death penalty and was imprisoned on the Isle of Man.

(ii) Richard Beauchamp, 13th Earl of Warwick (1382–1439). Son of the above. Although he was a godson of Richard II, he supported the claims of Henry IV, for whom he fought at the Battle of Shrewsbury in 1403. In later life, he was appointed lieutenant of Normandy and France and died in Rouen in 1439. Married to Cecily Neville, a sister of Warwick the King-maker.

(iii) Richard Neville, 16th Earl of Warwick, known as the "King-maker" (1428–1471). Son of Richard Neville, 5th Earl of Salisbury and brother of John Neville, Marquess of Montague. His marriage to Anne Beauchamp, daughter of the 13th Earl of Warwick, brought him great wealth and the Warwick title as well as making him one of the most powerful of the English magnates. One daughter, Isabel, married the Duke of Clarence, and the other, Anne Richard, married the Duke of Gloucester.

(iv) Edward Neville, 17th Earl of Warwick. (1475–1499). Son of the Duke of Clarence and grandson of the above. Executed for treason in 1499.

WELLES

(i) Lionel, 6th Baron Welles (c. 1406–1461). Lincolnshire landowner and Lancastrian commander. Through his third marriage to Margaret Beauchamp, he became the brother-in-law of Edmund Beaufort, Duke of Somerset. Killed at Towton.

(ii) Richard, 7th Baron Welles (1428–1470). Son of the above and a member of Salisbury family through his marriage to Elizabeth Montague, the earl's niece. Executed with his son Robert following the Lincolnshire rebellion against Edward IV in 1470.

WENLOCK

John Wenlock, Baron Wenlock (d. 1471). Diplomat and soldier and one of several prominent turncoats. Started in the Lancastrian camp but fought for the Yorkist cause at Mortimer's Cross and Towton. Joined Warwick in supporting Margaret of Anjou and was killed at Tewkesbury.

WESTMORLAND

(i) Ralph Neville, 1st Earl of Westmorland (1365–1425). He married twice, first Katherine Stafford and secondly Joan Beaufort, a daughter of John of Gaunt and Katherine Swynford. Between them, they produced 24 children. The eldest son of the second marriage became Earl of Salisbury.

(ii) Ralph Neville, 2nd Earl of Westmorland (c. 1407–1484). Eldest son of the above and Katherine Stafford. The bulk of the Neville lands passed to his stepbrother Salisbury.

WILTSHIRE: SEE ALSO ORMOND

William Scrope, Earl of Wiltshire (c. 1351–1399). Eldest son of the 1st Lord Scrope of Bolton and a favorite of Richard II. Executed by Bolingbroke and died without issue.

WORCESTER

John Tiptoft, 4th Earl of Worcester (1427–1470). Constable of England and deputy lieutenant of Ireland under Edward IV and also known as the "Butcher of England." Married Cecily Neville, widow of the 13th Earl of Warwick. Executed on Henry VI's readeption.

WOODVILLE (OR WYDEVILLE): SEE ALSO RIVERS

Elizabeth Woodville (1437–1492). Daughter of Sir Richard Woodville, later 1st Earl Rivers, and Jacquetta of Luxembourg. Widow of Sir John Grey of Groby, who was killed at the Second Battle of St. Albans in 1461. Married Edward IV in 1464.

YORK

(i) Edmund of Langley, Earl of Cambridge and 1st Duke of York (1341–1402). Fourth surviving son of John of Gaunt, he married Isabella, daughter of Pedro the Cruel of Castile.

(ii) Edward, Earl of Rutland and 2nd Duke of York (c. 1373–1415). Son of the above. Commanded the vanguard of Henry V's army at Harfleur and killed at Agincourt.

(iii) Richard, 3rd Duke of York (1411–1460). Son of the Earl of Cambridge executed in 1415 and nephew of the above. Served in France and Protector of the Realm 1454–1456. Killed at the Battle of Wakefield, 1460. Married to Cecily Neville, sister of the Earl of Salisbury.

(iv) Edward, Earl of March (1442–1483). Son of the above. Reigned as King Edward IV. Married to Elizabeth Woodville. His younger brother Edmund was Earl of Rutland (1442–1460).

SELECT BIBLIOGRAPHY

The period has produced one of the biggest bibliographies in British history, and the following suggestions for further reading can give only a brief general introduction to the literature of the late medieval period in England, Wales, Scotland, and Ireland. This bibliography is by no means exhaustive and does not list essays and articles published in learned journals.

THE CHRONICLES, PRINTED SOURCES

The main chronicles of the late fourteenth and fifteenth centuries are all available in modern English translations. They have provided the core for the historical narrative, although all should be read with care so far as their accuracy is concerned.

Adam of Usk, *Chronicon Adae de Usk 1377–1421*, ed. and trans. E. M. Thompson, London, 1904; *The Chronicle of Adam of Usk 1377–1421*, ed. and trans. C. Given-Wilson, Oxford, 1997

Benet, John, *Chronicle*, ed. G. M. Harriss and M. A. Harriss, Camden Society 4, London, 1972

Blacman, John, *Memoir of Henry VI*, ed. M. R. James, Cambridge, 1919

Bower, Walter, *The Scotichronicon*, 9 vols., ed. D. E. R. Watt, Aberdeen, 1987–1998

Brut, The, or Chronicles of England, ed. F. W. D. Brie, 2 vols., Early English Text Society, old series 136, 1906–1908

Calendar of State Papers and Manuscripts Existing in the Archives and Collections of Milan, vol. 1, ed. and trans. A. B. Hinds, London, 1912

Capgrave, John, *The Chronicle of England*, ed. F. C. Hingeston, Rolls Series 1, London, 1858

Castries, Duc de, *The Lives of the Kings and Queens of France (Rois et Reines de France)*, trans. Anne Dobell, London, 1979

Cely Letters, The, ed. A. Hanham, London, 1975

Chastellain, Georges, *Chronicles of the Duke of Burgundy, Oeuvres*, vols. 4 and 5, ed. Kervyn de Lettenhove, Academie Royal de Belgique, Brussels, 1863–1866

Chronicles of London, ed. C. L. Kingsford, Oxford, 1905

Chronicles of the White Rose of York, The, ed. J. A. Giles, London, 1845

Commines, Philippe de, *Memoires*, ed. Denis Godefroy and G. E. Cockayne, 13 vols., London, 1910–1959; *The Memoirs for the Reign of Louis XI 1461–1483*, trans. Michael Jones, Harmondsworth, 1972

Crowland Chronicle Continuations, The, 1459–1486, ed. Nicholas Pronay and John Cox, Richard III & Yorkist Historical Trust, 1986

English Chronicle of the Reigns of Richard II, Henry IV, Henry V, and Henry VI, ed. J. S. Davies, Camden Society London, 1856

English Historical Documents 1327–1485, ed. A. R. Myers, London, 1969

Eulogium Historiarium sive Temporis, 3 vols., ed. F. S. Haydon, Rolls Series 9, London, 1858

Fabyan, Robert, *New Chronicles of England and of France*, ed. Henry Ellis, London, 1811

Fordoun, John of, *Chronicle of the Scottish Nation* (*Chronica Gentis Scotorum*), 2 vols., ed. W. F. Skene, Edinburgh, 1871

Fortescue, Sir John, *The Governance of England*, ed. Charles Plummer, Oxford, 1885

Froissart, Jean, *Chronicles*, ed. and trans. Geoffrey Brereton, London, 1968

Gesta Henrici Quinti, The Deeds of Henry V, ed. and trans. Frank Taylor and J. S. Roskell, Oxford, 1975

Great Chronicle of London, The, ed. A. H. Thomas and I. D. Thornley, London, 1938

Gregory, William, "Gregory's Chronicle 1189–1469," *Historical Collections of a Citizen of London*, ed. James Gairdner, Camden Society, London, 1876

Hall, Edward, *Chronicle*, ed. Henry Ellis, London, 1809

Hardyng, John, *Chronicle*, ed. C. L. Kingsford, *English Historical Review*, 27, 1912

Historie of the Arrivall of Edward IV in England, ed. John Bruce, Camden Society 1, London, 1838

Ingulph's Chronicle of the Abbey of Croyland, with the Continuation by Peter of Blois, ed. and trans. Henry T. Riley, London, 1854

Journal d'un Bourgeois de Paris 1405–1449, Parisian Journal 1405–1449, trans. Janet Shirley, Oxford, 1968

Mancini, Dominic, *The Usurpation of Richard the Third: Dominicus Mancinus ad Angelum Catonem de Occupatione Regni Anglie per Ricardum Tercium Libellus*, ed. and trans. C. A. J. Armstrong, 2nd ed., Oxford, 1969

Monstrelet, Enguerrand de, *Chroniques*, ed. and trans. Thomas Johnes, London, 1840

More, Sir Thomas, *The History of King Richard the Third*, ed. R. S. Sylvester, *The Complete Works of Sir Thomas More*, vol. 2, Yale, 1963

Paston Letters, ed. James Gairdner, London, 1904

Paston Letters and Papers of the Fifteenth Century, 2 vols., ed. Norman Davis, Oxford, 1971–1976

Rous John, *Historia Regum Angliae*, ed. Thomas Hearne, Oxford, 1745; *The Rous Roll*, ed. Charles Ross, Stroud, 1980

St. Alban's Chronicle, The, 1406–1420, The Chronica Maiora of Thomas Walsingham, vol. I, 1376–1399, eds. John Taylor, Wendy R. Childs, and Leslie Watkiss, Oxford, 2003

Vergil, Polydore, *The Anglica Historia of Polydore Vergil*, ed. Denys Hay, 1950

Warkworth, John, *A Chronicle of the First Thirteen Years of Edward IV*, ed. J. O. Halliwell, Camden Society 10, 1839

Waurin, Jean de, *Chroniques*, ed. W. Hardy and E. Hardy, Rolls Series, 5 vols. (1864–1891), 1884

Westminster Chronicle 1381–1394, The, ed. L. C. Hector and B. F. Harvey, Oxford, 1982

Wyntoun, Andrew, *The Orygynale Cronikyl of Scotland*, ed. David Laing, 3 vols., Edinburgh, 1872–1879

The Historical Background, Secondary Sources

Baldwin, J. F., *The King's Council during the Middle Ages*, Oxford, 1913

Boardman, A. W., *The Medieval Soldier in the Wars of the Roses*, Stroud, 1998

Carter, Christine, *The Wars of the Roses and the Constitution of England c. 1437–1509*, Cambridge, 1997

Castor, Helen, *Blood and Roses: The Paston Family in the Fifteenth Century*, London, 2004

Chrimes, S. B., *Lancastrians, Yorkists, and Henry VII*, London, 1964

Cole, Hubert, *The Wars of the Roses*, London, 1973

Cook, D. R., *Lancastrians and Yorkists: The Wars of the Roses*, London, 1984

Gillingham, John, *The Wars of the Roses: Peace and Conflict in Fifteenth-Century England*, London, 1981

Goodman, A. E., *The Wars of the Roses: Military Activity and English Society 1452–1497*, London, 1981; *John of Gaunt: The Exercise of Princely Power in Fourteenth-Century Europe*, London, 1992

Griffiths, R. A., *The Wars of the Roses*, Stroud, 1998

Haigh, Peter A., *The Military Campaigns of the Wars of the Roses* (Stroud, 1995); *The Battle of Wakefield*, London, 1996

Hallam, Elizabeth, *The Chronicles of the Wars of the Roses*, London, 1988

Harriss, Gerald, *Shaping the Nation: England 1360–1461*, Oxford, 2005

Hicks, Michael, *Bastard Feudalism*, London, 1995

Horrox, R. E., *Fifteenth-Century Attitudes*, Cambridge, 1994

Jacob, E. F., *The Fifteenth Century 1399–1485*, Oxford

Keen, M. H., *England in the Late Middle Ages*, London, 1973

Kendall, P. M., *The Yorkist Age: Daily Life during the Wars of the Roses*, London, 1962

Lander, J. R., *The Wars of the Roses*, London, 1965; *Crown and Nobility 1450–1509*, London, 1976

Laynesmith, J. L., *The Last Medieval Queens: English Queenship 1445–1503*, Oxford, 2004

Macfarlane, K. B., *England in the Fifteenth Century*, London, 1981

McKisack, May, *The Fourteenth Century 1307–1399*, Oxford, 1959

Myers, A. R., *England in the Late Middle Ages 1307–1536*, London, 1936

Neillands, Robin, *The Wars of the Roses*, London, 1992

Pollard, A. J., *The Wars of the Roses*, London, 1988

Reid, Peter, *By Fire and Sword: The Rise and Fall of English Supremacy at Arms 1314–1485*, London, 2007

Richardson, Geoffrey, *The Hollow Crowns: History of the Battles of the Wars of the Roses*, London, 1996

Ross, Charles, *The Wars of the Roses*, London, 1976; ed., *Patronage, Pedigree, and Power in Late Medieval England*, Stroud, 1979

Rowse, A. L., *Bosworth Field and the Wars of the Roses*, London, 1966

Rubin, Miri, *The Hollow Crown: A History of Britain in the Late Middle Ages*, London, 2005

Seward, Desmond, *The Wars of the Roses and the Lives of Five Men and Women in the Fifteenth Century*, London, 1995

Strohm, Paul, *England's Empty Throne: Usurpation and the Language of Legitimation*, London, 2006

Vickers, K. H., *England in the Later Middle Ages*, London, 1937

Warren, John, *The Wars of the Roses and the Yorkist Kings*, London, 1995

Weir, Alison, *Lancaster and York: The Wars of the Roses*, London, 1995

The Reign of Richard II

Bevan, Bryan, *King Richard II*, London, 1990

Dobson, R. B., ed., *The Peasants Revolt of 1381*, London, 1983

Du Boulay, F. R. H. and Barron, C. M., eds., *The Reign of Richard II. Essays in Honour of May McKisack*, London, 1971

Given-Wilson, Chris, *The Royal Household and the King's Affinity: Service, Politics, and Finance in England, 1360–1413*, New Haven and London, 1986

Goodman, Anthony, *The Loyal Conspiracy: The Lords Appellant under Richard II*, London, 1971

Goodman, Anthony, and Gillespie, James L., eds., *Richard II: The Art of Kingship*, Oxford, 1999

Hutchison, H. F., *The Hollow Crown: A Life of Richard II*, London, 1961

Mathew, Gervase, *The Court of Richard II*, London, 1968

Saul, Nigel, *Richard II*, London, 1997

Tuck, J. A., *Richard II and the English Nobility*, London, 1973

The Reign of Henry IV

Bevan, Bryan, *Henry IV*, London, 1994

Castor, Helen, *The King, the Crown, Helen and The Duchy of Lancaster: Public Authority and Private Power 1399–1461*, London, 2000

Dodds, Gwilym, and Biggs, Douglas, *Henry IV: The Establishment of the Regime 1399–1446*, York, 2003

Kirby, J. L., *Henry IV of England*, London, 1970

Mortimer, Ian, *The Fears of Henry IV: The Life of England's Self-Made King*, London, 2007

Wylie, J. H., *History of England under Henry the Fourth*, 4 vols., London, 1884–1898

THE REIGN OF HENRY V

Allmand, Christopher, *Henry V*, rev. ed., London, 1997

Earle, Peter, *The Life and Times of Henry V*, London, 1972

Harriss, G. L., ed., *Henry V: The Practice of Kingship*, Oxford, 1985; *Cardinal Beaufort: A Study of Lancastrian Ascendancy and Decline*, Oxford, 1988

Hibbert, Christopher, *Agincourt*, London, 1964

Jacob, E. F., *Henry V and the Invasion of France*, London, 1947

Kingsford, C. L., *Henry V: The Typical Medieval Hero*, London, 1923

Labarge, M. W., *Henry V: The Cautious Conqueror*, London, 1975

Seward, Desmond, *Henry V as Warlord*, London, 1987

Wylie, J. H., and Waugh, W. T., eds., *The Reign of Henry V*, 3 vols., London, 1914–1929

THE REIGN OF HENRY VI

Bagley, J. J., *Margaret of Anjou*, London, 1948

Christie, M. E., *Henry VI*, London, 1922

Dockray, Keith, *Henry VI, Margaret of Anjou, and the Wars of the Roses*, Stroud, 2000

Griffiths, R. A., *The Reign of Henry VI: The Exercise of Royal Authority 1422–1461*, London, 1981

Johnson, P. A., *Duke Richard of York 1411–1460*, Oxford, 1988

Maurer, H. E., *Margaret of Anjou: Queenship and Power in Late Medieval England*, Woodbridge, 2003

Watts, J. L., *Henry VI and the Politics of Kingship*, Cambridge, 1996

Wolffe, B. P., *Henry VI*, London, 1981

THE REIGN OF EDWARD IV

Baldwin, David, *Elizabeth Woodville: Mother of the Princes in the Tower*, Stroud, 2002

Hicks, Michael, *Warwick the Kingmaker*, Stroud, 1998; *Edward V: The Prince in the Tower*, London, 2003; *Edward IV*, Stroud, 2004

Kendall, P. M., *Warwick the Kingmaker*, London, 1957

Macgibbon, David, *Elizabeth Woodville*, 1938

Myers, A. R., *The Household of Edward IV*, Manchester, 1959

Okerlund, Arlene, *Elizabeth Wydeville: England's Slandered Queen*, London, 2005

Ross, C. D., *Edward IV*, rev. ed., London, 1997
Scofield, C. L., *The Life and Reign of Edward the Fourth*, 2 vols., London, 1923
Simons, E. N., *The Reign of Edward the Fourth*, London, 1966

THE REIGN OF RICHARD III

Gairdner, James, *History of the Life and Reign of Richard III*, Cambridge, 1898
Gillingham, John, ed., *Richard III: A Medieval Kingship*, London, 1992
Hammond, P. W., ed., *Richard III: Loyalty, Lordship and Law*, London, 1986
Hammond, P. W., and Sutton, A. F., *Richard III: The Road to the Throne*, London, 1985
Hanham, A., *Richard III and His Earlier Historians*, London, 1975
Hicks, Michael, *False, Fleeting, Perjur'd Clarence: George, Duke of Clarence 1449–1478*, Gloucester, 1980; *Richard III and His Rivals: Magnates and Their Motives during the Wars of the Roses*, London, 1991; *Richard III*, rev. ed., Stroud, 2003; *Anne Neville: Queen to Richard III*, London, 2006
Horrox., R. E., *Richard III: A Study of Service*, Cambridge, 1989
Kendall, P. M., *Richard III*, London, 1955
Pollard, A. J., *Richard III and the Princes in the Tower*, Stroud, 1991; ed., *The North of England in the Reign of Richard III*, Stroud, 1999
Ross, C. D., *Richard III*, rev. ed., London, 1999
Storey, R. L., *The End of the House of Lancaster*, London, 1966
Tudor-Craig, Pamela, *Richard III*, Woodbridge, 1977
Weir, Alison, *The Princes in the Tower*, London, 1993

THE TUDOR SUCCESSION

Bindoff, S. T., *Tudor England*, London, 1950
Elton, G. R., *England under the Tudors*, Oxford, 1955
Griffiths, R. A., and Thomas, R. S., *The Making of the Tudor Dynasty*, Stroud, 1999
Gunn, S. J., *Early Tudor Government 1485–1558*, Basingstoke, 1995
Mackie, J. D., *The Earlier Tudors 1485–1558*, London, 1952
Pendress, Colin, *Henry VII and the Wars of the Roses*, London, 2003
Rees, David, *The Son of Prophecy: Henry Tudor's Road to Bosworth*, London, 1985

WALES

Davies, R. R., *The Age of Conquest: Wales 1063–1415*, Oxford, 1987; *The Revolt of Owain Glyn Dwr*, Oxford, 1995
Evans, H. T., *Wales in the Wars of the Roses*, Cambridge, 1915
Griffiths, R. A., *King and Country: England and Wales in the Fifteenth Century*, London, 1991

Lloyd, J. E., *Owen Glendower*, Oxford, 1931

Pugh, T. B., *The Marcher Lordships of South Wales 1415–1536*, Cardiff, 1963

Walker, D., *Medieval Wales*, Cambridge, 1990

SCOTLAND

Brown, J. M., ed., *Scottish Society in the Fifteenth Century*, London, 1977

Dickinson, W. C., and Duncan, A. A. M., *Scotland from the Earliest Times to 1603*, Oxford, 1977

Donaldson, Gordon, *The Auld Alliance: The Franco-Scottish Connection*, Edinburgh, 1985

Duncan, A. A. M., *Scotland: The Making of the Kingdom*, Edinburgh, 1975

Frame, Robin, *The Political Development of the British Isles 1100–1400*, Oxford, 1994

Grant, Alexander, *Independence and Nationhood: Scotland 1306–1469*, London, 1984

Laidlaw, James, ed., *The Auld Alliance: France and Scotland over 700 Years*, Edinburgh, 1999

Lesley, John, *History of Scotland from the Death of King James I in the Year 1436 to 1561*, Bannatyne Club, Edinburgh, 1830

Macdougall, Norman, *James III: A Political Study*, Edinburgh, 1982

Neville, C. J., *Violence, Custom, and Law*, Edinburgh, 1998

Nicolson, Ranald, *Scotland: The Later Middle Ages*, Edinburgh, 1974

Sadler, John, *Border Fury: England and Scotland at War 1296–1568*, London, 2005

Whyte, I. D., *Scotland before the Industrial Revolution: An Economic and Social History c. 1050–c. 1750*, London, 1995

IRELAND

Cosgrove, Art, *Late Medieval Ireland 1350–1541*, Dublin, 1981; ed., *A New History of Ireland*, vol. 2, *1169–1534*, Oxford, 1993

Curtis, Edmund, *History of Medieval Ireland 1110–1513*, Dublin, 1923

Lydon, J. F., *The Lordship of Ireland in the Middle Ages*, Dublin, 1972

Otway-Ruthven, A. J., *A History of Medieval Ireland*, Dublin, 1968

FRANCE

Allmand, Christopher, *The Hundred Years' War, England and France at War c. 1300–1450*, Cambridge, 1988; ed., *Society at War: The Experience of England and France during the Hundred Years War*, Edinburgh, 1973

Bates, David, and Curry, Anne, eds., *England and Normandy in the Middle Ages*, London, 1994

Burne, A. H., *The Agincourt War: A Military History of the Latter Part of the Hundred Years War 1369–1453*, London, 1956

Cleugh, James. *Chant Royal, the Life of King Louis XI of France 1423–1483*, New York, 1970

Curry, Anne, *The Hundred Years War*, New York, 1993

De Vries, K. R., *Joan of Arc: A Military Leader*, Stroud, 1999

Fowler, K. A., *The Age of Plantagenet and Valois: The Struggle for Supremacy 1328–1498*, London, 1967; ed., *The Hundred Years War*, London, 1971

Gies, Frances, *Joan of Arc, the Legend and the Reality*, New York, 1981

Kendall, P. M., *Louis XI*, London, 1971

Labarge, M. W., *Gascony: England's First Colony 1204–1453*, London, 1976

Macleod, E., *Charles of Orleans: Prince and Poet*, London, 1969

Newhall, R. A., *The English Conquest of Normandy 1416–1424: A Study in XV Century Warfare*, London, 1924

Palmer, J. J. N., *England, France, and Christendom, 1377–99*, London, 1972

Perroy, E., *The Hundred Years War* (*La Guerre de Cent Ans*), trans. W. B. Wells, London, 1951

Seward, Desmond, *The Hundred Years, the English in France 1337–1453*, London, 1978

Sumption, Jonathan, *The Hundred Years War*, 2 vols., *Trial by Battle*, London, 1990, *Trial by Fire*, London, 1999

Thompson, G. L., *Paris and Its People under English Rule: The Anglo-Burgundian Occupation 1420–1436*, Oxford, 1991

Vale, M. G. A., *English Gascony 1399–1453: A Study of War, Government, and Politics during the Later Stages of the Hundred Years War*, Oxford, 1970; *Charles VII*, Oxford, 1974

Vaughan, R., *Philip the Bold*, 1962; *John the Fearless*, 1966; *Philip the Good*, London, 1970; *Charles the Bold*, London, 1973

Shakespeare and the Wars of the Roses

Bates, Jonathan, and Rasmussen, Eric, *The RSC Shakespeare: The Complete Works*, London, 2007

Dockray, Keith, *William Shakespeare, the Wars of the Roses, and the Historians*, Stroud, 2002

Horsley, Richard, ed., *Shakespeare's Holinshed: An Edition of Holinshed's Chronicles*, New York, 1968

Kelly, H. A., *Divine Providence in the England of Shakespeare's History Plays*, Harvard, 1970

Norwich, John Julius, *Shakespeare's Kings*, London, 1999

Tillyard, E. M. W., *Shakespeare's History Plays*, London, 1944

Art and Literature

Bennett, H. S., *Chaucer and the Fifteenth Century*, Oxford, 1947

Brown, R. Colvin, H. M., and Taylor, A. J., *The History of the King's Works*, 2 vols., London, 1963

Chaucer, Geoffrey, *Works*, ed. F. N. Robinson, London, 1957

Green, R. F., *Poets and Princepleasers: Literature and the English Court in the Late Middle Ages*, Toronto, 1980

Harrison, F. L., *Music in Medieval Britain*, London, 1958

Kingsford, C. L., *English Historical Literature in the Fifteenth Century*, Oxford, 1913

Macaulay, G. C., *John Gower's English Works*, 4 vols., Early English Text Society, extra series 81, 1900

Malory, Sir Thomas, *Works*, ed. Eugene Vinaver, Oxford, 1954

Quiller-Couch, Arthur, ed., *The Oxford Book of Ballads*, London, 1910

Robbins, R. H., *Secular Lyrics of the XIVth and XVth Centuries*, rev. ed., Oxford, 1961

Scattergood, V. T., *Politics and Poetry in the Fifteenth Century*, London, 1971

Sisam, Kenneth, *Fourteenth Century Verse and Prose*, rev. ed., Oxford, 1962

INDEX